CONTENTS

Plan Your Trip

The Guide

Toolkit

Storybook

STRIKE FIRST/SHUTTERSTOCK

Aerial view, Echo Park (p94)

LOS ANGELES & SOUTHERN CALIFORNIA

THE JOURNEY BEGINS HERE

As a kid in California, I was addicted to TV – everything coming out of the box was magic. One time, I snuck into CBS Television City and watched Carol Burnett rehearse her hysterical Saturday night show. Another time, I found Bronson Caves in Griffith Park, where it all went to hell in the 1956 *Invasion of the Body Snatchers*. Then came a life-changing episode, literally: the 'Queen of Peru,' an episode of *The Rockford Files* written by a young David Chase, who 25 years later created *The Sopranos*, was so subversive, so funny, it made me want to be a writer. Researching this book, I went to Paradise Cove in Malibu, where they shot the exteriors for the show. It looks the same. I got chills, it was magic.

Ryan Ver Berkmoes

@ryanvb Bluesky

Ryan is a writer who has worked as a journalist covering everything from wars to bars. He prefers the latter. He's written over 170 books for Lonely Planet.

My favorite experience involves walking LA's neighborhoods – Echo Park and Los Feliz are favorites – but the **Academy Museum of Motion Pictures** (p107) has me coming back over and over.

lonely planet

Los Angeles & Southern California

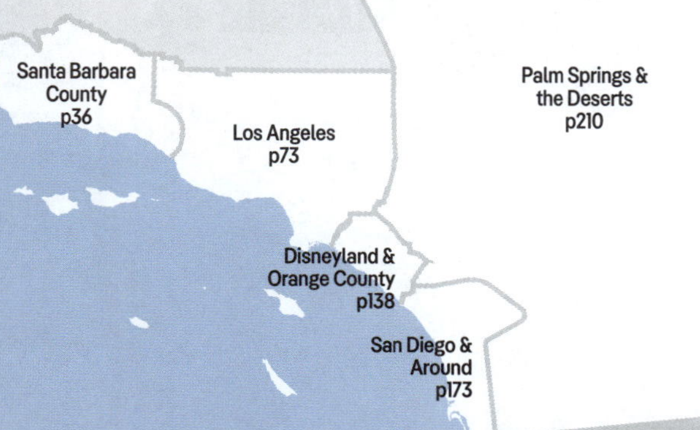

Alexis Averbuck, Amelia Mularz,
Julie Tremaine, Ryan Ver Berkmoes, Wendy Yanagihara

PANDORA PICTURES/SHUTTERSTOCK

Venice Beach (p123)

WHO GOES WHERE

Our writers and experts chose the places which, for them, define Los Angeles & Southern California.

J STEELE/SHUTTERSTOCK

The first time I drove down **Pacific Coast Highway** (p164; pictured), I felt like I was home – and I hadn't even moved to California yet. A million sunny days later, I still get the same thrill from driving the stunning stretch of coastline.

Julie Tremaine

@julietremaine

Julie Tremaine is a travel journalist and cookbook author. She wrote the Disneyland & Orange County and San Diego chapters.

KOJIHIRANO/SHUTTERSTOCK

Roaming through the **Mojave Desert** (p253; pictured), I marveled at the changes a month can bring. Even outside peak wildflower season, it was a joy to glimpse a stray pop of color – yellow, hot pink, orange.

Wendy Yanagihara

@wendyyanagihara

Wendy is a writer and artist living in coastal California who has co-authored over 60 Lonely Planet titles. She wrote the Santa Barbara and Palm Springs & the Deserts chapters.

BETTO RODRIGUES/SHUTTERSTOCK

One place I frequent is **Olvera St** (p91; pictured) in Downtown LA. This historic street and nearby plaza really shine during Dia de Muertos, with live music and dancing, and Easter, when locals line up with pups in hand for the annual Blessing of the Animals.

Amelia Mularz

@ameliamularz

Amelia is a California-based writer with a focus on travel and design. She wrote The Climate Crisis, Skating and Cruising California essays.

Pasadena
Splendid art museums with world-class collections (p132)
Los Angeles
Combine celebrity fantasy with vibrant neighborhoods (p73)
Ojai
Idyllic town renowned for new age living (p68)
Santa Ynez Valley
Wineries abound above Santa Barbara (p56)
Santa Barbara
Spanish Colonial Revival architecture, superb eating and fine beaches (p42)
Santa Monica
The beach city with a great pier (p119)
Seal Beach
Beguiling combo of a cute beach and town (p162)
Disneyland
Everyone wants to go at least once (p144)
Fresno
Lone Pine
Mt Whitney
Visalia
Sierra Nevada
Porterville
Paso Robles
Lake Isabella
Ridgecrest
Bakersfield
Randsburg
San Luis Obispo
Pismo Beach
Taft
Mojave
Santa Maria
Orcutt
Los Alamos
Big Pine Mountain
Lompoc
Solvang
Santa Ynez
Lancaster
Palmdale
Ojai
Santa Paula
Santa Clarita
Santa Barbara
Simi Valley
San Fernando
Ventura
Thousand Oaks
Oxnard
Hollywood
San Miguel Island
Channel Islands National Park
Pasadena
Santa Monica
Malibu
Venice
Los Angeles
Santa Rosa Island
Santa Cruz Island
Manhattan Beach
Long Beach
Anaheim
Torrance
Santa Ana
San Pedro
Channel Islands
Huntington Beach
Irvine
Newport Beach
Laguna Beach
Dana Point
Santa Catalina Island
Avalon
San Nicolas Island
Gulf of Santa Catalina
Pacific Ocean
San Clemente Island

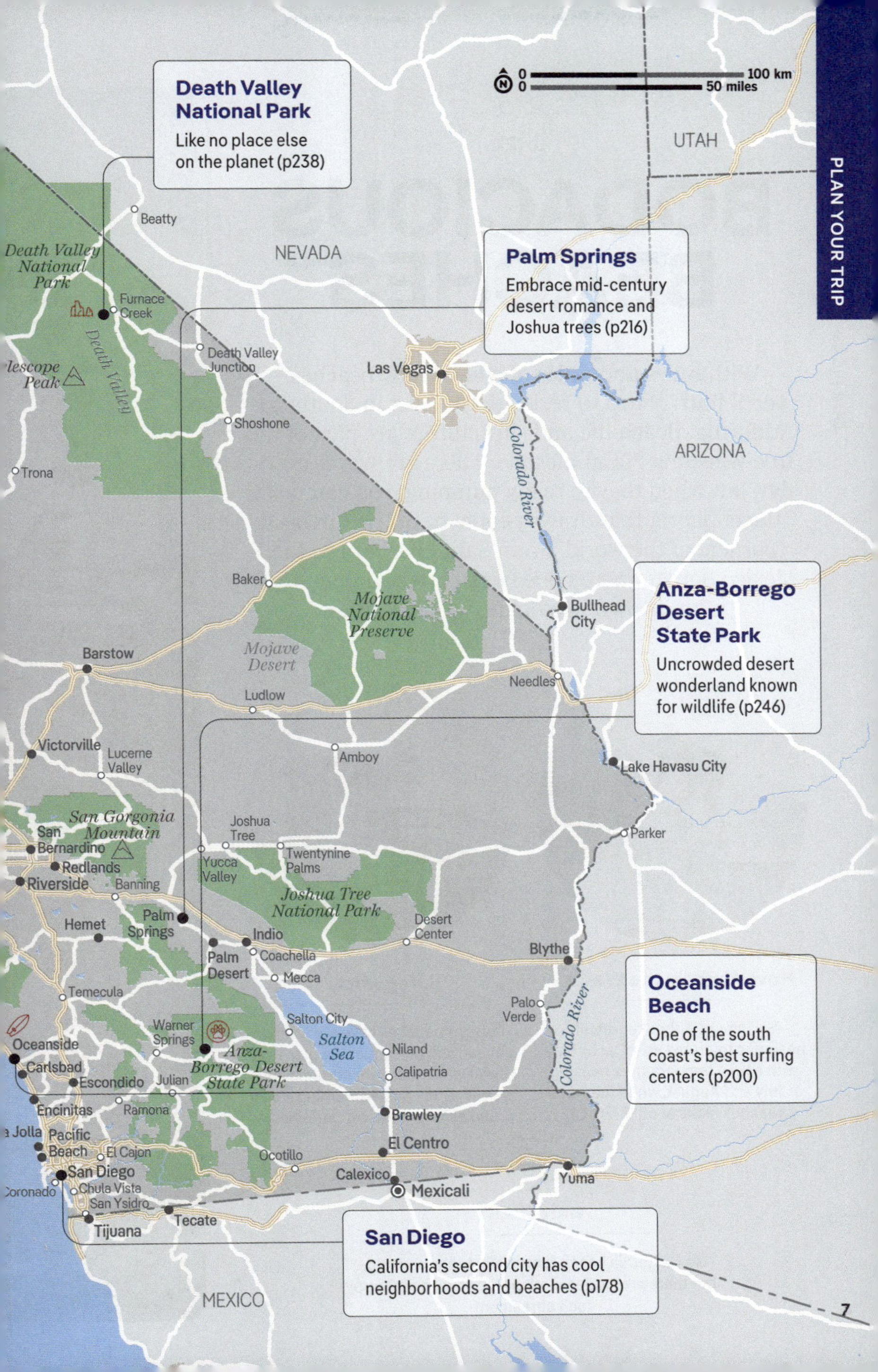
Death Valley National Park
Like no place else on the planet (p238)
Palm Springs
Embrace mid-century desert romance and Joshua trees (p216)
Anza-Borrego Desert State Park
Uncrowded desert wonderland known for wildlife (p246)
Oceanside Beach
One of the south coast's best surfing centers (p200)
San Diego
California's second city has cool neighborhoods and beaches (p178)
0 100 km
0 50 miles
UTAH
NEVADA
ARIZONA
MEXICO
Beatty
Death Valley National Park
Furnace Creek
Death Valley
Death Valley Junction
Telescope Peak
Las Vegas
Shoshone
Trona
Colorado River
Baker
Mojave National Preserve
Mojave Desert
Bullhead City
Barstow
Needles
Ludlow
Victorville
Lucerne Valley
Amboy
Lake Havasu City
San Gorgonia Mountain
San Bernardino
Redlands
Riverside
Banning
Joshua Tree
Yucca Valley
Twentynine Palms
Parker
Joshua Tree National Park
Hemet
Palm Springs
Palm Desert
Indio
Coachella
Mecca
Desert Center
Blythe
Temecula
Salton City
Salton Sea
Palo Verde
Colorado River
Oceanside
Carlsbad
Escondido
Warner Springs
Julian
Anza-Borrego Desert State Park
Niland
Calipatria
Encinitas
Ramona
Brawley
La Jolla
Pacific Beach
El Cajon
El Centro
Ocotillo
San Diego
Coronado
Chula Vista
San Ysidro
Calexico
Mexicali
Yuma
Tijuana
Tecate

BODACIOUS BEACHES

With miles and miles of wide, sandy beaches, you'll find it hard to resist getting wet in Southern California. Beach life and surf culture are part of the free-wheeling SoCal lifestyle. There are waves every day, but when they're really pumping, you can taste the euphoria that draws people from the furthest corners of the world. From Santa Barbara to the Mexico border, there's one beach after another, each with its own personality and qualities.

FROM LEFT: WONDERFUL NATURE/SHUTTERSTOCK, HOLBOX/SHUTTERSTOCK, ONEINCHPUNCH/SHUTTERSTOCK

How Warm is the Water?

Swimming without a wetsuit becomes tolerable in SoCal by May, with ocean temperatures peaking in July and August, when the water reaches highs of 68°F (20°C).

Lifeguards

Popular beaches have lifeguards, but can still be dangerous places to swim when there are currents and swells. Obey posted warning signs and ask about local conditions.

Bare it All?

No California beach is officially topless or nude, but there are hidden clothing-optional beaches by tacit agreement.

Santa Monica State Beach (p121)

BEST BEACH EXPERIENCES

Lounge around Santa Barbara's ❶ **Leadbetter Beach** (p46), where the slow-rolling waves make it popular for surf lessons and beginners.

Base yourself around ❷ **Santa Monica State Beach** (p121), where you can bike LA's shoreline, play volleyball or play on the pier.

Hang out at ❸ **Manhattan Beach** (p125), a classic LA South Coast idyll with powdery sand, endless good vibes and escape-proof allure.

Get charmed in ❹ **Seal Beach** (p162), where the cute beach is matched by the cute and walkable namesake town.

Surf ❺ **Oceanside Beach** (p200), which hosts the Super Girl Surf Pro, the largest all-female surf contest in the world.

Tacos

FABULOUS FOOD

Southern California offers unlimited bounty for good eating. Where else is the natural cornucopia fresher, the kitchen creativity more boundary-pushing or the flavors more international? Get adventurous with anything from food trucks to Michelin-starred gastronomic temples.

Everything's Local

California is the top US producer of vegetables and organic foods – expect everything from pistachios to hillside honey. For farmers markets, check cafarmersmkts.com and cdfa.ca.gov.

Taco Obsession

Tacos are a staple of the SoCal food scene, especially in LA and San Diego where the humble Baja-style fish taco is a local obsession.

BEST FOOD EXPERIENCES

Join posh diners for French-style cuisine at ❶ **Black Sheep** (p49) in russet-roofed Santa Barbara.

Surrender to dining joy under the stars at ❷ **Barn Kitchen** (p223) in Palm Springs.

Sample thoughtfully prepared fusion fare at ❸ **Danbi** (p110) in LA's Koreatown, a treasure trove of palate pleasures.

Mingle with hipsters and office jockeys at ❹ **Grand Central Market** (p91), a gourmet food hall in Downtown LA going strong since 1917.

Enjoy a fab night out at ❺ **Juniper & Ivy** (p189) in San Diego's Little Italy.

NATURAL WONDERS

In Southern California, Mother Nature has been more prolific than Picasso in his prime. And beyond the blissful beaches, there is unspoiled wilderness, big-shouldered mountains and desert sand dunes – this land is a mosaic that has inspired visionaries, artists and wanderers for centuries. You'll be astonished by Southern California's diversity – plunge in to create indelible memories.

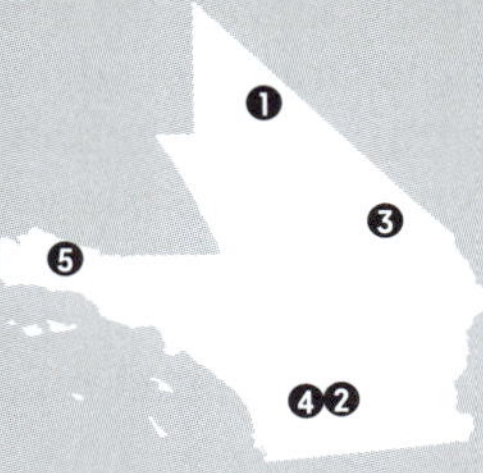

FROM LEFT: STEPHEN SIMPSON/GETTY IMAGES, BRIAN SWANSON/SHUTTERSTOCK

Camp by Starlight

Bed down under a blanket of stars at one of California's many desert parks. **Joshua Tree** (p227; pictured) is surrounded by moonlit boulders and fan-palm oases.

Winter Desert Pleasures

The inland deserts can kill the unwary in summer, but are ideal in the months that are off-season elsewhere when the temps make exploration more manageable.

Hidden Escapes

Find off-beat escapes from wilderness adventures in **Tecopa** (p245), with its inviting hot springs to soothe weary trail aches.

BEST NATURAL EXPERIENCES

Zoom across salt flats and stop at North America's lowest point in larger-than-life **1 Death Valley National Park** (p238).

Search for golden eagles and bighorn sheep at wonderfully under-visited **2 Anza-Borrego Desert State Park** (p246).

Find solitude and serenity at **3 Mojave National Preserve** (p253).

Venture into the mountains for hiking and camping in tiny **4 Julian** (p251), the purest expression of life's simple pleasures.

Hike to waterfalls along superb nature trails in **5 Los Padres National Forest** (p68), where the views reach the Pacific.

CLASSIC ROAD TRIPS

Road-tripping is the ultimate way to experience California, so fill the gas tank for unforgettable drives through scenery that tugs at your heart and soul. Wheel through epic desert expanses, endless miles of coastal highway and lonely, inland valleys tinged with wildflowers. Just make sure the rental car has unlimited miles – you'll need 'em.

Route 66

Get your kicks on America's 'Mother Road,' which brought Dust Bowl refugees, Hollywood starlets and hippies to California, the end of the rainbow.

Pacific Coast Hwy

The entire coastal road runs for an iconic 656 miles, but you'll have plenty of thrills on the 245 miles of Hwy 1 in Southern California.

Driving to SoCal from NoCal

If you're driving to SoCal from the north, choose Hwy 1, Hwy 395, or US 101 in that order. Avoid the bland, traffic-clogged I-5.

BEST ROAD-TRIP EXPERIENCES

Cruise Pinto Basin Rd through ❶ **Joshua Tree National Park** (p227), when springtime wildflowers light up the sere sands with a rainbow of colors.

Travel back to the hippie years on Topanga Canyon Blvd (Hwy 27), where your drive wends through ❷ **Topanga Canyon** (p121), a land of free spirits.

Explore LA's South Coast Beaches on meandering Hwy 1, where gorgeous strips of sand are backed by towns like fun-filled ❸ **Redondo Beach** (p127).

Coast through the wine-country back roads of the ❹ **Santa Ynez Valley** (p56), where the vines meander around rolling hills.

Ponder the frightening allure of the starkly forbidding ❺ **Death Valley** (p238) on a Hwy 190 driving tour.

FROM LEFT: NYOKKI/SHUTTERSTOCK, MARK SCHWETTMANN/SHUTTERSTOCK

ROLF_52/SHUTTERSTOCK

Getty Center (p118)

BEGUILING CITIES

California's urban areas will seduce you with a cultural kaleidoscope that whirls from art museums and vibrant theaters to tantalizing food scenes and high-octane nightlife. LA and San Francisco may hog the spotlight, but you'll find ample charm in smaller towns, too.

Diverse Metropolises

California cities run deeper than their reality-TV entourages might have you believe. Ultimately, it's the cultural diversity that makes the biggest impression.

No-Car Nirvana?

Every SoCal city has a good transport system and walkable neighborhoods, so though you're in the land of the car, you don't need one.

BEST CITY EXPERIENCES

Hit the wonderland that is ❶ **Los Angeles** (p72), with everything from Hollywood dives to the Getty Center.

Enjoy ❷ **San Diego's** (p173) breezy confidence – hit the beach, explore Balboa Park or just soak up the vibe.

Plan your move to ❸ **Santa Barbara** (p42), where the alluring downtown flows seamlessly to the beach.

Breathe deep in ❹ **Newport Beach** (p156), where Orange County's good life is permanently moored amid wide boulevards.

Keep smiling in carefree ❺ **Palm Springs** (p216), the desert-y idyll with one of the world's highest pool-to-resident ratios.

UNEXPECTED HIGHLIGHTS

Surprises across history abound in Southern California and some are just plain whimsical, as befitting the region's rep. After all, it's been quite a wild ride from the days of mammoths and saber-toothed tigers to the world's fourth-largest economy. Here, you can follow in the footsteps of countless generations that have shaped the state in ways unexpectedly dark and golden. And for every discovery that will delight, there's another that's a reminder of less noble inclinations.

FROM LEFT: STEVE CUKROV/SHUTTERSTOCK, KEN WOLTER/SHUTTERSTOCK, BILL MORSON/SHUTTERSTOCK

Native American Highlight

Amid the mid-century glitter, Palm Springs boasts the superb **Agua Caliente Cultural Museum** (p218; pictured), which tells the story of the Cahuilla Indians.

Diverse Downtown LA

Roam culturally rich Downtown Los Angeles from Olvera St to Chinatown (pictured) and then on to Little Tokyo, soaking up some of California's early influences.

History's Influences

Discover traces of Spanish Colonial forts, Catholic missions, Mexican pueblos and mining ghost towns.

Pumpkin patch, Solvang (p52)

BEST UNEXPECTED EXPERIENCES

Smell the tar, it's like a permanent new-roof installation at ❶ **La Brea Tar Pits & Museum** (p108), the graveyard of mammoths and other prehistoric unfortunates.

Witness a painful chapter of the USA's past at the ❷ **Japanese American National Museum** (p92), which details how citizens were sent to concentration camps in WWII.

Sample Danish flavors and local wines at ❸ **Solvang** (p52), a faux Danish village (of all things) in Santa Barbara's wine country.

Explore ❹ **Slab City** (p226), an off-grid community of artists and people seeking an alternative lifestyle that sprawls across a sun-scorched desert floor at the foot of Salvation Mountain.

Enjoy top theater in a venue where some of Hollywood's biggest names have performed and trained for over 100 years at the ❺ **Pasadena Playhouse** (p135).

MAGIC OF THE MOVIES

All the world may have been a stage to Shakespeare, but in California, it's actually more of a film set. And although movies were born in France, they certainly came of age in Hollywood. Here, you can stand in celebrities' footprints, take in famous filming locations or hop on a bus to see where the stars live.

Studio Tours

For a century California has made audiences laugh, cry and come back for more. To witness the magic, tour a movie studio in LA.

Hollywood Selfies

Snap a selfie with famous footprints at TCL Chinese Theatre, then duck onto Hollywood & Highland for a photo op with the iconic Hollywood sign.

Theme Park Magic

Meet beloved characters, ride movie-themed rides and more at Disneyland Resort and Universal Studios Hollywood.

FROM LEFT: CHIZHEVSKAYA EKATERINA/SHUTTERSTOCK, HAYK_SHALUNTS/SHUTTERSTOCK, SEAN PAVONE/SHUTTERSTOCK

Downtown skyline from Griffith Park (p94)

BEST MOVIE EXPERIENCES

Stand on the spot of the climactic scene of one of LA's iconic movies, *Chinatown*, where it was shot: ❶ **Chinatown** (p89).

Save a full day for the world's greatest movie museum, the ❷ **Academy Museum of Motion Pictures** (p107), which celebrates the arts with original memorabilia.

Gaze out on the City of Angels from the favored location of *Rebel Without a Cause* and many more films at the ❸ **Griffith Observatory** (p94).

Live your (romantic) *Top Gun* fantasy and enjoy a piece of tasty pie at the bungalow used as Charlie's home in ❹ **Oceanside** (p200).

Drink merlot if you dare on a *Sideways* road trip to the ❺ **Santa Ynez Valley wineries** (p56) where the 2004 film still resonates.

REGIONS & CITIES

Find the places that tick all your boxes.

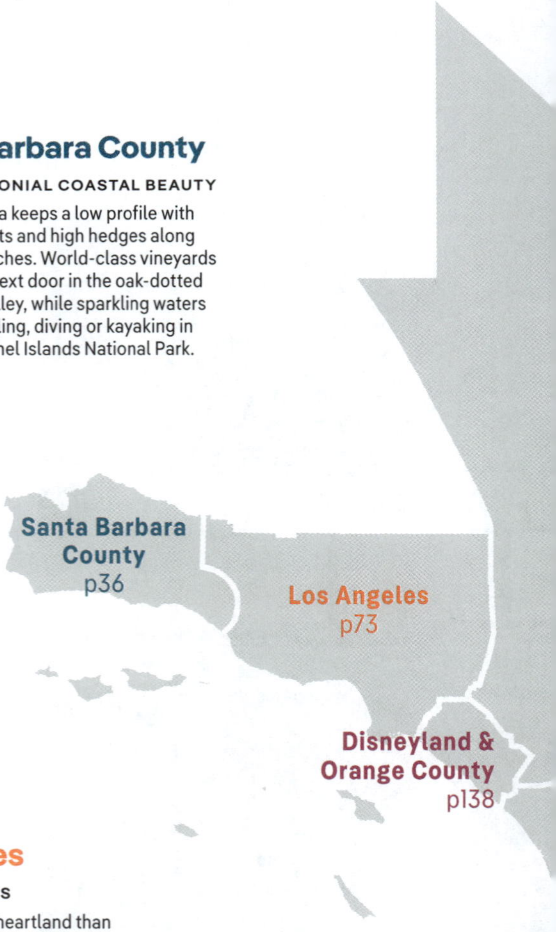

Santa Barbara County

SPANISH-COLONIAL COASTAL BEAUTY

Santa Barbara keeps a low profile with pristine streets and high hedges along white-sand beaches. World-class vineyards beckon right next door in the oak-dotted Santa Ynez Valley, while sparkling waters invite snorkeling, diving or kayaking in nearby Channel Islands National Park.

Los Angeles

CITY OF DREAMS

There's more to life in SoCal's heartland than just sunny beaches and air-kissing celebrities. Take the time to dive deeper and explore its bounty of art and architecture, and revel in the sheer diversity of its cuisines and neighborhoods, each with rich histories dating from the earliest days of Spanish colonization.

Palm Springs & the Deserts

DESERT CULTURE, ART AND EXPANSIVE WILDERNESS

The desert gets hot, but Palm Springs has kept its cool since the '50s when stars like Sinatra and Elvis came out to play. Nowadays you can pair Coachella festival, a thriving LGBTQ+ scene, speakeasies and restored mid-century-modern motels with hiking or climbing in Joshua Tree and desert solitaire in Death Valley.

Disneyland & Orange County

THE MOST QUINTESSENTIALLY CALIFORNIA EXPERIENCE

The OC's beaches are packed with strapping surfers, volleyball champions and retouched reality stars. If you think this scenery is surreal, check out the hyper-reality of the Disneyland Resort which, along with the rest of the theme parks, keeps the kids enthralled as they meet life-size characters from their favorite movies.

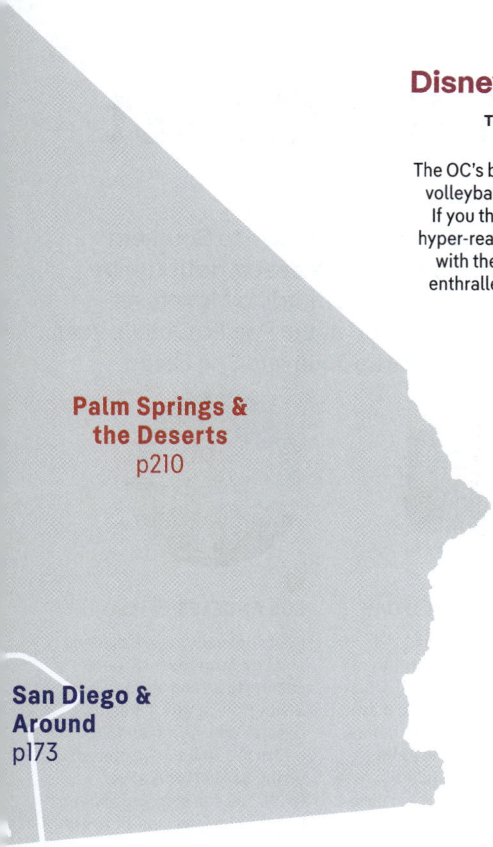

San Diego & Around

EXPLORE CALIFORNIA'S SUNNIEST CITY

California's southernmost city seems like it's on permanent vacation, with a near-perfect year-round climate, beaches and a booming craft-brewery scene. Explore Balboa Park's quirky museums and experience the pleasures of Coronado's beaches, or wander laid-back beach towns in search of the ultimate fish taco.

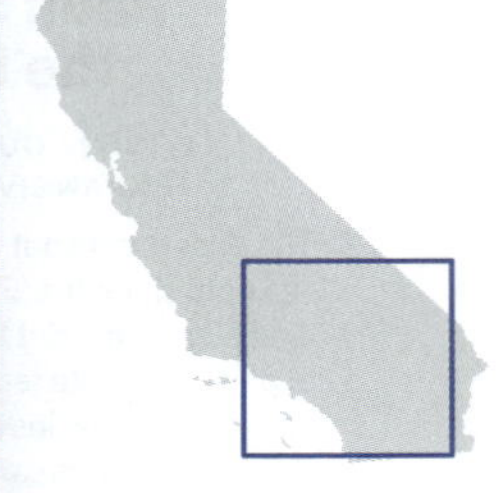

Roy's Motel & Cafe (p257) on Route 66

ITINERARIES

Route 66 & the Coast

Allow: 5 days **Distance:** 365 miles

You'll know you've found Route 66, the legendary road to Southern California, when you're cruising through the stark desert dotted with kitschy roadside attractions. Play in the San Bernardino Mountains, then get a Santa Monica pleasure-pier payoff at the Pacific Ocean. Veer south to hit the OC beaches, then explore La Jolla and San Diego.

1

MOJAVE DESERT 1 DAY

The Golden State was once the promised land at the end of a long and sometimes lonesome road. Today, motoring across the stark beauty of the **Mojave Desert** (p253; pictured) is a relative breeze compared to times of yore. Get a diner lunch in famous Western towns like Barstow and Daggett.

Detour: *Feeling the desert mood? Head north to austere* ***Death Valley National Park*** *(p238).*

2

PALM SPRINGS 1 DAY

Take a turn off Route 66 to reach the **San Bernardino National Forest** (p224), where you can hike, camp and play at Big Bear and its lake before reaching retro-glam **Palm Springs** (p216; pictured), where poolside cocktails meet desert oases and Joshua trees.

3

LOS ANGELES 1 DAY

Route 66 emerges in Pasadena and **Los Angeles** (p73) before coming to an end at Hwy 1 in Santa Monica with a grand coastal-view payoff and the End of the Trail sign (pictured) on the **Santa Monica Pier** (p119). You can stop and explore LA for as long as time allows or breeze through on your way to the coast.

0 100 km
0 50 miles
Death Valley National Park
NEVADA
CALIFORNIA
Bakersfield
Mojave National Preserve
Mojave
58
Barstow
15
Mojave Desert
1 START
Daggett
2hr
40
5
15
Pasadena
2hr
10
3
Malibu
Santa Monica
Los Angeles
Anaheim
½hr
Indio
2 Palm Springs
10
Huntington Beach 4
45min
5
Laguna Beach
Colorado Desert
Santa Catalina Island
5
Salton Sea
Oceanside
½hr
Imperial Valley
Gulf of Santa Catalina
San Clemente Island
La Jolla 6 END
San Diego

4

HUNTINGTON BEACH ½ DAY

In **Huntington Beach** (p160; pictured), aka 'Surf City USA,' SoCal's obsession with wave riding hits its frenzied peak. If you look down, you'll see the names of legendary surfers in the sidewalk Surfers' Hall of Fame. On Huntington Beach Pier, catch up-close views of daredevils barreling through tubes.

5

LAGUNA BEACH ½ DAY

On your way south, **Crystal Cove State Park** (p167) is a wonderland of more than 3 miles of open beach, an underwater scuba park and 2400 acres of undeveloped woodland. Emerge at **Laguna Beach** (p164; pictured), an early-20th-century artist colony of secluded coves, romantic cliffs, arts-and-crafts bungalows, galleries and the acclaimed Laguna Art Museum.

6

LA JOLLA 1 DAY

Sitting pretty on one of SoCal's loveliest sweeps of coast, **La Jolla** (p192; pictured) is a ritzy town of shimmering beaches, fashionista boutiques and clifftop mansions. Kayak at La Jolla Cove or snorkel in the offshore marine reserves which harbor a variety of marine life and reefs. It's the perfect base for exploring the area and **San Diego** (p178), too.

FROM LEFT: STEVE CUKROV/SHUTTERSTOCK, JOSH GUNTER/SHUTTERSTOCK, DANITA DELIMONT/SHUTTERSTOCK

WHEN TO GO

Outside of the deserts, weather is rarely a concern in Southern California – so pick your corner and enjoy.

Southern California's sunny reputation is deserved. The climate's variations across the year are mere shadings rather than the dramatic highs and lows found elsewhere. Nonetheless, it's high season almost everywhere from June through August with tourists arriving from around the state, nation and world. Spring in the Southland is brilliant after winter rains, when the hills turn an iridescent shade of green and are accented by blooming wildflowers such as the golden California poppy. While it's equally sunny and cloudless in the fall, the dry months from summer to winter are increasingly known as 'fire season.' Stay vigilant about the danger – light no open flames, ever – and keep an eye on the sky for smoke.

Looking for a Bargain?

In summer high season (and on the coast on weekends) accommodation prices are 50% to 100% higher on average than the rest of the year. If you can, travel at another time.

I LIVE HERE

ANNUAL MIGRATION

LA journalist Adam Skolnick is author of American Tiger, set in Southern California. @adamskolnick

Every spring they swim north from the lagoons in southern Baja to Alaska. But it was mid-May and we assumed the gray whale migration was over as we swam a quarter mile offshore from Malibu. Then we saw six of them rolling in the tides. We floated on the surface mesmerized, as one by one they swam out to us. Then they were under us: a flotilla of power and beauty just passing through.

FROM LEFT: ARTUR DEBAT/GETTY IMAGES, ONEINCHPUNCH/SHUTTERSTOCK

Route 66 (p257)

DESERT DRIVING

Southern California's roads dwindle to two-lane strands of sun-blasted blacktop as they cross the deserts. Drivers should not take these routes lightly, given that any unplanned stop can prove dangerous. Always carry water for a few days and if you're going off a major road, tell someone.

Weather through the Year: Los Angeles

JANUARY	FEBRUARY	MARCH	APRIL	MAY	JUNE
Avg. daytime max: 69°F (21°C)	Avg. daytime max: 69°F (21°C)	Avg. daytime max: 70°F (21°C)	Avg. daytime max: 73°F (23°C)	Avg. daytime max: 74°F (23°C)	Avg. daytime max: 79°F (26°C)
Days of rainfall: 5	Days of rainfall: 5	Days of rainfall: 4	Days of rainfall: 3	Days of rainfall: 2	Days of rainfall: 0

DESERT SEASONS

Unlike in the rest of Southern California, summer is low season in the deserts where temperatures exceed 100°F (38°C). It's blistering to even try to walk around, let alone hike the gorgeous trails. Go in spring instead, when wildflower blooms can be mind-blowing, or high-season winter.

The Big Festivals

Pasadena's **Tournament of Roses Parade** (p132) has been filling the streets with sweet smells and rolling floral beauty since 1890, all in honor of a fabled college football game, the Rose Bowl. **January**

Headliners, indie rockers, rappers and DJs converge outside Palm Springs at the **Coachella Valley Music & Arts Festival** (p237) for an annual musical extravaganza. **April**

Southern California celebrates LGBTQ+ pride with parades, events and parties. Major events happen one after the other in LA, West Hollywood and Long Beach during May and June. **Palm Springs** (p217) celebrates in November. **May, June & November**

The Maritime Museum of San Diego preserves the 150-year-old *Star of India*, the world's oldest active sailing ship. It's the star of the thrilling annual **Festival of Sail** (p181), which attracts dozens of tall ships from around the world. **September**

Local & Quirkier Festivals

The Arlington Theatre is the center of the **Santa Barbara International Film Festival** (p48), which gives Hollywood luminaries an excuse to escape north in the weeks before the Oscars. **February**

To be or not to be Newport Beach. During the summer months, **Shakespeare By the Sea** (p158) performs the Bard's works in pop-up performances around the city. **June to August**

The best **Halloween party** in California fills the streets of West Hollywood with over half a million revelers, gawkers and partiers. There's a big LGBTQ+ component which adds to the color. **October**

Desert X (p220) is an outdoor art biennale in the Coachella Valley. International artists create arresting art installations in unexpected locations on odd-numbered years. **March to May**

I LIVE HERE

SPRING PUPS

Caz Shen, LA transplant and artist, describes the Spring fido culture in SoCal. @studio_caz

Spring in LA means everyone brings their dogs to the cafe. Pups of all shapes and sizes bask in the warm afternoon sun and lap water out of paper cups set out by their owners. A great reminder that even in LA, where the perfect weather feels like a guarantee, one must appreciate the gentle sunshine. A beautiful day should never go unappreciated.

Skaters with dog, Santa Monica (p119)

COASTAL FOG

Even Southern California gets the fog Northern California is famous for. It's more likely in the cooler months, but when it does roll in, it can turn a beach into a refrigerator. Venice might be socked in and chilly, but just inland in Downtown LA, it's a sunny 75°F (24°C).

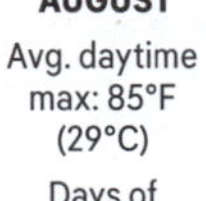
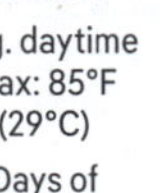

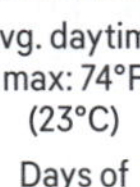

JULY	AUGUST	SEPTEMBER	OCTOBER	NOVEMBER	DECEMBER
Avg. daytime max: 83°F (28°C)	Avg. daytime max: 85°F (29°C)	Avg. daytime max: 84°F (29°C)	Avg. daytime max: 79°F (26°C)	Avg. daytime max: 74°F (23°C)	Avg. daytime max: 68°F (20°C)
Days of rainfall: 0	Days of rainfall: 0	Days of rainfall: 0	Days of rainfall: 3	Days of rainfall: 4	Days of rainfall: 8

FROM LEFT: MAGRAPHY/SHUTTERSTOCK, MAXIMUM FILM/ALAMY IMAGES

Hikers and dogs, Griffith Park (p94)

GET PREPARED FOR SOUTHERN CALIFORNIA

Useful things to load in your bag, your ears and your brain.

Clothes

Casual layers Southern California is a laid-back, anything-goes kind of place, especially when it comes to fashion (outside of a narrow strip of chic LA). Note, however, that the balmy weather of clichés is mostly true, but be prepared for surprises along the coast, where marine fog reprimands anyone in shorts in the morning, rolls back in the afternoon to make you wish you'd worn sweat-proof sunscreen, and may return by evening to mock skimpy night-out outfits. The mountains can be cold and deserts blazing hot: have layers at the ready.

Local Language

In California, language goes way beyond 'dude.' Many Californians are multilingual – more than 200 different languages are spoken here. The top five are English, Spanish, Chinese, Tagalog and Vietnamese. Around 43% of state residents speak a language other than English at home. Dive in and go for it, you may find someone who speaks your native tongue.

Shoes Walking shoes and sandals are essential for cities and trails alike. Even on nights out, stilettos or natty Oxfords are not necessary – just dress however you like.

READ

Where I Was From (Joan Didion; 2003) California-born essayist shatters palm-fringed fantasies.

Devil in a Blue Dress (Walter Mosley; 1990) First of a series of acclaimed Easy Rawlins LA noirs. Great in audiobook format.

City of Quartz (Mike Davis; 1990) Landmark book details every wart in the Southland's development; 2006 update captures more.

The Big Sleep (Raymond Chandler; 1939) Iconic Phillip Marlowe mystery set in Los Angeles sets the bar for detective fiction.

Courtesies

Southern Californians are casual by nature, but a few (unspoken) rules still apply.

Friendliness Smiles go a long way. Be friendly, even in a disagreement.

Greetings Shaking hands when meeting is a tad formal, but it's expected for business dealings and by some older adults.

Bargaining Haggling usually isn't appropriate, except at outdoor markets and with sidewalk vendors.

Smoking Don't light up indoors (it's illegal) or anywhere else you don't see others doing it. Some restaurants have patios or sidewalk tables where smoking is tolerated (ask first), but don't expect your neighbors to be happy about it.

Cannabis While people aged 21 and older can buy cannabis, smoking or consuming marijuana in public or on federal land (national parks, Joshua Tree etc) is illegal.

Dining out Californian restaurant etiquette tends to be informal. Only a handful of restaurants require more than a dressy shirt, slacks and shoes that aren't flip-flops. At other places, T-shirts, shorts and sandals are fine.

Tipping (p266) At restaurants, 20% to 25% is expected for table service. Takeaway service can still rate 10%, though it's not obligatory.

Driving It is illegal to drive under the influence of anything or to carry open alcohol containers. If wine tasting, have a designated driver and keep open bottles in the trunk.

WATCH

LA Confidential (Curtis Hanson; 1997; pictured) Neo-noir tale of corruption and murder in 1950s LA.

Boyz n the Hood (John Singleton; 1991) Groundbreaking coming-of-age story set in South Central.

Laurel Canyon (Lisa Cholodenko; 2002) Gripping tale unfolds in the '60s and '70s music scene.

Chinatown (Roman Polanski; 1974) Semi-fictional account of LA's successful grab of water from hundreds of miles away, which continues today.

La La Land (Damien Chazelle; 2016) Two plucky kids try to sing and dance their way to fame.

LISTEN

Drop It Like It's Hot (Snoop Dogg; 2004) His first single to hit number one went quadruple platinum, not bad for a rapper from Long Beach...

Blood Sugar Sex Magik (Red Hot Chili Peppers; 1991) Seminal album by iconic punk pioneers, kin to bands like No Doubt and Green Day.

L.A. Woman (Doors; 1971) The song was thought to be Jim Morrison's farewell to Los Angeles; he died in Paris three months after its release.

La Bamba (Los Lobos; 1987) Famed interpretations by East LA band of classic songs from the biopic about California teenage star Ritchie Valens.

HEIDI BESEN/SHUTTERSTOCK

Grand Central Market (p91)

THE FOOD SCENE

Southern California cuisine is a team effort that changes with every season – and it reflects the way the world eats.

As you graze your way around the most populated part of the Golden State, you'll often want to compliment the chef – and they will pass it on to the staff, local farmers, fishers, ranchers, winemakers and artisan food producers who make their menu possible. 'Let the ingredients speak for themselves!' is the rallying cry of California cuisine. Most of America's fruit and specialty vegetables are grown in the state, and those not grown in SoCal are drawn down by the huge market.

Southern California dining also reflects the contributions of some of the world's top food cultures. The state's rich Mexican and Latin American heritage means burritos regularly outshine burgers. And SoCal has some of the best Asian cuisine available outside Asia. The regional stew is peppered, too, with Mediterranean traditions – where the climate and soil are similar to Southern California's – and Afro-Caribbean and southern soul cooking.

Thus, fusion is not a fad but second nature in the Southland, where international takes blend beautifully with seasonal, local ingredients.

Mix & Match From the Start

California was part of Mexico before it became a US state in 1850, and almost 40% of the population today is Latinx. It's no surprise, then, that Mexican classics remain go-to comfort foods, and upscale restaurants add novel twists to staple enchiladas and tacos. This blend of local

Best Californian Dishes

CALIFORNIA BURRITO
Mega-meal bursting out of a giant flour tortilla.

DOUGHNUTS
This humble fried treat is an art form.

SALMON
Freshly caught, prepared in myriad ways.

AVOCADOS
One of SoCal's most popular fruits, eaten at all meals.

produce and international cuisines defines California's great culinary advantage: an experimental attitude toward food. Even in its Wild West days, when immigrants from around the world were pouring into LA, necessity and proximity meant everyone ate adventurously and cross-culturally, pairing whiskey and wine with tamales and Chinese noodles. Similarly, as other groups with distinct cuisines immigrated, their cuisines joined the pot.

The Many Hearts of SoCal Food

Ruth Reichl, the one-time California chef and former *New York Times* restaurant critic, observed LA's real culinary treasure is its ethnic restaurants. With more than 180 nationalities in LA County alone, you will only be scratching the surface with the next great Korean barbecue truck, Japanese ramen shop or Persian ice-cream parlor.

You'll find Mexican restaurants all over SoCal. Japanese eateries are concentrated in LA neighborhoods, such as Downtown's Little Tokyo and Torrance inland from the South Bay. Downtown LA's Chinatown and communities in the San Gabriel Valley are the epicenter of Chinese cooking. LA's Koreatown and Orange County's Little Saigon are each the largest respective ethnic immigrant communities outside their countries of origin, while Anaheim's Little Arabia is best for Middle Eastern fare. San Diego has a thriving Little Italy, too.

If you want to taste all of SoCal in just one place, head to Downtown LA's **Grand Central Market** (p91). It's crammed with energetic vendors dishing up street food from around the globe, from Latin American *pupusas* to tangy Thai barbecue.

Japanese dish of Shoyu Ramen

Green Truck, Los Angeles

FOOD-TRUCK FAVES

If you can think of a cuisine, somewhere in SoCal there's a food truck for it.

Dim sum Chinese small plates and dumplings.

Kalbi Korean flavor-bursting marinated, grilled beef short ribs.

Jollof rice Spicy West African rice.

Cuitlacoche Mexican corn smut, a sort of mold – a delicacy the world over.

Korean tacos Grilled, marinated beef and spicy pickled kimchi.

Pho Vietnamese noodle soup.

Fish tacos Grilled fish tacos, ideally fresh.

Birria Meat stew from Jalisco, sometimes goat, often beef.

Expect every type of fusion and comfort food. Many food trucks also offer sweets, such as churros.

FORAGED FOOD
Wild chanterelles found beneath hillside oaks.

RANCH DRESSING
This ubiquitous flavoring was invented in Santa Barbara.

COBB SALAD
Popular 1940s Hollywood lunch dish with multiple ingredients.

CALIFORNIA ROLL
Invented in 1960s LA using crab, avocado and cucumber.

TACOS IN MYRIAD WAYS
Anything stuffed into a corn or flour tortilla.

Specialties

Food Trucks

For affordable, innovative cooking, make raids on food trucks. Southern California's legendary trucks serve up everything from tacos *al pastor* (marinated pork) and Indian curry-and-naan wraps to Chinese buns packed with roast duck and fresh mango. People trade the names of favored food trucks the way IPO tips are traded in Silicon Valley.

As a casual visitor, if you see a truck and you see a crowd, stop! Otherwise, the best ones have huge social followings, which is also how you locate them. In LA, the definitive source for Cal-Mex street food, LA Taco *(lataco.com)*, is always up on the best trucks.

Vegan Lifestyle

Seasonal, produce-forward, locavore eating has become so mainstream it verges on cliché, but California started the movement over 50 years ago when much of the country was eating packaged foods.

Tacos & nachos

To all those accustomed to making do with dressed-up side salads, relax – your needs are not an afterthought here.

Los Angeles, with its laser focus on healthy eating, has been exploring the boundaries of a vegan diet for decades.

You won't have to go out of your way to find vegetarian and vegan options: bakeries, bistros and even mom-and-pop joints in workaday neighborhoods are ready for meat-free, dairy-free, eggless requests.

MEALS OF A LIFETIME

Providence (p82) Wild-caught and sustainably-sourced seafood takes center stage in LA.

Barbareño (p49) Fresh, locally-harvested produce, seafood and meats prepared with playful creativity in Santa Barbara.

My 2 Cents LA (p107) TV chef Alisa Reynolds has a loyal following for her Southern Fusion fare.

Danbi (p110) Korean-fusion fine dining, thoughtfully prepared and artfully served in LA's Koreatown.

Addison (p194) Three Michelin-starred tasting menus focused on the flavors of Southern California in Del Mar.

Bar Cecil (p221) In-demand, stylish French-Californian spot in Palm Springs. Book months ahead.

THE YEAR IN FOOD

SPRING

When the sun comes out, farmers markets fill city streets with salad makings, fish-taco trucks flock to beaches, and lines bend around the block for organic ice cream studded with just-picked berries.

SUMMER

Markets of all kinds overflow with California's incredible bounty of produce. Strawberries are an early arrival, right before the avalanche of stone fruit. Avocados come from farms in Ventura County.

FALL

Experience your first crush at harvest in all the wine regions and give thanks for California's bounty of fresh-fruit pies. Many of the little food and wine festivals that enliven small towns happen now.

WINTER

Make the most of long nights with seafood feasts of Dungeness crab and salmon. Celebrate Lunar New Year with lucky mandarins, and warm yourself with citrus-spiked cocktails.

CHECUBUS/SHUTTERSTOCK

Venice Beach (p123)

HOW TO... Pick a Beach

With miles of super beaches and waves made for surfing, there's a beach to suit everyone in Southern California. Whether you're hoping to hit the waves, looking for a chilled spot, seeking family fun or fancy mingling with the in-crowd, SoCal has a beach for you.

Good Sand

Picking a beach in Southern California means deciding what style of sandy strand you want. One constant compared to other parts of the world is the quality of the sand: it is light and powdery, from the Santa Barbara County line to the Mexican border. You won't find a rocky field pretending to be a beach anywhere. Otherwise, your choices, broadly, are as follows...

A Scene

Famous beaches where the crowds are the reason to go. Think **Venice** (p123), **Laguna** (p166) or **Coronado** (p188). You go to see and be seen and to revel in the vibe. If finding your own patch of sand on a weekend is a challenge, that's part of the deal. Especially at LA County beaches such as **Will Rogers** (p121) and starting at **Manhattan** (p125) and going south, there are intense volleyball matches.

Fun for the Kids

Quieter but easily accessed beaches with gentle surf, bathrooms, access to drinks, snacks and other diversions. Santa Barbara's **West Beach** (p46) at the bottom of State St is a prime example of a family-friendly beach. **Seal Beach** (p162) in Orange County is another.

Nature

Plenty of SoCal beaches are windows into the rich Pacific habitat, from tide pools at the shore to habitats for dolphins and seals off shore. They are often away from built-up areas and harder to reach. You may have to clamber down cliff-face steps and park a distance away, but the added benefit is fewer crowds. The coast north of Santa Barbara is good as is the coast north of the San Diego region. Close to Malibu, **El Matador State Beach** (p121) is a gem.

TIPS FOR SOCAL BEACHES

- Bring lots of water.
- Bring a Frisbee.
- They're all free, but parking may cost.
- Nobody owns any beach.
- Few allow open fires.
- Carefully note if there are lifeguards or not.
- They all face the sunset.
- And, finally, if you find yourself being carried offshore by a riptide, don't panic or try to swim against the current. Instead, swim parallel to the shoreline and once the current stops pulling you out, swim back toward shore.

FROM LEFT: RON AND PATTY THOMAS/GETTY IMAGES, ED FREEMAN/GETTY IMAGES

Wildflowers, Anza-Borrego Desert State Park (p246)

THE OUTDOORS

Hike through deserts sprinkled with spring wildflowers, dive into the Pacific in summer, cycle through fall foliage and ski wintry mountain slopes.

Southern California is an all-season magnet for outdoor fun. Beach life and surf culture define the region's freewheeling lifestyle, so consider this permission granted to hit the waves. Amble on smooth coastal bluff trails or hike on multiday backpacking treks into the desert. If you want to get your adrenaline pumping, try scuba diving past coastal shipwrecks, cycle the coast or kitesurf the bays.

Swimming & Surfing

With miles of wide, sandy beaches between Santa Barbara and San Diego, you can be living the dream at least six months of the year. Ocean temperatures are tolerable by May or June, peaking in July and August. During the **Los Angeles 2028 Olympic Games** *(la28.org)*, the surf competitions will be at Lower Trestles Beach, off San Clemente. Every year, Huntington Beach (p160) hosts the **US Open of Surfing** *(usopenofsurfing.com)*.

Experienced windsurfers tear up the waves along the coast, while newbies and those who want a mellower ride skim along calm bays and protected beaches. There's almost always a breeze, but the best winds blow from September through November.

Walking & Hiking

With epic scenery, Southern California is the perfect place to explore iconic highlights on foot. Stroll the beach at sunset

Adrenaline Sports

CAVING
Descend into a desert cavern with a lava tube at the end of a lonely road in **Mojave National Preserve** (p253).

OCEAN KAYAKING
Exploring the sea caves and isolated coves along the coastlines of the **Channel Islands** (p66) is a privilege and an uncommon pleasure.

WATER SKIING & KITESURFING
San Diego's **Mission Bay** (p190) has the ideal combination of water protected from currents and open to winds.

FAMILY ADVENTURES

Kayak in warm water at **Laguna Beach** (p166) where the shallow coves are good for paddling.

Take surf lessons on beaches around **Santa Barbara** (p46), at **Dana Point** (p168) or many more SoCal beaches.

Explore tide pools on the nature-rich coast at **La Jolla** (p192). The entire California coast is dotted with these rich cradles of sea life.

Go for a horseback ride in **Julian** (p251) on trails through the colorful high desert.

Loop-de-loop on rides at **Disneyland Resort** (p144), **Knott's Berry Farm** (p164) and **Pacific Park** (p121) on the Santa Monica Pier.

Pedal the beachfront on the 22-mile **Marvin Braude Bike Trail** (p119), which links most LA beaches. Rent bikes for the family in **Venice** (p123).

or trek past Joshua trees in desert oases. In spring and early summer, the Golden State is touched with a painter's palette as wildflowers bloom down coastal hillsides, across mountain meadows and along desert sands.

Even urban areas are close to good ambling. In LA, **Griffith Park** (p94) is a natural wonderland laced with trails, including some to famous movie locations, while many of the city's neighborhoods, such as **Echo Park** (p94), are tailor-made for walking.

Cycling, Santa Barbara (p49)

Cycling & Mountain Biking

California's outstanding cycling terrain calls for leisurely spins along the beach, adrenaline-fueled mountain rides or multiday road-cycling tours down the coast. Even heavily trafficked urban areas may have good cycling routes. For example, cycle downtown Santa Barbara and the beachfront are perfect for peddling (p49). Avoid SoCal's deserts in summer, due to comfort and safety considerations.

Whale-Watching

Every summer, an estimated 20,000 gray whales feed in the Arctic waters between Alaska and Siberia, and every fall they start moving south down the west coast of Canada and the USA to sheltered lagoons in the Gulf of California off Baja California. In spring, these whales turn around and head back to the Arctic. During their 12,000-mile round-trip, the whales pass just off the California coast, typically between late December and early April.

It's not only gray whales that make appearances in SoCal. Blue, humpback, sperm and killer whales, as well as schools of dolphins and porpoises, can be seen swimming offshore throughout the summer and fall, but spotting these marine mammals is not quite as predictable. Still, most SoCal towns with a large marina will have boats leaving on well-publicized tours in season.

SCUBA DIVING
Artificial reefs and sunken ships are an underwater playground for scuba divers at **Wreck Alley** (p189), off the San Diego coast.

DESERT HIKING
Hike into the canyons for otherworldly geological wonders in **Death Valley National Park** (p238); note, expertise is required.

WHALE-WATCHING
Spot migrating gray, blue, humpback and sperm whales, plus orca, on trips from **Santa Barbara** (p46).

CLIMBING
Rock climbing abounds in **Joshua Tree National Park** (p227). The namesake town has hundreds of guides and there are myriad routes.

ACTION AREAS

Where to find Los Angeles' and Southern California's best outdoor activities.

Beach

1. Seal Beach (p162)
2. El Capitán State Beach, Gaviota Coast (p50)
3. Venice Beach (p125)
4. Zuma Beach (p121)
5. Carlsbad (p195)
6. Encinitas (p201)

Snorkeling/Diving

1. Diver's Cove, Laguna Beach (p166)
2. Little Corona del Mar Beach, Newport Beach (p159)
3. Channel Islands (p66)
4. San Diego-Scripps Coastal Marine Conservation Area (p192)
5. Matlahuayl State Marine Reserve (p192)
6. Wreck Alley (p189)

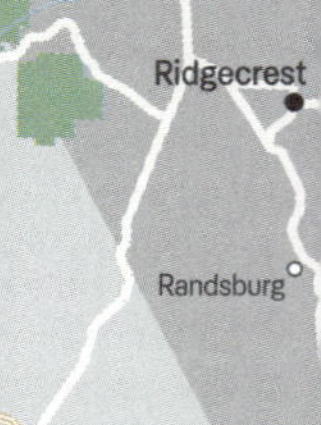

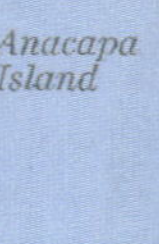
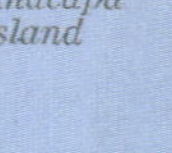

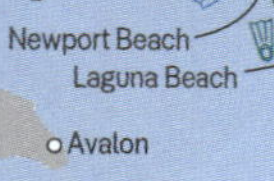

Surfing

1. Huntington Beach (p160)
2. Laguna Beach (p166)
3. Dana Point (p168)
4. Malibu (p119)
5. Del Mar (p193)
6. Oceanside (p200)
7. Ventura (p63)

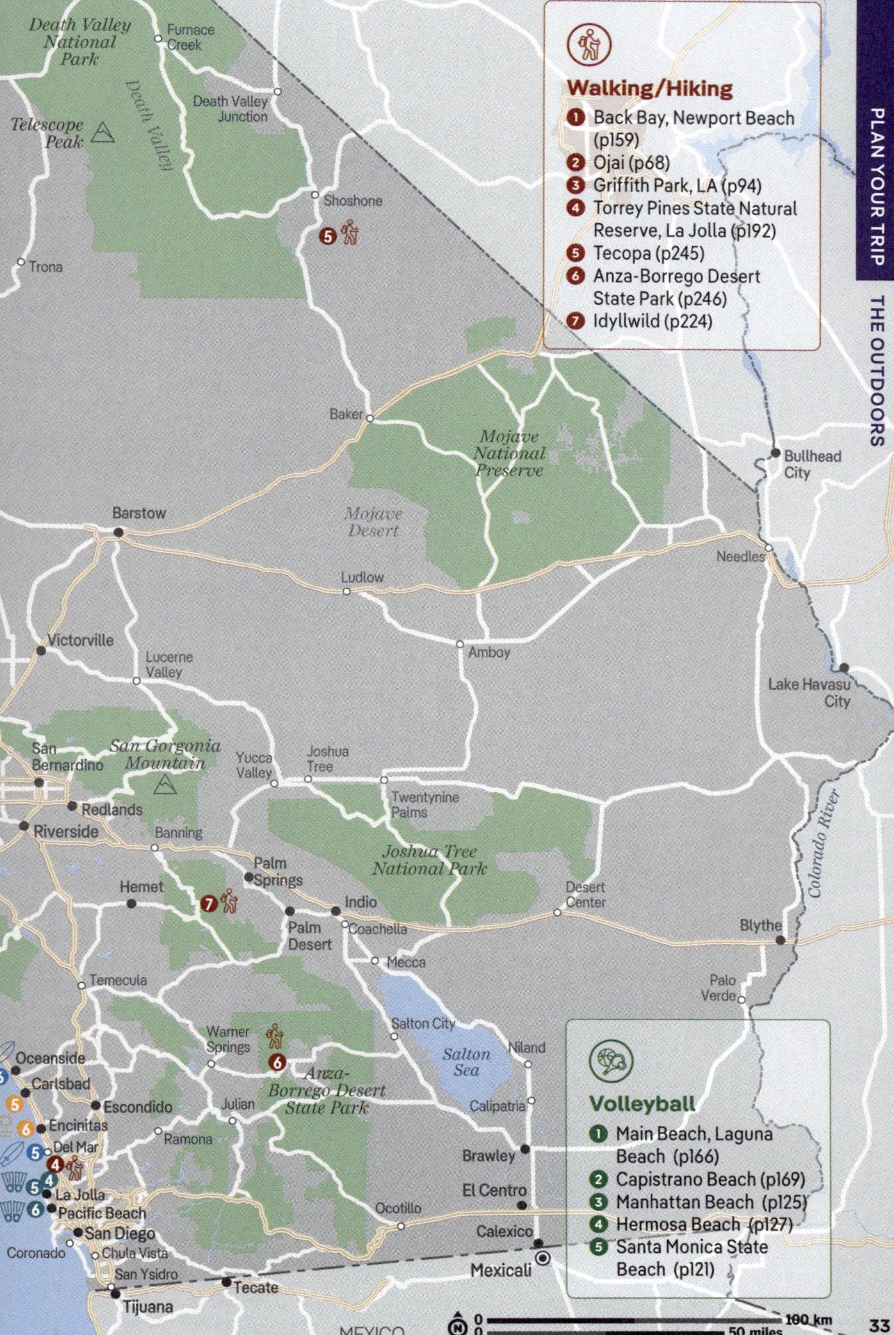
Walking/Hiking
1 Back Bay, Newport Beach (p159)
2 Ojai (p68)
3 Griffith Park, LA (p94)
4 Torrey Pines State Natural Reserve, La Jolla (p192)
5 Tecopa (p245)
6 Anza-Borrego Desert State Park (p246)
7 Idyllwild (p224)
Volleyball
1 Main Beach, Laguna Beach (p166)
2 Capistrano Beach (p169)
3 Manhattan Beach (p125)
4 Hermosa Beach (p127)
5 Santa Monica State Beach (p121)
Death Valley National Park
Furnace Creek
Death Valley
Death Valley Junction
Telescope Peak
Shoshone
Trona
Baker
Mojave National Preserve
Mojave Desert
Bullhead City
Barstow
Needles
Ludlow
Amboy
Victorville
Lucerne Valley
Lake Havasu City
San Bernardino
San Gorgonia Mountain
Yucca Valley
Joshua Tree
Twentynine Palms
Redlands
Riverside
Banning
Joshua Tree National Park
Colorado River
Palm Springs
Hemet
Indio
Desert Center
Palm Desert
Coachella
Blythe
Mecca
Temecula
Palo Verde
Salton City
Warner Springs
Niland
Salton Sea
Oceanside
Carlsbad
Anza-Borrego Desert State Park
Escondido
Julian
Calipatria
Encinitas
Ramona
Del Mar
Brawley
La Jolla
El Centro
Pacific Beach
Ocotillo
San Diego
Calexico
Coronado
Chula Vista
Mexicali
San Ysidro
Tecate
Tijuana
MEXICO
0 100 km
0 50 miles

LOS ANGELES & SOUTHERN CALIFORNIA

THE GUIDE

Chapters in this section are organized by hubs and their surrounding areas. We see the hub as your base in the destination, where you'll find unique experiences, local insights, insider tips and expert recommendations. It's also your gateway to the surrounding area, where you'll see what and how much you can do from there.

Death Valley National Park (p238)

NAGEL PHOTOGRAPHY/SHUTTERSTOCK

Researched by
Wendy Yanagihara

Santa Barbara County

SPANISH COLONIAL COASTAL BEAUTY

Hike, bike and surf year-round in a Mediterranean climate where pinot noir, Pixie tangerines and avocados thrive, on the southern end of California's Central Coast.

The Santa Barbara coastline was originally inhabited by the Chumash people, who harvested and hunted from the oak-studded hills and the rich waters of the Santa Barbara Channel. Using tar from natural beach seeps, they built seafaring canoes that allowed them to settle on the northernmost of the Channel Islands.

In 1786, Spanish Franciscan missionaries dedicated the tenth California mission on the feast day of Santa Barbara, thereby blessing the city with its name and one of its most famous landmarks. With its island-sheltered beaches, front-country foothills and mild year-round climate, SB has forever attracted visitors and new residents. Over the last two decades, Santa Barbara County has developed into a wine country destination. With its transverse mountain range and unique patterns of fog and diurnal shift, a wealth of high-quality, small-production wines are yet another pleasure to savor.

Besides wine, the region's bountiful produce is celebrated with local festivals centered around the lemon and avocado. Appreciation for farmers, and what they literally bring to the table, continues to be an undercurrent of life here. That, and a commitment to the land and ocean in which 'Santa Barbarians' love to play.

Join the locals in enjoying a slower pace of life, watching dolphins leap, and squinting for the green flash at sunset, unfussed by tar blobs staining their toes.

RON THOMAS/GETTY IMAGES

THE MAIN AREAS

SANTA BARBARA
What California dreaming is made of.
p42

SOLVANG
Danish-kitsch gateway to wine country.
p52

VENTURA
SB's secret cute sister city.
p63

For places to stay in Santa Barbara County, see p70

EMSON/GETTY IMAGES

Left: Old Mission Santa Barbara (p43); Above: Stearns Wharf (p46)

Find Your Way

Santa Barbara occupies an easily navigable slice of coastal plain between mountains and ocean. Outlying areas of interest are reached by scenic drives along the coast or through the foothills of the Santa Ynez and Topatopa mountain ranges.

Solvang, p52
Danish-heritage tourist destination that has evolved into a serious but perenially fun intro to Santa Barbara wine country.

PACIFIC OCEAN

San Miguel Island

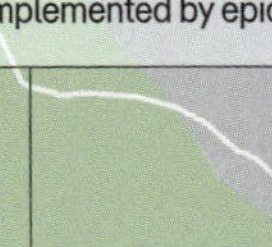

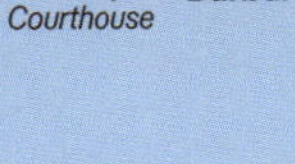
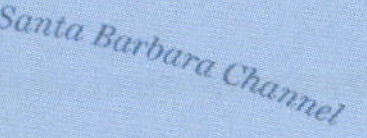
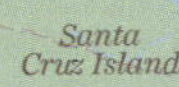
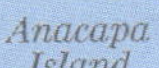

Santa Barbara, p42

Streets of Spanish Colonial architecture stretch from the foothills to Pacific beaches, offering outdoor fun on trail and ocean, complemented by epicurean pleasures.

BUS

Santa Barbara MTD buses cover the city proper, with service as far as Goleta and Carpinteria. Santa Ynez Valley Transit runs buses between Buellton and the town of Santa Ynez, while Gold Coast Transit has a route between Ventura and Ojai.

BICYCLE

The city of Santa Barbara has bicycle-friendly crosstown routes with painted bike lanes on some major streets, but for the most part its bike lanes are narrow or shared with vehicle traffic. Santa Ynez Valley is more spread out and suitable for bicycle touring.

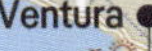

CAR

To visit outlying destinations from Santa Barbara, it's most convenient to drive, although most towns are small enough to explore on foot once you've arrived. Street parking is free or inexpensive throughout the region.

Ventura, p63

Alluringly retro beach town with under-the-radar appeal in its beaches, harbor and downtown; and it's the launch point for Channel Islands National Park.

Plan Your Time

Santa Barbara makes the most beautiful base for easy access to beach, foothills and city. Stay in Solvang or Los Olivos if wine tasting is your mission, or retreat in low-profile style to Ojai.

NADEZDA AUDIGIE/SHUTTERSTOCK

Butterfly Beach (p51)

If You Have Only One Day

- Start in the **Funk Zone** (p47), a compact neighborhood packed with fun, even for kids – check out the **MOXI** (p47) science museum and pet some rays at the **Sea Center** (p46) on Stearns Wharf. Savor an ocean-air seafood lunch, or pair wine tasting (or beer, or spirits) with a bite at one of the excellent neighborhood eateries.

- Next, check out SB's landmarks: the gorgeous Spanish Colonial **Santa Barbara County Courthouse** (p42), with the 3rd-floor clock tower affording 360-degree views of the city. Head several blocks up, stroll the peaceful courtyard and cemetery at the Queen of the Missions, **Old Mission Santa Barbara** (p43), then end your evening with super-casual tacos at **La Super-Rica Taquería** (p49) and live music at **Soho** (p49).

Seasonal Highlights

California poppies start bursting in joyous orange in mid-February or March, followed in April or May by the jacaranda trees. Year-round, different whale species travel through the Santa Barbara Channel.

FEBRUARY

The **Santa Barbara International Film Festival** (p48) lights up the historic Arlington Theatre with red-carpet screenings and talks with filmmakers and celebrities.

MAY

Artists create a patchwork of amazing chalk art squares at the Santa Barbara Mission for the **I Madonnari Italian street painting festival** (p43). The artwork remains until it gets scuffed or rained away.

JUNE

Since 1974, the only-in-SB **solstice celebration** (p49) revolves around a whimsically artsy parade continuing into a weekend festival in the park.

A Long Weekend to Play

- After exploring **Santa Barbara** (p42) on the first day, head farther afield the next.

- Take a country drive to an estate winery or two in the **Santa Ynez Valley** (p56), or to the small towns of **Los Alamos** (p60) or **Los Olivos** (p57) for sipping and exploring on foot; don't forget to pick up a tin of Danish cookies in **Solvang** (p52).

- Or, while away a day in **Ojai** (p68) to soak up sunshiny, new-agey vibes and diverse, healthy cuisine. Make time to venture outdoors to hike Santa Barbara's front country, or paddle a kayak or stand-up paddleboard (SUP) around the **harbor** (p46) for close encounters with seals, pelicans and bat rays.

Five Days or More to Explore

- Spend a day or two exploring **Santa Barbara** (p42) and get on the water, whether it's with a surf lesson, a paddle around the harbor or a whale-watching cruise. Try catching an SB farmers market on Tuesday afternoon or Saturday morning to pick up snacks and see locals at their most relaxed.

- Take advantage of a longer stay with forays to **Ojai** (p68) for hiking, horseback riding or a spa day. Consider hiring a local guide for a wine-tasting tour in the **Santa Ynez Valley** (p56), and stop in **Solvang** (p52) to feed ostriches, find the taproom speakeasy and feast like a California-style Viking.

AUGUST

Santa Barbara's biggest annual fiesta, **Old Spanish Days** (p49) celebrates the city's Spanish, Mexican and Chumash heritage with parades, street food and traditional performances at the Courthouse sunken garden, the Mission and De La Guerra Plaza.

SEPTEMBER

Kick up your dancing clogs at **Danish Days** (p54) in Solvang with music, parades, food and celebration of all things Danish.

OCTOBER

Little Carpinteria swells with visitors in early October for the **California Avocado Festival** *(carpinteriaca.gov/visitor-info/california-avocado-festival/)*, which of course features bountiful guacamole, tri-tip sandwiches and free live music.

DECEMBER

Winter is a wonderful time to be in the region, when tourist crowds have ebbed significantly. The coastal climate remains pleasantly cool, while the inland valleys aren't as blazingly hot as in summer.

Santa Barbara

RED-TILE ARCHITECTURE | BEACHES & FOOTHILLS | COASTAL CHIC

TOP TIP

Check your feet after beach visits, as SB shores have naturally occurring tar seeps that ooze up through the sand. If you've been tarred, give it a good dab of sunscreen and wipe it off with a paper towel. Plain cooking oil works best if you happen to have some handy.

Santa Barbara has long been a weekend getaway for Angelenos, for obvious reasons – only an hour-and-a-half drive up the coast from LA, it's cozily nestled between the picturesque Santa Ynez Mountains and the Pacific Ocean, with tiled Spanish Colonial architecture and chill, beach-town vibes. The self-branded American Riviera inarguably hits a sweet spot of beautiful natural setting, plentiful outdoor and cultural activities, and great dining experiences. In one day it's easy to hike into sunshine above the marine layer, frolic in the ocean and rinse off your sweaty, sandy day with world-class wine tasting. SB retains a small-town feel while still being a university city with diverse cultural events, a gorgeous outdoor music venue and thriving arts scene. The city's background is rooted in agriculture and a vibrant Mexican heritage, both of which remain proudly and visibly integral to its identity today.

Classic Santa Barbara Landmarks

Architecture, gardens and natural history

Does it sound weird that the **Santa Barbara County Courthouse** *(sbcourthouse.org; free)* is a must-visit? Once you see

GETTING AROUND

The **Amtrak station** conveniently places passengers a couple of blocks from Stearns Wharf, the beach, downtown and the Funk Zone. In this part of town, most visitors get around on foot or bike; traveling further afield within SB or outside city limits, rideshare or driving yourself gets you where you need to go. Getting to and from LAX is a breeze on the **Santa Barbara Airbus** *(www.sbairbus.com; per person one-way prepaid $60)*, which stops in Goleta, Santa Barbara, Carpinteria and Camarillo (Ventura County). The trip between SB and LAX takes 2½ hours.

Downtown SB is crisscrossed with one-way streets parallel and perpendicular to State St. Look out for wrong-way drivers, whizzing e-bikes and pedestrians crossing streets in out-of-office mode. Parking at city lots is free for the first 75 minutes, after which it's $3 an hour (or any part thereof).

NAGEL PHOTOGRAPHY/SHUTTERSTOCK

Santa Barbara County Courthouse

it, you'll understand why couples plan courthouse weddings here. Taking up an entire city block, the Spanish Colonial Revival stunner is surrounded by inviting lawn and sunken garden. **Docent-led tours** *(weekdays at 10.30am, except for court holidays)* give details on the Moorish-style tile work and intricately painted Mural Room (where former VP Kamala Harris got hitched). You can simply turn up during the day and ride up to the 3rd-story clock tower to take in 360-degree views of the surrounding city, ocean and foothills.

Next up: the Queen of the Missions. Founded in 1786, **Old Mission Santa Barbara** *(santabarbaramission.org; adult/youth $17/12)* is only one of two California missions that have continuously operated since their establishment. Self-guided and docent-led tours explore the church, courtyard garden and cemetery where white settlers and unnamed Chumash lie. The Mission lawn and rose garden below are a local favorite for picnics. If you're here during Memorial Day weekend, be sure to check out the chalk-painting festival **I Madonnari** *(@imadonnari)* as it transforms the Mission sidewalk into art.

Head a little farther toward the foothills to the **Santa Barbara Museum of Natural History** *(sbnature.org; adult/child $19/14)* in its creekside nook amid oak habitat. Find natural context in exhibits ranging from Chumash culture, indigenous wildlife and geology, then complement it with forest bathing at the nearby **Santa Barbara Botanic Garden** *(sbbotanicgarden.org; adult/child $20/12)* – reservations required. The Channel Islands sector offers spectacular views and native island flora if you can't get to the islands themselves.

BUILDING A CHUMASH CANOE

Alan Salazar, Ventureño Chumash and Tataviam Tribal Elder.

We established the Chumash Maritime Association in January 1997 to oversee construction of a *tomol* (plank canoe) for the Chumash community. We had to relearn the skills of building, paddling and navigating. In 1912 Fernando Librado Kitsepawit, whose family was of the *tomol* brotherhood, built one as a demonstration; our research relied on extensive notes taken by anthropologist JP Harrington from interviews with Librado.

In 1997 we built the first working *tomol* in modern times, with the help of the Santa Barbara Maritime Museum, and paddled it across the Santa Barbara Channel in 2001. Our goal was to revitalize the Chumash maritime culture, especially to involve our young people. Conditions permitting, we now do the channel crossing annually.

HIGHLIGHTS
1 Santa Barbara County Courthouse

SIGHTS
2 Leadbetter Beach
3 MOXI
4 Santa Barbara Maritime Museum
5 Santa Barbara Museum of Art
6 Sea Center
7 Sullivan Goss

ACTIVITIES
8 Condor Express
9 Paddle Sports Center
10 Santa Barbara Sailing Center

SLEEPING
11 Canary
12 Castillo Inn
13 Harbor House Inn
14 Hotel Californian
15 Marina Beach Motel

EATING
16 Arigato Sushi
17 Barbareño
18 Bibi ji
19 Corazón Cocina
20 Helena Avenue Bakery
21 La Super-Rica Taquería
22 Loquita
23 Sama Sama Kitchen
24 The Black Sheep
25 The Lark
26 Zaytoon

DRINKING & NIGHTLIFE
27 Cajé
28 Cutler's Artisan Spirits
29 Draughtsmen Aleworks
30 Dune
31 EOS Lounge
32 Handlebar Coffee Roasters
33 Lama Dog Tap Room
34 M Special
35 Margerum Wine Company
36 Municipal Winemakers
37 Night Lizard
38 Santa Barbara Roasting Company
39 Test Pilot

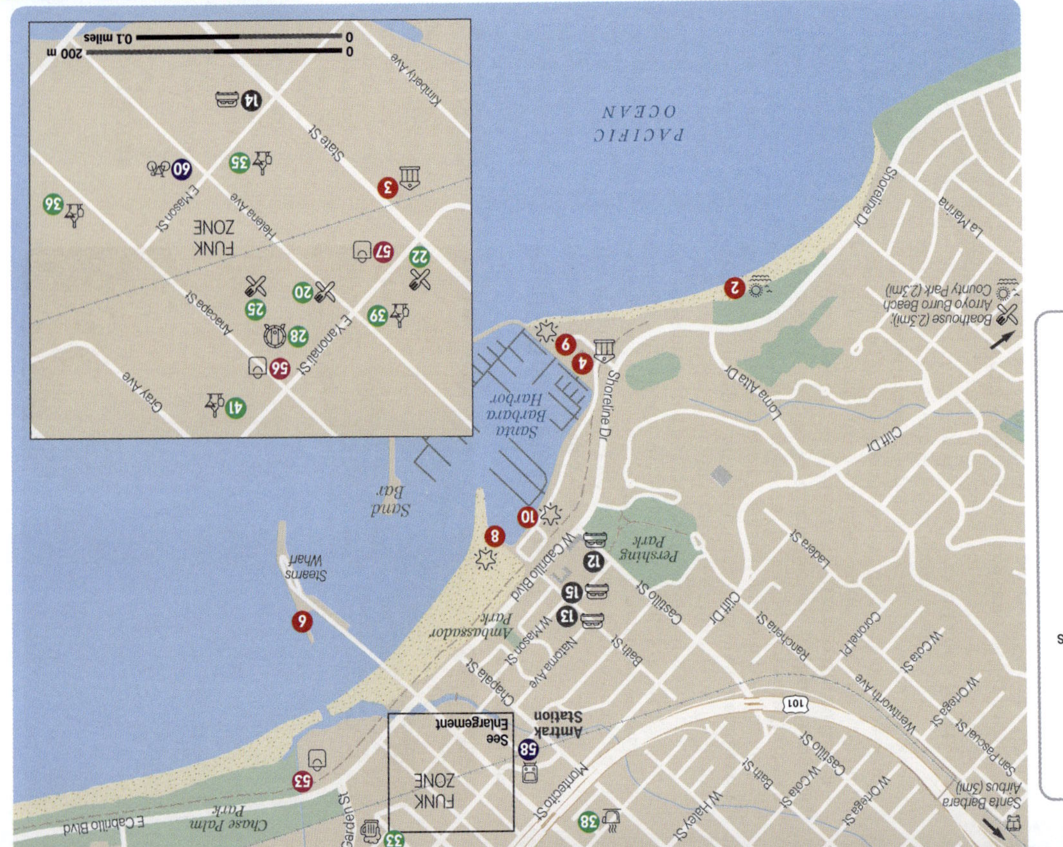

40 The Red Piano
41 The Valley Project
42 Third Window Brewing
43 Wildcat Lounge

ENTERTAINMENT
44 Arlington Theatre
45 Granada Theatre
46 Lobero Theatre
47 Old Spanish Days
48 Santa Barbara Bowl
49 Soho
50 Summer Solstice Celebration

SHOPPING
51 Farmer and the Flea
52 Mujeres Makers Market
53 Santa Barbara Arts & Crafts Show
54 Santa Barbara Certified Farmers Market
55 Santa Barbara Company
56 Shopkeepers
57 The Blue Door

TRANSPORT
58 Amtrak
59 Cal Coast Adventures
60 Wheel Fun Rentals

ARCHITECTURE WALKS

For an exceptionally insightful look at Santa Barbara's architectural highlights, take a walking tour with a docent from the **Architectural Foundation of Santa Barbara** *(afsb.org; suggested donation $20)*. Reserve a two-hour walk and talk every Saturday and Sunday at 10am. The DIY **Red Tile Walking Tour** *(santabarbaraca.com/itinerary/red-tile-walking-tour)* stops at the most significant historical sites downtown, including El Presidio de Santa Bárbara, with remnants of its original adobe structure.

Lest you think the American Riviera takes its red tile too seriously, check out a few of the playful, Seussian takes on the local vernacular with architect **Jeff Shelton** *(jeffsheltonarchitect.com/santa-barbara-map)*. Download a walking tour map or book a guided tour that includes a visit to Shelton's studio.

GERI LAVROV/GETTY IMAGES

Leadbetter Beach

Pacific Ocean Pleasures

Swim, surf, paddle, whale-watch

You could visit Santa Barbara without dipping a toe in the ocean...but why would you? Buffered from open ocean by the Channel Islands, the south-facing coastline offers a string of beautiful protected beaches for free saltwater therapy.

Novice surfers will appreciate the smaller swell of summer; most surf spots are best during the winter. **Leadbetter Beach** has a slow-rolling wave that makes it popular for lessons and beginners. Book surf lessons with **Santa Barbara Surf School** *(santabarbarasurfschool.com)* or **Surf Happens** *(surfhappens.com)* to feel the stoke. **Arroyo Burro Beach** – also known as Hendry's – is a consistent surf spot with both rights and lefts. Added bonuses: it's SB's sanctioned **dog beach**, and the **Boathouse** *(boathousesb.com)* provides the perfect setting for post-beach lunch or happy hour.

At the harbor, rent an SUP or a kayak at **Paddle Sports Center** *(paddlesportsca.com)*. Even within the breakwater, you'll encounter harbor seals, pelicans and rays on your paddle. Explore farther, steering between the pilings of **Stearns Wharf**, or upwind toward Leadbetter Beach. Wildlife-watchers can book a whale-watching tour on the *Double Dolphin* of the **Santa Barbara Sailing Center** *(sbsail.com)* or with **Condor Express** *(condorexpress.com)*, to cruise the Santa Barbara Channel in search of over 30 species of cetaceans, including migrating humpbacks, blue or gray whales and orcas (depending on the season).

Back on land, learn about SB's marine history, going back to its Chumash heritage, at the **Santa Barbara Maritime Museum** *(sbmm.org; adult/child $12/6)*. On Stearns Wharf, get to know the local marine life in the touch tanks and try out some actual research tools on the Wet Deck at the Santa Barbara Museum of Natural History's **Sea Center** *(sbnature.org; adult/child $15/12)*.

Tasting in the Funk Zone

Santa Barbara's urban wine trail

While the Funk Zone is ground zero for SB wine tasting, consider it a starting point (maybe also an ending point – your mileage may vary). The high concentration of tasting rooms, eateries, breweries and galleries could entrap you for an entire day.

There's limited street parking but large pre-pay lots are on Garden St and Cabrillo Blvd. Pick up divine pastries and coffee at **Helena Avenue Bakery** *(helenaavenuebakery.com)* and pop into vintage shops like **The Blue Door** *(thebluedoorsb.com)* and lifestyle purveyors **Shopkeepers** *(shopkeeperssb.com)*. If you've got kids with you, the excellent museum of science and innovation **MOXI** *(moxi.org; adult/child $20/15)* is a delight, with sensory exhibits and interactive exploration for all ages.

If you don't have specific wineries in mind, start at **The Valley Project** *(thevalleyprojectwines.com)* on Yanonali St, where the chalkboard art gives a quick primer on the lay of the wine-country land. Nearby, **Margerum Wine Company** *(margerumwines.com)* has an elegant feel while **Municipal Winemakers** *(municipalwinemakers.com)* offers a fun, approachable vibe. Ask your tasting room host for onward recommendations based on your tastes.

Not into wine? **Lama Dog Tap Room** *(lamadog.com)* pours a rotating selection of craft beers, with a bottle shop and convivial little patio to boot. Sample cocktails made with house-distilled bourbon, vodka and gin at **Cutler's Artisan Spirits** *(cutlersartisan.com)*. And mingle with the beautiful people at postmodern tiki bar **Test Pilot** *(testpilotcocktails.com)*, serving tropical-themed cocktails and seasonal, shrub-based non-alcoholic mocktails.

Reservations are recommended if you're set on dining at **The Lark** *(thelarksb.com)* or **Loquita** *(loquitasb.com)*.

OUTSIDE THE ZONE

The Funk Zone may be the densest, but other tasting nooks are clustered around SB's downtown area. Pick up a **Santa Barbara Urban Wine Trail map** *(urbanwinetrailsb.com)* to find worthwhile gems along the Haley St corridor, along State St and around the bougainvillea-laced **El Paseo arcade** on Anacapa St.

The purchase of an Urban Wine Trail tasting card *($200)* entitles you to one-time free tastings at participating wineries as well as day-of-tasting discounts. You can also simply use the map as an orientation tool, as many worthwhile wineries aren't part of the Urban Wine Trail program but are located in the highlighted neighborhoods.

Arts & Culture

Theater, live music, visual art

Local landmarks themselves, many of SB's arts venues enhance their events with their own architectural beauty.

Entering the historic **Arlington Theatre** *(thearlingtontheatre.com)* under its archways and sitting in a trompe l'oeil courtyard almost makes it feel like you're watching performances under a Spanish sky, complete with twinkling ceiling

DRINKING IN SANTA BARBARA: CRAFT BEER

Third Window Brewing: Beautiful Belgian-style beers, and smashburgers using beef from the family ranch. *11.30am-9pm Mon-Thu, to 11pm Fri, 11am-11pm Sat, to 10pm Sun*

Night Lizard: Great range of beers named for endangered species, plus occasional live music. *3-9pm Mon, noon-10pm Tue-Thu, noon-midnight Fri & Sat, noon-8pm Sun*

M Special: Good beer, regular live music and Mexican eats from the Beast Taquería window in back. *noon-9pm Tue, Wed & Sun, to 10pm Thu, to 11pm Fri & Sat*

Draughtsmen Aleworks: Up State St in the theater district, you'll find this taproom in the Mosaic Locale food and beverage collective. *11.30am-8pm Sun-Wed, to 9pm Thu-Sun*

BEST SPOTS TO SHOP LOCAL

Santa Barbara Arts & Crafts Show: Every Sunday since 1965, along half a mile of beachfront Chase Palm Park, artists and craftspeople sell their creative work.

Mujeres Makers Market: Regularly scheduled pop-up market run by women of color, fostering community and celebrating seasonality at El Presídio de Santa Bárbara.

Farmer and the Flea: Another beautifully curated pop-up also taking place at the Presídio, on a quarterly schedule.

Santa Barbara Company: Find locally made gifts, edible goodies and flowers at this cute little cottage on East Victoria St.

Santa Barbara Certified Farmers Market: Downtown on Tuesdays and Saturdays. Locally grown bounty includes chile-spiked pistachios, toffee-studded almond butter and sage honey.

LOGAN BUSH/SHUTTERSTOCK

Granada Theatre

stars. Or you can come out to watch film stars walk the red carpet here at the **Santa Barbara International Film Festival** *(sbiff.org)* every February.

On the next block, the ornate Spanish Moorish-style **Granada Theatre** *(granadasb.org)* occupies the ground floor of the low-scale city's tallest building, topping out at 116ft, and is home to local institutions like the **State Street Ballet** *(statestreetballet.com)* and **Santa Barbara Symphony** *(thesymphony.org)*.

A little farther down State St, the elegant neoclassical **Santa Barbara Museum of Art** *(sbma.net)* houses visual inspiration, occasionally holding workshops and events. Nearby, the art gallery **Sullivan Goss** *(sullivangoss.com)* focuses on American artists of varying genres.

The **Lobero Theatre** *(lobero.org)*, a few blocks down, is the oldest continuously operating theater in California. Originally founded in 1873, it was renovated in Spanish Colonial Revival style in 1924, and its acoustics make it perfect for chamber, folk and jazz performances.

From spring to fall, it's a special treat to see a show at the **Santa Barbara Bowl** *(sbbowl.com),* the city's beloved outdoor music venue tucked into a residential hillside. A shuttle runs from the entrance to the amphitheater, but part of the magic is walking up the woodsy path in shared anticipation with your fellow concertgoers.

DRINKING IN SANTA BARBARA: CAFFEINATION STATIONS

Dune: Minimalist, light-flooded space with a spacious patio and excellent coffee in the Lower State area. *6am-5pm Mon-Sat, from 7am Sun*

Handlebar Coffee Roasters: Friendly, efficient espresso bar established by former cycling pros, with an appealing interior and a street-side patio. *6.30am-5pm*

Cajé: This cozy space along the Haley St corridor concocts elaborate, craft-cocktail-style coffee drinks as well as the basics. *7am-6pm*

Santa Barbara Roasting Company: Since 1989, this old-school coffeehouse has been roasting beans and keeping SB whirring. *6.30am-6pm Mon-Sat, from 7am Sun*

SB's unique cultural celebrations are the biggest community parties of the year. The **Santa Barbara Summer Solstice** *(solsticeparade.com)* sambas and sashays up State St in riotous color and creativity in June, while **Old Spanish Days** *(sbfiesta.org)* – known simply as 'Fiesta' locally – celebrates the city's Chumash, Mexican and Spanish heritage with parades, dance, music and food in early August.

Check the **UCSB Arts & Lectures** *(artsandlectures.ucsb.edu)* website for current listings, or keep it casual and discover the lively local music scene at the many breweries and cafes around town.

BEST LIVE-MUSIC VENUES

Santa Barbara Bowl: Even the nosebleeds are a sweet place to be, with spectacular views of city and ocean from the upper bar.

Soho: Going strong since 1994, this intimate venue hosts live local and touring bands.

The Red Piano: It does have a red piano, with 'Church on Monday' blues and live music every night of the week.

EOS Lounge: Long-running club with DJs spinning a range of styles – this being SB, the vibe is casual.

Wildcat Lounge: Teeny, busy and always a winner for people-watching in the wild. Sister lounge **Bobcat**, out back, is a more chilled-out space.

Cycle Santa Barbara

See SB on two wheels

Santa Barbara is a great place to pedal around, whether meandering along the Cabrillo Blvd beachfront or taking a serious road tour into the foothills. Downtown SB is generally flat with some gentle climbs, and you can rent a bicycle to stitch together sightseeing stops.

Cal Coast Adventures *(calcoastadventures.com)* rents bicycles and also runs guided bike tours around the city. Additionally, their website links to bike maps of longer road cycling tours, mountain-biking trails and a great self-guided tour of downtown and the waterfront.

For short, low-commitment jaunts, **Santa Barbara BCycles** *(santabarbara.bcycle.com)* rents e-bikes for $8.70 per 30 minutes, with docks located in multiple locations around town.

Rent a bike at **Wheel Fun Rentals** *(wheelfunrentals.com; beach cruiser half-day $34)* in the Funk Zone and ride along the palm-lined Cabrillo bike path southward about 2½ miles to local favorite Butterfly Beach, or north past the harbor about a mile to Leadbetter Beach and on to Shoreline Park on the Mesa.

Mountain bikers will find plenty of technical singletrack to negotiate after the thigh-burning climbs. Etiquette tip: pick up and drop off a bike bell at the trailhead, as trails in the front country are multiuse and very popular with hikers.

EATING IN SANTA BARBARA: FROM A TO Z

Arigato Sushi: Popular Arigato has been around for decades and still pulls them in. *5.30-9:45pm Sun-Thu, to 10:15pm Fri & Sat* $$

Barbareño: Showcasing fresh, locally harvested produce, seafood and meats. Lunch is a more casual affair. *5-8.30pm Sun-Thu, to 9pm Fri & Sat* $$$

Bibi ji: Santa Barbara-style Indian food, with an extensive natural-wine list. *5-10pm Thu-Tue* $$

Corazón Cocina: It's worth the long line at SB Public Market for bright, fresh ceviches and regional-specialty tacos. *11am-9pm* $

La Super-Rica Taquería: There's always a line at this cash-only shack beloved by Julia Child. *11am-9pm Mon, Thu & Sun, to 9.30pm Fri & Sat* $

Sama Sama Kitchen: Southeast Asian fusion, paired with cocktails. *noon-3pm Tue-Sun & 5-9.30pm Tue-Thu & Sun, to 10.30pm Fri & Sat* $$

The Black Sheep: French-style cuisine with a California accent. The tasting menu is a solid bet. *5-9pm Wed, Thu & Sun, to 10pm Fri & Sat* $$$

Zaytoon: Good Middle Eastern food and a romantic, twinkling ambience. *5-9pm Tue-Thu & Sun, to 10pm Fri & Sat* $$

Beyond Santa Barbara

Hwy 101 north opens up to coastline ranches, while to the south you'll discover some of the county's best underrated small towns.

Places

GETTING AROUND

It's easiest to drive, whether heading north to the Gaviota Coast or to Montecito and Summerland, but once there you can explore on foot. Santa Barbara MTD runs regular express buses through to Carpinteria. Less frequently, you can catch local train services on Amtrak, with a platform mere blocks from Carpinteria State Beach.

Note that the Santa Barbara coastline runs east–west, but locals give directions in reference to Hwy 101 – putting Summerland south and Goleta north of SB.

Northbound 101 moves through Goleta – 'The Good Land' – and branches off to Santa Barbara Municipal Airport, the University of California, Santa Barbara (UCSB) and the community of Isla Vista. After that it rolls through scenic ranchlands and the wild Gaviota coastline before turning inland to Buellton and Santa Ynez Valley wine country.

Southbound, the highway cuts through the rarefied enclave of Montecito, land of low-key lavish estates but accessible foothill trails and village restaurants. A smidge south is hillside Summerland, with its crescent of gorgeous beach and strip of cute boutiques, followed by the throwback beach town of Carpinteria. Easy to bypass on your way elsewhere, these small towns have their allures for those who detour through.

Gaviota Coast

TIME FROM SANTA BARBARA: **25 MINS**

Windswept tidepools & trails

The wild coast north of Goleta is a wealth of coastal open space, much of it privately owned, working ranchland with some parcels purchased by conservation organizations to protect these rare oceanfront lands from future development.

Of three state parks along Hwy 101, the first is **El Capitán State Beach** *(parks.ca.gov)*. The campground is closed for renovation through 2025, but the beach is open to pedestrian access for day use. Explore tidepools, the nature trail along El Capitán Creek and miles of empty beach, stretching east and west from a south-facing point. A paved trail from the west leads all the way to **Refugio State Beach** *(parks.ca.gov; vehicle entry $10)*, about 3 miles further northbound on Hwy 101. This crescent of beach is lined with stately palm trees and has over 60 campsites.

Furthest north, at the coastline where Hwy 101 veers inland, find **Gaviota State Park** *(parks.ca.gov; vehicle entry $10)*, with interesting tilted shale beds embedded in the beach sand. Offshore, the park's waters form part of the **Kashtayit State Marine Conservation Area**. The trestle bridge above the beach is still used by Amtrak and freight trains, and camping is also available here.

Day hikers can access the **Gaviota Wind Caves trail** from the green gate past the state park entrance; the five-mile out-and-back takes you up to the caves for beautiful windswept views of the coast below.

WAYNE VIA/SHUTTERSTOCK

El Capitán State Beach

South County

TIME FROM SANTA BARBARA: **10 MINS**

Not-so-secret small towns

Begin in Montecito with coffee and real French croissants at **Bree'osh** *(breeosh.com)* or **Renaud's** *(renaudsbistro.com)* and stroll **Coast Village Rd** boutiques, keeping an eye out for mononymous luminaries like Oprah, Harry and Meghan roaming under the radar. Cross over the freeway at Olive Mill Rd and walk to **Butterfly Beach** to while away your morning before a wood-fired pizza at **Bettina** *(bettinapizzeria.com)* or Mexican favorite **Los Arroyos** *(losarroyos.net/montecito)*.

Then head into the foothills for a hike through front-country ceanothus and chaparral to reach views of the coastline as far south as Malibu. Find trail information at the website of the **Montecito Trails Foundation** *(montecitotrailsfoundation.info)*. Pursue more meditative walks through the wondrous landscape of **Lotusland** *(lotusland.org; adult/youth $60/25)* – by appointment only – a lavish, eccentric botanical garden on the former estate of opera singer Ganna Walska. End with a fancy cocktail at **Honor Bar** *(honorbar.com)* or **Lucky's** *(luckys-steakhouse.com)*.

A few miles further south lies the hillside beach town of **Summerland**, where Lillie Ave boutiques like **Porch** *(porchsb.com)* and **Botanik** *(botanikinc.com)* are stuffed with chic coastal decor and succulent art. On the ocean side of the freeway, bluff-top **Lookout Park** *(countyofsb.org/822/Lookout-Park)* has a great playground, bocce court, picnic tables and path down to the beautiful slice of **Summerland Beach**.

Beyond Summerland, the little beach town of **Carpinteria** is at heart an agricultural community, growing avocados, citrus and cherimoyas, and celebrating the **California Avocado Festival** *(avofest.org)* every October.

Downshift into small-town gear and cruise **Linden Ave** down to **Carpinteria State Beach** *(parks.ca.gov)*, browsing the indie shops and homegrown restaurants. Little kids love running around the **Tomol play area**, after which you can grab burgers at old-timey shack **The Spot** and take them over to **Island Brewing Co** *(islandbrewingcompany.com)* to enjoy with a sunset beer.

CARPINTERIA FERMENTATION OPERATIONS

Bordering the **Carpinteria Salt Marsh**, the industrial park at the west end of Carpinteria Ave is not visually inspiring. But walk around the back alley and you'll find a bubbly social zone with miniscule tasting rooms, empanadas, a specialty wine store and boutique chocolate.

The dreamy **Apiary** *(theapiary.co)* brews beautiful and complex mead, cider and kombucha from local honey, flowers, herbs and fruit.

Next door, nanobrewery **BrewLAB** *(brewlab craft.com)* always has a creative selection of top-notch small-batch beers on tap, from sours to stouts brewed with locally grown flora.

At the end of the line, **Rincon Mountain Winery** *(rinconmtn.com)* pours tastings of their Carpinteria-farmed and -produced wine. Weekends are liveliest with food trucks, live tunes and kids running around underfoot.

Solvang

DANISH KITSCH | WALKABLE VILLAGE | WINE-COUNTRY BASE

GETTING AROUND

Solvang has an eminently walkable downtown – park in one of the free public lots south of Mission Dr and roam on foot. Copenhagen Dr is the main shopping and restaurant strip, with the surrounding streets fanning out to tasting rooms, hotels and the residential area to the south. Many local lodgings offer free bicycles for their guests to borrow.

From red-tiled Spanish Colonial Santa Barbara, arriving in Solvang ('sunny fields' in Danish) is like experiencing a mildly kooky bout of culture shock. Founded in 1911 by three Danish-American educators, Solvang shows its authentic Danish influence even if the decorative motif is over the top. Before the Danes, the Spanish established Mission Santa Inés here in 1804, and before that, it was the ancestral land of the Native Chumash people.

Nowadays the Chumash tribe not only runs the nearby casino resort, but also tends vineyards and makes wine, as is the contemporary tradition of the Santa Ynez Valley. Long a destination for its butter cookies and Disneyfied Scandinavian window dressing, Solvang does make a convenient central base for exploring Santa Ynez Valley wine country. And don't worry, there's plenty of good food besides *aebleskiver* and *pandekager* (Danish fritters and pancakes).

☑ TOP TIP

Solvang makes a great base for exploring Santa Barbara's wine country, but if you're seeking a more low-key vibe during your stay, the nearby towns of Santa Ynez and Los Olivos are stellar choices. Los Alamos is another option, though it's slightly more removed.

Solvang's Danish Heritage

Local insight into Danish culture

Solvang's Danishness runs deeper than the scent of sugary confections and its ersatz windmills – details like stork statues on rooftops and the gabled rooftops themselves are nods to the town's actual Danish roots. Learn more at the charming **Elverhøj Museum of History & Art** *(elverhoj.org; adult/child $5/free)*, open Thursday to Monday. It was formerly the residence of an artist couple; the beautiful tongue-and-groove construction of the home was modeled after an 18th-century Danish farmhouse design and is itself a work of art.

Back on main drag Mission Dr (Rte 246), you'll find the **Hans Christian Andersen Museum** *(bookloftsolvang.com; free)* upstairs at The Book Loft bookstore. The museum houses a small collection of the author's handwritten letters, first-edition copies of his illustrated books and a model of

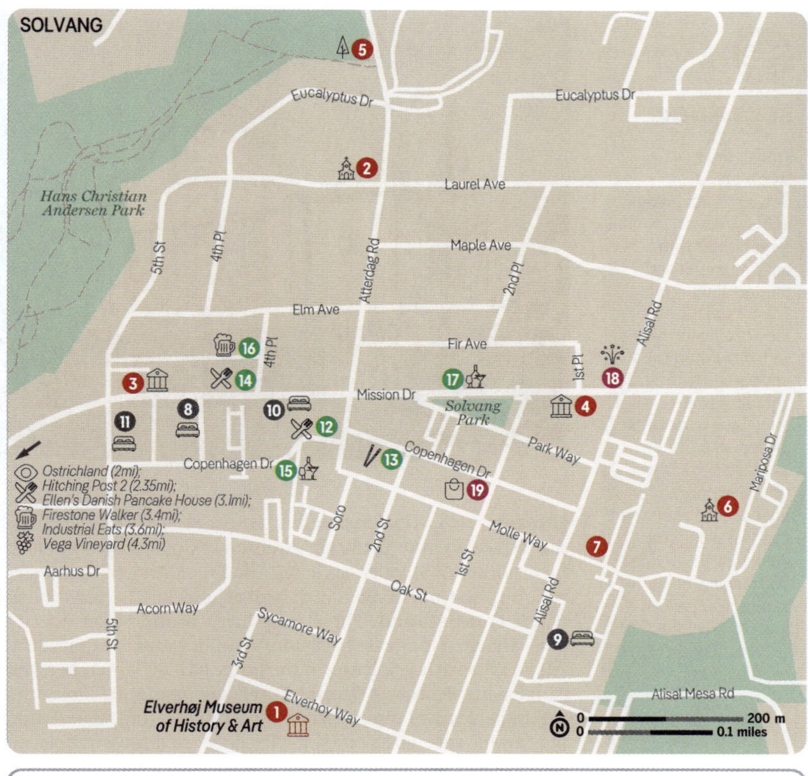

HIGHLIGHTS
1 Elverhøj Museum of History & Art

SIGHTS
2 Bethania Lutheran Church
3 California Nature Art Museum
4 Hans Christian Andersen Museum
5 Hans Christian Andersen Park
6 Old Mission Santa Ínes
7 Rundetaarn

SLEEPING
8 Hamlet Inn
9 Hotel Corque
10 The Landsby
11 Viking Inn

EATING
12 peasants FEAST
13 Ramen Kotori
14 The Gathering Table

DRINKING & NIGHTLIFE
15 Lost Chord Guitars
16 The Backroom
17 Vaquero Bar

ENTERTAINMENT
18 Danish Days

SHOPPING
19 Copenhagen House

his childhood home. A scaled-down replica of Copenhagen's *Little Mermaid* statue sits in contemplative repose in the fountain across the road.

On narrow Copenhagen Dr, the **Copenhagen House** *(thecopenhagenhouse.com)* imports Danish furniture and jewelry as well as high-end kitchenware and designy trinkets. The shop's comings and goings are supervised by the stern-faced wooden figures of Solvang's founders, Reverend Benedict Nordentoft, Reverend JM Gregersen and Professor PP Hornsyld, standing sentry out front.

Several notable buildings around town were also inspired by monuments in Denmark, including **Bethania Lutheran**

AEBLESKIVER

Translated as 'apple slice,' Solvang's ubiquitous *aebleskiver* is a round, sweet fritter with a crispy exterior and a tender, doughy bite. Fresh from the pan, they're usually dusted with powdered sugar and served with jam.

It takes some technique to make the perfect *aebleskiver*, as they need to be turned evenly on their special stovetop pan to get uniform doneness on all sides. You can buy cast-iron *aebleskiver* pans in town to make these festive balls of carby happiness at home.

Church *(bethanialutheran.net)* whose stucco design echoes the more elaborate Gruntvig's Church in Copenhagen but also incorporates a Spanish-style red-tiled roof. Also taking inspiration from Copenhagen is Solvang's one-third-scale replica of the **Rundetaarn**. The stately brick round tower doesn't have an astronomical observatory but does house a pizzeria.

If you're visiting Solvang in the latter half of September, you can join in celebrating **Danish Days** *(solvangdanishdays.org)*, a cultural festival replete with *aebleskiver* eating, beer drinking, parade spectating and some friendly axe throwing. You can also throw your name into the drawing for a trip to the real Denmark, in case Solvang piques your interest in Scandinavia.

Slow Solvang

Low-speed sights and delights

As tourist-saturated as Solvang can get, it has quiet corners worth finding. East of downtown along Mission Dr, the driveway to Solvang's **Old Mission Santa Inés** *(missionsantaines.org; free)* is an immediate escape. Fringed with olive trees, the mission garden is a peaceful spot to retreat for a moment. Pause in the cemetery to remember the Chumash people who were conscripted to build the mission here.

EATING & DRINKING IN SOLVANG: OUR PICKS

peasants FEAST: Seasonal, local American classics with an emphasis on freshness; superb picnic takeout at their deli across the street. *11am-6pm Wed-Sun* $

Ramen Kotori: Authentic ramen, gyoza and Japanese-style small plates like poke with fresh local seafood and farmers-market produce. *noon-3pm & 4.30-8pm Wed-Sun* $

The Gathering Table: Chef Budi Kazali's Asian-inflected French menu is executed beautifully for memorable seasonal cuisine. *5-9pm Wed, Thu & Sun, 8am-2pm & 5-9.30pm Fri & Sat* $$$

Vaquero Bar: Squeeze in at the bar for a cocktail, and order a grilled artichoke or rib-sticking ribeye off the Coast Range menu. *10am-midnight Wed-Mon, from 5pm Tue*

TRAVELVIEW/SHUTTERSTOCK

Solvang

At the other end of town, visit with room-sized troll Lulu Hyggelig at the nonprofit **California Nature Art Museum** *(calnatureartmuseum.org; adult/child $5/free)*, formerly the Wildling Museum. Lulu is the museum's latest ambassador who, in her inimitably enchanting selfness, explores how art can foster a closer relationship with nature. The troll, one in a worldwide series (see *trollmap.com*) by Danish recycling artist Thomas Dambo, will remain in residence until 2035. After visiting with Lulu, wander off through the museum's current exhibits, often featuring local artists whose work is deeply connected with nature.

One block over, turn off of Mission Dr at 4th Pl and leave the tourist traffic behind. Stop into the home-brewing supply shop **Valley Brewers**, where the carboys and bags of hops may not hold any thrall for you. But you're here to pass the owner a fiver for the privilege of being led down the hallway of illusory bookshelves and let in – speakeasy-style – to **The Backroom** *(valleybrewers.com/the-backroom; over-21 adult entry $5)*. This tiny taproom always has interesting craft beers, meads and ciders on rotation and a quiet patio to enjoy them in the sunshine.

End your evening with first-rate live music of the singer-songwriter bent at **Lost Chord Guitars** *(lostchordguitars.com; cover varies)*, a guitar shop and music venue on Copenhagen Dr.

BEST SANTA YNEZ VALLEY KIDS FUN

Ostrichland: Few thrills are cheaper than $1 feed bowls for the resident ostriches and emus that will come calling, all legs and necks and delightfully prehistoric *(ostrichlandusa.com; adult/child $7/3)*.

Vega Vineyard: For more animal encounters, stop at family-friendly Vega Vineyard, where kids can feed all sorts of animals: look for rabbits, sheep, llamas, potbellied pigs and a mini Highland bull *(vegavineyard andfarm.com; free)*.

Hans Christian Andersen Park: Let the kids enjoy themselves at this lovely Solvang park, with an oak-shaded, creekside trail, a playground, skate park and interactive sensory play areas. Take Atterdag Rd north from Mission Dr, veering left onto Chalk Hill Rd. A castle gate marks the entrance in true Solvang style.

EATING & DRINKING IN BUELLTON: MORNING TO NIGHT

Ellen's Danish Pancake House: Established in 1947, this comfortingly old-timey diner is where locals come for the best Danish pancakes and all-day breakfasts. *6am-2pm* $

Industrial Eats: Wood-fired pizzas with ever-changing toppings, innovative small plates and creative specials concocted from local producers. *noon-8pm* $$

Hitching Post 2: Dark-paneled chophouse serving oak-grilled steaks, lamb, quail and such. Pair with one of their own popular wines. *4.30-9pm Wed-Mon* $$

Firestone Walker: This gastropub, taproom and barrel room celebrates wild ferments. A Buellton beer institution. *noon-8pm Mon-Thu, to 9pm Fri, 11am-9pm Sat, to 8pm Sun*

Beyond Solvang

All roads lead to wine from gingerbread village Solvang. Westward, the landscape opens into the rolling hills of the Santa Ynez Valley.

Places

GETTING AROUND

Regular bus services with **Santa Ynez Valley Transit** *(syvt.com)* connect Buellton, Solvang, Santa Ynez and Los Olivos from Monday through Saturday. If you're roaming beyond town, you'll need private transportation to explore the rest of the Santa Ynez Valley.

Santa Barbara wine country fans out from the Solvang area, its local appellations ranging west along Santa Rosa Rd to Lompoc and northward through Los Olivos, Los Alamos and Santa Maria. Each of the little hamlets anchoring the Santa Ynez Valley have their own look and vibe – Los Alamos with its Old Western storefronts that include a Michelin-starred restaurant among its good culinary company, and Los Olivos' clapboard-ranch-chic aesthetic and oak-lined lanes. A drive along Santa Rosa Rd or Rte 246 is the simplest way to visit some of the region's best wineries while also enjoying a slow day trip through the valley's picturesque rolling hills cultivated in rows of vines.

Santa Ynez Valley

TIME FROM SOLVANG: **7 MINS**

Un-wine in the SYV

Wine is queen around here, but there are other pleasures to savor in the Santa Ynez Valley. These rolling hills have traditionally sustained the Chumash people and supported agriculture and ranching that have nothing to do with the relatively new fermented-grape industry.

Begin with an introduction to the region's indigenous background at the newly-opened **Chumash Cultural Center** *(sychumashmuseum.org; adult/teen/child $15/12/10)* in Santa Ynez. The museum's contemporary architecture incorporates the dome shape of the traditional Chumash *'ap* house, and has a garden element landscaped with grasses, herbs and other native flora used for medicine and weaving. Inside, the wonderful interactive exhibits teach visitors about Chumash folklore, Samala language, maritime culture, history and the many cultural contributions of its tribal members. Even the tile work leading to the museum entrance features illustrations of native animals with their Samala names.

Then, inhabit your inner *vaquero/a* (cowboy/girl) on a horseback ride with **Vino Vaqueros** *(vinovaqueros.com)*. To be fair, the ride does end with a wine tasting, but the main event is riding through ranch and vineyard with experienced guides and horses; kids eight and up can ride, too. Reservations must be made in advance; walk-ins are not accommodated.

Local tasting isn't limited to wine: try lavender honey and pick up lavender baking mixes and teas at **Clairmont Farms**

BILLYHANKEJR/SHUTTERSTOCK

Vineyard, Los Olivos

(clairmontfarms.com). Its small shop also sells housemade skincare and mists, and visitors are free to enjoy the shade and walk amid the lavender; blooming season is in June and July.

Local olive farmers offer estate-grown tastings of their grassy, fruity and peppery olive oils in beautiful ranch settings, including at **Rancho Olivos** *(ranchoolivos.com)* just outside of downtown Los Olivos.

Los Olivos

TIME FROM SOLVANG: **11 MINS**

Walking & wine tasting

Wine tasting in Los Olivos is a delicious reminder that life is good. Its petite size makes this appealing town the perfect choice if you've only got an afternoon to taste in the valley, as you can walk to two dozen tasting rooms within a few blocks. Tastings generally run around $25, and wineries may waive the tasting fee if you purchase multiple bottles – policies vary by individual business.

Although there's no need to drive anywhere once you've parked, do plan ahead for getting safely to your onward destination. If you're cruising around with others, a good strategy for hitting several wineries is to split your tastings with someone so you're not consuming the entirety of each pour. When tasting solo, sip and spit. (The dump bucket is there for a reason; no one will be offended if you use it.)

THE SIDEWAYS EFFECT

In the 2004 film *Sideways*, whose story took place in the Santa Ynez Valley, wine-snob protagonist Miles famously declared he didn't want to drink merlot, and almost as famously helped trigger a real-world decline in merlot sales. But though the 'Sideways Effect' did contribute to the 2% drop, a glut of merlot plantings and subsequent production of lower-quality wines had already set that effect in motion.

Though pinot noir is still a local darling around here, it's worth giving a good merlot another try. Either way, you can follow in the fictional footsteps of the wayward Miles and Jack on your own *Sideways*-based tour *(solvangusa.com/solvang-wine-country/sideways)* for tasting stops, scenic drives and ostrich encounters.

EATING & DRINKING IN SANTA YNEZ: OUR PICKS

Santa Ynez Billiards & Café: A falafel or shawarma wrap plus cool drink on the shaded patio: the best deal in town. *11am-8pm Sun, to 9pm Mon, Tue, Thu-Sat* $

Maverick Saloon: Santa Ynez's go-to for late-night cocktails, live music and line dancing with the locals. *11am-midnight Sun-Thu, to 2am Fri & Sat* $

SY Kitchen: Reservations recommended for standout, authentic Italian farm-to-table cuisine in the bustling modern farmhouse dining room or fairy-lit veranda. *11.30am-2pm & 4.30-9pm* $$

Pony Cocktails + Kitchen: Get a coffee fix and brunch in the morning, craft cocktails and fresh takes on comfort food later on. *8am-2.30pm daily & 4.30-10pm Tue-Sat* $$

PUTTING THE OLIVES BACK IN LOS OLIVOS

Los Olivos comes by its name honestly. In the 1880s, a young rancher planted 5000 olive trees near Ballard. When the Pacific Coast Railway built its rail line from Los Alamos down to its new station, it eventually bequeathed the stop with the name Los Olivos in homage to the trees. Unfortunately, a harsh winter in 1889 killed most of the young olive trees.

In the mid-1990s, observing that the latitude and climate are similar to olive-growing regions in Spain and Italy, a few intrepid souls began planting olive trees in the Santa Ynez Valley expressly to produce olive oil. The happy, full-circle result is that you can now taste olive oil in Los Olivos.

If you have no clue where to start, you'll find a super-approachable vibe at **Carhartt Family Wines** *(carharttvineyard.com)*, which is open 11am to 6pm and often has live music on their spacious patio, or at family-run **Saarloos + Sons** *(saarloosandsons.com)*, who also do cupcake pairings *(open 11am to 5pm)*. Try the region's cool-climate Burgundian and Rhône varietals like chardonnay, pinot noir and syrah at the amazing small producers here. These include **Blair Fox Cellars** *(blairfoxcellars.com)*, open noon to 5pm Sunday to Thursday and to 6pm Friday and Saturday, **Storm Wines** *(stormwines.com)*, open 11am to 5pm Wednesday to Monday, **Liquid Farm** *(liquidfarm.com)*, open from 11am, and women-run **Holus Bolus** *(holusboluswine.com)*, open noon to 5pm, and **Story of Soil** *(storyofsoilwine.com)*, by reservation only Monday to Thursday. Sample less common varietals like interesting Austrian skin-contact grüner veltliner at **Solminer** *(solminer.com)*, open 11am to 5pm Sunday to Friday, to 6pm Saturday, and be sure to taste at heavy-hitters like **Brewer-Clifton** *(bygregbrewer.com)*, open 10am to 4pm Thursday to Tuesday, and **Stolpman** *(stolpmanvineyards.com)*, open 11am to 4pm.

This town is mostly (OK, all) about the wine, but Los Olivos has boutiques and galleries to browse between tastings. Weekends often feel like a block party, with live bands and a festive atmosphere. Arrive early to find parking closer in.

Lompoc

TIME FROM SOLVANG: **30 MINS**

Tasting at the Wine Ghetto

There's nothing hidden about Lompoc's **Wine Ghetto**, but it feels like you've discovered a local secret when you park among the nondescript industrial buildings in this warehouse complex. It's just off the intersection of Hwy 1 and 12th St in the city of Lompoc (pronounced 'Lom-poke'); you could easily spend a day here tasting a representative spectrum of Santa Rita Hills terroir.

Each tasting room has its own creative feel reflective of its resident winemaker: from the self-effacing cartoon goats of **Flying Goat Cellars** *(flyinggoatcellars.com)* labels (belying the artistry inside the bottle), to the bright and friendly **Fiddlehead Cellars** *(fiddleheadcellars.com)*, pouring estate-grown wines made by pioneering winemaker Kathy Joseph.

Family-run **Ampelos Cellars** *(ampeloscellars.com)* uses grapes from organically and biodynamically farmed vineyards to make their pinot noir and Rhône varietals. Also sourcing from

EATING IN LOS OLIVOS: WINE-COUNTRY PAIRINGS

Panino: Take a break from tasting with a takeout sandwich and a cool non-alcoholic beverage. *10am-4pm* $

Mattei's Tavern: There's cozy elegance at the coffee shop, atmospheric bar and tavern serving California cuisine. *6.30am-2pm & 5-9pm* $$

Los Olivos Wine Merchant & Cafe: Elevated but relaxed dining created with organic ingredients from the restaurant's own farm. *11.30am-8.30pm Sun-Thu, to 9pm Fri & Sat* $$

Bar Le Côte: The couple who brought us Bell's in Los Alamos has set up shop here, with Euro-style seafood on the menu. *noon-8.30pm* $$

SANTA RITA HILLS VINEYARD SOJOURN

Roll through the terroir of the green hills and curves of the Santa Rita Hills AVA (American Viticultural Area).

START	END	LENGTH
Buellton	Melville Winery	29 miles; 50 mins

Drink in the beauty of these vineyards, planted mostly with pinot noir and chardonnay, though other varietals like grenache, syrah and viognier are cultivated. Start the loop in 1 **Buellton** with your picnic fixings packed, taking Santa Rosa Rd to the west. About 6 miles down the bucolic, winding road, stop to taste at 2 **Peake Ranch**, in its contemporary, airy tasting room with an outdoor patio looking out to the vineyard. On the same road offshoot, try the beautiful wines of 3 **Alma Rosa Winery & Vineyards** (reservations required), which organically farms its grapes in an intentional commitment to sustainability. Alma Rosa was founded by Richard Sanford, the first vintner to plant pinot noir in Santa Barbara County in 1971.

Just before Santa Rosa Rd intersects with Hwy 1, 4 **The Hilt Estate** offers sublime tastings (appointment only). Turn right on Hwy 1 to drive the two miles to Lompoc's industrial 5 **Wine Ghetto**, where you can sample multiple wineries' offerings efficiently if you're pressed for time. Return to Buellton on Rte 246 heading east. You'll find the tasting experience to be relaxed and playful at the multigenerational, family-run 6 **Babcock Winery**, which often has live music and other fun events. Next-door neighbor stalwart 7 **Melville Winery** offers a more elegant setting, either in the civilized tasting room or in the front vineyard.

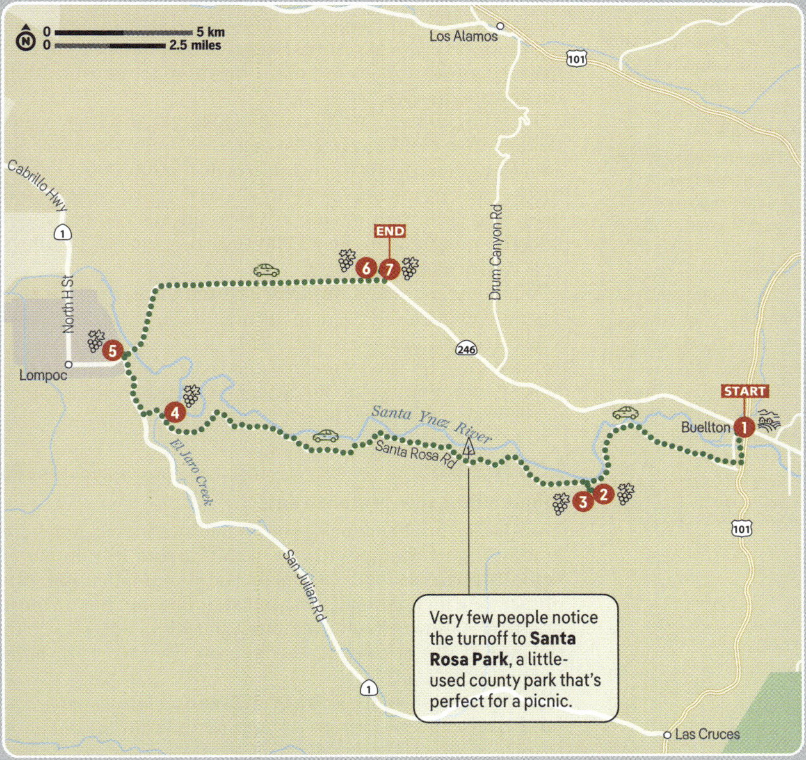

BEST WINE TOURS

Sustainable Wine Tours: This small company brings guests to private tastings at wineries that aren't open to the public.

Destination Vine: A concierge-style outfit with personable guides and customizable tours, run by two women who have long-standing relationships with valley wineries.

Santa Barbara Wine Country Cycling Tours: More of a cycling than a tasting tour, though it includes a seasonal lunch and wine tasting. E-bikes are available.

Santa Barbara Wine Country Tours: Private or shared group tours include tastings at three wineries and lunch, plus pickup from your accommodations.

Coastal Concierge: Private, custom wine tours; you can also incorporate sailing, horseback riding or even a private flight over wine country into your experience.

biodynamic and regenerative-minded vineyards, the women- and Native-run **Camins 2 Dreams** *(camins2dreams.com)* has an inclusive tasting room here.

Find a map of the Wine Ghetto at *explorelompoc.com*, and let your tasting-room hosts suggest neighboring wineries to discover something new to you, just steps away.

At some point you'll probably want to grab a bite, in which case you should head straight to **Eye on I** *(theeyeoni.com)*, about 1.5 miles from the Ghetto on North I St. A cousin to local fave **Industrial Eats** (p55), it consistently offers wood-fired pizza on the menu, which otherwise changes seasonally and is hand-written on butcher paper on the wall. Open Tuesday through Saturday, it has a cluttered, industrial feel that extends to its funky back patio.

San Marcos Pass

TIME FROM SOLVANG: **20 MINS**

Detours off Highway 154

The drive over San Marcos Pass (Hwy 154) between Santa Barbara and the Santa Ynez Valley is a gorgeous one, with a few detours worth making if you have time for a relaxed drive. Along much of the way, the winding mountain pass has only two lanes, so it's particularly important to be or designate a sober driver.

About 12 miles from Solvang, **Cachuma Lake Recreation Area** *(countyofsb.org/693/Marina; vehicle entry $10)* has several easy trails, kayak and boat rentals and fishing opportunities for bass, rainbow trout and other freshwater species.

Ten miles further east along Hwy 154, take the Stagecoach Dr turnoff to **Cold Spring Tavern** *(coldspringtavern.com)*, a former stagecoach stop established in 1868. This historic little forest haven serves Central Coast tri-tip sirloin and beer, and with live music on weekend afternoons you'll find the tavern at its best. The tavern is closed Tuesdays and Wednesdays.

Finally, the stunning **Chumash Painted Cave** *(parks.ca.gov)* sits right above a side road up the mountain, its interior viewable through a protective gate. Note that the 2-mile drive up Painted Cave Rd is very narrow and twisty, squeezing to one lane at a few points – do not attempt the drive with a trailer or recreational vehicle (RV).

Los Alamos

TIME FROM SOLVANG: **25 MINS**

High-caliber, low-pretense eats

Los Alamos might surprise you. What looks like a nowhere kind of highway stop with a gas station and hilltop motel actually possesses four blocks of rustic sophistication. Appropriately nicknamed Lost Almost, it may not be the most practical gateway to wine country, but it's definitely worth the stop if you're passing through on Hwy 101 with hunger pangs.

Your first stop should be **Bob's Well Bread** *(bobswellbread.com)* for a transcendent *kouign amann* (Breton butter cake) or

FOXEN CANYON WINE TRAIL

The winding Foxen Canyon Rd invites you to drink in the scenery of bucolic ranches and a sea of vineyard rows.

START	END	LENGTH
Demetria Estate	Presqu'ile	27 miles; 1 hr

Foxen Canyon, the region's oldest AVA (American Viticultural Area), is home to some of Santa Barbara County's most venerable vineyards. Its hilly topography and microclimates create ideal conditions for different varietals to thrive: you'll travel from Rhône-heavy territory to a Burgundian clime as you head closer to the coast.

Tastings at 1 **Demetria Estate** are by appointment only, but visiting this estate is like scoring the cheapest ticket to Tuscany you'll ever find. Grapes here are organically and biodynamically grown, an added bonus at this gorgeous estate tasting experience. Next on the road northward, one of the oldest wineries in the Santa Maria AVA, 2 **Foxen Winery** runs a sustainable operation and a ranch-style, solar-powered tasting room serving spectacular pinot noir, syrah and chardonnay. Half a mile up the road, their 3 **Shack** pours Bordeaux and Italian varietals. Continue almost two miles to the sharp right onward to 4 **Rancho Sisquoc Winery** – reserve picnic boxes ahead of your tasting and soak in the historic atmosphere. End by pairing a picnic with delicate pinot noir and/or pinot bubbles at peaceful, female-run 5 **Riverbench Vineyard & Winery**. The cozy ranch house and outdoor tables are lovely settings. Or opt for a more energizing finish to your day with live music, bites and wine at 6 **Presqu'ile**, whose scene-stealing tasting room and amphitheater complement their beautiful wines.

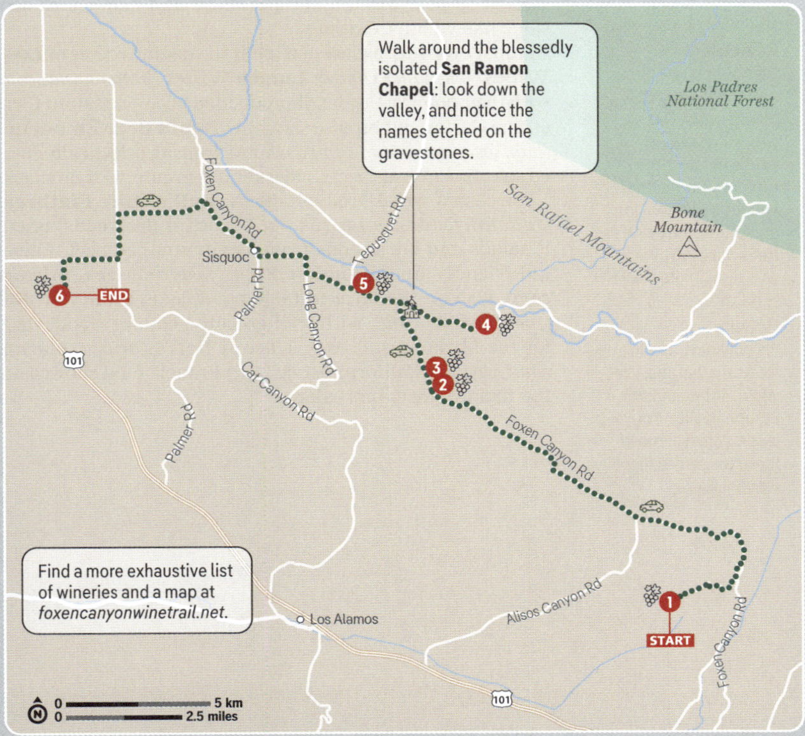

Walk around the blessedly isolated **San Ramon Chapel**: look down the valley, and notice the names etched on the gravestones.

Find a more exhaustive list of wineries and a map at *foxencanyonwinetrail.net*.

PICNICKING AT ESTATE WINERIES

Amy Christine, co-owner and winemaker at Holus Bolus & The Joy Fantastic, shares her picks for winery picnics.

Peake Ranch
Their tasting room is in the vineyard, which is not the case everywhere. So you're sitting in the vines, away from the highway – it's quiet, modern, very comfortable and stunningly beautiful.

Demetria
Demetria is remote, up a really rugged private road. Once you're back there you're nestled into this cozy Santa Ynez environment, looking out at the vines with trees hanging over you, right in the midst of nature.

Melville
It's polished, a little more aristocratic, like you're sitting outside a European villa. You're tasting amid some of the vines, with a more elegant feel.

BUYENLARGE/GETTY IMAGES

Chumash Painted Cave (p60)

sit-down breakfast. For the gluten-free, the hearty brick of seeded GF bread is worth picking up. From here, roam along **Bell St** to poke around antique shops and make hard decisions like where to eat next.

Mull it over with a glass of wine at the tasting rooms of **Lo-Fi Wines** *(lofi-wines.com)* or **Lumen Wines** *(lumenwines.com)*, with their noteworthy, small-production juice. Or taste at Clementine Carter and browse sister biz **Babi's Beer Emporium** *(babisbeeremporium.com)* to choose from an eclectically curated selection of craft beers, ciders and charcuterie-style snacks.

For casual wood-fired goodness, **Full of Life Flatbread** *(fulloflifefoods.com)* turns out beautiful flatbreads, organic salads and burnt ends from locally sourced beef. There's kid-friendly fine dining at **Pico** *(losalamosgeneralstore.com)*, also on the farm-to-table train, as is **Plenty on Bell** *(plentyonbell.com)*, with well-executed comfort food. Or go for the Michelin-star experience at **Bell's** *(bellsrestaurant.com)*, serving California-style 'very Franch' food showcasing the region's fresh ingredients.

Ventura

LOW-KEY VIBES | COASTAL CULTURE | OCEAN RECREATION

Often overlooked by visitors in favor of Santa Barbara, Ventura is SB's more salt-of-the-earth sister, underrated only because she lacks the movie-star sheen. This coastal city (officially known as San Buenaventura) has an attractive old town anchored by the Mission San Buenaventura, plus a beachfront promenade and slightly retro little harbor village.

Ventura and its surrounding area were originally occupied by the Ventureño Chumash people, who built seafaring canoes and were skilled at spear-fishing. During the era of Spanish colonialization, Junípero Serra established Mission San Buenaventura in 1782, the last of the California missions. In the early 1900s, oil drilling boomed, and some of East Main St's architecture has survived from that period.

Ventura harbor is the jumping-off point for Channel Islands National Park, about an hour's boat ride across the Santa Barbara Channel. It's also the coastal gateway to Ojai, nestled in the Topatopa mountain range.

GETTING AROUND

Downtown Ventura is walkable, with plenty of free or cheap parking. Because so many people who work in Santa Barbara live in Ventura County, the $4 (one-way) Coastal Express bus runs several trips daily during commuting hours from Ventura to Santa Barbara. It's also possible to take the local Amtrak service between Ventura and Santa Barbara County towns.

TOP TIP

Adjacent to Ventura, the agricultural city of Oxnard is California's biggest strawberry producer. Pick up fresh, juicy berries from farmstands, such as those at the T-junction of Telephone Rd and Olivas Park Dr.

EATING IN VENTURA: SEAFOOD SPOTS

Spencer Makenzie's: This casual counter-service joint slings ceviche, fish tacos, ahi pockets and poke a little eastward of old town. *11am-8pm* $

Brophy Bros: Upstairs institution with harbor views and a busy, boisterous atmosphere for huge platters of seafood and strong drinks. *11am-9pm Sun-Thu, to 10pm Fri & Sat* $$

Rumfish y Vino: Lovely patio whisks you to coastal Spain, with excellent seafood and a Latin twist in old-town Ventura. *from 11.30am Mon-Sat, from 11am Sun* $$

Lure Fish House: Sustainably caught fresh fish, organic regional farm produce and California wines. *11.30am-9pm Sun-Thu, to 10pm Fri & Sat* $$

SIGHTS

1 Mission San Buenaventura
2 San Buenaventura State Beach
3 Surfers Point
4 Ventura Botanical Gardens
5 Ventura River Estuary

ACTIVITIES

6 Ventura Promenade

SLEEPING

7 Crowne Plaza Ventura Beach
8 Hotel San Buena

EATING

9 Jolly Oyster
10 Lure Fish House
11 Rumfish y Vino
12 Spencer Makenzie's

DRINKING & NIGHTLIFE

13 Bank of Italy Cocktail Trust
14 Leashless Brewing
15 Rocks & Drams
16 Topa Topa Brewing Company

SHOPPING

17 Patagonia

Old-Town Ventura

Visit the mission, old town and botanical garden

Ventura's retro old town lies along East Main St, with the beaux-arts **City Hall** looming on the hill above and the beach a few blocks below. Closed to vehicle traffic, this section of East Main St is a pleasant stretch for window-shopping, with gobs of indie and thrift shops, and places for a bite of Thai food or tacos.

Mission San Buenaventura welcomes visitors on the western end of Main St and remains a community parish church. In the peaceful garden area, its olive mill and brick filtering tank from the mission's aqueduct still stand.

For a short hike you can do right from downtown, **Ventura Botanical Gardens** *(venturabotanicalgardens.com; $7)* – free on Fridays, closed on Mondays – has a 2-mile graded trail zigzagging up a ridge. The steep path shows off expansive views of the city and ocean as you climb through South American and South African garden areas.

Otherwise, walk along the **Ventura Promenade** to soak up salt air with the cyclists, skaters, joggers and dog-walkers enjoying the paved pathway. A bike and pedestrian path begins off Main St (park in the small lot just west of the Hwy 33 overpass), following the Ventura River down to the **Ventura River Estuary** before heading east along the beach. Watch the surfers – or paddle out into the lineup yourself – at **Surfers Point**. From here, you can walk two to three miles to **San Buenaventura State Beach**, where on weekends you can top off your beach day with freshly shucked oysters at the **Jolly Oyster** *(thejollyoyster.com)*, a seafood shack in the state park.

GREAT PACIFIC ENV(IRON)MENTAL WORKS

Yvon Chouinard founded pioneering outdoor clothing brand **Patagonia** *(patagonia.com)* in Ventura. In 1972, he set up shop in the distinctive yellow **Great Pacific Iron Works** building, where Patagonia's HQ still operates today, as does its flagship retail shop.

Chouinard's unconventional business practices always dovetailed with his core beliefs – he is an environmentalist to his bones.

The nonprofit 1% for the Planet was co-founded in 2002; its member companies donate 1% of their profits to collectively support environmental causes. In 2022 Patagonia announced its partnership with the purpose-built nonprofit Holdfast Collective to which Patagonia's excess profits are plowed, to fund environmental conservation and address climate change.

DRINKING IN VENTURA: DOWNTOWN

Bank of Italy Cocktail Trust: Named for the historic building it occupies; also serves Italian-style bites. *4pm-midnight Mon-Thu, 2pm-1am Fri & Sat, 2pm-midnight Sun*

Rocks & Drams: Craft cocktails, great happy hour specials and regularly programmed live music and DJs. *5-10pm Mon-Thu, 5pm-midnight Fri, 3pm-midnight Sat, 3-9pm Sun*

Leashless Brewing: Organic, beer in the Belgian style, including gluten-free options. Occasional live music. *4-9pm Tue & Wed, 4-10pm Thu, 4-11pm Fri, 1-11pm Sat, 1-8pm Sun*

Topa Topa Brewing Company: Good vibes and ethics on so many levels besides the great beer; check the calendar for events. *noon-9pm Mon-Thu, to 10pm Fri & Sat, to 8pm Sun*

Beyond Ventura

From Ventura, journey inland to Ojai for slow living and sunshine, or cross the channel to windswept Channel Islands National Park.

Places

GETTING AROUND

Downtown Ojai is small enough to explore on foot once you've arrived (it's a 25-minute drive from Ventura). Journeys beyond, from Meiners Oaks (3 miles) to nearby trailheads, require a car drive or bicycle ride.

On the Channel Islands, you'll rely on your own feet on land or paddle power on the water.

When the coast is cool and tinged with fog, chances are good that the sun is shining in Ojai. About 20 minutes' drive into the oaky inland valley transports you to a different world altogether, where citrus groves and horse country meet spiritual seekers and Hollywood refugees. The lovely nest of a valley exudes good energy for rejuvenating and recreating.

Offshore, the Channel Islands topography defines the horizon line. Traveling across the channel is a 1½-hour journey over marine wilderness, where dolphin and whale encounters are the norm. Hiking on the wild, windswept islands is witnessing what the coastal mainland might have looked like a thousand years ago.

Channel Islands National Park

TIME FROM VENTURA: **1½ HRS** 

Day-tripping to Santa Cruz Island

Harbor seals bark your way out as your boat departs Ventura Harbor into the **Santa Barbara Channel**. From there, it's all eyes on the ocean's surface as you scan for whale spouts or dolphins racing your vessel. It's not that unusual to find your boat in the middle of a superpod of dolphins numbering in the hundreds, or to have a curious humpback whale approach as the boat idles.

Once you dock at the island, it's yours to explore on foot. **Santa Cruz Island** is the most accessible of the five-island chain, with the most frequent boats making daily trips in high season. At **Scorpion Anchorage**, displays explain the island's human history, flanked with antique ranching equipment rusting in the sun. The 2-mile **Cavern Point Loop** heads through the campground and up to a bluff trail to a lovely overlook of offshore arches, ocean and distant mainland California. A longer 5-miler goes to a viewpoint on **Potato Harbor** and the islands beyond.

Alternatively, meet up with your guide and suit up for **kayaking** into sea caves and isolated coves, exploring the ecosystem on the island's fringe. As you paddle, you'll marvel at the coppery blades of kelp swaying in contrast with the clear blue water, poppy-orange garibaldi (California's state marine fish) darting within the kelp bed and bristling reef beneath.

BRAM REUSEN/SHUTTERSTOCK

Scorpion Anchorage

Island camping

Imagine waking up to the tranquility of central California's landscape as it was when wild and in ecological balance. Camping on the Channel Islands gifts you with the luxury of immersing yourself in something akin to that.

Exploring one of these offshore sanctuaries after day-trippers have departed for the mainland you'll get a taste of the rugged survival of the original Channel Islands people and the peace with which they lived. In fact, the name Chumash is derived from these island inhabitants, who were the 'makers of shell-bead money.'

In the Chumash creation story, the first people lived on **Limuw** (Santa Cruz Island) but had become too numerous to all remain there. Hutash (Mother Earth) told the people that they must cross over to the mainland on a rainbow she had created for them. Some of the people looked down as they crossed the rainbow bridge and were dizzied by the height, falling into the water. Hutash, not wishing to see them perish, turned them into dolphins, now considered by the Chumash as family – beautiful context for your channel passage.

Scorpion Canyon Campground on Santa Cruz Island has the most campsites (31), only a half-mile from the boat dock with potable water and vault toilets. If you're backcountry camping, you'll have to bring your own water and haul it to the designated campgrounds. Reserve campsites up to six months ahead at recreation.gov; cancellations do happen, so keep checking in.

Regardless of location, the super-intelligent ravens know how to unzip zippers and fearless little island foxes will steal silently away with unattended snacks, so it's key for wildlife health to lock down your food in the fox boxes.

ISLAND TOUR OPERATORS

Island Packers Cruises is the national park concessionaire running public transportation to and from the Channel Islands, departing from Ventura Harbor. If you rent or bring your own kayaks, they can also transport them with prior notice. They're also a fantastic choice for whale-watching trips on the channel.

To explore the waters of the national park, you can arrange kayaking and snorkeling day trips with **Channel Islands Adventure Company**. For divers and those with the time for deeper exploration, **Channel Islands Expeditions** operate their own vessels for multiday liveaboard trips to several of the islands.

BEST DAY SPAS

Spa Ojai: The full-on, decadent resort experience at Ojai Valley Inn, with private outdoor terraces, desert clay mud treatment, guided meditation and light-flooded common areas.

Day Spa of Ojai: Owner Kim Wachter's Chumash heritage influences her treatments at this cozy downtown spa offering massages and skincare.

Ojai Garden Spa: Gazebo massages outdoors in the garden of the Lavender Inn downtown; also offers skincare treatments.

Ojai Massage: Experienced professionals providing a range of bodywork and therapeutic massage. Outcalls to your accommodations can also be arranged.

Ojai Skin Revision: With a customized approach to skincare, Ojai's oldest day spa (formerly known as Body Essentials) has an infrared sauna and offers facial treatments and massage.

Ojai

TIME FROM VENTURA: **25 MINS**

Roaming the valley of the moon

Holiday with Hollywood escapees in the magical place that is Ojai. Taking its name from the Chumash word *'awhay'* for 'moon' (some say 'nest'), this valley has always attracted seekers, from spiritual philosopher Krishnamurti to contemporary urban dwellers lured, possibly, by the spiritual energy of Ojai's vortexes.

Downtown is defined by Ojai Ave. **Libbey Park**, with its pretty archways, has a fantastic playground, walking paths and picnic tables under the trees. Further back, catch outdoor concerts at **Libbey Bowl** *(libbeybowl.org)* amphitheater.

Along this side of Ojai Ave and its side streets you'll find wine-tasting rooms, local boutiques like the indoor/outdoor **Fig** *(figojai.com)*, and the gallery and theater of the **Ojai Art Center** *(ojaiartcenter.org)*, established in 1939.

People-watch from the corner patio of **Topa Topa Brewing Company** *(topatopa.beer)* with Asian pub fusion food (like *okonomiyaki* tots) from **Little Sama Ojai**. Try the Burmese tea-leaf salad at the sustainably minded **Dutchess** *(thedutchessojai.com)*, which also tempts with sumptuous pastries and an excellent wine list.

Across Ojai Ave, find art galleries, shops and honey tastings along the **Ojai Arcade**, which opens out to a plaza behind. The spectacular, cheerfully jam-packed Sunday morning **farmers market** sets up shop in the parking lot on East Matilija St just beyond the plaza. Stroll a few more blocks west along East Matilija St to browse the maze of aisles at cherished landmark **Bart's Books** *(bartsbooksojai.com)*, known as the 'world's largest outdoor bookstore,' founded in 1964.

Oh hi, outdoors

Hiking is the leisure activity of choice in Ojai, backed as it is by the Topatopa Mountains and Los Padres National Forest.

Easily accessed from town is the **Shelf Rd Trail** in the **Valley View Preserve** *(ovlc.org/valley-view-preserve)*, at the north end of Signal Rd in Ojai. This is a mostly flat hike with excellent views of the valley; make it an out-and-back or return through town. You'll also find the **Fox Canyon Trail** in the preserve, which you can connect with others for a more challenging loop hike.

Use your America the Beautiful parks pass or pay the day-use fee *($10)* for the easy, short hike to a waterfall (best in springtime) on the **Rose Valley Falls Trail** in the Sespe

EATING & DRINKING IN OJAI: OUR PICKS

Ojai Tortilla House: The window of opening hours at this authentic, hole-in-the-wall Mexican spot is limited, as is the menu. Cash only. *11am-2pm* $

Ojai Beverage Company: OBC is the place to refuel post-hike with a salmon salad or burger and a beer. *11am-9pm Tue-Thu & Sun, to 10pm Fri & Sat* $

Ojai Rôtie: Farm-to-picnic-table fare shines here, with housemade sourdough, roast chicken and local wine. *7.30-11am Sun, noon-3pm & 4-8pm Wed-Sun, to 8.30pm Fri & Sat* $$

Rory's Place: Locally sourced, fresh ingredients assembled in simple, sophisticated style. Oysters, roasted beets, salt-and-vinegar martinis: yes please. *5-10pm Wed-Mon* $$

JAY L CLENDENIN VIA GETTY IMAGES

Ventura River, Ojai

Wilderness, about 15 miles from Ojai on Hwy 33. Another Sespe hike is the **Piedra Blanca Trail**, with beautiful white sandstone boulders at the end, about 5 miles round trip with a creek crossing. Call or visit the **Ojai ranger station** *(fs.usda.gov/detail/lpnf)* for detailed info.

Closer to town, a kid-friendly trail is the flat, close to 1-mile hike at **Ojai Meadows Preserve** *(ovlc.org/omp)* that's good for birding as it passes wetlands and meadows with views of the mountains.

Rent bicycles at the **Mob Shop** *(themobshop.com)* on W Ojai Ave and ride along the **Ojai Valley Trail**, the Ojai section of the Ventura River Parkway Trail. Or take a trail-only sunset horseback ride in the Ventura River Valley Preserve to enjoy Ojai's 'pink moment' with **Ojai Valley Trail Riding Company** *(ojaivalleytrailridingcompany.com)*.

VENTURA RIVER PARKWAY TRAIL

Cycling the 16-mile **Ventura River Parkway Trail** from the Ventura River Estuary to Ojai is a fantastic way to experience the changing landscape from coast to inland valley. Running through local parks and natural preserve lands, the pedestrian-and-bike trail passes historical sites such as the **Ortega Adobe** and **mission aqueduct** along the way. Climbing through agricultural and open space before emerging into oak chaparral woodland, the trail eventually connects with the Ojai Valley Trail and heads into the heart of Ojai. Find a trail map at *friendsofventurariver.org*.

EATING IN MEINERS OAKS: RURAL GEMS

Farmer & the Cook: Run by an Ojai farmer/poet and cook couple, serving some of the most direct farm-to-table food at its cafe/market. *8am-4pm Mon-Wed, to 8pm Thu-Sun* $

Ojai Noodle House: Vietnamese food (not just noodles), with a covered patio and moody Southeast Asian bar. *11am-3pm & 4-9pm Wed-Sun* $

Ojai Deer Lodge: Ojai's oldest restaurant, serving panzanella and shishito peppers alongside burgers. *noon-8pm Wed-Thu, noon-9pm Fri, 11am-9pm Sat, 11am-8pm Sun* $$

The Ranch House: The original owners' ethos purportedly inspired Alice Waters' farm-to-table philosophy. Reservation only. *5-9pm Tue-Sun* $$$

Places We Love to Stay

$ Budget $$ Midrange $$$ Top End

Santa Barbara

MAP p44

Agave Inn $ Playful Mexican accents and a sun-splashed color palette create warm ambience in this updated Uptown motel. Family-size rooms have a kitchenette and pullout sofa beds.

Marina Beach Motel $ This whitewashed, pet-friendly motor lodge is a block from the beach, with tidy remodeled rooms, some with kitchenette, and complimentary beach cruisers to borrow.

Castillo Inn $ One of the best of the West Beach bunch. Rooms are large and bright, some with private terraces, with the Funk Zone, Stearns Wharf and harbor a short walk away.

Harbor House Inn $ Two blocks from the beach, this meticulously run inn offers bright, individually decorated studios and rooms, plus free loaner beach gear and bicycles.

Canary $$$ Stylish downtown Kimpton joint with rooftop pool and sunset-watching perch for cocktails. In-room spa services and Saturday yoga soothe away stress, but be aware of ambient street noise.

Hotel Californian $$$ This upscale spot puts the Funk Zone and waterfront within strolling distance, with a glamorous blend of Spanish Colonial and North African Moorish style.

El Encanto $$$ This enchanting 1920s classic in the Riviera neighborhood looks out over the city from its foothill perch, a real Santa Barbara refuge.

Gaviota Coast

Refugio State Beach Campground $ A lovely beachside campground with palms fringing the beach and tidepools to poke around in at low tide. Walk-in only from December 1 to March 31.

El Capitan Canyon $$ Glamp in cedar cabins with covered porches, or in canvas yurts with skylights for stargazing. All have picnic tables and firepits for barbecuing.

South County

Inn on Summer Hill $$ This cute Summerland B&B has a prime location with ocean views on one side, but be aware that it also overlooks the freeway and Amtrak railway.

Rosewood Miramar Beach $$$ An exceedingly enviable beachfront locale on Miramar Beach for a truly splurgy Montecito stay, with a range of luxurious garden and beachside rooms.

Solvang

MAP p53

Viking Inn $ A friendly little family-run motel done up in in bright white and astroturf lawn with Adirondack chairs on the western end of main street, Mission Dr.

Hamlet Inn $ A modern motel makeover with a bit of Danish flavor, crisp, comfortable rooms and a location right on Mission Dr in the heart of Solvang.

Hotel Corque $$ On the eastern end of town and adjacent to open space, the Corque has spacious and quiet rooms and a pool, and offers a visual break from all things Scandinavian.

The Landsby $$ Contemporary style and spacious suites surround a welcoming courtyard, with live music often featured at the lobby bar. Central location on Mission Dr.

Buellton & Santa Ynez

Flying Flags $ Hook up your own RV, check into a kitted-out Airstream, or choose a glamping tent, cabin or cottage at this Buellton RV resort that feels like summer camp.

Sideways Inn $ The Scandinavian design ends with the big windmill out front – enjoy modern accommodations, a pool, firepit and lounge after a day exploring.

Pea Soup Andersen's Inn $ The neighboring historic restaurant may have closed, but this Buellton hotel is still a great, reasonably priced choice for families, with a pool and outdoor games.

Hotel Ynez $$ Upstyled wine-country motel with an airy ranch feel and a relaxed garden setting between Santa Ynez and Solvang, with bocce, an adults-only pool and outdoor spaces for lounging.

Los Olivos

Fess Parker Wine Country Inn $$$ Find low-key luxury in the center of Los Olivos, where fireplaces come standard in spacious rooms, as do breakfast and a wine tasting.

The Inn at Mattei's Tavern $$$ Originally a stagecoach stop, Mattei's is now an eminently softer landing spot if you can swing it. It's also de rigueur for morning coffee.

Los Alamos

Alamo Motel $ A hip little Western-themed spot, centrally located on Bell St, with an inviting lawn, a firepit and a bar shack for socializing outdoors.

Skyview Los Alamos $$ Another remodeled retro number, this hilltop motel has a pool, restaurant and bar – it's near Bell St, but across the highway.

Victorian Mansion B&B $$ This attractive Victorian has a unique and ornate interior with themed rooms that go all-in, from a pirate lair to a hobbit hole.

Ventura

MAP p64

Crowne Plaza Ventura Beach $$ Yes, it's a chain hotel, but pickings are slim in Ventura, and you can't argue with beachfront property and easy access to old-town Ventura.

Hotel San Buena $$ From the bones of a former Elks Lodge springs a blend of modern and Spanish Revival design at this lovely boutique hotel, steps from old-town Ventura.

Ojai

Ojai Rancho Inn $ On the western approach into Ojai, this modernized mid-century motel has a pool and sauna, plus free bicycles that are useful for getting into town.

Hummingbird Inn $ A peaceful stucco-and-tile inn at the eastern end of Ojai on the edge of a residential neighborhood, with a pool, shaded lawn and little outdoor sitting nooks.

Caravan Outpost $$ Airstreams outfitted with modern comforts and a Southwestern aesthetic are arranged within little garden havens for privacy, with communal showers and toilets, a firepit and a fun community vibe.

Emerald Iguana Inn $$ Close to downtown Ojai, this boutique inn has comfortably boho rooms and standalone cottages in an attractive woodsy setting, with a pool and Jacuzzi.

Ojai Valley Inn & Spa $$$ A relaxed luxury resort with Spanish Colonial architectural style, a golf course and a dreamy spa, but also culinary classes and events celebrating regional bounty.

STEVE CUKROV/SHUTTERSTOCK

Hotel Californian

For places to stay in Los Angeles, see p136

UVL/SHUTTERSTOCK

Above: Downtown Los Angeles (p84); Right: Hollywood Boulevard (p78)

THE MAIN AREAS

HOLLYWOOD
The dream, the reality, the fame.
p78

DOWNTOWN
History, culture, strolling and food.
p84

GRIFFITH PARK, LOS FELIZ & ECHO PARK
Family fun, nature, hipster fun and nightlife.
p94

EXPOSITION PARK & SOUTH LA
Museums, sports, music, arts and culture.
p100

KOREATOWN, MIRACLE MILE & FAIRFAX
Nonstop delight, top museums, edgy shopping.
p105

Researched by
Ryan Ver Berkmoes

Los Angeles

CITY OF DREAMS

Balmy weather warms wave-kissed beaches at the Pacific edge of a vast tapestry of neighborhoods, holding sights and surprises that endlessly delight.

Los Angeles is many things to many people. It is a city of dreams, but has too much traffic. It enjoys perfect weather, but there are so many wildfires. It has the best sunsets, but the smog is terrible. And while all of this rings true in this vast metropolis, what's absolutely for sure is that nothing beats the pulsating, vivacious and infamous flair of Los Angeles.

For many, LA is Hollywood. The sign on a hillside. Famous faces behind sunglasses. The studio magic that captures hearts and minds. LA is also home to music legends: rap is synonymous with South LA and rock and roll is symbiotic with the Sunset Strip. It's where creatives bivouac in Downtown and the Arts District. Melrose is where shopping trends begin, while Koreatown never sleeps. Free-spirit vibes flourish in Venice and everyone celebrates the beaches over 75 miles of coast all the way to Malibu.

SEAN PAVONE/SHUTTERSTOCK

LA is also a kaleidoscope of cultures from over 140 countries, with nearly 220 languages spoken, creating an intricate web of diversity that connects deep beneath the surface. Can't travel abroad? Travel north, south, east and west in LA and you'll find a vibrant enclave for almost any culture you can name.

And that's part of LA's endless appeal for any visitor – it's so many places in one. Boyle Heights is not like Pasadena, Burbank is different from Compton, Los Feliz is not Beverly Hills and Chinatown is not West Hollywood. You get the idea. You can experience so many different places and never leave LA. Once you get the hang of the Metro and the freeways, you can range wide and you'll make the startling discovery that LA is one of the great walkable cities. Yes! Pick a neighborhood and you'll likely find a compact center with shops, sights, history and food and drink and, probably, more than one famous film location.

Looking ahead, LA is working hard to shake off 2025's wildfire and prep for the 2028 Summer Olympics. It has an incredible new building coming at LACMA and more exciting developments in its ceaseless reinvention.

Find Your Way

Los Angeles is a vast city known for its traffic with a side of chaos. It's simply not easy to get from here to there. In late afternoon, Santa Monica to Los Feliz (14 miles) can take 90 minutes. Use the expanding network of subways and light rail when possible.

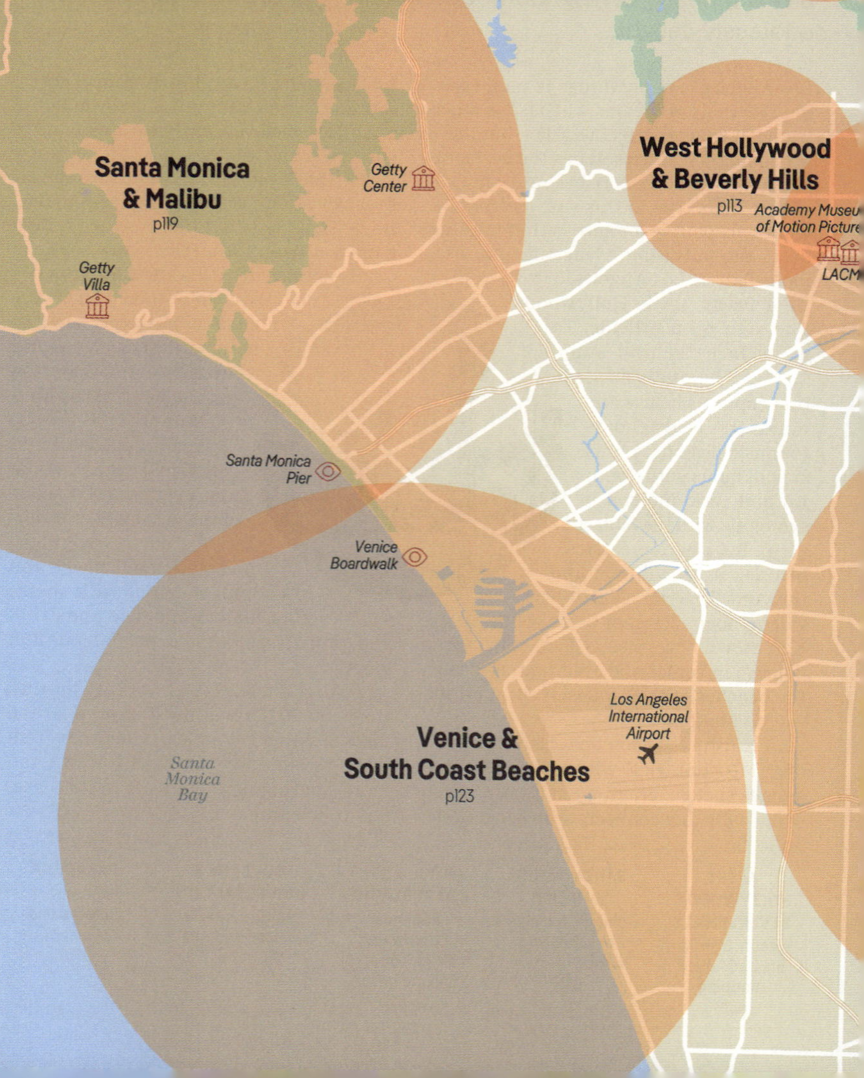

Burbank & Universal Ci
p128
Universal Studios Hollywood

Santa Monica & Malibu
p119
Getty Center
Getty Villa

West Hollywood & Beverly Hills
p113
Academy Museu of Motion Picture
LACM

Santa Monica Pier
Venice Boardwalk

Venice & South Coast Beaches
p123
Santa Monica Bay
Los Angeles International Airport

FROM THE AIRPORT

Huge Los Angeles International Airport (LAX) is the main airport, located in Inglewood. It's right off the I-405, which is often traffic-choked. The new Metro Rail K Line, due to open in 2026, will connect to the airport's elevated shuttle.

CAR

A car offers flexibility and the freedom to travel to the many corners of LA that are not easily reached by public transportation. But it also handcuffs you to being stuck in traffic, paying usurious parking lot rates or simply trying to find parking.

PUBLIC TRANSPORTATION

Billions are being spent to stitch together LA with a network of subways, light rail and commuter trains. Buses fill in the gaps and the entire system can be surprisingly efficient. Use map apps to plan trips. Use the TAP app to pay for rides.

RIDESHARE

Services like Uber and Lyft are great for providing the last mile of transportation after you've covered the bulk of the distance on Metro Rail. Once you see the cost of car rental and parking, rideshare fees become palatable.

Plan Your Days

Los Angeles is like the best of burritos: it's huge and filled with delights, so go slow and enjoy it one bite at a time.

PANDORA PICTURES/SHUTTERSTOCK

Venice Boardwalk (p123)

Day 1

Morning

- Walk all over your favorite stars on the **Hollywood Walk of Fame** (p78) and size up their handprints outside the **TCL Chinese Theatre** (p80).

Afternoon

- Hasten over to the **Original Farmers Market** (p110) and graze your way to a fresh and wonderful lunch. Just south, dig into movie magic at the extraordinary **Academy Museum of Motion Pictures** (p107). Next door, get a dose of fine art in the striking new building at **LACMA** (p107).

Evening

- After dinner at historic old Hollywood **Musso & Frank Grill** (p81), laugh it up with live comedy at the **Laugh Factory** (p115) or **Improv** (p112).

You'll Also Want To...

With about a million things to do in LA, here are a few things to do that give an idea of all the options.

HIT THE PIÑATA DISTRICT

Head to the busy **Piñata District** (p93), just south of the Arts District. The high ceilings are loaded with colorful characters and you can have lunch, a snack or a drink in the big open-air cafeterias.

GO ON A STUDIO TOUR

See where they filmed *Casablanca* and hundreds of other films and TV shows like *Friends* on the **Warner Bros Studio Tour** (p129) in Burbank. It's the best of the offerings from the major studios.

SEE AFRICAN AMERICAN LA ART

See what's on at **CAAM** (California African American Museum; p102), which has ever-changing exhibits by top artists and photographers. Then get wowed at the nearby California Science Center.

Day 2

Morning

- Explore Downtown LA (DTLA), reserving tickets in advance to the spectacular modern art at **Broad** (p85) and discover the city's Spanish heritage at **El Pueblo de Los Ángeles** (p91).

Afternoon

- Following lunch at **Grand Central Market** (p91), wander **Little Tokyo** (p92) and walk the busy streets of **Chinatown** (p89). Browse the galleries and shops in the **Arts District** and **Row DTLA** (p93).

Evening

- Have cocktails at **Everson Royce Bar** (p91) and then a sublime, modern meal at **Bavel** (p88). Enjoy an evening of music in the great acoustics of **Walt Disney Concert Hall** (p88). Book your tickets in advance.

Day 3

Morning

- Spend the morning using your prebooked admission at the **Getty Center** (p118), a spectacular synergy of art, architecture, landscaping and panoramic views.

Afternoon

- Have lunch at the innovative, produce-driven **Gjusta** (p125) in ever-eclectic Venice. Satiated, hunt down unique fashion, accessories and art along **Abbot Kinney Boulevard** (p125), then stroll, pedal or skate along the **Venice Boardwalk** (p123), taking in its street art, goofball souvenirs and acres of powdery sand.

Evening

- Wrap up the day in neighboring Santa Monica, catching a perfect SoCal sunset from **Santa Monica Pier** (p119) before heading up the coast to dinner with a view at **Nobu Malibu** (p122).

OBSERVE THE SUNSET

Head up to the landmark **Griffith Observatory** (p94) to watch the sun sink over the city in sprawling Griffith Park. It's a famous LA architectural treasure – and a good place to see the cosmos too.

WALK EVER-CHANGING BOYLE HEIGHTS

Go for a walk near Downtown in **Boyle Heights** (p90), the neighborhood built by waves of immigrants over the decades. See how it evolved from Eastern European Jews 100 years ago to Mexican Americans today.

CATCH A DODGERS GAME

Play ball! Get your tickets well ahead, then go see LA's much-loved **Dodgers** (p99) play at Dodger Stadium near Echo Park. Have a Dodger Dog in the park.

TOUR LA ON FOOT OR BIKE

See LA on a bike or on a hike with a tour by **Bikes & Hikes LA** (p117). One of its most popular is a 32-mile cycling jaunt that shows you 'LA in a Day.'

Hollywood

THE DREAM, THE REALITY, THE FAME

TOP TIP
Come early to Hollywood Blvd for the strictly Hollywood sights (Walk of Fame, forecourt of the Chinese Theatre), then skedaddle before the crowds swell during the day, filling the many attractions that aren't unique to the area (wax museums and the like).

GETTING AROUND

Hollywood is well-served by the Metro Rail B Line with three stations along Hollywood Blvd, including iconic Hollywood/Vine.

Otherwise, Hollywood is easily walked. And you'll want to be on foot for spotting some of those 2800 names on the Walk of Fame. The only hills are the Hollywood Hills, where the stars live. Street parking is competitive and parking lots are expensive.

The Hollywood area might be past its heyday, but its history is rich in stories of Californian glamour. The neighborhood is filled with iconic monuments, including the Egyptian and TCL Chinese Theatres, that even the excessive souvenir shops and tour buses can't taint. The Walk of Fame is part of the bread and butter of Hollywood and millions of visitors come each year to stroll down the tawdry but bustling city blocks to see the terrazzo sidewalks with their celebrity stars.

Look beyond the tourist-magnet landmarks of Hollywood Blvd and you'll discover a nuanced, multifaceted neighborhood where sometimes gritty streets are punctuated by edgy galleries, swinging bistros and the homes of long-gone movie stars. There are good restaurants and bars to be found here. And, yes, you can see a great movie – new or classic – in a golden-age movie palace or join Angelinos at a beloved venue like the Hollywood Bowl.

Hollywood's Galaxy of Stars

Follow the Walk of Fame

Hollywood Blvd is just tawdry enough that having an excuse to stare at the ground can be a good thing. The **Hollywood Walk of Fame** *(walkoffame.com)* gives you over 2800 reasons to keep your eyes down.

Jennifer Lopez, Bob Hope, Marilyn Monroe and Aretha Franklin are among the luminaries being sought out, worshipped, photographed and stepped on. Or, in the case of many names, pondered over, since production staff and writers are also honored. They've been adding the brass and pink-terrazzo stars since 1960.

Follow the galaxy along Hollywood Blvd between La Brea Ave and Gower St and on Vine St between Yucca St and Sunset Blvd. At least 30 new stars are added each year and the ceremonies often draw famous faces. Check the website for the schedule.

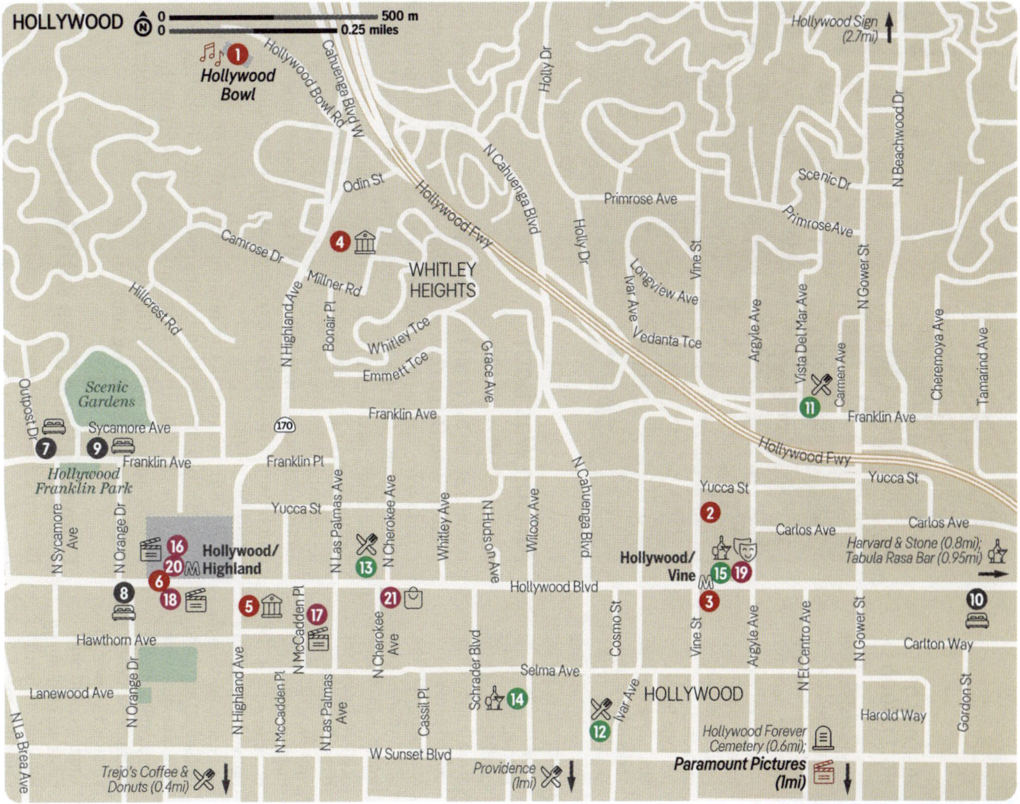

HOLLYWOOD
500 m
0.25 miles
Hollywood Bowl
Hollywood Sign (2.7mi)
WHITLEY HEIGHTS
HOLLYWOOD
Scenic Gardens
Hollywood Franklin Park
Hollywood/ Highland
Hollywood/ Vine
Harvard & Stone (0.8mi); Tabula Rasa Bar (0.95mi)
Hollywood Forever Cemetery (0.6mi);
Paramount Pictures (1mi)
Providence (1mi)
Trejo's Coffee & Donuts (0.4mi)
Hollywood Fwy
Hollywood Blvd
Franklin Ave
Yucca St
Selma Ave
W Sunset Blvd
N Cahuenga Blvd
N Highland Ave
Vine St
N La Brea Ave
Hollywood Bowl Rd
Cahuenga Blvd W
Outpost Dr
Hillcrest Rd
Camrose Dr
Odin St
Milner Rd
Bonair Pl
Whitley Tce
Emmett Tce
Grace Ave
Holly Dr
Primrose Ave
Longview Ave
Ivar Ave
Vedanta Tce
Argyle Ave
Vista Del Mar Ave
Carmen Ave
N Gower St
Scenic Dr
N Beachwood Dr
Cheremoya Ave
Tamarind Ave
Carlos Ave
Carlton Way
Harold Way
Gordon St
N El Centro Ave
Cosmo St
Wilcox Ave
N Hudson Ave
Whitley Ave
N Cherokee Ave
N Las Palmas Ave
N McCadden Pl
Franklin Pl
Sycamore Ave
N Sycamore Ave
N Orange Dr
Hawthorn Ave
Lanewood Ave
Schrader Blvd
Cassil Pl
170

HOLLYWOOD

HIGHLIGHTS
1 Hollywood Bowl

SIGHTS
2 Capitol Records
3 Hollywood & Vine
4 Hollywood Heritage Museum
5 Hollywood Museum
6 Hollywood Walk of Fame
see 3 Taft Building

SLEEPING
7 Highland Gardens Hotel
8 Hollywood Roosevelt
9 Magic Castle Hotel
10 Vibe Hotel Hollywood

EATING
11 Clark Street Diner
12 Grandmaster Recorders
13 Musso & Frank Grill

DRINKING & NIGHTLIFE
14 Bar Lis
15 Frolic Room

ENTERTAINMENT
16 Dolby Theatre
17 Egyptian Theatre
18 El Capitan Theatre
19 Pantages Theatre
20 TCL Chinese Theatre

SHOPPING
21 Larry Edmunds Bookshop

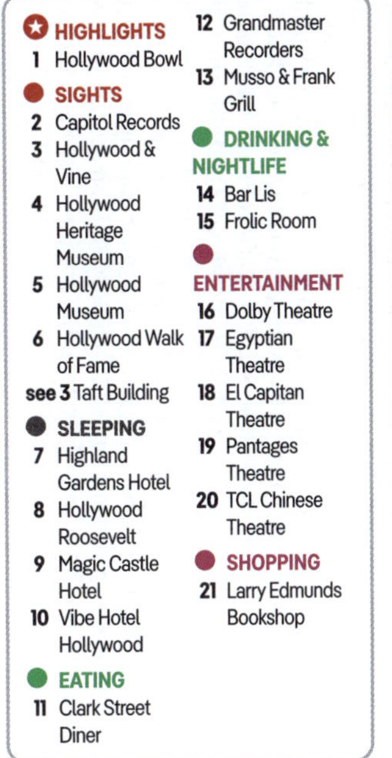

HISTORY OF HOLLYWOOD

Few industries have symbolized California, and especially Los Angeles, more than movie-making. Independent producers were attracted here from the former film centers of New York and Chicago beginning in 1908 for Southern California's sunny climate, which allowed indoor scenes to be shot outdoors – essential given the unsophisticated photo technology of the day. And any location, from ocean to desert to alpine forest, could be realized nearby.

By the 1920s, the major studios were established and Hollywood continued as a company town for decades. This lasted until recently and the area is still dotted with independent studios. However, AI, streaming and high costs are challenging Hollywood's hold like never before.

GABRIELE MALTINTI/SHUTTERSTOCK

TCL Chinese Theatre

An Icon Was Born

Spot the Hollywood Sign

Perched at the top of Mt Lee in the Hollywood Hills is the iconic **Hollywood Sign** *(hollywoodsign.org)*. The story goes that *Los Angeles Times* publisher and real estate developer Harry Chandler erected the sign in 1923 (back then it said 'Hollywoodland') as a way to advertise luxury homes in the hills.

What was only supposed to be there for 18 months became a permanent landmark that has come to symbolize a place, an industry and a mythology. The sign is now trademarked; don't even think of trying to use a similar typeface for your smoothie shop.

The 50ft-tall letters can be spotted easily from the Griffith Observatory and myriad other spots in LA – including possibly on your flight in. Three hiking trails lead to the sign: Brush Canyon Trail, Mt Hollywood Trail and Cahuenga Peak Trail. Or go on a **hiking tour** (p117).

Compare Shoe Sizes with George

Big and small impressions at the Chinese Theatre

Compare your shoe size to George Clooney's in the famous forecourt of **TCL Chinese Theatre** *(tclchinesetheatres.com; forecourt free)*. Or why not try standing in Tom Hanks' shoes? Just find his footprints among the many in front of this world-famous movie palace. The exotic pagoda theater once known as Grauman's (first name Sid, who you'll see mentioned in the older imprints) – complete with temple bells and stone heaven dogs from China – has shown movies since 1927, when Cecil B DeMille's *The King of Kings* first flickered across the screen.

And it's not all feet. There's Betty Grable's legs, Whoopi Goldberg's braids, Daniel Radcliffe's wand and R2-D2's wheels. Inside, the cinema lives up to the promise. The main theater is one of the world's few that can show 70mm film prints on an Imax screen.

Dine Like a Star

Famous Musso & Frank

Hollywood history hangs in the thick air at **Musso & Frank Grill** *(mussoandfrank.com)*, Tinseltown's oldest eatery (since 1919). Charlie Chaplin came here to knock back vodka gimlets, Raymond Chandler penned scripts in the high-backed booths and movie deals were made on the old phone at the back. The menu favors old American classics like steaks, lobster thermidor and huge salads. It's in constant use as a shooting location; recent appearances include *Once Upon a Time in Hollywood* and anything associated with writer Michael Connelly and his detective Harry Bosch.

Mixed drinks like the famous martinis come with sidecars on ice so your chaser is right at hand. Note that Musso's has never been more popular, so be sure to book ahead. It's open from 5pm to 10pm Tuesdays through Sundays.

Hear Stars under the Stars

The magical Hollywood Bowl

The Hollywood Hills stalwart **Hollywood Bowl** *(hollywood bowl.com)* hosted its first concert in 1922. Top headliners have ranged from Billie Holiday to the Beatles and it's still the summer home of the LA Philharmonic. The amphitheater stands out for its silhouette, which is reminiscent of – you guessed it – a bowl, with concentric shell-like arches. This is a live-show summer haven for Angelenos and although food and beverage prices can hit a high note (you can bring your own), the Hollywood Hills backdrop, the acoustics and the views make up for it all.

Tinseltown's Unmissable Attic

Star at the Hollywood Museum

Something of Hollywood's attic, the musty **Hollywood Museum** *(thehollywoodmuseum.com; adult/child $15/5)* is a temple to the stars and a mishmash of props, memorabilia and movie and TV costumes chaotically spread across four floors. The museum is housed inside the Max Factor Building, which launched in 1935 as a glamorous beauty salon for Hollywood's leading ladies. Track down the toupees worn by Frank Sinatra and John Wayne. A must-see is the 'Real to Reel' exhibit on LGBTQ+ issues in the industry. You'll also encounter various props, scripts, movie posters and even Marilyn Monroe's million-dollar dress, in addition to changing exhibits.

HOLLYWOOD'S BEST THEATERS

TCL Chinese Theatre: This legendary 1927 cinema is one of the world's few that can show 70mm film prints on an IMAX screen. *tclchinesetheatres.com*

El Capitan Theatre: Disney premieres blockbusters at this 1926 movie palace and the *Jimmy Kimmel Show* is produced here – book tickets at *liota.com.*

Pantages Theatre: A 1930 art deco showplace and home of the Oscars through the 1950s. *broadwayinhollywood.com*

Egyptian Theatre: The first of Hollywood's opulent movie palaces. Lavishly restored, with hieroglyphs and sphinx heads. Netflix uses it for premieres and classic films. *egyptiantheatre.com*

Dolby Theatre: State-of-the-art theater in a shopping mall. The Oscars have been held here since 2001. *dolbytheatre.com*

DRINKING IN HOLLYWOOD: OUR PICKS

Frolic Room: This Hollywood dive has served everyone from Judy Garland to Charles Bukowski. Toast the fabulous cartoon mural. *11am-2am*

Harvard & Stone: Lures partiers with bands, DJs and burlesque troops working their saucy magic. It's ski lodge meets steampunk factory, with a rockabilly soul. *9pm-2am*

Bar Lis: Hollywood's all around the rooftop lounge of the hip Thompson Hollywood. There's a bit of a posh Med vibe (Cannes, anyone?). *6pm-midnight*

Tabula Rasa Bar: Away from the glitz, this unpretentious wine bar gets everything right with well-picked tunes and regular live gigs. Rear terrace. *2pm-midnight*

THE 'FIRST' BEVERLY HILLS

For a taste of Old Hollywood, walk north up Ivar Ave from Hollywood Blvd to the narrow streets of **Whitley Heights**, an area peppered with beautiful Moorish, Renaissance and Italianate-style villas. This was the city's first 'Beverly Hills' and it was close to the silent-era movie studios. Developed in the early 1900s, the neighborhood was home to all the A-listers of silent-era Hollywood. Stories abound of famous names racing horses on the hilly streets and tying them up in front of Hollywood Blvd watering holes. By the 1930s, Beverly Hills was luring everyone west. Innumerable films were shot here. The Alto Nido Apartments (1851 N Ivar Ave) were used for the initial home of the ill-fated Joe Gillis in *Sunset Boulevard*.

Hollywood's Last Great Studio

Tour Paramount Studios

Indiana Jones, The Godfather and *Ironman* are among the blockbuster series that originated at **Paramount Pictures**, the country's second-oldest movie studio (1914) and the only major one still in Hollywood proper.

Two-hour golf-cart **tours** *(paramountstudiotour.com; from $69)* of the studio complex are offered year-round, taking in the back lots and sound stages. Passionate, knowledgeable guides offer fascinating insights into the studio's history and the movie-making process in general. VIP tours include a meal, but are not worth the much higher fee. Fans of *Star Trek* will want to follow Leonard Nimoy Way to the sound stages where the original TV show was shot.

Resting Place for the Stars

Stroll Hollywood Forever Cemetery

Paradisiacal landscaping, vainglorious tombstones and epic mausoleums (plus a view of Paramount Studios over the wall) at **Hollywood Forever Cemetery** *(hollywoodforever.com; free)* make for an appropriate resting place for some of Hollywood's most iconic dearly departed. Residents include Rudolph Valentino, Cecil B DeMille, Mel Blanc (his tombstone reads, 'That's all folks'), Jayne Mansfield, Judy Garland, punk rockers Johnny and Dee Dee Ramone, *Golden Girls* star Estelle Getty, Burt Reynolds and David Lynch.

Recalling Hollywood's Early Days

When movies were silent

Hollywood's first feature-length film, Cecil B DeMille's *The Squaw Man* (1914), was shot in this building, which was originally set at the corner of Selma and Vine Sts. DeMille went on to co-found Paramount and had the barn moved to the lot in the '20s. The building is now the fascinating **Hollywood Heritage Museum** *(hollywoodheritage.org; adult/child $14/free)*, which does a deep dive into pre-talkie history.

Mid-Century Landmark

Spot the Capitol Records building

You'll have no trouble recognizing the iconic 1956 **Capitol Records** tower, one of LA's great mid-century buildings. Designed by Welton Becket, it resembles a stack of records

EATING IN HOLLYWOOD: OUR PICKS

Providence: Michael Cimarusti's fine dining is the ultimate LA experience, offering the finest seafood, service and stunt-free cuisine. *6-9pm Tue-Sat* $$$

Grandmaster Recorders: Buzzing bistro with Italian flavors; the airy dining room was once home to the namesake recording studio. Rooftop bar. *5-10pm Tue-Sat* $$$

Clark Street Diner: Legendary coffee shop has been in movies *(Swingers)* and served actors and writers nursing bottomless cups of java. *7am-9pm* $$

Trejo's Coffee & Donuts: Standout in a town known for doughnuts. Owned by Danny Trejo *(Heat)*, the goods reflect his Mexican heritage. *7am-4pm* $

ALEX MILLAUER/SHUTTERSTOCK

Paramount Pictures

topped by a stylus blinking out 'Hollywood' in Morse code. Some of music's biggest stars have recorded hits in the building's basement studios, including Nat King Cole, Frank Sinatra, the Beatles, Katy Perry and Sam Smith. Outside on the sidewalk, Garth Brooks and John Lennon have their stars.

Hollywood's Literary Hub

Find it at Larry Edmunds Bookshop

For decades, the **Larry Edmunds Bookshop** *(larryedmunds.com)*, a cluttered old-school shop, has been the place to go for all types of entertainment industry books, new and used. You can find out-of-print bios of long-dead celebs mixed with classic tomes on acting and scriptwriting techniques. Browse the bins of lobby cards for classic films and studio stills. They have a huge range of TV and movie scripts.

It hosts events with industry luminaries who have books to sign. Look on the walls for notable mementos, such as a check for a book purchase from Lucille Ball.

Find a Famous Corner

Hollywood and Vine

If you'd turned on the radio in the 1920s and '30s, chances were you'd hear a broadcast 'brought to you from **Hollywood and Vine**.' The corner still has some cachet even if the reality pales. However, take a moment at the southeast corner of the intersection for Hollywood's first high-rise office tower, the 12-story **Taft Building**. Dating back to 1923, its former tenants include Charlie Chaplin and the Academy of Motion Picture Arts and Sciences.

BEST FILMS ABOUT HOLLYWOOD

Sunset Boulevard (1950): Director and screenwriter Billy Wilder at his best, plumbing the dark side of fame and Hollywood's delusions.

The Player (1992): Robert Altman brings decades of experience on the front lines to this biting satire about the moral rot at the heart of studio execs.

La La Land (2016): Timeless musical of plucky kids hoping to make it big in Hollywood.

The Artist (2011): Won the Oscar for best picture for its story of the often-brutal late-1920s transition from silent pictures to talkies.

A Star Is Born: Pick your version (1937, 1954, 1976, 2018) of the classic drama about fame and tragedy.

Downtown

HISTORY, CULTURE, STROLLING AND FOOD

TOP TIP

LA's intractable housing issues manifest fully here. There are many people living on the streets. This is also the original home of Skid Row (it's the neighborhood between 4th and 7th Sts east of Los Angeles St). The usual cautions about personal safety apply across Downtown.

Downtown Los Angeles is not your typical downtown area: it's relatively small compared to others in the US and is made up of smaller, diverse neighborhoods that all converge together.

Take Manhattan, add a splash of Mexico City, a dash of Tokyo, shake and pour. Your drink: Downtown LA. Rapidly evolving, DTLA (the preferred moniker) is the city's most intriguing patch, where cutting-edge architecture and killer modern-art museums contrast sharply with blaring mariachi tunes, Chinese grocers, abject poverty, old architectural gems and intriguing restaurants, bars, galleries and boutiques, especially in the Arts District.

It's a place of surprises: one corner can be full of life, the next could be struggling; another turn could lead you to spectacular museums and art exhibits and still another could take you to what feels like a different country and time. It's a place where shops hawking $99 suits mix with an artist's personal vision for the future.

GETTING AROUND

Downtown is the hub of LA's transit. All the Metro Rail Lines come together here, from the subways to the light rail. At beautiful Union Station, there are regional Metrolink commuter trains and local Amtrak trains north to Santa Barbara and south to San Diego, plus various long-distance trains.

Pricey parking is easily found, although the surrounding freeways are often traffic-clogged – try to take Metro Rail. LA's center is flat and walkable, although distances can add up, like from the Arts District to Chinatown (2½ miles). DASH buses provide local service around Downtown (50¢).

Walt Disney Concert Hall (p88) and the Broad

DTLA's Striking Museum

Be dazzled at the Broad

The **Broad** (rhymes with 'road'; *thebroad.org; free*) is a must-visit for anyone with the slightest interest in postwar and contemporary artworks. It houses the world-class collection of the Broads, local philanthropists and billionaire real-estate developers. They amassed more than 2000 postwar pieces by dozens of heavy hitters, including Cindy Sherman, Jeff Koons, Andy Warhol, Roy Lichtenstein, Robert Rauschenberg, Keith Haring and Kara Walker.

Among the many blockbuster exhibits here is Yayoi Kusama's immersive **Infinity Mirrored Room**. When it's your turn to view the installation, you'll enter a room that's both an artwork and an entire world of light and color. With your reservation to see the work, you can tour the museum and you'll receive a text message when there's an opening for you to go in. Wait times are dynamic, as some people spend less time inside than you'd think.

Once you've eyed up the temporary exhibitions on the lobby floor, an escalator whisks you up through a narrow tunnel to the 35,000-sq-ft 3rd-floor gallery, where Jeff Koons charms visitors with his giant bunch of stainless-steel tulips. The surrounding galleries rotate works from the Broad's permanent collection, considered one of the world's most prominent holdings of postwar and contemporary artworks. These include a second interactive installation by Yayoi Kusama.

Longing for Eternity.
The museum docents are knowledgeable. The Broad has an excellent website geared toward the browsers on phones that

(continued on p88)

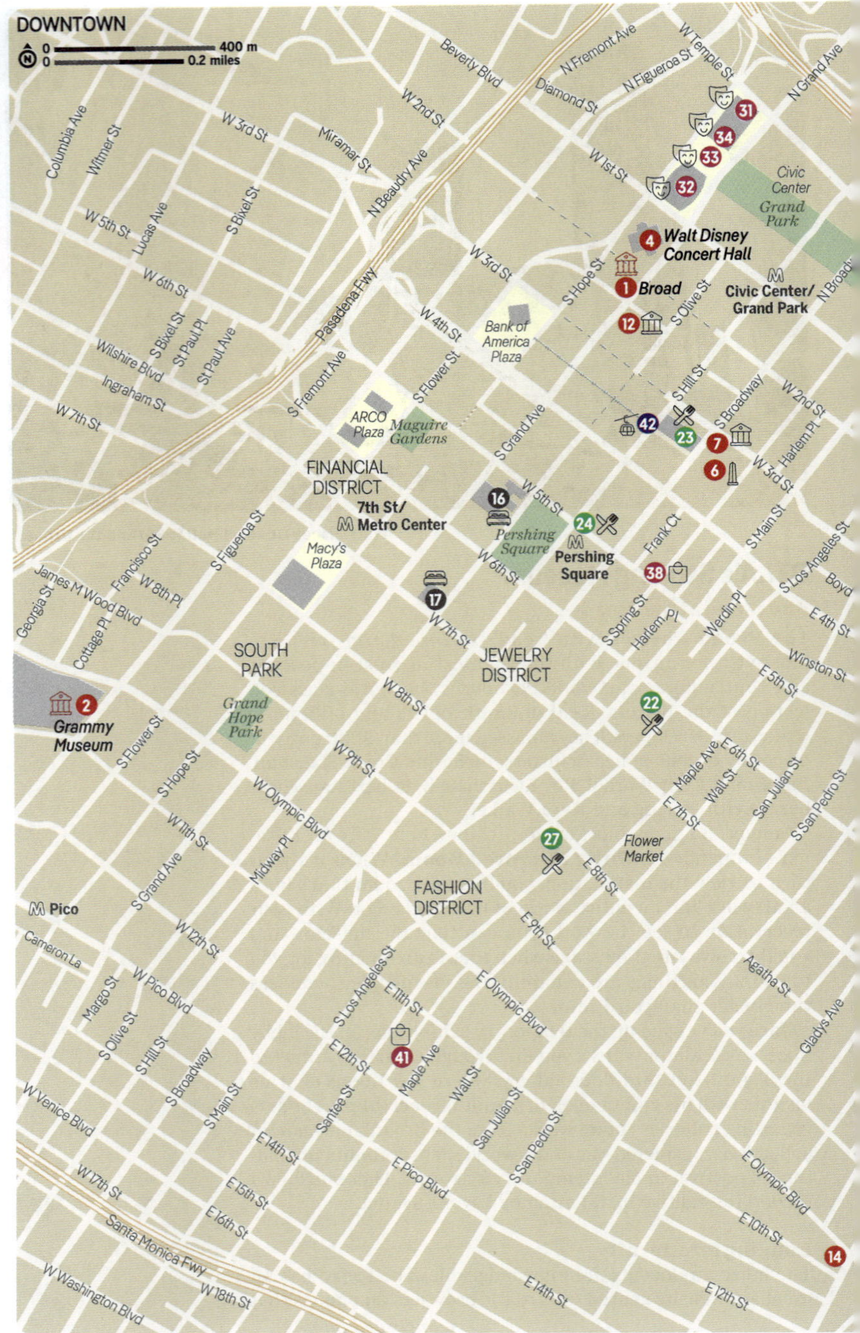
DOWNTOWN
0 400 m
0 0.2 miles
Walt Disney Concert Hall
Broad
Civic Center/ Grand Park
Civic Center
Grand Park
Bank of America Plaza
ARCO Plaza
Maguire Gardens
FINANCIAL DISTRICT
7th St/ Metro Center
Macy's Plaza
Pershing Square
Pershing Square
SOUTH PARK
Grand Hope Park
Grammy Museum
JEWELRY DISTRICT
FASHION DISTRICT
Flower Market
Pico

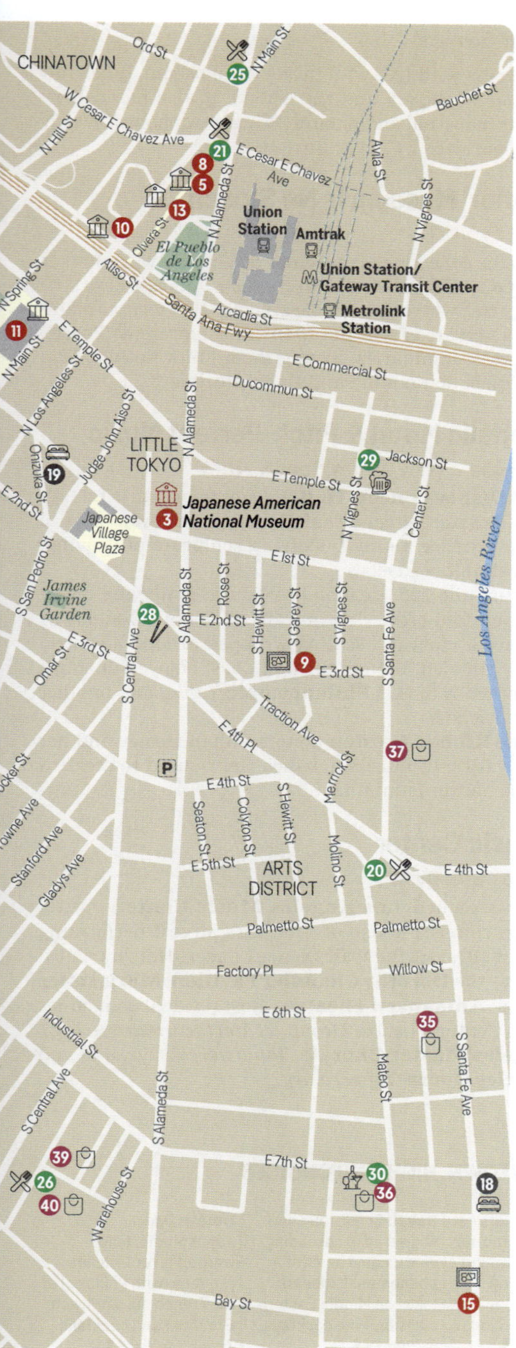

HIGHLIGHTS
1 Broad
2 Grammy Museum
3 Japanese American National Museum
4 Walt Disney Concert Hall

SIGHTS
5 Avila Adobe
6 Biddy Mason Memorial Park
7 Bradbury Building
8 El Pueblo de Los Ángeles
9 Hauser & Wirth
10 LA Plaza
11 Los Angeles City Hall
12 MOCA Grand Ave
13 Museum of Social Justice
14 Piñata District
15 Webber 939

SLEEPING
16 Biltmore Los Angeles
17 Hotel Per La
18 Kodō Hotel
19 Miyako Hotel Los Angeles

EATING
20 Bavel
21 Cielito Lindo
22 Cole's
see 23 Eggslut
23 Grand Central Market
24 Perch
25 Philippe the Original
26 Pizzeria Bianco
27 Sonoratown
see 23 Sticky Rice
28 Sushi Gen

DRINKING & NIGHTLIFE
29 Boomtown Brewery
30 Everson Royce Bar

ENTERTAINMENT
31 Ahmanson Theatre
32 Dorothy Chandler Pavilion
33 Los Angeles Music Center
34 Mark Taper Forum

SHOPPING
35 Dover Street Market
36 Good Liver
37 Hennessey + Ingalls
38 Last Bookstore
39 Omami Mini
40 Row DTLA
41 Santee Alley

TRANSPORTATION
42 Angels Flight

THE BROAD'S ARTFUL ARCHITECTURE

The **Broad's building** (p85) is as much a talking piece as the collection within. Costing $140 million, the 120,000-sq-ft showpiece was completed in 2015. It's 'shrouded' in a white lattice-like shell, complete with a dimple (an oculus looking out onto Grand Ave) and corners that lift sharply at street level to let art lovers and the curious in and out. Inside, the building bucks the museum tradition of hiding away its storage facilities. Here, the Vault becomes an integral part of the visit. Hovering between the 1st- and 3rd-floor galleries, it's pierced by the 105ft escalator connecting the gallery floors and visible through glass panels, offering visitors a voyeuristic peek at hibernating artworks.

(continued from p85)

you can access with free wi-fi inside the museum. It has full descriptions of the art and the artists. It also has gallery guides plus maps and audio tours (bring headphones). A tour for kids is narrated by LaVar Burton.

The 'Other' Museum Is No Slouch

Be moved by MOCA

Adding to the collection of museums on Grand Ave in Bunker Hill is **MOCA Grand Ave** *(Museum of Contemporary Art; moca.org; free)*, where the notable art collection focuses mainly on works created from the 1940s to the present. There's no shortage of luminaries, among them Mark Rothko, Dan Flavin, Willem de Kooning and David Hockney.

Psychedelic Metal & Pitch-Perfect Music

The unmissable Walt Disney Concert Hall

The **Walt Disney Concert Hall** *(musiccenter.org)* is DTLA's eye candy. It's starchitect, Frank Gehry, played every note to the hilt to produce a gravity-defying sculpture of heaving, billowing stainless steel.

In contrast, the 2265-seat auditorium feels like the inside of a finely crafted cello, clad in walls of smooth Douglas fir with terraced 'vineyard' seating wrapped around a central stage. You can visit, though the hall's best enjoyed during a concert, either by the **LA Philharmonic** *(laphil.org)* or other visiting musicians.

The **Blue Ribbon Garden** honors Lillian Disney and her love of Royal Delft porcelain, which Gehry used to create a mosaic-like flower fountain.

LA's Music Center

The venues with Disney

The county-owned **Los Angeles Music Center** *(music center.org)* complex is one of America's largest performing arts centers. Besides the Walt Disney Concert Hall, its multiple venues – the **Dorothy Chandler Pavilion**, **Mark Taper Forum** and **Ahmanson Theatre** – host resident companies including Center Theatre Group *(centertheatregroup.org)*, **Los Angeles Master Chorale** *(lamasterchorale.org)* and **Los Angeles Opera** *(laopera.org)*.

EATING & DRINKING DOWNTOWN: HIGH-END CHOICES

Sushi Gen: Grab a lunch seat in Little Tokyo; chefs carve slabs of the freshest fish. Dinner is less frenetic. *11am-2pm & 5-8.30pm Tue-Sat* $$

Perch: Two-elevators get you to this French rooftop bar-restaurant crowning the vintage Pershing Square Building. Gatsby-esque vibe; bewitching views. *4pm-1am* $$

Bavel: Sleek, loud and showered in cascading vines, come here for phenomenal, modern takes on Middle Eastern classics. Fine cocktails. *5-11pm* $$$

Cole's: Dark, atmospheric, time-warped tavern, claims progeny (with Philippe) of the French dip sandwich. Great bar and cocktails. *3pm-midnight* $$

STROLLING DOWNTOWN'S CHINATOWN

Discover today's Chinatown and its vibrant mix of shops, restaurants and galleries on this walking tour, which stops for treats.

START	END	LENGTH
Union Station	Chinatown Metro Rail stop	1.85 miles; 2hr

In the 1920s, LA's white leaders maneuvered to replace the city's Chinatown, which was deemed too close to the center of power, with a new **1 Union Station**. The Chinese population was moved several blocks north to today's Chinatown. From the station, cross through **El Pueblo de Los Ángeles** (p91) to N Broadway, where there's the dragon-topped **2 Gateway Monument** (2001). Cut around to N Spring St and **3 Long's Family Pastry**, where people line up for the $1.50 leek cakes.

Return to Broadway and walk north. Note the vendors, some with little more on offer than oranges they may have found on a tree. **4 Far East Plaza** is worth a pause for the Now Serving cookbook store, the vintage muumuu of your dreams at the East/West Shop, the fanatical coffee preparation at Endorffeine and the exciting Filipino fare at Lasita Rotisserie & Natural Wine.

Continue on Broadway until you see the **5 East Gate**. Enter **6 Central Plaza** (1938). Note the Bruce Lee Statue (his martial arts studio was at 628 W College St). Cross Hill St to **7 West Plaza**, an appealing collection of small galleries. Back on Broadway, stop at **8 Phoenix Bakery** for a slice of its famous strawberry cake. Across the street, **9 Steep LA** holds regular tea ceremonies and classes. Finish at the **10 Chinatown Metro Rail stop**.

You might see baseball fans walking to nearby **Dodgers Stadium**. It also was used as a form of urban renewal.

The final shot in *Chinatown* – 'Forget it, Jake, it's Chinatown' – was filmed looking south in front of **Long's Family Pastry**.

The **Chinese American Museum** *(camla.org; adult/child $3/2)* near Union Station has full details on LA's Chinatown. It's in the 1890 Garnier Building.

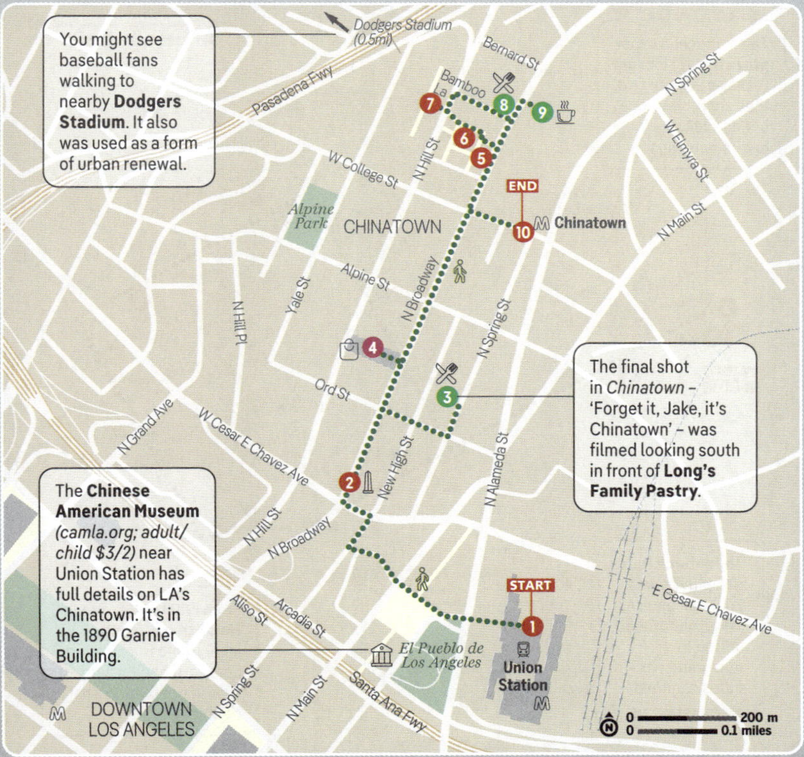

GETTING TO KNOW BOYLE HEIGHTS

See where LA's mariachi bands wait for gigs, then wander a neighborhood built on immigration, filled with unique businesses run with heart.

START	END	LENGTH
Mariachi Plaza Metro Rail stop	Mariachi Plaza Metro Rail stop	1.6 miles; 2hr

Begin at ❶ **Mariachi Plaza Metro Rail stop**, where mariachi bands often wait in the shade of the gazebo for work. Hungry? ❷ **Un Solo Sol** serves vegan Latin American dishes. The banana date shakes are a rich treat. Nearly next door, the glittery House of Trophies and Awards produces mantelpieces for amateur leagues. Another couple of doors down, you can see where the mariachis get their embroidered suits at La Casa del Mariachi. Across 1st St, ❸ **Espacio 1839** is a community arts space.

Back across the street, the ❹ **Women's March Store** supports the group's political activities with merch, including ever-popular tote bags. Cross under I-5 and walk up the 1920s residential Cummings St to Cesar Chavez Ave and turn east. ❺ **Other Books** is packed with comics and zines. A series of blocks follow packed with mom-and-pop retail. ❻ **Las Fotos Project** *(lasfotosproject.org)* teaches teenage women of color about the power of photography.

Turn south on N Breed St to step back to a previous era at the ❼ **Breed Street Shul Project**, which is restoring the 1922 Byzantine synagogue. Back at 1st St, turn west and go two blocks. Tiny ❽ **Al & Bea's Mexican Food** is so old (1966) it was a burrito pioneer in LA. Close by, Botanica Olokun stocks spiritual candles. Return to Mariachi Plaza Metro Rail stop.

The mariachis at the **plaza** are not looking to play a song or two, they are professional bands available for last-minute gigs.

Hollenbeck Park in the 1890s was a palatial gem. As the neighborhood shifted to immigrants, its status changed.

From 1910 to 1950, **Boyle Heights** was mostly immigrants from Eastern Europe; it had the largest Jewish population west of Chicago.

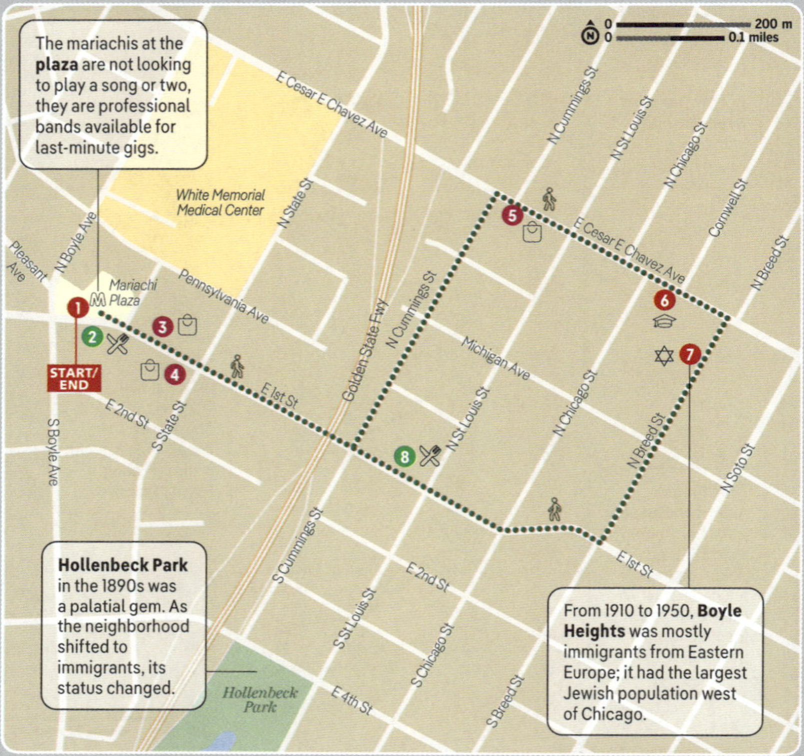

Taste Grand Central Market

A global culinary feast

Designed by prolific architect John Parkinson and once home to an office occupied by Frank Lloyd Wright, LA's beaux arts **Grand Central Market** *(grandcentralmarket.com; hours vary)* has been satisfying appetites since 1917 and today is DTLA's always-busy hub of food culture. Lose yourself in its bustle of neon signs, stalls and counters, which peddle everything from fresh produce to sizzling Thai street food at **Sticky Rice**, hipster breakfasts at **Eggslut**, modern deli classics, artisanal pasta and specialty coffee.

For a digestive interlude, exit and cross S Hill St for a quick ride on **Angels Flight** *(angelsflight.org; $1)*, the famous short funicular up to Bunker Hill. It's another local star in many TV and film productions.

Two Iconic Stars

Gaze at the Bradbury and City Hall

The **Bradbury Building** (1893) is one of LA's heritage jewels. Behind its Romanesque-lite facade lies a whimsical galleried atrium that wouldn't look out of place in New Orleans. Inky filigree grillwork, rickety birdcage elevators and yellow-brick walls glisten golden in the afternoon light, which filters through the peaked glass roof. Such striking beauty hasn't been lost on Hollywood; it's been used in hundreds of productions, including *Blade Runner.*

Two blocks north is another instantly recognizable icon, **Los Angeles City Hall** (1928), the phallic-shaped star of *Dragnet*, *LA Confidential* and countless other films and TV shows. It hides a surprise on its 27th floor: a free **observation deck** with incredible views of the city – when the smog allows. The observation deck is open from 9am to 5pm, Monday through Friday.

Where Modern LA Was Born

Dig down in El Pueblo

Compact and popular, **El Pueblo de Los Ángeles** *(elpueblo.lacity.org)* is the historic district where LA's first colonists settled in 1781. Wander through narrow **Olvera St**'s vibrant and family-owned Mexican-themed stalls and check out the district's museums, the best of which is **LA Plaza** *(lapca.org; free)*, offering snapshots of the local Mexican American

DTLA'S BEST SHOPPING

Last Bookstore: LA's largest new-and-used bookstore. Rare tomes, terrific vinyl, good prices and staff recs. Display of books banned in parts of the US.

Omami Mini: In Row DTLA, fashion-forward clothing for the under-12 set (though it's really aimed at parents).

Hennessey + Ingalls: Light-filled new-and-used bookstore focuses on design, from architecture to graphics and photography.

Good Liver: Carefully curated, museum-like space sells beautiful artisan objects you're unlikely to find elsewhere; each displayed with its story and craftsmanship.

Santee Alley: Scores of alley vendors with bargains in clothing, bling and eyewear between Santee St and Maple Ave, from Olympic Blvd to 12th St.

TOP CHOICES FOR AFFORDABLE EATING & DRINKING DOWNTOWN

Boomtown Brewery: Great brews served inside and out downtown, with a parade of food trucks turning up. Pool tables, party atmosphere and local art. *4-10pm* $

Philippe the Original: Famous old-fashioned joint renowned for French dip sandwich (try the pastrami instead). Always busy; don't miss beets on the side. *6am-10pm* $

Sonoratown: Straddles the Fashion District and DTLA. Superb northern Mexican street food, like buttery tortillas with succulent, mesquite-grilled meats. *11am-10pm* $

Everson Royce Bar: Arts District bar that puts the happy in happy hour. Suitably artful cocktails, best enjoyed in the shady backyard. *4-10pm* $$

AN INCREDIBLE LIFE

Stretching along a green, inviting alley behind the Bradbury Building and across from Grand Central Market, the easily overlooked **Biddy Mason Memorial Park** tells the remarkable story of an early LA resident. Historical displays detail the incredible life of Bridget 'Biddy' Mason, who was born an enslaved person in Mississippi in 1818. She eventually moved to California, walking much of the way, where she won a landmark court case in 1856 confirming her freedom. Working as a midwife and nurse, she saved her money and began buying land – including this part of DTLA. As her wealth grew, she became a philanthropist to African Americans, the poor and the sick and founded an elementary school. Before she died in 1891, she was worth $3 million.

experience. The **Avila Adobe**, built in 1818, is one of the region's oldest buildings. The heartfelt **Museum of Social Justice** *(museumofsocialjustice.org; free)* examines LA's history through the filters of poverty, women's suffrage and civil rights. Have a *taquito* (rolled taco, fried crispy) at the **Cielito Lindo** *(9am-8pm)*, the stand that claims their invention in 1923.

One of LA's First Communities

Deeply enriching Little Tokyo

To the north of Downtown lies Little Tokyo, a robust Japanese community that's been around since the early 1900s. Scores of shops and restaurants thrive across several blocks and there is a traditional Buddhist temple. It's a rewarding cultural immersion to stroll, browse and dine.

At the center is the impressive **Japanese American National Museum** *(janm.org)*, which focuses on the evolution of Japanese American culture and gives moving insight into the mass incarceration of over 125,000 American citizens of Japanese descent in remote internment camps during WWII. Watch for temporary exhibitions; it's undergoing renovations through late 2026.

LA's Sound of Music

Listen in at the Grammy Museum

The highlight of the LA Live entertainment complex, the **Grammy Museum**'s *(grammymuseum.org; adult/child $23/free)* features interactive exhibits that explore the evolution of popular music and the famous awards. Rotating exhibits might include iconic threads worn by Whitney Houston,

RUBEN A MARTINEZ/SHUTTERSTOCK

Arts District

Peggy Lee and Beyoncé; scribbled words from the hands of Count Basie and Taylor Swift; and instruments once played by music legends. Top names often perform.

Where the Surprises Never Stop

Explore the Arts District

The **Arts District** is one of DTLA's most intriguing places. Blocks of old warehouses and gritty industrial areas have been cleaned up and you never know what you'll find behind those big metal roller doors: a gallery? A designer shop? Or perhaps something more esoteric?

Start at the vast **Row DTLA** *(rowdtla.com)*, a curated garden of specialty retail and dining delights across several big warehouses next to a produce market. Among the chic boutiques is beloved **Pizzeria Bianco** *(11am-9pm)*. Less elevated is **Dover Street Market** *(doverstreetmarket.com)*, a sprawling, off-the-radar warehouse in which bleeding-edge fashion and art collide to spectacular effect and TikTok kids shoot videos out front.

Among the swanky galleries, **Hauser & Wirth** *(hauserwirth.com)* displays contemporary art; **Webber 939** *(webberrepresents.com)* has exhibits by famous names like Yorgos Lanthimos.

For the ultimate in single-use colorful art, head to the busy **Piñata District**, where high-ceiling emporiums display legions of aliens, animals and other characters waiting for the big moment to spew forth candy when burst with a stick. It's a carnival for the eyes; the other senses also get in on the action as stores sell treats and there are several delicious open-air Mexican cafeterias with full bars.

HISTORY OF LA: PART 1

LA's human history begins with the Gabrielino and Chumash, who roamed the area as early as 6000 BCE. Their hunter-gatherer existence ended in the late 18th century with the arrival of Spanish missionaries and Mexican settlers who founded **El Pueblo de Los Ángeles** (p91). The Gold Rush in Northern California also opened up LA to US influence, which soon forcibly pushed aside the Mexicans. The city was incorporated on April 4, 1850. A series of seminal events caused LA's population to grow exponentially: the railroad's arrival in the 1870s, the birth of the citrus industry in the late 1800s and the discovery of oil in 1892. But that was nothing compared to the 20th century (p135).

Griffith Park, Los Feliz & Echo Park

FAMILY FUN, NATURE, HIPSTER FUN AND NIGHTLIFE

TOP TIP

Enjoy touring Griffith Park by bike, from the flat trails near the river to the hillsides. Rent all types of bikes at **Spokes 'N Stuff**, located just southwest of the LA Zoo. The bike paths are geared to all levels and are family-friendly.

GETTING AROUND

Individual portions of this large area are walkable. Overall, it is hilly, especially in Griffith Park. Each of the neighborhoods is good for strolling.

Transit access is mostly by bus with the exception of Los Feliz, which is near the Metro Rail B station Vermont/Sunset. Outside of the parks, parking is mostly on streets and is always at a premium.

From the natural heights and artificial diversions of Griffith Park, the trendy neighborhoods of Los Feliz, Silver Lake and Echo Park offer hipsterism, laid-back vibes and urban charms unlike anywhere else in the sprawling city.

Griffith Park, one of the US largest municipal parks, is a refreshing escape from the hustle and bustle, with its rugged, trail-laced hills and iconic Griffith Observatory offering some of the best views of the Hollywood sign and the LA Basin.

South is walkable Los Feliz with its shops and nightlife along Vermont Ave and Sunset Blvd. The latter flows right into ever-trendy Silver Lake. Its diversity of food, people, LGBTQ+ history and constant reinvigoration keep residents staying put.

Echo Park nears Downtown and mixes heritage with natural beauty and funky urban charms. Its many independent shops, beautiful architectural monuments and namesake lake offer a great excuse to plunge deep – even if you don't get wet.

Observe LA!

And the universe from the Griffith Observatory

The universe aside, the rooftop viewing platform of the **Griffith Observatory** *(griffithobservatory.org; free)* offers boffo – and free – views of LA and the Hollywood Hills. The uber-popular art deco observatory is no stranger to the spotlight itself, having made cameos in numerous movies and TV shows, among them *La La Land, Terminator, 24* and *Alias*. The film it's most associated with, however, remains *Rebel Without a Cause,* commemorated with a bust of James Dean on the west side of the observatory lawn.

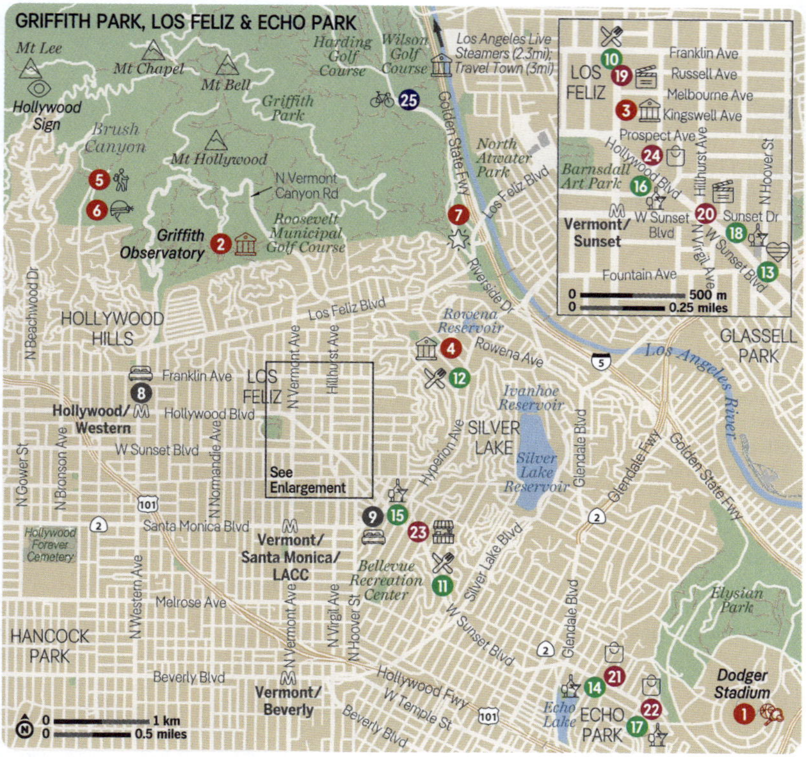

GRIFFITH PARK, LOS FELIZ & ECHO PARK

HIGHLIGHTS
1 Dodger Stadium
2 Griffith Observatory

SIGHTS
3 Disney's First Studio
4 Snow White Cottages

ACTIVITIES
5 Bronson Canyon
6 Bronson Caves
7 Griffith Park & Southern Railroad

SLEEPING
8 Cara Hotel
9 Silver Lake Pool & Inn

EATING
see 19 Figaro Bistrot
10 House of Pies
see 20 Pam's Coffy
11 Playita Mariscos
12 Speranza

DRINKING & NIGHTLIFE
13 Akbar
14 Bar Flores
15 Black Cat
16 Covell
see 3 Dresden Lounge
17 Ototo
18 Tiki-Ti

ENTERTAINMENT
19 Los Feliz Theatre
20 Vista Theater

SHOPPING
see 3 Kingswell
21 Reverie Bookstand
22 Sick City Records
23 Silver Lake Farmers Market
see 19 Skylight Books
24 Wacko

TRANSPORTATION
25 Spokes 'N Stuff

WHERE TO EAT & DRINK IN LOS FELIZ: OUR PICKS

Figaro Bistrot: A culinary trio includes a boulangerie, bistro and lounge. Figaro channels Paris with sidewalk tables and Gallic-inspired fare. *8am-midnight* $$

House of Pies: Indomitable survivor of a chain that once swept California, the House serves top diner fare plus its namesake desserts. *7am-1am* $$

Covell: Over 150 wines by the glass, showcasing interesting producers, unusual grapes and lesser-known regions. *4pm-midnight* $$

Tiki-Ti: Channeling Waikiki since 1961, this tiny tropical tavern packs in everyone from stylish slummers to 'non-ironic' partiers in Hawaiian shirts. *6pm-midnight Wed-Sat* $$

BEST LOCAL SHOPS

Skylight Books: Los Feliz institution with an incredible selection. Frequent top author appearances. *skylightbooks.com*

Kingswell: Los Feliz skate shop is one of SoCal's best. Custom boards, gear and art exhibits. *kingswell.tv*

Silver Lake Farmers Market: The best locally sourced produce, plus artisan coffee, vintage clothing and more. *1.30-7pm Tue, 6am-1.30pm Sat*

Reverie Bookstand: Find treasures, from used Joyce to Chekov's *Guide to Acting,* at this Echo Park gem. *reverie bookstand.com*

Sick City Records: Get your punk groove on at this used album shop in Echo Park.

Wacko: Sprawling Los Feliz carnival of pop, kitsch and camp is always a fun browse. *wackola.com*

ENGEL CHING/SHUTTERSTOCK

Griffith Observatory (p94)

Inside, there's a **planetarium** and all sorts of unmissable exhibits on the cosmos.

Owing to its popularity, finding parking here can be akin to finding life on another planet. It's best to arrive on a weekday before noon. Otherwise, especially on weekends, you may park so far away that you might as well hike up the hillside from Los Feliz (it *is* a great trail). Or, take the DASH Observatory/ Los Feliz shuttle bus from the Vermont/Sunset metro station.

Famed Film Location in the Park

Hike to Bronson Caves

With more than 50 miles of trails, **Griffith Park** is LA's great hub of hiking. It's accessible from all directions and offers all types of experiences. A good start is the family-friendly jaunt (0.75 miles one-way) up **Bronson Canyon** off Canyon Dr to **Bronson Caves**. The latter are legit stars: among many appearances, they served as the Bat Cave in the old *Batman* TV series and were the climactic location in the still-relevant *Invasion of the Body Snatchers* (1956). From here, more challenging trails lead to sights like the Hollywood Sign (p80).

Choose Your Choo-Choo

Griffith Park has three train rides

Families can spend a day riding miniature trains in Griffith Park; each of the three options comes with a distinct appeal.

Closest to Los Feliz, the **Griffith Park & Southern Railroad** *(griffithparktrainrides.com; adult/child $4/3)* has ferried generations of parents and kids on pint-sized trains around a 1-mile loop past an old Western town since 1948. Everyone loves the soft-serve ice cream stand.

Travel Town *(traveltown.org; free)* is the park's railroad museum, with a collection of moth-eaten railcars and locomotives that once rolled along the tracks that crossed the Western US. There's a **miniature train** *(griffithparktrainrides.com; adult/child $4/3)* you can ride that meanders around the full-size collection.

Right next door, **Los Angeles Live Steamers** *(lalsrm.org; $4)* is a group of hobbyists who give rides most Sundays on their own miniature loop of track.

Screen Gems

Feel the magic of classic cinemas

Dating back to 1923, the single-screen **Vista Theater** *(vistatheaterhollywood.com)* received a 100-year anniversary revamp of its wonderfully kitsch 'ancient Egyptian' interior from owner Quentin Tarantino. Like his other cinema, the acclaimed New Beverly (p111), he programs an eclectic lineup of mostly classic films (many from his own collection) projected in 35mm as opposed to digital. The director also runs the adjoining **Pam's Coffy** *(8am-7pm)*, a cafe dedicated to the actor Pam Grier.

For more movie magic just up the road, the century-old **Los Feliz Theatre** *(vintagecinemas.com)* is a gem of a neighborhood cinema. It screens first-run movies and a good mix of classics and arthouse films.

Lounge Acts

Hear timeless tunes at the Dresden

This institution has been serving the LA crowds since 1954. You may have seen it in the film *Swingers*, where the line, 'You're so money' was made famous. The **Dresden** *(thedresden.com; no cover)* is an old-school, retro-style bar and restaurant with dimly lit rooms, arched walkways and red-wine-colored booths. Once known for singers Marty and Elayne, today their tuneful traditions are carried on nightly by an array of talented crooners. This is definitely the place to savor a traditional cocktail – try the Sidecar. It's open 5pm to midnight.

Iconic Bar

Make your own history at the Black Cat

New York City has the Stonewall Inn, Los Angeles has the **Black Cat**. Look for the winsome logo on Sunset Blvd in

SNOW WHITE'S INSPIRATION

LA had a secret love for storybook and fairy-tale houses between the 1920s and '30s – look no further than the **Snow White Cottages**. Built by fantastical developer Ben Sherwood in 1931, the eight white houses have thatched roofs, sweet window boxes and chimneys. They are said to be the inspiration for *Snow White and the Seven Dwarfs* (1937) and were built in ersatz Tudor style. Coincidentally (!), the cottages stand just around the corner from the site of Walt Disney's studios on Hyperion Ave from 1926 until 1940 (now a supermarket).

Disney's first studio, however, still stands modestly at 4647 Kingswell Ave in Los Feliz. Now a copy shop, Mickey's face peers out the window. Employees claim they sense the ghost of Walt every day.

EATING & DRINKING IN SILVER LAKE & ECHO PARK

Playita Mariscos: Homemade tortillas and fresh seafood star at a simple Mexican cafe with a short menu. Plenty of seating outside. *11am-9pm* $

Speranza: Feels like a secret club but it's not – it's just sign-challenged. The verdant patio is the spot for Italian fare like handmade pastas. *5.30-11pm* $$

Ototo: Japanese craft beer bar does big business with Dodgers fans pre-game. Great snacks; vaunted Tsubaki restaurant adjoins. *5-10pm* $$

Bar Flores: Upstairs cantina faces Sunset Blvd, providing views of the 'hood with a candlelit glow. Mellow vibe, delicious drinks and snacks. *4pm-2am* $$

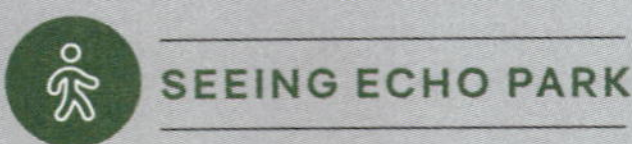

SEEING ECHO PARK

From old Victorians to an iconic lake, Echo Park is a star on screen and off. Its shops and views are bonuses.

START	END	LENGTH
Bob's Market	Angels Point	3.1 miles; 3hr

Begin at ❶ **Bob's Market** (1913), aka Toretto's Market & Deli, owned by Vin Diesel's character in the *Fast & Furious* franchise. Look for the shelf of merch. It was also in *LA Confidential*. Walk uphill to Angelino Heights, established in the mid-1880s as one of LA's first suburbs. Its most charming street is the ❷ **1300 Block of Carroll Avenue**, home to the largest concentration of Victorian-era homes in the city. A few house numbers of note: 1300 is the grandest on the block; 1316 captures the look of the 1880s with its old-style drapes; 1329 is the most original and was Halliwell Manor in the TV series *Charmed;* 1330 has Asian details like the lion dogs below the arch; and 1337 is the oldest house on the block (1872).

Walk down via Bellevue Ave to ❸ **Echo Park Lake**, anchor of the namesake park. One block of Sunset Blvd has a thicket of cool retail like the literature-rich ❹ **Stories** and the indescribable Time Travel Mart, where the slogan is 'Whenever you are, we're already there.' You won't regret a minute you spend inside.

Walk north up Portia St and use your map app to wander through leafy ❺ **Elysian Park** and up to ❻ **Angels Point**. Under towering public art, you'll enjoy uncommon views of LA, including Dodger Stadium, downtown and Hollywood.

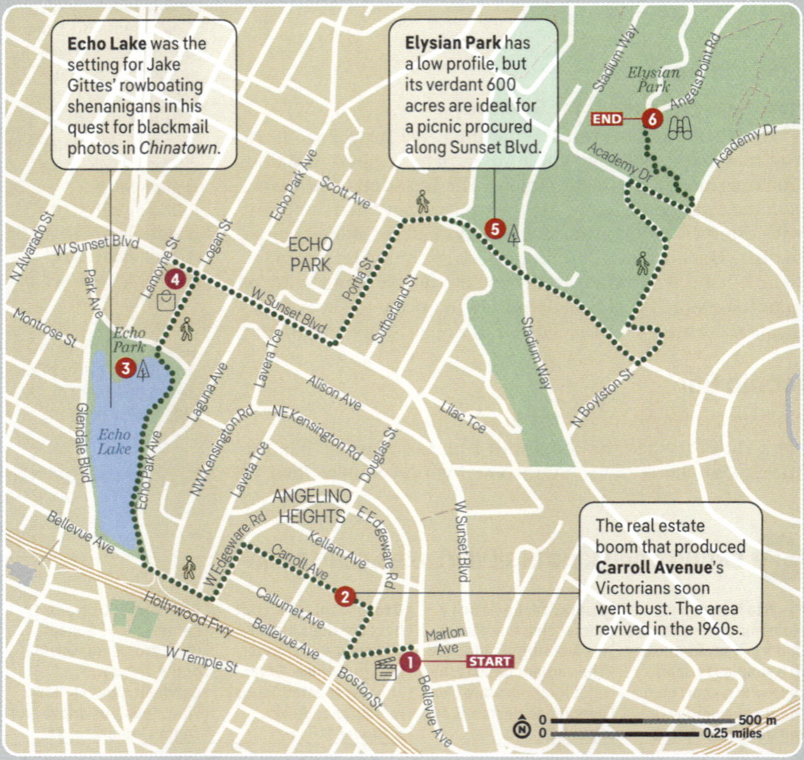

Echo Lake was the setting for Jake Gittes' rowboating shenanigans in his quest for blackmail photos in *Chinatown*.

Elysian Park has a low profile, but its verdant 600 acres are ideal for a picnic procured along Sunset Blvd.

The real estate boom that produced **Carroll Avenue**'s Victorians soon went bust. The area revived in the 1960s.

Silver Lake, which leads to this historic tavern, which became a symbol for LGBTQ+ civil rights.

The Black Cat was the site of an early LGBTQ+ civil rights demonstration in 1967 after being raided by the LA police during New Year's Eve celebrations. Now recognized as a Los Angeles Historic-Cultural Monument for its significant role in the LGBTQ+ movement, look for the plaque outside the building that honors the tavern's place in the fight for human rights.

Today, the Black Cat continues to be an inclusive neighborhood hangout with a loyal following. Casual bar food is paired with great cocktails in a woodsy, vintage interior with seating for fab people-watching out front.

After a visit, head to nearby **Akbar** to dance the rest of the night away. Both Black Cat and Akbar are open from 4pm to 2am.

Take Me Out to the Ballgame

LA is crazy for the Dodgers

Few teams can match the **Los Angeles Dodgers** *(mlb.com/dodgers)* for history (Jackie Robinson, Sandy Koufax, Fernando Valenzuela and sportscaster Vin Scully), success and fan loyalty, especially after they won an eighth World Series title in 2024. You see Dodger blue everywhere and current sensation Shohei Ohtani is LA's most popular person.

Mid-century **Dodger Stadium**, between Echo Park and Chinatown (built on what was once the vibrant Mexican American neighborhood of Chavez Ravine), is considered one of baseball's most scenic, framed by views of palm trees and the San Gabriel Mountains. Buy tickets well ahead as games sell out.

THE FATE OF CHAVEZ RAVINE

Chavez Ravine, the piece of land where Dodger Stadium sits, has the sort of tangled past that's not uncommon in LA.

In the 1940s, it was a Mexican American neighborhood, filled with residents who'd been unable to own homes elsewhere due to racist land covenants. Eyeing this prime land near downtown, the city declared it 'blighted' (it wasn't) and bought out homeowners with the claim that the land would be used for public housing (it wasn't).

Repeating the fate of the old Chinatown in the 1930s, Chavez Ravine was bulldozed and some homes were sold to the studios for their backlots. In 1958, the land was given to Walter O'Malley, who broke a million Brooklyn hearts and moved the Dodgers to LA.

Exposition Park & South LA

MUSEUMS, SPORTS, MUSIC, ARTS AND CULTURE

TOP TIP

For a wonderful read that transports you back to South Central in 1948, check out *Devil in the Blue Dress*, the first of the best-selling, hardboiled Easy Rawlins novels by South LA native Walter Mosley.

GETTING AROUND

The Metro Rail E Line has stops at Expo Park. There is also a DASH bus route from downtown (50¢). The A Line serves Compton and Watts. The K Line serves Downtown Inglewood and the LAX area.

Otherwise, South LA is the stereotypical Southern California sprawl of suburbia. You'll need a car to get around. None of the privately built stadiums in the SoFi Stadium area were located near mass transit. Expo Park is the one ideal place for extended walking.

The massive area south of the I-10 Fwy and straddling the I-110 Fwy comprises dozens of neighborhoods collectively called South LA. On its north end is Exposition Park, home to LA's iconic Memorial Coliseum, popular museums and the University of Southern California (USC).

A couple of miles west, Leimert Park is the thriving, beating heart of LA's African American community and east of the 110 is Watts, known for Watts Towers, a masterpiece of folk art.

South LA (formerly known as South Central) burst into global consciousness with the rat-a-tat-tat rhythm and rhyme of some of hip-hop's greatest pioneers. With infectious beats and sharp tongues, folks such as Ice T, Ice Cube, Eazy E, Dr Dre and Tupac Shakur broadcast gangsta life to the suburbs and beyond.

Today, as transit lines snake into the area and vast projects like SoFi Stadium spawn further investment, South LA continues its evolution.

LA's Olympic Games Home

Get lost in Exposition Park

Exposition Park – or Expo Park – began as an agricultural fairground in 1872, devolved into a magnet for the down-and-out, before finally emerging as a patch of public greenery in 1913. It contains three big-time museums (the California Science Center, California African American Museum and Natural History Museum) and will soon host a fourth (p104).

The centerpiece is the grand 1923 **Los Angeles Memorial Coliseum** *(lacoliseum.com)*. This vast bowl has hosted the 1932 and 1984 Summer Olympic Games, various Super Bowls, NFL teams and the USC Trojans college football team. It's due for another round of international fame in 2028 when the Olympics return to town. **Guided tours** *(adult/child $28/22)* are available.

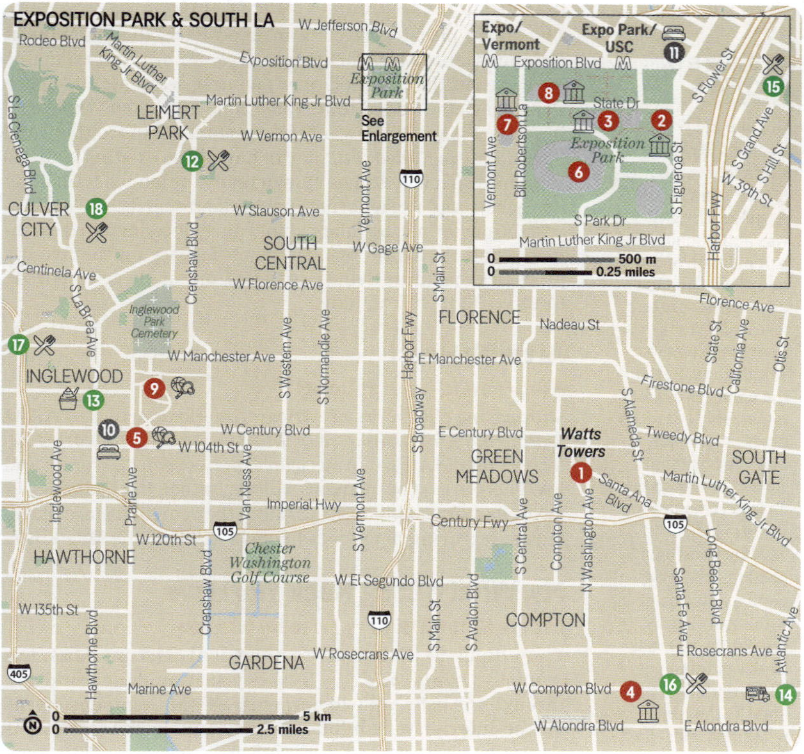

EXPOSITION PARK & SOUTH LA

HIGHLIGHTS
1 Watts Towers

SIGHTS
2 CAAM
3 California Science Center
4 Compton Art and History Museum
see 4 Compton City Hall
5 Intuit Dome
6 Los Angeles Memorial Coliseum
7 Lucas Museum of Narrative Art
see 4 Martin Luther King Memorial
8 Natural History Museum
9 SoFi Stadium

SLEEPING
10 Crestridge Inn
11 USC Hotel

EATING
see 4 Alma's Place
12 Dulan's On Crenshaw
13 Foster's Freeze
14 Kitchen's Corner
15 Mercado La Paloma
16 Patria Coffee Roasters
17 Randy's Donuts
18 Somerville

TOP CHOICES FOR EATING & DRINKING IN SOUTH LA

Dulan's On Crenshaw: Soul food mainstay in a lovely space near Leimert Park. Great mac 'n cheese. *11am-8pm* **$$**

Kitchen's Corner: This top Compton BBQ food truck is so popular it's double-size. Texas-style fall-off-the-bone: enjoy at the big park across Atlantic Ave. *11am-7pm* **$$**

Alma's Place: Near Compton City Hall, Alma cooks 'food for the soul' and her pork chops and catfish are just that. Lunch specials. *11am-5pm* **$$**

Somerville: Evoking a 1940s supper club, elegance is the theme where soul meets steakhouse and cool jazz plays. Book well ahead. *6-11pm Wed-Sun* **$$**

LA'S 1932 & 1984 OLYMPICS

Hosting the 1932 Summer Olympics was a real coup for boosters in Los Angeles. The city was approaching a population of two million and the city's power brokers were ready to take their place on the world stage. Getting the games proved remarkably easy – no other cities made a bid. The Memorial Coliseum hosted the main ceremonies for the first time.

LA's second time hosting – the 1984 games – also came with several lucky breaks. Its only real rival was Tehran, which ended up sidelined by the Islamic revolution. Most Eastern Bloc countries wound up boycotting the games, which ensured that the US won the most medals. In addition, minimal new construction and tight budgets meant that the games turned a sizable profit.

From Amoebae to the Stars

Blast off at the California Science Center

The crowd-pleasing favorite in Expo Park, the **California Science Center** *(californiasciencecenter.org; free)* remains open even as the enormous new Samuel Oschin Air and Space Center is being added to it. Some time after 2026, this soaring new wing will show off the museum's pride and joy, the Space Shuttle *Endeavour,* one of only three existing shuttles to go into space. It will be shown ready for launch with all of its rockets and the external fuel tank attached.

In the meantime, popular exhibits include a simulated earthquake and the World of Life, which focuses on the five life processes that unite living creatures from single-cell amoebae to 100 trillion-cell humans.

Art with Heart

Find a new favorite at CAAM

Showcasing the works of African American artists, **CAAM** *(California African American Museum; caamuseum.org; free)* focuses on the African American experience in California and LA. There are no permanent exhibits; rather, the five galleries have changing exhibitions through the year. Some are blockbuster, featuring big names like folk artist Nellie Mae Rowe.

My, What a Long Neck You Have

Let the Natural History Museum bite you

From dinos to diamonds, the **Natural History Museum** *(nhm.org; adult/child $18/7)* takes you around the world and through the eons. A huge new wing, NHM Commons, opens up the interior to exhibits outside. Among the features is Gnatalie, a long-necked dinosaur measuring over 70ft long. It's all housed in a beautiful 1913 Spanish Renaissance-style building that stood in for Columbia University in the first Tobey Maguire *Spider-Man* movie – where Peter Parker was bitten by the radioactive arachnid.

All That Glitters Isn't Good

SoFi Stadium and Intuit Dome

Flying into LAX, you'll likely spot the new and growing complex of corporate-financed stadiums east of the airport in Inglewood. Largest is **SoFi Stadium** *(sofistadium.com),* a huge, flashy NFL stadium that some would say has a split personality and others would say has no personality. That's because the 70,200-seat arena serves two teams, the LA Rams and the LA Chargers, and thus can't show allegiance to either. So while Lambeau Field is all about the Green Bay Packers and Arrowhead Stadium is all about the Kansas City Chiefs, SoFi Stadium isn't about anything (SoFi is a 'financial technology company').

Just south, past a growing mall, the glitzy **Intuit Dome** *(intuitdome.com)* puts on a nighttime light show and is home to the NBA's LA Clippers. By day, you can see that when they

WALTER CICCHETTI/SHUTTERSTOCK

SoFi Stadium

bought up the land to build the arena, they didn't buy up all the land, eg there's an old cut-rate liquor store near the entrance as well as a tawdry mini-storage facility.

Soaring Folk Art

Marvel at the Watts Towers

The three 'Gothic' (or is it Gaudí-esque?) spires of the fabulous **Watts Towers** *(wattstowers.org; tour adult/child $7/3)* rank among the world's greatest monuments of folk art. In 1921, Italian immigrant Simon Rodia set out to 'make something big' and then spent 33 years cobbling together this whimsical free-form sculpture from concrete, steel and a motley assortment of found objects: green 7-Up bottles, seashells, tiles, rocks and pottery.

The towers reach up to 99.5ft in height, just below the city's legal limit of 100ft. You can admire Watts Towers from beyond the fence 24/7 (and there's good explanatory signage), but to get inside, you must take the tour.

The adjacent **Watts Towers Art Center** has rotating exhibitions of important artists such as David G Brown, who created searing political cartoons. The campus is a short walk from the Metro Line A 103rd St/Watts Towers station.

THE 2028 OLYMPICS

For its Summer Olympics hat trick *(la28.org)*, the city once again had great luck. It came down to just two candidates for the 2024 games – LA and Paris – and so the International Olympic Committee suggested a compromise: Paris in 2024 and LA in 2028. *Voila!*

Like the profitable 1984 games, events will be held at existing venues, including the **SoFi Field** (Opening Ceremony, Swimming), the **Memorial Coliseum** (Track & Field, Closing Ceremony), the **Expo Park 1932 Pool** (Diving), along with the **Intuit Dome**, **Crypto.com Arena**, **Dodger Stadium**, **UCLA** and the **Pasadena Rosa Bowl**. The games will be held in LA July 14–30. Besides prepping venues and finishing new transit lines, many hope the city will scrub itself up.

TOP CHOICES FOR A QUICK BITE IN SOUTH LA

Mercado La Paloma: A walk under the I-110 from Expo Park, this fabulous food hall has everything from Yucatán cuisine to Thai. *9am-9pm* $

Patria Coffee Roasters: Only a block from Compton's City Hall, this art-filled coffee house is a standout for top-end coffee drinks. Next to a park. *8am-3pm* $

Foster's Freeze: Time-warp Inglewood soft-serve emporium. Order a hot fudge sundae and enjoy it at a picnic table. *10am-8pm* $

Randy's Donuts: Famously excellent doughnuts are your first or last memory of LA going to/from LAX. Simple flavors, like glazed old-fashioned, are best. *24hr* $

THE LUCAS MUSEUM OF NARRATIVE ART

An enormous, sinuous blob rising west of the Coliseum, the **Lucas Museum of Narrative Art** *(lucasmuseum.org)* is the dream of George Lucas, creator of *Star Wars*. However, exactly what his hundreds of millions of dollars will buy is more labyrinthine than the plot of *The Phantom Menace*.

Both San Francisco and Chicago rebuffed efforts to locate the museum in those cities. Ground was broken in Expo Park in 2018. However, the original 2021 opening has been pushed back repeatedly amid massive staff upheavals and layoffs. As for what will be inside the metallic shell, the official line is that the mission is 'to inspire and connect people through the exploration of visual stories and their influences in society.'

WALTER CICCHETTI/SHUTTERSTOCK

Watts Towers (p103)

Compton's Anthem

See the site of 'Not Like Us'

West Coast rap and hip-hop have been part of Southern California since NWA's 1988 album *Straight Outta Compton* launched the careers of Eazy E, Ice Cube and Dr Dre and established gangsta rap.

Jump ahead and Compton remains relevant, as megastar Kendrick Lamar showed in 2024 with his music video 'Not Like Us.' Viewed millions of times, it features scenes shot at the striking modernist **Martin Luther King Memorial** on the wide open plaza at the **Compton City Hall**.

Lamar invited the people of Compton to show up for the shoot and they did. The results are joyous and vivacious. It's worth visiting the location while watching the video on your phone. After, cross S Acacia Ave and see what's on at the **Compton Art and History Museum** *(comptonmuseum.org; adult/child $5/3)*. Exhibits regularly change.

Koreatown, Miracle Mile & Fairfax

NONSTOP DELIGHT, TOP MUSEUMS AND EDGY SHOPPING

And the Oscar goes to...the swath of gridded streets from Koreatown in the east to the trendy zone butting up against Beverly Hills in the west. This area claims some of LA's top cultural and retail assets. It's here that you'll find the 'Miracle Mile' and its string of blockbuster museums, the Orthodox Jewish-meets-hipster Fairfax district and once-trendy-now-funky Melrose Ave.

Sometimes called Mid-City, though that's really a specific neighborhood down by the Santa Monica Fwy, you'll find every aspect of LA here. The unbeatable cluster of museums includes the Academy Museum of Motion Pictures, otherwise known as the Oscar Museum, and the city's boffo main art museum, LACMA, which has a stunning new building. Running through the middle of it all is a new subway line that's been years in the digging.

The eating, drinking, shopping and entertainment run almost around-the-clock, especially in Koreatown, LA's tireless enclave of frenetic day and night action.

TOP TIP

With many LA neighborhoods and nightspots going quiet by midnight, Koreatown remains the city's most vibrant and exciting nightlife district. An ever-changing line-up of bars and clubs keeps the action going well past the witching hour. As the venues of choice are always changing, ask around for what's hot.

GETTING AROUND

Metro's D (Purple) Line subway serves Koreatown with the Wilshire/Normandie and Wilshire/Western stations. The big news is the extension that was due to open in 2025 covering stops on Wilshire at La Brea Ave, Fairfax Ave and La Cienega Blvd. The Wilshire/Fairfax stop promises to be the best transit development in LA for visitors in decades as it will serve several top sights like the Oscar museum and LACMA. Further extensions will serve Rodeo Dr in Beverly Hills (by 2027) and Westwood (before the 2028 Olympics). Individual neighborhoods in this area, such as Koreatown, are all enjoyably walkable.

HIGHLIGHTS
1 Academy Museum of Motion Pictures
2 LACMA

SIGHTS
3 La Brea Tar Pits & Museum
4 Little Ethiopia
5 Petersen Automotive Museum

SLEEPING
6 Banana Bungalows Hotel and Hostel West Hollywood
7 Hotel Normandie LA
see 7 Line Los Angeles
8 Palihouse West Hollywood

EATING
9 Ahgassi Gopchang
see 4 Buna
10 Canter's
11 Danbi
12 Guelaguetza Restaurant
see 16 Happy Ice
13 My 2 Cents LA
14 Pink's Hot Dogs
15 République

DRINKING & NIGHTLIFE
16 Be Bright Coffee
17 Dan Sung Sa
18 El Carmen
19 Lock & Key
see 7 Normandie Club
20 Pips on La Brea
21 Rosen Karaoke
22 Snake Pit
23 Stir Crazy

ENTERTAINMENT
24 El Rey Theatre
see 16 Groundlings
25 Improv
26 Largo at the Coronet
27 New Beverly Cinema

SHOPPING
28 Golf Wang
29 Melrose Trading Post
30 Original Farmers Market
31 Polkadots & Moonbeams
32 Posers Hollywood
33 Ripndip

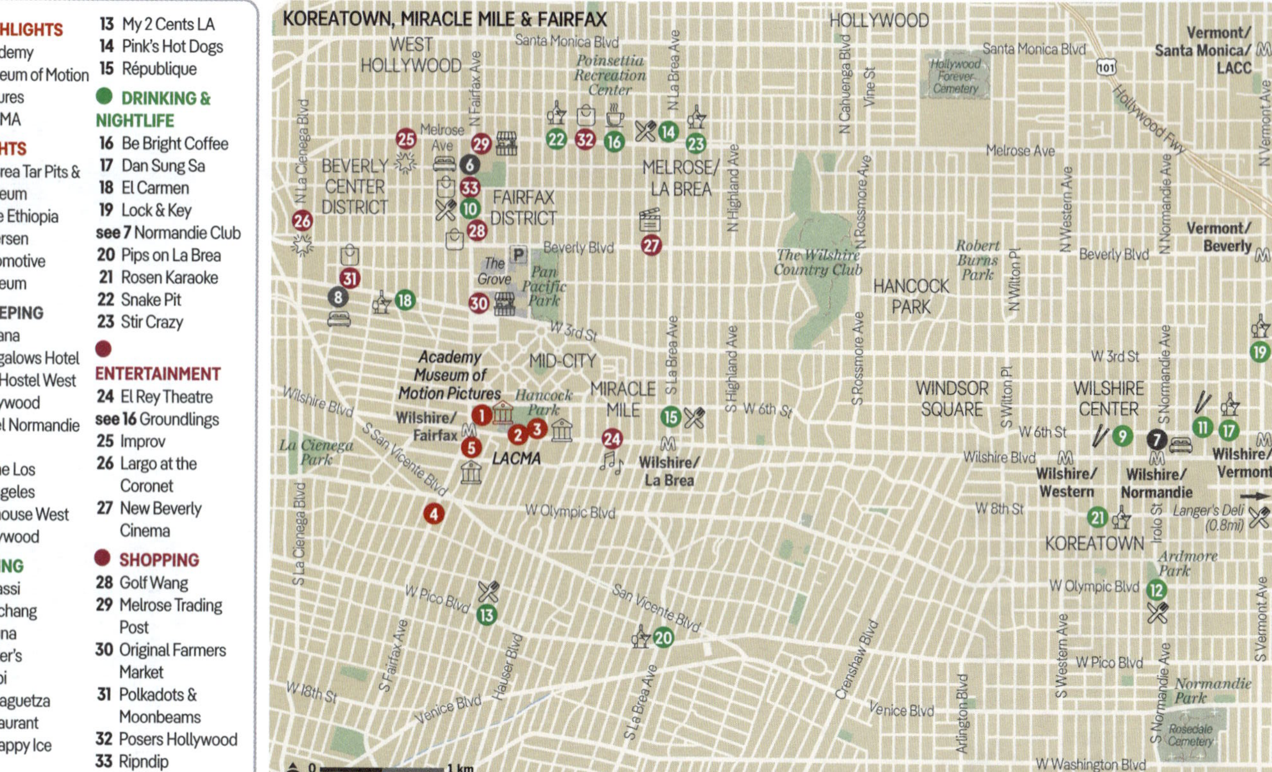

Stunning New Home for Art

Take in the wealth at LACMA

Soaring across Wilshire Blvd, the new **LACMA** *(Los Angeles County Museum of Art; lacma.org; adult/child $28/13)* is set to open for visitors by mid-2026. The $720 million David Geffen Galleries will replace the museum's four aging buildings and with the new real estate will come an entirely new philosophy for exhibiting the largest collection of art in the western United States.

The depth and wealth of LACMA's collection is stunning. It includes millennia worth of Chinese, Japanese, pre-Columbian and ancient Greek, Roman and Egyptian sculpture, plus treasures across media from every continent except Antarctica. From Europe and North America come stars like Rembrandt, Cézanne, Magritte, Mary Cassatt and Ansel Adams.

Permanent collection highlights include Chris Burden's outdoor installation *Urban Light* (a surreal selfie backdrop of hundreds of vintage LA street lamps) and Michael Heizer's *Levitated Mass,* a surprisingly inspirational 340-ton boulder perched over a walkway. Other high points: *Cold Shoulder* by Roy Lichtenstein and *Flower Day* by Diego Rivera. Two works are iconic LA: *Mulholland Drive* by David Hockney and *105 Freeway* by Catherine Opie.

LACMA's Zen-like **Pavilion for Japanese Art** houses pieces ranging in origin from 3000 BCE to the 21st century. Several cafes are planned for admission-free public spaces on both sides of Wilshire Blvd once the new galleries open.

Movie Magic's Home

See the blockbuster Academy Museum of Motion Pictures

You'll be channeling your inner movie-lover at LA's lavish **Academy Museum of Motion Pictures** *(academymuseum.org; adult/child $25/free)*. Spectacular and expansive, it's a cutting-edge ode to film, with thought-provoking exhibits, priceless memorabilia and a dynamic program of movie screenings and talks delving deep into celluloid culture. If you only have time for one museum in town, make it this one.

Designed by Italian starchitect Renzo Piano, this 300,000-sq-ft blockbuster's permanent exhibition offers an immersive, state-of-the-art journey through cinema's evolution. The core **Stories of Cinema** galleries explore the many aspects of filmmaking, as well as showcasing movie memorabilia that includes Dorothy's ruby slippers from *The Wizard of*

DISPLAYING ART IN A NEW WAY

LACMA's new building is the bold vision of Swiss architect Peter Zumthor. The curvaceous, airy, cantilevered galleries straddle Wilshire Blvd and floor-to-ceiling windows will make the most of LA's natural beauty, highlighting its hills and celebrated natural light.

Inside, LACMA's curators have challenged themselves to utterly rethink how their huge and rich collection is displayed. They want to dispense with the Eurocentric and chronological narrative that dominates art museums and instead show how works spanning mediums, cultures and time interrelate. As they readily admit in interviews, this new paradigm is a 'challenge.'

EATING IN MIRACLE MILE & FAIRFAX: OUR PICKS

République: Artisan bakery, light-filled cafe and bistro. The kitchen whips up delectable French-accented dishes and desserts. *8am-2pm & 5.30-10pm* **$$**

Canter's: The veteran deli isn't closed despite the appearance. Legendary pastrami and other standards. Comfy booths, knowing servers and parking. *6am-11.30pm* **$$**

My 2 Cents LA: Acclaimed restaurant of TV-chef Alisa Reynolds has a loyal, A-lister following for her Southern fusion fare. Book. *11.30am-9.30pm Thu-Sun* **$$$**

Pink's Hot Dogs: Famous doggeria (since 1939) with glacially moving lines thanks to the garlicky all-beef frankfurters drenched in chili. *9.30am-midnight* **$**

BEST SHOPPING

Golf Wang: Tyler, the Creator, known for his alternative hip-hop, owns this clothing store that reflects his vision of cool. *golfwang.com*

Polkadots & Moonbeams: Whimsical vintage shop stocked with affordable designer dresses, shades, scarves and hats. *polkadotsandmoonbeams.com*

Ripndip: Streetwear, skatewear and skateboards. The witty logo will look familiar to tire buyers. *ripndipclothing. com*

Melrose Trading Post: Every Sunday, over 250 vendors sell threads, jewelry, crafts and other offbeat items in the Fairfax High parking lot. *melrosetradingpost.org*

Posers Hollywood: Embodies the old Melrose Ave. Dr Martens, Fred Perry and other punkish wear. *posersonline.com*

Oz. Iconic items from films are all here, including a surviving Rosebud sled from *Citizen Kane*. Scripts for blockbusters are dissected and annotated to explain the creative process. Temporary exhibitions have depth, such as Oscar-winner Bong Joon Ho (*Parasite*; 2019) detailing how he creates his films.

The Academy Museum occupies two sharply contrasting buildings. Entry is via the restored **Saban Building**, a 1939 Streamline Moderne landmark that once housed a May Company department store, which was a popular shopping location for many of the stars now memorialized within. Directly behind it is Piano's addition, a commanding space-age sphere featuring a dome with 1500 glass panels. A terrace offers sweeping views of the Hollywood Hills.

The museum's theaters host year-round film screenings and discussions. Oscar Sundays brings out award-winning blockbusters, while Silent Sundays screens long-forgotten classics. Branch Selects sees Academy members curating films significant to their specific craft. Watch for films hosted by Academy members who worked on them.

Use the Bloomberg Connects app, which offers insight to greatly enhance your experience in the galleries. There's a good cafe-restaurant with outdoor seating.

Smell the Ice Age

Get stuck at the La Brea Tar Pits

Mammoths, saber-toothed cats and other critters roamed LA's savanna in prehistoric times. The **La Brea Tar Pits & Museum** *(tarpits.org; adult/child $18/7)* preserve a trove of skulls and bones and are one of the world's most famous fossil sites. Generations of young dino hunters have come to learn about paleontology in the museum.

Outside, the smell of asphalt permeates the air as the tar pits still bubble away and beloved models show mammoths stuck in the gooey crude oil bubbling up from deep below Wilshire Blvd. A life-size diorama of a mammoth family dramatizes the cruel fate of countless thousands of animals between 50,000 and 10,000 years ago. Nearby, you can observe pits where fossils are still being discovered.

Not Just for Gearheads

Zoom into the Petersen Automotive Museum

The **Petersen Automotive Museum** *(petersen.org; adult/child $21/12)* is a treat even for those who can't tell a piston from a crankshaft. Inside the museum's body of undulating

DRINKING IN MIRACLE MILE & FAIRFAX: OUR PICKS

El Carmen: Loud, dimly lit and festooned with bull heads and *lucha libre* wrestling memorabilia, this tequila tavern pulls in an industry-heavy crowd. *5pm-2am*

Stir Crazy: Neighborhood favorite with sociable tables out front and rare California wines by the glass. Daily specials and small plates. *5-11pm Mon-Fri*

Be Bright Coffee: Storefront cafe roasts its own beans, used by restaurants across LA. Expertly crafted coffee drinks; plenty of tea options. *8am-4pm*

Snake Pit: Long-running dive bar serving the Dr Martens crowd on Melrose. Good drink prices and big selection of whiskey. Popular burgers. *3am-midnight*

FOLLOW THE PAST IN CULVER CITY

Hollywood's workaday sibling, Culver City, produced scores of movies. Now a burgeoning tech hub, it's a walkable pleasure.

START	END	LENGTH
Metro E Line, Culver City Station	Sony Pictures	2 miles; 2hr

Cross over from the Metro line E, Culver City Station ❶ **Platform**, a buzzing outdoor development that harbors niche boutiques and eateries. Loqui offers creative Mexican you can enjoy on the back patio. Hidden behind an inconspicuous door on Venice Blvd, the ❷ **Museum of Jurassic Technology** *(mjt.org; $15)* is LA's most idiosyncratic museum. Its labyrinth of curiosities would be right at home in a carnival sideshow. Book ahead.

Many iconic movies were filmed at ❸ **Culver Studios**, including the original *A Star Is Born*. It's now home to Amazon Studios. The ❹ **Culver Hotel** (1924) is a National Historic Landmark. From here, Washington Blvd is lined with many shaded cafes. A striking example of Streamline Moderne architecture, the 1946 ❺ **Kirk Douglas Theatre** *(centertheatregroup.org)* showcases new works by local playwrights. Across the intersection, diminutive Village Well Books attracts writers who tap away at communal tables. Stop into the ❻ **Backstage Bar & Grill**, the long-running dive bar popular with studio workers in for a shot.

MGM, arguably the most storied of the old major studios, was not in Hollywood but in Culver City. Today, it's known as ❼ **Sony Pictures** and you can visit the locations of famous films. In-depth tours *(sonypicturesstudiostours.com; from $55)* depart from Overland Gate on Overland Ave.

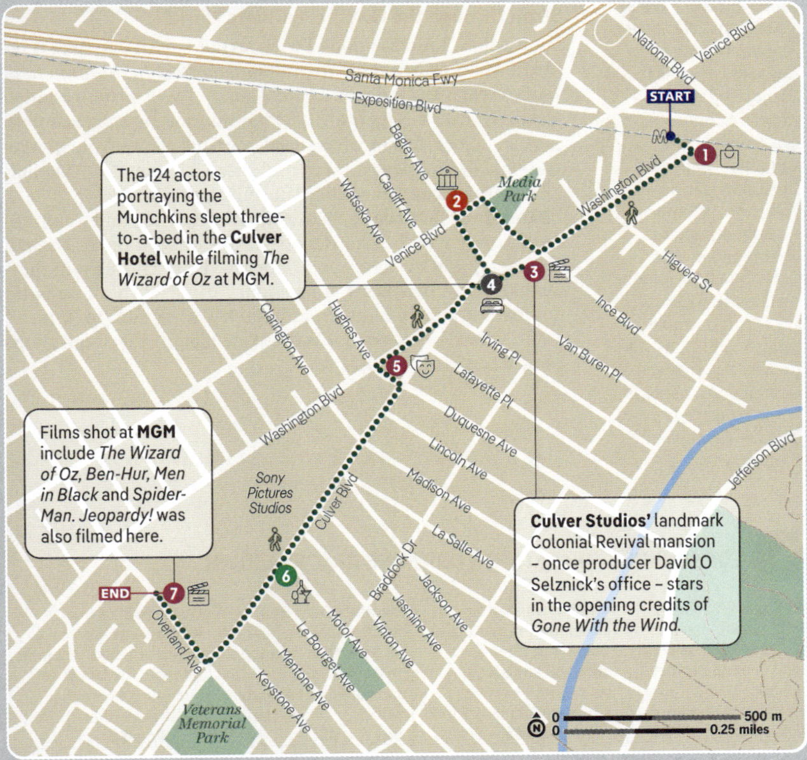

The 124 actors portraying the Munchkins slept three-to-a-bed in the **Culver Hotel** while filming *The Wizard of Oz* at MGM.

Films shot at **MGM** include *The Wizard of Oz, Ben-Hur, Men in Black* and *Spider-Man. Jeopardy!* was also filmed here.

Culver Studios' landmark Colonial Revival mansion – once producer David O Selznick's office – stars in the opening credits of *Gone With the Wind*.

HANCOCK PARK

Century-old mansions flank the tree-lined streets of **Hancock Park**, a genteel neighborhood roughly bounded by Highland, Rossmore and Melrose Aves and Wilshire Blvd. In the 1920s, LA's leading families, including the Dohenys and Chandlers, hired famous architects to build their cribs and numerous celebrities have lived here amid the curving lawns.

It's a lovely area for a stroll or a drive, such that you'd never be aware of the ugly aspects of its history. Long whites-only, it was a center of redlining, the practice pioneered by California Realtors of keeping neighborhoods segregated. When Nat King Cole bought a house here in 1948, his dog was poisoned. Today, it's a wealthy, diverse community, popular with bankers, lawyers and entertainment industry types.

bands of stainless steel on a hot-rod-red background are four floors exploring the history, industry and artistry of motorized transportation.

Vehicles are rotated through the exhibitions regularly. Start your visit on the history floor, loaded with classic and concept cars. In the Cars of Film and Television gallery, you might see the DeLorean from *Back to the Future,* the Durango 95 from *A Clockwork Orange* and a Batmobile or two.

The industry floor is devoted to how cars are designed and built. The kids' section is inspired by Disney's *Cars;* there's a custom-built Lightning McQueen. The ground floor focuses on the art of the automobile, mostly in special exhibits.

New for 2025, the extra-admission basement **Vault** *(adult/child $28/12)* displays over 300 rare cars and motorcycles. Here you won't find cars that ran on the open road; rather, you'll discover rare concept cars and vehicles designed for special purposes. Many are exquisite works of art. Expect anything from Pope John Paul II's Popemobile to cars decades ahead of their time, like the 1953 Cadillac Series 62 by Ghia.

The Petersen is the perfect stop if you've arrived in LA via Route 66, which passes to the north on Santa Monica Blvd and ends at the Santa Monica Pier.

Taste Delight

Stroll through the Original Farmers Market

Long before LA was flooded with farmers markets, the **Original Farmers Market** *(farmersmarketla.com; hours vary)* was *the* farmers market. Once a dusty lot of produce-laden pickup trucks, the open-air 1934 landmark is now packed with casual choices for a meal or snack any time of day, from gumbo and bakery classics to tacos and pizza, sit-down or takeout. There are even a few stalls still selling produce.

Monsieur Marcel has a gourmet market and seafood-centric sidewalk bistro. It's open 9am to 9pm daily. Fans of Michael Connelly books and Detective Harry Bosch will thoroughly enjoy **Du-par's**, a legendary diner with a fine patio and memorable banana cream pie. It's open 6am to 9pm.

The upscale **Grove** mall next door has all the same shops as other upscale malls.

TOP CHOICES FOR EATING & DRINKING IN KOREATOWN

Ahgassi Gopchang: Popular with families; get here early to avoid long lines. Many pics of happy luminaries enjoying the bulgogi. *11.30am-midnight* **$$**

Danbi: In historic Chapman Plaza, Korean fusion fine dining, thoughtfully prepared and artfully served. Changing menu. *6-10pm Wed-Sun* **$$$**

Langer's Deli: By MacArthur Park, famous for Sandwich 19 (peppery pastrami, Swiss cheese and coleslaw on double-baked rye). *8am-4pm Mon-Sat* **$$**

Guelaguetza Restaurant: Serves award-winning, rich mole. Anchors the Oaxacan community here that dates back to the 1990s. *9am-9pm* **$$**

KIT LEONG/SHUTTERSTOCK

Original Farmers Market

High Style & Street Pleasures

Prowl Melrose Ave and 3rd St

This legendary rock-and-roll shopping strip is as famous for its epic people-watching as it is for its retail pleasures. The strip between N Poinsettia Pl and N Fairfax Ave gets a lot of the buzz thanks to the boutiques stuck together like block-long hedgerows. Most of its gear is rather low-end, so amuse yourself browsing, then get sweet at **Happy Ice**, which is open from noon to 9pm.

If you're after hipper, higher-end stuff, explore the long stretch of Melrose between N Crescent Heights Blvd and Santa Monica Blvd. Stop for selfie joy at the Paul Smith clothing store's Barbie-pink wall. Or hit 3rd St in the same area, which is the current place to find attitude outpacing style and cars with sticker prices beyond the means of the 99% idling in traffic.

Tarantino's Features

Nightly film fests at New Beverly Cinema

Quentin Tarantino owns the vintage 1920s **New Beverly Cinema** *(thenewbev.com)*, which screens classic, cult, current and art films. All are projected in 35mm, with many of the restored prints from the owner's collection. He also owns the Vista Theater (p97) in Los Feliz. Some programs are double

VIBRANT LITTLE ETHIOPIA

Starting with Little Armenia near Los Feliz, you can run right through the alphabet of LA's great diversity of cultures. Ever-changing, these enclaves are both old (Downtown's Little Tokyo) and new, like **Little Ethiopia**. Along a block of Fairfax Ave south of Olympic Blvd, it started with one shop around 1990. As is often the case, this attracted other immigrants and everyone's success became symbiotic. Soon, it was a hub for LA's Ethiopian community and in 2002 the city officially named the neighborhood Little Ethiopia. Browsing the many stores, cafes and markets makes for a fine walk. The green, yellow and red of the Ethiopian flag colors storefronts. Sidewalk displays offer yams and other staples. Cafes like **Buna** are indicative of the neighborhood's vibrancy.

TOP CHOICES FOR EATING & DRINKING IN KOREATOWN

Normandie Club: This dimly lit bar is cool and approachable. Talented staff whip up creative cocktails for pre-dinner imbibers and first dates. *6pm-2am*

Rosen Karaoke: Popular spot for great service and private rooms in varying sizes. Sing, snack and drink yourself happy. Good tunes selection. *7pm-2am*

Dan Sung Sa: In a tatty strip mall, mimics a Seoul street bar with tight wooden booths, potent soju cocktails and ribald revelry. *4pm-2am*

Lock & Key: Look for the neon key sign and enter. Classy, with candles on tables and a cool dance patio. The dress code eschews most bro-wear. *7pm-2am*

HUN YOUNG LEE/SHUTTERSTOCK

Koreatown

features and many include classic Bugs Bunny cartoons. The crowd is heavy with industry types who stand up front before the lights go down, discussing projects and deals.

No Ending to the Happy

Prowl the action in Koreatown

Koreatown is as close as LA gets to being the 'city that never sleeps.' Sprawling and vibrant, it's a platter of sizzling BBQ joints, buzzing malls and karaoke bars, all splashed with a dash of glorious Moderne architecture from the area's gilded past when it was a bastion of Golden Age Hollywood.

Koreatown is roughly bounded by Beverly and Olympic Blvds north and south, plus Western Ave on the west. The east side abuts MacArthur Park, the one that 'melts in the dark' in the eponymous Jimmy Webb song made famous by Donna Summer. Wilshire Blvd is the main artery, along with W 6th St, S Vermont Ave and W 8th St.

Koreatown has a vast number of eateries. Enjoy swilling *soju* (rice alcohol) or *makgeolli* (rice wine) at a sweaty drinking den or in a *noraebang* (private karaoke room) hangout.

And, just to keep things geographically off-kilter, there's a cluster of superb Oaxacan restaurants.

BEST VENUES FOR LIVE ACTS

Groundlings: Improv alums include Will Ferrell, Maya Rudolph and Melissa McCarthy. On Thursdays, the main company and surprise guests riff together. *groundlings.com*

Improv: Launch pad for countless stand-up comics from Richard Pryor to Ellen DeGeneres. Mixes headlines with improv. *improv.com*

El Rey Theatre: This 1936 art deco dance hall is a brilliant live-music venue, with a killer sound system. *theelrey.com*

Pips on La Brea: Beautiful heated patio in Mid-City that's the scene for near-nightly jazz. Trees with fairy lights add to the date-night ambience. *pipsonlabrea.com*

Largo at the Coronet: Incubator of high-minded pop culture. It features edgy comedy and nourishing night music. *largo-la.com*

West Hollywood & Beverly Hills

WEALTH, LGBTQ+ LIFE AND FABLED SHOPPING

Famous worldwide, the 90210 zip code is a symbol for wealthy A-list celebrities, luxe hotels and top-of-the-line shopping. In the 1920s, actors Douglas Fairbanks and Mary Pickford built their home in Beverly Hills, turning the neighborhood into an immediate status symbol. Today, visitors flock here to get a taste of the fantasy and to take in the opulent real estate and swaying palm trees.

Nudging up alongside, but a world apart, West Hollywood (aka WeHo) is distinctly, proudly independent. With some of LA's finest bars, renowned live music, hedonistic nightlife and the famous (albeit faded) Sunset Strip, WeHo has a draw to rival the famous zip code. More importantly, WeHo is a thriving LGBTQ+ community, making West Hollywood one of the nation's most influential cities on LGBTQ+ issues. Of course, there is a little fun to be had; just drop by in June for Pride and October for Halloween.

TOP TIP

Superb walking tours of Rodeo Dr and celebrity homes are easily followed in the free **Beverly Hills Experience** app from the Beverly Hills Historical Society. The fact-filled routes are clearly marked. The home tour includes houses used by Frank Sinatra, Barbra Streisand, Eddie Murphy, Lucille Ball, George Clooney and many others.

GETTING AROUND

When the Metro Rail Line D Wilshire/Rodeo station opens – possibly in 2026 – it will revolutionize public transit access to Beverly Hills. Until then, Metro Bus Line 4 runs frequently along Santa Monica Blvd in West Hollywood and Beverly Hills, also reaching Hollywood, Silver Lake, Echo Park and Downtown LA. Metro Bus Line 2 connects Sunset Blvd in West Hollywood to Westwood, Hollywood, Silver Lake, Echo Park and Downtown LA.

Parking in WeHo and Beverly Hills is never easy and usually expensive. Both areas are enjoyably walkable, although WeHo is hilly at the edges.

SIGHTS
1 Greystone Mansion & Gardens

ACTIVITIES
see 13 Bikes & Hikes LA

SLEEPING
2 Andaz West Hollywood
3 Beverly Hills Hotel
4 Beverly Wilshire
5 Chateau Marmont
6 Crescent Hotel Beverly Hills
7 Mondrian Los Angeles
8 Sunset Tower Hotel

EATING
9 Hamburger Mary's
10 Nate'n Al's
11 Spago
12 Sugarfish
13 Tail O' the Pup
see 8 Tower Bar
14 Wally's Beverly Hills

DRINKING & NIGHTLIFE
15 Bar Next Door
16 Barney's Beanery
17 Micky's WeHo
18 The Abbey

ENTERTAINMENT
19 Comedy Store
20 Jazz Café at Cipriani Beverly Hills
21 Laugh Factory
22 Roxy Theatre
23 Whisky-a-Go-Go

SHOPPING
24 Book Soup
25 Cheese Store
26 Edelweiss Chocolates
see 24 Mystery Pier Books
27 Pleasure Chest

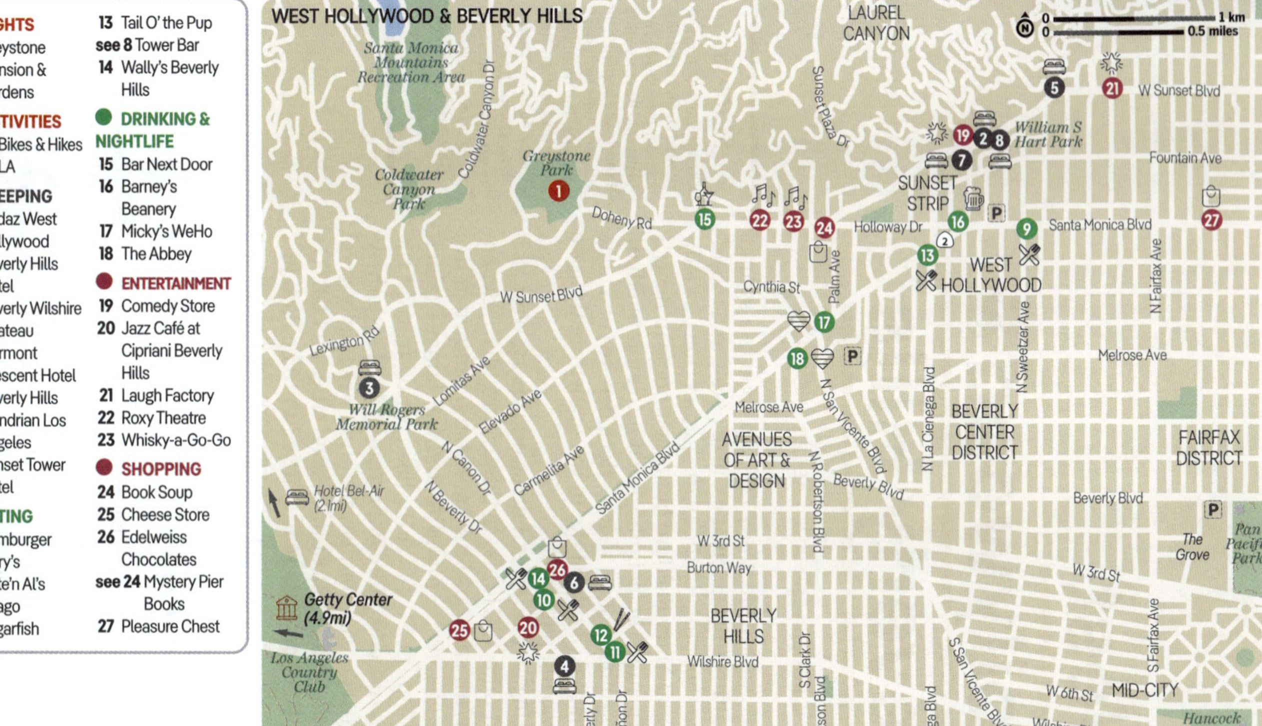

A Neighborhood Like No Other

Do the West Hollywood Walk

Santa Monica Boulevard is the main drag of West Hollywood (WeHo) and barhopping its length is one of the LA region's great joys. The LGBTQ+-centric bars and clubs heave through the weekends, with Sunday brunch being a must. Weeknights are busy as well.

Central to WeHo is one of the most iconic gay nightclubs on the West Coast today, **The Abbey**, which serves the community as a cultural center as well as being a bar and nightclub. With over three decades in the game, it's been called the best gay bar in the world. Match your mood to the space: thumping dance floor, outdoor patios, Goth lounge or chill space. It's open from 11am to 2am daily.

The boulevard abounds with choices like the iconic **Micky's Weho**, with long-running drag shows and great DJ sets. It's open noon to 2am. **Hamburger Mary's** is the Sunday afternoon brunch go-to. It's open from 11am to 10 pm.

If You Were Rich & Famous

The Beverly Hills experience

Beverly Hills is as much a state of mind as a place. Its name is so often used as shorthand for ostentatious wealth, conspicuous consumption and celebrity that it can get reduced to cliché. Ultimately, however, it's a rich, tidy place without a plethora of must-see sights; rather, you go to soak up the vibe, nibble off a bit of the fantasy and think about what life would be like if that was your Lamborghini parked on Rodeo Dr.

On a short walk (p116), you can take in the heart of Beverly Hills, including Rodeo Dr. Spoiler alert: the big-name retailers here all exist to serve free-spending tourists; the rich and/or famous shop at the private boutiques.

Stop at the **Beverly Hills Hotel**, the famed 'pink palace' that's never lost its sheen of glamour and where the **Polo Lounge** or **Cabana Cafe** remain the ultimate Beverly Hills experience. Have a martini and mourn the arrival of cell phones, which ended the tradition of fading celebs calling the hotel and having themselves paged to remind producers of their existence.

Note: don't bother with **Bel Air**, which is all 16ft hedges and fences.

WEHO'S BEST LIVE VENUES

Whisky-a-Go-Go: Trades on its legendary status when the Doors were the house band and go-go dancing was invented here. *whiskyagogo.com*

Roxy Theatre: A Sunset Strip fixture since 1973. This small venue puts you close to the bands, with some big-name surprises. *theroxy.com*

Comedy Store: The club with cred. Richard Pryor, George Carlin, Eddie Murphy and Robin Williams were all nurtured here. *thecomedystore.com*

Laugh Factory: The Marx Brothers used to keep offices at this institution. Gets big names, up-and-comers and surprise celebs. *laughfactory.com*

Jazz Café at Cipriani Beverly Hills: In Beverly Hills this luxe jazz bar caters to a refined crowd in the swank Cipriani Hotel. Top acts. *cipriani.com*

WHERE TO EAT & DRINK IN WEHO

Tail O' the Pup: Look for the big weenie in a bun – it's right beside the road. Hot dogs served in myriad ways. *noon-10pm* **$**

Barney's Beanery: Burger and beer bar that has fronted Santa Monica Blvd since it was known as Route 66 and Studebakers steamed out front. *11am-2am* **$$**

Tower Bar: Old-school Hollywood luxury in an indoor-outdoor setting at the swank Sunset Tower Hotel. Vaunted martinis and high-end burgers. *7am-10pm* **$$$**

Bar Next Door: Enticing cocktail bar with a solid backlist of creations going back more than a century. Has rare libations; cheery, mellow vibe. *5pm-2am* **$$**

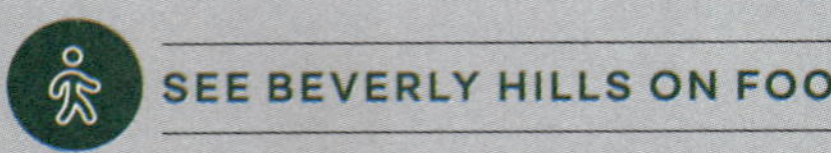

SEE BEVERLY HILLS ON FOOT

Stroll Rodeo Dr and discover notable art and iconic architecture and get your picture taken: yep, you're in Beverly Hills!

START	END	LENGTH
Rodeo Dr and Wilshire Blvd	Beverly Gardens Park	0.75 miles; 2hr

Standing at the corner of ❶ **Rodeo Drive and Wilshire Boulevard**, begin your walk up the three-block ribbon of consumption that features every major luxury brand on the planet. Architecturally, nothing is especially noteworthy – even the Frank Lloyd Wright ❷ **Anderton Court Shops** at number 328 are ho-hum. Rather, a successful day here is measured by the number of glossy brand-name shopping bags you can carry. Note: celebs go to private boutiques, so don't expect to see any famous faces.

When you reach inner-Santa Monica Blvd, turn right for one block. ❸ **Mr Brainwash Art Museum** *(mrbrainwashartmuseum.com; adult/child $20/free)* is the namesake project of the French-born Banksy protege who's based in LA. It's crammed with his whimsical kitsch-meets-fine art; eg, the Hollywood Sign pops up in a Van Gogh.

Two streets east is a mid-century icon: the ❹ **Union 76 Gas Station**. Its swooping, back-to-the-future canopy is a world-famous example of Googie architecture and is spectacular at night. Swing around to Rexford Dr and the ❺ **Beverly Hills Civic Center**, a grand 1932 Spanish Revival edifice. Cross into ❻ **Beverly Gardens Park**. At nearly 2 miles, this green swath is the manicured, flower-filled border to commercial Beverly Hills. The 40ft-long 'Beverly Hills' sign might as well spell s-e-l-f-i-e.

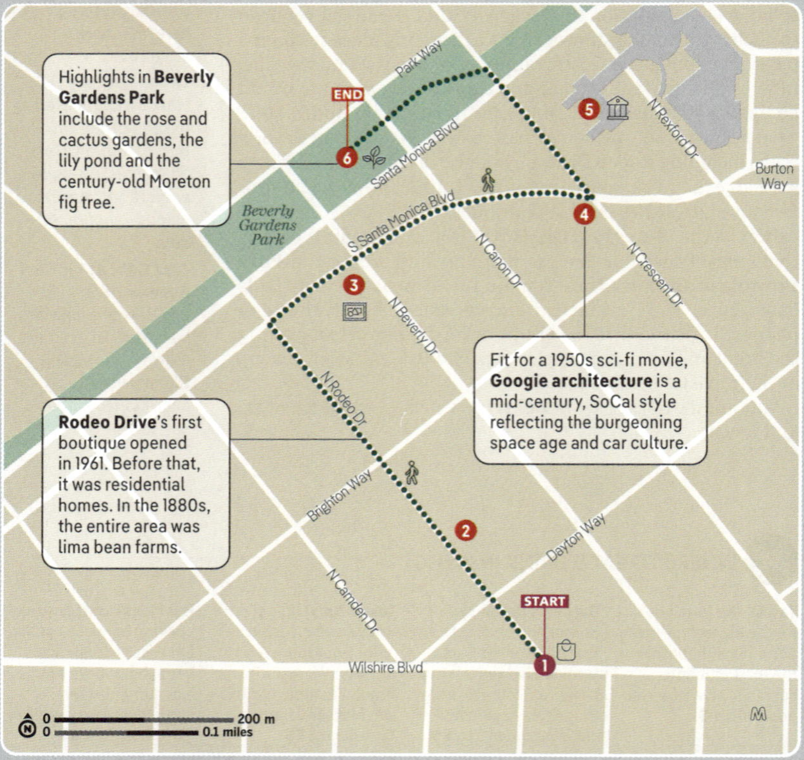

Highlights in **Beverly Gardens Park** include the rose and cactus gardens, the lily pond and the century-old Moreton fig tree.

Fit for a 1950s sci-fi movie, **Googie architecture** is a mid-century, SoCal style reflecting the burgeoning space age and car culture.

Rodeo Drive's first boutique opened in 1961. Before that, it was residential homes. In the 1880s, the entire area was lima bean farms.

Touring the Active Way

Hiking and biking the sights

See Hollywood, Beverly Hills and greater LA on highly recommended tours with **Bikes & Hikes LA** *(bikesandhikesla.com)*. Its signature ride is the 32-mile 'LA in a Day,' which takes in celebrity homes, swank shopping streets, inspiring architecture and the Pacific *(from $187 on an e-bike)*. Other options include shorter tours and e-bikes. Hiking tours include a 1½-hour jaunt to the Hollywood Sign (p80).

A Vital Experience

The compelling Museum of Tolerance

Learning the hard lessons of humanity's past so they aren't repeated is at the core of the **Museum of Tolerance** *(museumoftolerance.com; adult/child $18/13.50)*. The human cost of intolerance is relentlessly detailed on each floor. Among the museum's many fascinating artifacts are original diary entries written by Anne Frank as well as the first record of Hitler's anti-Semitic beliefs.

Visitors, including many school groups, are given the persona of a child who died in the **Holocaust** and then follow an effective and gripping exhibit about the events that shows the influence of major donor Steven Spielberg. In the basement, the **Social Lab** is an immersive and interactive exploration of how we are driven apart through prejudice and bigotry. It's effective and timely.

One BIG House

Be dazzled at Greystone Mansion & Gardens

Looking just like you'd expect a Beverly Hills mansion to look, the **Greystone Mansion & Gardens** *(free)* has featured in countless movies and TV shows *(The Big Lebowski, There Will Be Blood)*. This 1927 Tudor Revival pile was a gift from oil tycoon Edward Doheny to his son Ned. In 1929, the oil heir and his male secretary were both found dead in an alleged murder-suicide – a notorious mystery that has been debated endlessly ever since.

The elegant grounds with their perfectly coiffed lawns, Italian Renaissance fountains and 166ft walkway with enormous cypress trees offer commanding views of LA. The lavish interior is often open the first Saturday or Sunday each month.

THE BEST NON-DESIGNER SHOPPING

Cheese Store: Featured in one of the final episodes of *Curb Your Enthusiasm;* has a section for 'Larry David's cheese.' *cheesestore.com*

Edelweiss Chocolates: Old-school shop; that woman buying chocolates looks like the one who played Mom on a classic sitcom. *edelweiss chocolates.com*

Pleasure Chest: The perfect boutique to accessorize your soiree in WeHo. Most tastes are catered for in this adult novelty store. *thepleasure chest.com*

Book Soup: Great indie bookstore with thoughtful staff recs. The source for eclectic, edgy and LA-based fiction. *booksoup.com*

Mystery Pier Books: Signed scripts from blockbusters and rare 1st editions. Curated selection of mystery and detective fiction. *mysterypierbooks.com*

EATING IN BEVERLY HILLS: TOP CHOICES

Spago: Wolfgang Puck's heart remains where his empire started and most evenings he still turns up. The smoked salmon pizza is an icon. *5.30-9.30pm* **$$$**

Sugarfish: Quality sushi in a small space; always packed with talent agents and local residents. The 20-course tasting menu is pure pleasure. *11.30am-10pm* **$$$**

Nate'n Al's: Get a bowl of piping-hot matzo-ball soup and a Brentwood sandwich at this Beverly Hills institution, which shines after a refresh. *8am-9pm* **$$**

Wally's Beverly Hills: Wine bar and restaurant with outdoor seating and a huge choice of wine, mescal and champagne. Cheese platters too. *10am-12.30am* **$$**

GETTY CENTER TIPS

- Book a timed entry reservation in advance. Parking is $25 ($15 after 3pm); a space is reserved for all reservation holders.
- Visit early morning or mid-afternoon. Sunsets create a remarkable alchemy of light and shadow. Saturday nights are usually less crowded.
- Get the essential GettyGuide app. Free audioguides are available in the lobby. Bring a photo ID.
- There's a modern American restaurant and two casual cafes. The food is fine, but consider bringing a picnic lunch to enjoy on the beautiful grounds.
- The 16,000 tons of travertine cladding the Getty came from the same Italian quarry used for Rome's ancient Colosseum. Look closely to spot fossilized shells, fish and foliage.
- Tours and special events are invariably worth the time.

WALTER CICCHETTI/SHUTTERSTOCK

Getty Center

Treasures on a Hill

Experience the Getty Center

Straddling a hilltop in the Santa Monica Mountains off the 405, the palatial **Getty Center** *(getty.edu; entry free)* offers an irresistible feast of art, design and botanical beauty. Ponder the myths and landscapes of Dossi, Van Gogh and Cézanne, gaze out over the City of Angels and kick back in a verdant wonderland of gurgling water, lush lawns and world-famous sculptures.

The Getty's collections focus on European art, with a concentration on works from the 19th and 20th centuries. There are genuine treasures here. In the east pavilion, seek out Gentileschi's *Danaë and the Shower of Gold* and Rembrandt's self-portrait, *Rembrandt Laughing*. In the west pavilion, look for Van Gogh's *Irises*, Monet's *Wheatstacks, Snow Effect, Morning*, Manet's *Jeanne (Spring)* and Turner's *Modern Rome – Campo Vaccino*. The south pavilion's outdoor terrace is home to Marino Marini's excitable bronze *Angel of the Citadel*, while the grounds themselves are studded with prized sculptures, including three works by Henry Moore.

On Saturday evenings in summer, the center hosts **Off the 405**, a popular series featuring top progressive pop and world-music acts in the Getty courtyard.

Santa Monica & Malibu

SUNSETS, FUN PIERS, BEACHES, SURFING AND LIFESTYLE

Santa Monica is LA's little sister: its smaller, beachier twin, with glass towers abutting the famous pier and amusement park. Surrounded by the city on three sides and the Pacific on the fourth, here boarders bob in the waves, laid-back dudes sip hazy brews next to martini-swilling Hollywood producers and celebrity chefs rub elbows with on-point soccer moms at bountiful farmers markets.

With the Pacific as the canvas, the vermilion spectacle at sunset extends along the Pacific Coast Hwy (PCH) to Malibu, the fabled beach town. Although the entire region is working hard to recover from the devastating 2025 Palisades wildfires, there is much to engage the visitor. Unmissable sights like the Getty Villa and the Malibu Pier still amaze and delight. And the near-endless ribbon of beaches are as welcoming as ever with famous names like Zuma ready to allow any comer to join in the Southern California dream.

TOP TIP

Tour LA's world-famous beaches by riding the 22-mile-long **Marvin Braude Bike Trail**. The paved coastal path starts at Will Rogers Beach in Santa Monica and passes through Venice, Hermosa and Redondo Beaches before ending at Torrance Beach. Rent a cruiser or an e-bike from **Joyride** *(joyridesantamonica.com; all-day rentals from $30).*

Go for a Ride

The unmissable Santa Monica Pier

No visit to LA is complete without a stroll on historic **Santa Monica Pier** *(santamonicapier.org; free)* that features on just about every LA tourist ad. Stretching almost a quarter-mile

GETTING AROUND

Santa Monica is well-served by the Metro Rail E Line, which goes right downtown and provides easy links to LAX and beyond. Going north, transit options dwindle quickly to one Metro bus line, the 134 along the Pacific Coast Hwy to Malibu. There's a stop for the Getty Villa. Topanga Canyon has no service.

Beachside parking fees add up quickly along the coast. For Santa Monica, take the train. Santa Monica is also enjoyably walkable, especially on the bluff overlooking the beaches, which seamlessly flow right into Venice. Malibu sprawls, with no real center to walk.

SANTA MONICA & MALIBU

HIGHLIGHTS
1 Getty Villa
2 Santa Monica Pier

SIGHTS
3 Bergamot Station Arts Center
4 El Matador State Beach
5 Getty Center
6 Malibu Lagoon State Beach
7 Malibu Pier
8 Santa Monica State Beach
9 Topanga Canyon
10 Will Rogers State Beach
11 Zuma Beach

SLEEPING
12 Georgian Hotel
13 HI Los Angeles Santa Monica Hostel
14 M Malibu
15 Malibu Beach Inn
16 Sea Shore Motel
17 Shutters on the Beach

EATING
18 Bay Cities Italian Deli & Bakery
19 Cafe on 27
20 Duke's Malibu
see 7 Malibu Farm Restaurant
see 15 Nobu Malibu
21 Paradise Cove
22 Santa Monica Farmers Markets
23 Sunny Blue

DRINKING & NIGHTLIFE
24 Divine Vintage

ENTERTAINMENT
25 Pacific Park

TRANSPORTATION
26 Joyride
27 Marvin Braude Bike Trail

over the Pacific, it's the exclamation point on iconic Route 66, which began 2400 miles east in Chicago.

Dating to 1908, the pier is the city's most compelling landmark. Every angle is dominated by the **Pacific Park** *(pacpark.com; rides from $8)* amusement park and its family-friendly arcades, carnival games, soaring **Ferris wheel** and tame roller coaster. Nearby is a vintage 1922 carousel and an aquarium. The pier is most photogenic when framed by California sunsets and when it comes alive with free concerts and outdoor movies in the summertime.

BEST BEACHES: SANTA MONICA TO MALIBU

El Matador State Beach: Park on the bluffs and stroll down to sandstone rock towers rising from emerald coves.

Zuma Beach: Easily accessed from the PCH (and Metro bus), with parking and long stretches of sand. Find privacy at Pirate's Cove.

Malibu Lagoon State Beach: Where Malibu Creek meets the ocean, migratory birds proliferate, attracting human spotters. To the north are popular surf breaks.

Will Rogers State Beach: The quiet alternative to the famous strands to the south. This was the beach used for *Baywatch*.

Santa Monica State Beach: There are endless ways to enjoy this 3.5-mile stretch of sand, running seamlessly into Venice Beach (p125) in the south.

Year-Round Creative Festival

Discover the Bergamot Station Arts Center

A former trolley yard, **Bergamot Station Arts Center** *(bergamotstation.com)*, has been converted to one of LA's best arts centers. More than 20 private galleries show the works of well-regarded (and often famous) artists and photographers. The free exhibitions are always changing, so just wander around to see what's on. The Metro E Line stops right outside.

Ancient Treasures by the Sea

Visit the extraordinary Getty Villa

Located just north of Santa Monica in Pacific Palisades is the remarkable **Getty Villa** *(getty.edu; entry free)*. This stunning place was built in 1974 when billionaire J Paul Getty decided to recreate Herculaneum's Villa dei Papiri, a Roman villa that was buried in the eruption of Mt Vesuvius in 79 CE. The focus here is on the art and cultures of ancient Greece, Rome and Etruria and there's also a vast collection of classical and Renaissance-era artworks on display. Corinthian columns surround perfectly manicured gardens and an elongated pool. Don't miss the Pompeii fountain and Temple of Herakles.

An advance, timed ticket is required; parking costs $25 ($15 after 3pm). Note: the **Getty Center** (p118) is one of LA's premier cultural highlights. The parking fee can be used at both institutions on the same day.

Back to a Beautiful Past

Drive Topanga Canyon

The sinuous 12 miles of Hwy 27 that cut north through **Topanga Canyon** from the namesake beach to Woodland Hills in the San Fernando Valley are a scenic time warp. The road

EATING & DRINKING IN SANTA MONICA: OUR PICKS

Bay Cities Italian Deli & Bakery: Best Italian deli in LA, period. Signature sandwich is the spicy Godmother (piled with Italian meats). *9am-6pm Wed-Sun* **$**

Sunny Blue: *Omusubi* (rice balls, aka *onigiri*) made to order from dozens of filling choices, from seaweed to salmon. One of the best waterfront options. *11am-8pm* **$$**

Santa Monica Farmers Markets: You haven't really experienced Santa Monica until you've explored one of its outdoor farmers markets. *8am-1pm Wed & Sat* **$**

Divine Vintage: Charming wine bar in a cute cottage. Most choices are organic. Nearby is Father's Office, a welcoming gastropub. *noon-8pm* **$$**

THE 2025 PALISADES FIRE

On January 7, 2025, a small brush fire near Pacific Palisades, fueled by drought and high winds, erupted into a raging inferno. Before the end of the month, the fire had burned nearly 23,500 acres, destroyed over 6800 structures and killed at least 12 people. Much of the affluent community of Pacific Palisades and parts of Malibu were destroyed. The flames reached the beaches and entire swaths of the famous cheek-to-jowl oceanfront homes along the Pacific Coast Hwy (Hwy 1) burned. In the aftermath of LA's worst wildfire to date, the region struggled with recovery. The cleanup lasted for months and many beloved businesses that weren't destroyed went bankrupt during the months the PCH was closed.

CHIZHEVSKAYA EKATERINA/SHUTTERSTOCK

Malibu Pier

first passes through a primordial cleft cut deep in the Santa Monica Mountains before reaching heights that afford sweeping views of the valley.

The road is shadowed by lazy oaks and glimmering sycamores and the whole thing smells of wind-blown black sage and 'cowboy cologne' (artemisia). Along the way, you'll pass vendors selling new-agey wares and signs depicting pigs with wings.

About halfway to the pass, the cute country town of **Topanga** sprouts on both sides of the road. A bit further on, popular **Cafe on 27** has tables in the trees. The cafe is open from 9am to 5pm.

Gangway to the Pacific

Stroll Malibu's great little pier

Besides the extraordinary beaches, Malibu's one real highlight is its namesake wooden **pier**, which traces its history to 1905. Strolling its 700ft length is a delight and there is a good restaurant, **Malibu Farm** at the base. Some of the best views of the Malibu coast are from the pier, as the wall-to-wall beach houses (even after the 2025 fires destroyed so many) cut off views from the Pacific Coast Hwy.

EATING & DRINKING WITH A VIEW IN MALIBU

Malibu Farm Restaurant: Dining rooms at Malibu Pier are a perfect place to munch on farm-to-table brunches, lunches and snacks. *9am-7pm* $$

Duke's Malibu: A beachfront legend known to employ minor Malibu celebs. The cocktail-seafood-steak menu is a crowd-pleaser. *11.30am-9pm* $$

Paradise Cove: Famous semi-private beach with expensive parking controlled by this cafe. Have lunch on the sand to avoid high fees. *8am-9pm* $$

Nobu Malibu: Chef Nobu Matsuhisa's empire of luxe Japanese restaurants includes this celeb-favored hotspot where tables overlook the sea. *noon-10pm* $$$

Venice & South Coast Beaches

BOHEMIAN BOARDWALKS, CANALS, STREET ART AND THE BEACH

For many, Venice Beach is synonymous with the Boardwalk. It embodies a clichéd California vibe that mixes carefree beach life, post-hippie weirdness and general funkitude. And that's all true, but Venice is much more. It's about good food and drink, good shopping and adapting hip trends to your own good life. You'll discover that the name isn't random as there really are canals and, in their own way, they embody all of Venice's qualities.

Heading south, you pass through the string of South Bay beach towns for which LA is also famous. The long sandy swath never ends as you pass through one volleyball-and-bacchanalia haven after another.

Manhattan Beach has so much to offer that it's hard to leave. Hermosa Beach and Redondo Beach add their own unique charms. At the south end, the Palos Verdes Peninsula crowns the coastline as it angles from south to east.

TOP TIP

Get gear for the boardwalk, the coastal Marvin Braude Bike Trail and getting around town at **Venice Boardwalk Bike Rental** *(veniceboardwalkbikerental.com)*. It rents all types of bikes, skateboards and in-line skates.

Living Life on the Sand

Venice's beach and boardwalk

Prepare for a sensory overload on the **Venice Boardwalk**, one of LA's essential experiences. Buff bodybuilders brush elbows with street performers and sellers of sunglasses, ribald

GETTING AROUND

The Metro Rail E Line to Downtown Santa Monica is a nice beach stroll 1.5 miles north of Venice. Otherwise, take Metro Bus Line 33 and Santa Monica's Big Blue Bus Lines 1, 3 and 18 from the station south into Venice. The South Bay beach towns all have minimal bus service and are best reached by car, which also allows you to bounce from one town to the next along the PCH.

Venice is wonderfully walkable and that's one of the prime reasons for coming. Use the 22-mile-long Marvin Braude Bike Trail to cycle the entire coast.

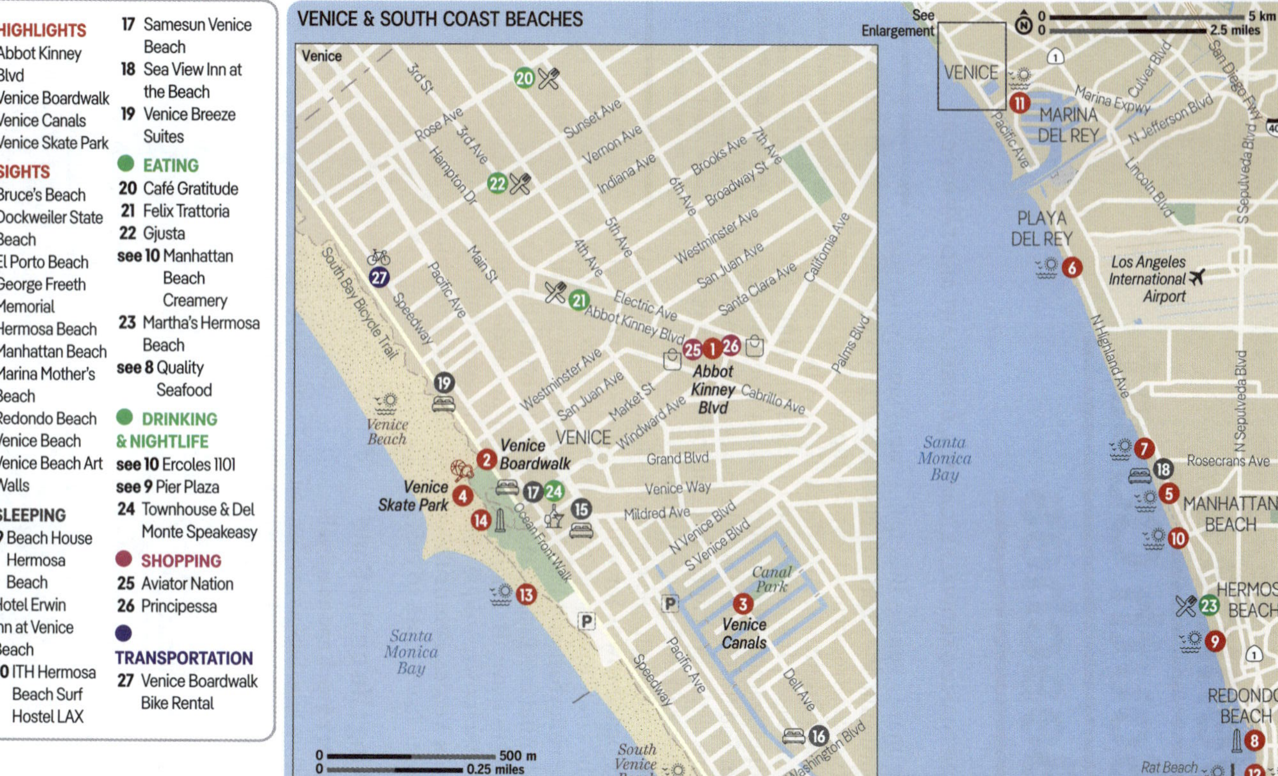

HIGHLIGHTS
1 Abbot Kinney Blvd
2 Venice Boardwalk
3 Venice Canals
4 Venice Skate Park

SIGHTS
5 Bruce's Beach
6 Dockweiler State Beach
7 El Porto Beach
8 George Freeth Memorial
9 Hermosa Beach
10 Manhattan Beach
11 Marina Mother's Beach
12 Redondo Beach
13 Venice Beach
14 Venice Beach Art Walls

SLEEPING
see 9 Beach House Hermosa Beach
15 Hotel Erwin
16 Inn at Venice Beach
see 10 ITH Hermosa Beach Surf Hostel LAX
17 Samesun Venice Beach
18 Sea View Inn at the Beach
19 Venice Breeze Suites

EATING
20 Café Gratitude
21 Felix Trattoria
22 Gjusta
see 10 Manhattan Beach Creamery
23 Martha's Hermosa Beach
see 8 Quality Seafood

DRINKING & NIGHTLIFE
see 10 Ercoles 1101
see 9 Pier Plaza
24 Townhouse & Del Monte Speakeasy

SHOPPING
25 Aviator Nation
26 Principessa

TRANSPORTATION
27 Venice Boardwalk Bike Rental

underwear, Mexican ponchos and cannabis, while cyclists and in-line skaters whiz by on the bike path and skateboarders and graffiti sprayers get their own domains.

Venice Beach has long been associated with street art. Proof are the tagged-up towers and the freestanding concrete wall of the **Venice Beach Art Walls** *(veniceartwalls.com)* that have been covered by graffiti painters from 1961 to the present.

Gym rats with an exhibitionist streak can get a tan and a workout at this famous **outdoor gym** right on the Venice Boardwalk, where Arnold Schwarzenegger and Franco Columbu once bulked up. Nearby **volleyball nets** and **basketball courts** also get a workout.

When Angelenos drained their swimming pools during a 1970s drought, board-toting teens made their not-quite-welcome invasion and modern skateboarding culture was born. Today, the public 17,000-sq-ft ocean-view **skate park** is a destination for both high flyers and gawking spectators. There are regular competitions.

Venice's Characterful Shopping Strip

Browse Abbot Kinney Blvd

Abbot Kinney Boulevard between Venice Blvd and Main St is full of upscale boutiques (both indie and chain), galleries, lofts and cafes and restaurants. Many shops are housed in reconstructed old wooden beach shacks. Favored shops include **Aviator Nation** *(aviatornation.com)* and **Principessa** *(principessavenice.com)*. The parallel stretch of Lincoln Blvd four blocks north is also good shopping territory.

Home of Beach Volleyball

Surf and sand at Manhattan Beach

A bastion of surf music and the birthplace of beach volleyball, **Manhattan Beach** may have gone chic, but that salty-dog heart still beats. Downtown's trendy restaurants and boutiques still mix with dive bars.

Ditch the shoes on the wide sweep of golden sand at the **beach**. You'll find pick-up **volleyball courts**, a **pier** with sweeping sea views and a consistent sandy bottom. The volleyball nets start here and run right through Hermosa Beach.

Founded in 1912, **Bruce's Beach** was a popular private African American beach. Driven by racism, the town of Manhattan Beach seized the beach from the Bruce family in 1924. In 2022, LA County returned the area bounded by Highland

VENICE CANALS

The **Venice Canals** are uniquely embedded in the heart of a now desirable residential area. The picturesque canals were created in 1905 by developer and conservationist Abbot Kinney, who wanted to replicate Italy's famed waterways, dubbing the area the 'Venice of America.'

What was once an expansive place of bridges and canals has shrunk in size, with only six canals remaining, comprising a length of 3 miles. Having become decrepit after WWII, the canals have reclaimed their beauty and charm, especially with the architecturally diverse homes that line the canalside paths.

A popular film and TV location, the canals' apex may have been toward the end of *Touch of Evil* (1958) when a dissolute Orson Wells dies, flopping around in the then-polluted waters.

BEST PLACES TO EAT & DRINK IN VENICE

Felix Trattoria: People flock here for maestro chef Evan Funke's *rigatoni all'amatriciana* and other artfully invented new forms of pasta. *5-9.30pm* $$$

Café Gratitude: Cutting-edge vegan dishes are paired with an open patio and fresh sea breezes. Sustainable, locavore and always surprising. *10am-9pm* $$

Gjusta: A *very* local bakery, cafe and deli behind a nondescript storefront on a hidden side street. Great patio. Food to go is ideal for picnics. *7am-4pm* $$

Townhouse & Del Monte Speakeasy: Upstairs: a cool, dark bar with a history dating to 1915. Downstairs: a speakeasy with DJs and bands. *5pm-2am* $

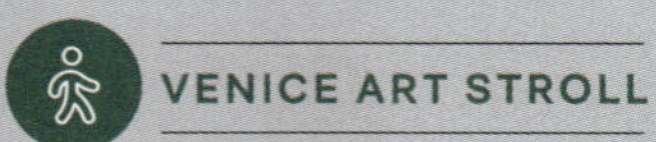

VENICE ART STROLL

Step into the Venice lifestyle and see the art that helps give the area its idiosyncratic vibe.

START	END	LENGTH
Venice Pier	Venice Ale House	2¼ miles; 2hr

Start at 1 **Venice Pier**. Here nature's golden sands unfurl and the blue sea churns. Walk inland to the 2 **Venice Canals** (p125). This idyllic neighborhood preserves 3 miles of waterways lined with a warren of cool waterside houses with cute little gardens, many featuring outdoor sculptures. Take time to wander at will. Exit the enclave and turn left on S Venice Blvd.

Pause at 3 **LA Louver**, a modern and contemporary art gallery featuring rotating, museum-quality exhibitions. Now, it's time for the main event, the 4 **Venice Boardwalk** (p123), where free expression is de rigueur. Look for Rip Cronk's epic 30ft-tall 5 **Jim Morrison Mural** on your right. Then see the Cronks of tomorrow in action at 6 **Venice Beach Art Walls** (p125), a vortex for the loony, the free-spirited and the hip. Head away from the sand briefly on Windward Ave until you see 7 **Venice Reconstituted**, a Cronk ode to Botticelli's *Birth of Venus*.

Back on the boardwalk, stop into 8 **Small World Books** and its artfully curated stock. Continuing north, nose around the 9 **narrow lanes** just off the walk between Wavecrest Ave and Brooks Ave; the area is rich with ever-changing murals. Finish at the 10 **Venice Ale House**, which has boardwalk seating.

In 1965, Jim Morrison was crashing at his friend Ray Manzarek's Venice apartment, where they plotted to start **The Doors**.

Since 1994, **LA Louver** – one of LA's top galleries – has been housed in a landmark building designed by Frederick Fisher.

The **Venice Art Walls** are part of a public foundation that maintains them. Permits are free; apply online.

JW_PNW/SHUTTERSTOCK

Hermosa Beach Pier Plaza

Ave and 27th St to the family, who then sold it back to the county so it can continue to serve as the popular public park it is today. Markers recall the saga.

Fun Day & Night

Party in Hermosa Beach

Strolling down **Hermosa Beach Pier Plaza** on a summer weekend, you'll notice everyone's wearing flip-flops, tiny tees and a tan and they all seem to be having way too much fun. The short, car-free strip is the South Bay's party central. Out on the **sand**, watch for international volleyball contests throughout the year.

Sandy Joy for Everyone

Diverse Redondo Beach

Redondo Beach is the most economically and ethnically diverse beach town and the largest in the South Bay. King Harbor interrupts the sweep of sand and is the place to find info about excursions on the bay. To the south, the **Palos Verdes Peninsula** is wealthy and notorious for having a land-slip problem that is causing an enormous portion of it to slowly erode into the ocean.

BEST BEACHES OF THE SOUTH BAY

Marina Mother's Beach: Childminders love it: a wave-free, half-crescent of sand that's safe for the tiniest of tots.

Dockweiler State Beach: Almost 4 miles of sand in the shadow of departing LAX jets. Backed by dunes, it's a rare beach with fire rings.

El Porto Beach: At the north end of Manhattan Beach, this is a good patch of sand for surf lessons, or renting a lounger and doing nothing.

Redondo Beach: Surfing was brought here from Hawai'i by George Freeth in 1907. Look for his memorial on the pier.

Rat Beach: Standing for Right-After-Torrance, this beautiful sandy patch (aka Malaga Cove) is right against the start of the Palos Verdes Peninsula.

EATING & DRINKING IN THE SOUTH BAY: OUR PICKS

Manhattan Beach Creamery: Housemade ice creams served in cones or pressed between two cookies for a 'Cream'wich.' Worth the line. *10am-9pm* $

Ercoles 1101: In Manhattan Beach; dark, neon-lit and cozy. Beloved by everyone from salty barflies to yuppie pub crawlers to volleyball stars since 1927. *10am-2am*

Martha's Hermosa Beach: The first stop before a day on the sand. Residents swear by the omelets at this beachside patio joint. *7am-3pm* $

Quality Seafood: Big seafood market on the Redondo pier, since 1953. Choose from a huge selection and they'll cook it your way. *10.30am-8pm* $$

Burbank & Universal City

STUDIOS, THEME PARK AND CULTURE

Angelenos from the other side of the Hollywood Hills think of two things first when it comes to 'the Valley': major studios and urban sprawl. One, they think, is worth visiting. The other, not so much.

Snootiness aside, the Valley (principally the communities of Sherman Oaks, Studio City, Universal City, North Hollywood, Burbank and Glendale) does sprawl. It's the place where car culture was invented, along with the mini-mall, drive-in movie theater, drive-in bank and drive-in restaurant.

But look closer and you'll see there's a lot of there's a lot of the real here. This is where the real folk live, making it more laid-back and down-to-earth than other areas in the city. There's plenty of culture, to the extent that North Hollywood has its own moniker, 'NoHo,' and its own arts district. One of the studios offers an excellent tour, while the other comprises a major theme park.

TOP TIP

California's microclimates are on full display in summer when moderating ocean breezes can't penetrate the valley. On sunny days, temps can be 20°F (11°C) higher – and pollution levels worse – than on the Downtown and Hollywood side of the Hollywood Hills.

GETTING AROUND

Take the Metro B Line from Downtown LA and Hollywood to the Universal City/Studio City and the North Hollywood Stations. The former has shuttle buses up the steep hill to the Universal Studios theme park.

Much of the San Fernando Valley is flat, but it defines suburbia and is so spread out that there are few areas that are worth walking. When Dionne Warwick sang 'LA is a great big freeway...,' she could have been describing the Valley.

Harry Potter, Mario & Bart

Thrill to Universal Studios Hollywood

Although Universal is one of the world's oldest continuously operating movie studios (since 1912), it's best known for the theme park in and around the studio's backlot. Despite the ebbs and flows of showbiz, the park has remained a draw for generations of visitors and residents alike, thanks to an entertaining, ever-changing mix of thrill rides, live-action shows and a tram tour.

The theme park is officially known as **Universal Studios Hollywood** *(universalstudioshollywood.com)* to differentiate it from the other parks around the globe – many of which are much larger, if you're an aficionado. Here, the most popular ride is the **Flight of the Hippogriff** roller coaster and the 3-D **Harry Potter and the Forbidden Journey**. Buy wizarding equipment and 'every-flavour' beans in the fantasy-themed shops, then quaff mugs of butterbeer at **Three Broomsticks** restaurant.

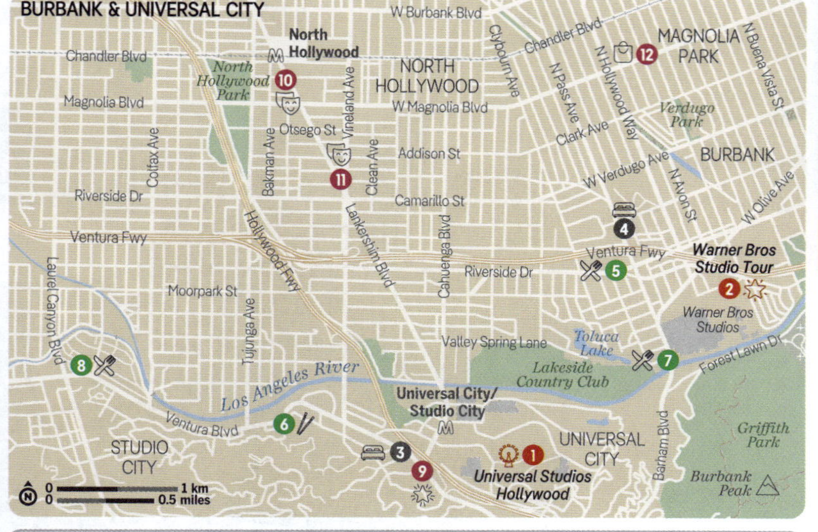

HIGHLIGHTS
1 Universal Studios Hollywood
2 Warner Bros Studio Tour

SLEEPING
3 BLVD Hotel & Studios
4 Hotel Amarano Burbank-Hollywood

EATING
5 Bob's Big Boy
6 Daichan
7 Smoke House
8 Tuning Fork LA

ENTERTAINMENT
9 Baked Potato
10 El Portal
11 Zombie Joe's Underground Theatre

SHOPPING
12 It's a Wrap!

Over in **Super Nintendo World**, the big ride is **Mario Kart: Bowser's Challenge**, which uses virtual reality to put riders inside the game. Elsewhere, the **Jurassic World** ride is a float back to dinosaur days before a tumble through a land of raptors and T rexes. A ride based on **The Simpsons** goes rocketing along through Springfield. While in this area, stop off for the top-notch doughnuts at **Lard Lad** (get the Big Pink).

The theme park also includes the original **tram tour of the studio backlot**, although over the years this has morphed into more of a theme-park ride than an actual behind-the-scenes tour.

Flashing video screens, oversized facades and garish color combos (think *Blade Runner* meets *Willy Wonka*) animate **Universal CityWalk**, the outdoor shopping concourse adjacent to Universal Studios. Under the glitz, CityWalk's shops and restaurants will be mostly familiar to anyone who has visited a US suburban mall, although the **Hello Kitty and Friends Cafe** is a hit.

Tour It Again, Sam

Thrill to the Warner Bros Studio Tour

The **Warner Bros Studio Tour** *(wbstudiotour.com; tours adult/child from $76/65)* offers a fun, mostly authentic look behind the scenes of a major movie studio. Much of the lot dates

TIPS FOR UNIVERSAL STUDIOS HOLLYWOOD

Universal Studios Hollywood uses demand pricing, which varies significantly throughout the year. At non-peak times, one-day admission is adult/child $109/103. At peak times, such as school holidays, it's adult/child $154/148. Buy tickets online for possible savings and watch for two-for-one offers, which give you free admission on a second non-consecutive day. Once the park reaches capacity, the ticket booths will close. You can cut the often long lines for rides at busy times by purchasing an Express Pass one-day admission for a significant premium: $329 at peak periods.

Parking costs $35 to $75. The Metro Rail B Line to Universal City/Studio City and the free shuttle combo is efficient and traffic-free.

back to 1926 and large parts of it feel surprisingly unchanged since the days when Jack Warner was cutting deals and trying to steal credit from his brothers.

The two-hour standard tour kicks off with a video of WB's greatest hits (*Rebel Without a Cause,* many versions of *Batman*), before a tram whisks you around 110 acres of sound stages, legacy sets for TV shows like *Friends* and the *Big Bang Theory* and technical departments, including props, costumes and a collection of Batmobiles. It's awe-inspiring as you encounter the places where legendary films like *The Big Sleep, Blade Runner* and *La La Land* were shot.

Tour variations include our favorite, the **TCM Classic Films Tour** *(adult/child $99/85),* which focuses on the studio's history and the production of films like *Casablanca.* The six-hour **Deluxe Tour** *($330)* includes an in-depth guided tour and lunch.

Nightlife in the Valley

NoHo is where you want to be

The **NoHo** (aka North Hollywood) **Arts District** along Lankershim Blvd is sprinkled with theaters and venues known for their edgy live theater, music and comedy.

Dating to 1926, **El Portal** *(elportaltheatre.com)* is a three-stage mainstay of the district with top-name acts. **Zombie Joe's Underground Theatre** *(zombiejoes.com)* is part theater, part haunted house. Shows are at turns creepy, campy, deranged and critically lauded.

ATTILA ADAM/SHUTTERSTOCK

NoHo Arts District

A bit south, **Baked Potato** *(thebakedpotato.com)* is an intimate jazz-and-blues hall – LA's oldest – where the schedule mixes no-names with big-timers.

Dress Like a Star

Browse wardrobes at It's a Wrap!

Industry legend **It's a Wrap!** *(itsawraphollywood.com)* is the outlet used to unload on-screen wardrobes and props. Besides the cachet, you get great prices on designer labels. Items are racked by show affiliation. Near Halloween, there are displays of authentic costumes from productions.

GUIDE TO STUDIO TOURS

Four of the five surviving major studios in LA offer public tours. Some are better than others.

Paramount Pictures: Unfussy tours of the historic Hollywood lot, which is pretty quiet these days.

Sony Pictures: Once the MGM Studios, but not an overwhelming sense of history with all the intellectual rights musical chairs.

Universal Studios: Turned its tours into a theme park in the 1970s. The 'backlot' really isn't, but it's a spectacle.

Warner Bros: Fascinating tours of a busy studio with palpable history all around.

Walt Disney Studios: In Burbank, it now includes 20th Century Studios. It only rarely gives tours.

EATING IN BURBANK & THE VALLEY: TOP CHOICES

Bob's Big Boy: Famous survivor of a once-ubiquitous chain of diners renowned for a winsome mascot plus a burger that's like a Big Mac. *6am-midnight* $

Daichan: Ventura Blvd's Sushi Row in Studio City is a hub of top choices, including this affordable Japanese diner. *11.30am-2.30pm & 5.30-8.30pm Mon-Sat* $$

Tuning Fork LA: Has a music industry vibe; staff spin tunes most nights. Casual bistro defines the California cuisine ethos: fresh, simple and creative. *5-9.30pm* $$

Smoke House: Located just outside Warner Bros and serving luminaries since 1948. George Clooney allegedly started his production company here. *11.30am-10pm* $$

Pasadena

GENTEEL, ART, CULTURED AND PLEASANT

TOP TIP

Old Pasadena is a 20-block downtown shopping and entertainment district of historic brick buildings south and east of Walnut St and Pasadena Ave. It mixes national chains with local businesses. In the 1950s, Route 66 came from the east on Colorado Blvd before turning south on Arroyo Pkwy.

GETTING AROUND

The Metro Rail A Line serves Pasadena and connects it to Downtown LA. Stations are on the west and north edges of downtown. Metro bus line 662 serves the Rose Bowl. The Huntington is not near transit; you'll need a rideshare from a transit stop.

Downtown Pasadena is pleasantly walkable and mostly level, though some distances, such as to the Rose Bowl (2.5 miles), are long.

You'll find a lot of things in Pasadena: a community with a button-down soul, a historical perspective, an appreciation for art and jazz, an old-school conservative undercurrent and a reverence for tradition. Its Rose Bowl college football game has been played annually since 1916, the namesake stadium dates to 1923 and the Rose Parade that perfumes the streets before the game began in 1890.

Pasadena's genteel streets are the home of old money, some of it from fortunes made in California, which funded two extraordinary local museums. Some of it came from fortunes made elsewhere and were brought here for the warmer climes (you'll find old mansions with names like Wrigley and Gamble).

On clear days, the San Gabriel Mountains to the north are a stunning backdrop, although they also hold peril. In January 2025, the Eaton fire began in the hills and went on to destroy the vibrant community of Altadena and threaten Pasadena.

A Wealth of Beauty

Be awe-struck by the Huntington

One of the most delightful, inspirational spots in LA is the century-old **Huntington** *(huntington.org; adult/child $29/13).* It is rightly a highlight of any trip to California, thanks to a world-class mix of art, literary history and over 120 acres of themed gardens (any one of which would be worth a visit on its own), all set amid stately grounds. There's so much to see and do that it's hard to know where to begin; allow three to four hours for a basic visit.

Start at the **Orientation Gallery**, where you can try to prioritize your visit. Pick up the laughably misnamed 'I have an hour tour' guide, which takes at least two hours.

The **library** could be next. Only a fraction of the six million rare books are on display at any one time, but the highlights are impressive: a Gutenberg Bible, a manuscript of *The Canterbury Tales* by Geoffrey Chaucer, plus books by Marco Polo and Christopher Columbus.

HIGHLIGHTS
1 Huntington

SIGHTS
2 Norton Simon Museum

SLEEPING
3 Langham Huntington Pasadena
4 Saga Motor Hotel

EATING
5 Artisanal Goods by CAR
6 Bistro 45
7 Fair Oaks Pharmacy

DRINKING & NIGHTLIFE
8 The 1894

ENTERTAINMENT
9 Pasadena Playhouse

SHOPPING
10 Gold Bug
11 Homage
see 10 Lather
see 10 Neo 39
see 8 Vroman's Bookstore

In the **galleries** of European and American art, you can lose yourself in the brushstrokes of Thomas Gainsborough's *The Blue Boy* and Thomas Lawrence's *Pinkie*. Other artists here include Mary Cassatt, Edward Hopper, Andy Warhol and Frank Stella.

Note the dour portraits of the patrons Henry and Arabella Huntington. They partly made their immense fortune by owning the 'Red Cars,' the trolley system that stitched the LA region together 100 years ago (and which is now being partly reconstituted for untold billions).

The extensive **gardens** – about a dozen – are as meticulously curated as the museums themselves. Don't miss the roses, the Chinese Garden, the Japanese Garden and the lush Jungle Garden.

Reserve your visit in advance at busy times.

Pasadena's Treasure

Savor the Norton Simon Museum

Rodin's *The Burghers of Calais* and *The Thinker* near the entrance are only an overture to the full symphony of art in store at the exquisite **Norton Simon Museum** *(nortonsimon.org; adult/child $20/free)*. Norton Simon (1907–93) was an

PASADENA'S BEST SHOPPING

Gold Bug: An amazing boutique with a steampunk vibe, Gold Bug shows work created by over 100 area artists. *goldbugpasadena.com*

Lather: Pasadena-based body-care showcases natural hand creams, exfoliants and other treatments at its flagship store. *lather.com*

Neo 39: In the Old Town Pasadena shopping district, this sneaker depot stocks the rare, the imported and the stylish. *neo39.com*

Vroman's Bookstore: Since 1894, Vroman's claims to be the largest and oldest bookstore in SoCal. Regular events. *vromansbookstore.com*

Homage: A Pasadena treasure with a selection of gifts, stationery, jewelry, accessories and more that includes many local items. *homagepasadena.com*

entrepreneur with a passion for art who parlayed his fortune into a remarkable collection.

The galleries teem with choice works by Renaissance and impressionist artists, including Rembrandt (eg *Self-Portrait*), Renoir *(Young Woman in Black),* Canaletto *(Piazzetta in Venice Looking North)* and Van Gogh, as well as an outstanding array of works by Degas. Twentieth-century masterpieces span Picasso and LA's own Sam Francis.

Asian sculpture – principally Buddhist and Hindu imagery in stone, bronze and copper – is another highpoint. The outdoor **sculpture garden** inspired by Monet's home in Giverny, France, is superb. A massive revamp of the museum's external grounds began in 2025.

EATING & DRINKING IN PASADENA: TOP CHOICES

Artisanal Goods by CAR: The best $6 chocolate croissant you'll ever eat. The cafe does other treats too, as well as coffee. *8.30am-5pm Tue-Sun* $

Fair Oaks Pharmacy: Nostalgic 1915 ice cream fountain where 'soda jerks' dish out 'phosphates' (flavored syrup and soda water) and malts. *9am-5pm Mon-Sat* $

Bistro 45: Sample fine California cuisine in an art deco–inspired dining room. Elegant yet not stiff, with the best local ingredients. Lovely patio. *5-8.30pm Tue-Sun* $$$

The 1894: Excellent wine bar adjoining Vroman's Bookstore, with literary-themed cocktails, microbrews and a quality selection of California wines. *3-9pm Wed-Sun* $$

ANGEL DIBILIO/SHUTTERSTOCK

Pasadena Playhouse

California's State Theater

Thrill to the Pasadena Playhouse

Fully deserving of the word legend, the **Pasadena Playhouse** *(pasadenaplayhouse.org)*, an attractive Spanish Colonial complex, was founded in 1917 and by 1937 had developed such a reputation that it was named the State Theater of California. It ran a lauded acting school in the 1930s and 1940s and has premiered hundreds of works. Grads include Dustin Hoffman, Gene Hackman and Leonard Nimoy. It won the Tony Award in 2023 for the best regional theater in the US.

Far Out

Visit other worlds at NASA's JPL

The world's premier space exploration agency, the **Jet Propulsion Laboratory** *(JPL; jpl.nasa.gov; free)*, has commanded robot explorers on Mars and interplanetary probes leaving our solar system from this campus on the north side of Pasadena.

The accomplishments of the scientists and engineers here, working in conjunction with CalTech and, at times, international space agencies, are extraordinary. And it's all done with cool professionalism and a lack of bombast or overhyped claims. Fascinating tours of the facility that birthed the Mars rovers and which is plotting the first ever return of Martian soil – among other feats – can be arranged at least three weeks in advance via the website.

HISTORY OF LA: PART 2

The opening of the LA aqueduct in 1913 turned the spigot on the region's growth. The bounty of water procured by dubious means (there's plenty of truth in the movie *Chinatown*) fueled fortunes like that of the Huntingtons in Pasadena.

During WWI, the Lockheed brothers and Donald Douglas established aircraft manufacturing plants in LA. Two decades later, aviation and then aerospace – helped along by billions of federal dollars for contracts first for WWII, then for the Cold War and then the space race – were among the industries that contributed to a real-estate boom and sparked suburban sprawl. And freeways and more freeways. And more...

Then there's the film biz, which took root in 1908 and gave LA and Hollywood their public persona.

Places We Love to Stay

$ Budget $$ Midrange $$$ Top End

Hollywood Map p79

Vibe Hotel Hollywood $ Blue-hued motel-style units come with a tiki-style outdoor lounge. Some have kitchens; Hollywood Blvd is out front.

Highland Gardens Hotel $ Famous landing spot for future celebs. Motel-style accommodations are only one block from the first star on the Walk of Fame.

Magic Castle Hotel $$ Solid hotel comes with an unmatched perk: access to the members-only Magic Castle private club where magicians ply their trade.

Hollywood Roosevelt $$ Hollywood lore lives large at its most famous hotel (tip: get a pool room). Celebrity stories abound.

Downtown Map p86

Biltmore Los Angeles $$ Grand old dame awash with history, grandeur and legend. The Academy Awards were founded in the Crystal Ballroom in 1927.

Kodō Hotel $$ A treasure in the Arts District. It blends Japanese and Western sensibilities in eight serene rooms.

Miyako Hotel Los Angeles $$ In the heart of Little Tokyo, right Downtown. Modern rooms with Japanese style have serene comfort and good transit connections.

Hotel Per La $$$ Vintage interiors and a rooftop pool in a restored Downtown palazzo that was once the grand digs of the Bank of Italy. Plush rooms.

Los Feliz & Silver Lake Map p95

Cara Hotel $$ Med-style in a small courtyard hotel on a quieter street with a convenient location between Los Feliz and Hollywood. Good, jazzy bar.

Silver Lake Pool & Inn $$$ Channeling Palm Springs, effortlessly hip, chilled and awash in SoCal light. The design credentials include locally produced art and bright rooms.

Exposition Park & South LA Map p101

Crestridge Inn $ Good, indie motel in Inglewood that's convenient to the SoFi Stadium area and LAX. Basic, budget-friendly rooms.

USC Hotel $$$ Wear your Trojan gear with pride at this luxe campus hotel in the shadow of Exposition Park. Rooms are comfortable.

Koreatown Map p106

Line Los Angeles $$ In the heart of Koreatown, this mid-century high-rise has exposed concrete walls and smallish rooms (some with sweeping views).

Hotel Normandie LA $$ Dating to 1926 when the neighborhood was awash in movie swells, the Normandie has vintage luxuries and a famous bar (p111).

Fairfax & Mid-City Map p106

Banana Bungalows Hotel and Hostel West Hollywood $ Budget digs in a primo location. Private rooms are a great deal, especially those with full kitchens.

Palihouse West Hollywood $$$ In the W 3rd St shopping district. Everything here is calming. Lovely pool area; some rooms are on the courtyard and offer watery serenity.

Culver City

Palihotel Culver City $$ What was a 1920s boarding house is now a fashionable boutique hotel. Art deco accents, smallish rooms and eclectic artwork.

Culver Hotel $$$ A 1924 heritage hotel with a tradition of serving MGM and the other Culver City studios. Renovated and luxurious.

West Hollywood Map p114

Andaz West Hollywood $$ Known as the Riot House in the '60s and '70s for the rock stars who partied hard and the hotel still has an industry vibe.

Mondrian Los Angeles $$$ Celeb-magnet landmark. The rooftop pool has the sweeping views you'd expect, and the cream-and-blue rooms welcome you home after a long day.

Sunset Tower Hotel $$$ A striking high-rise icon rich in showbiz history – it was once luxury apartments for the stars. Has a restaurant (p115) lauded for its martinis.

Chateau Marmont $$$ Where else? Looming over the Sunset Strip, storied hotel mixes Gothic details with a mishmash of French Loire Valley chateau inspiration.

Beverly Hills

Map p114

Crescent Hotel Beverly Hills $$ Basic hotel with limited service and smallish rooms, but it's an incredible value near Rodeo Dr. Part of the Sonder chain.

Beverly Wilshire $$$ Has corked Rodeo Dr since 1928. It exudes a formal elegance in the original Wilshire wing. Less of a laid-back LA vibe.

Beverly Hills Hotel $$$ The revered 'Pink Palace' packs more Hollywood lore than any other hotel in town. Slumber in an elegantly appointed hotel room or self-contained bungalow.

Hotel Bel-Air $$$ Tranquil, 12-acre Spanish Colonial estate that's a popular hideaway for royalty – Hollywood or otherwise.

Santa Monica

Map p120

HI Los Angeles Santa Monica Hostel $ Near the beach and promenade, these budget-friendly digs rival facilities at properties costing many times more. Single-sex dorms and private rooms.

Sea Shore Motel $$ Family-run lodgings at this comfy motel put you a Frisbee toss from the beach.

Shutters on the Beach $$$ A New England–style retreat in Santa Monica. Slink into a lounge chair on the ocean-view deck around the pool.

Georgian Hotel $$$ Across the street from Palisades Park and the Pacific beyond, the eye-catching 1933 art deco landmark has a snug ocean-view veranda.

Malibu

Map p120

M Malibu $$ Minimalist cool, the 2nd- and 3rd-floor rooms have views of the ocean across the street (which provides some noise).

Malibu Beach Inn $$$ Adult-oriented hacienda with coveted art and ocean views. Interiors make designers rave. First-floor rooms have decks.

Venice

Map p124

Samesun Venice Beach $ In a refurbished 1904 building with spectacular rooftop views of Venice Beach. Dorms, private rooms and a cool travelers' vibe.

Hotel Erwin $$ Unremarkable-seeming 1970s beachfront hotel offers fab place for sunset at the High Rooftop Lounge. Guests get bikes, coolers and volleyballs.

Inn at Venice Beach $$ Close to the beach, the Venice Canals, bars and restaurants. This mid-century-themed motel is comfortable and has a central courtyard.

Venice Breeze Suites $$$ Beachfront studios and suites right on the boardwalk. Good rates out of peak season. The Rooftop features big views and a communal barbecue area with sofas.

South Coast Beaches

Map p124

ITH Hermosa Beach Surf Hostel LAX $ In the heart of Hermosa Beach's party zone. The pier, the sand and the shots are all close by. Dorms and private rooms.

Sea View Inn at the Beach $$ Low-key motel with a variety of rooms spread over several buildings close to the sand in a low-key part of Manhattan Beach.

Beach House Hermosa Beach $$$ Upscale beachfront inn epitomizing California's laid-back lifestyle. Ocean-view suites let in the breezes. Located away from the frenetic center of Hermosa Beach.

Burbank & Universal City

Map p129

BLVD Hotel & Studios $$ A fun boutique property that's walking distance to Universal Studios. Large rooms and a heated indoor pool.

Hotel Amarano Burbank-Hollywood $$ Close to Warner Bros; rooms at this boutique hotel are inspired by movie sets.

Pasadena

Map p133

Saga Motor Hotel $ East of the center, this Route 66–era motel boasts a cool sign and comfortable rooms around a relaxing, palm-shaded pool.

Langham Huntington Pasadena $$$ Dating to 1906, this elegant 23-acre, palm-dappled, beaux-arts country estate has every luxury, from rambling gardens to a giant swimming pool.

Researched by
Julie Tremaine

Disneyland & Orange County

A QUINTESSENTIALLY CALIFORNIA EXPERIENCE

Laid-back and ultra-chic, Orange County shines with the magic of Disneyland and gem-like beaches.

Orange County is the most glamorized part of California. You've almost definitely seen it on television before, whether it's in reality shows like *The Hills* or *The Real Housewives of Orange County,* dramas like *The OC* or comedies like *Orange County.* Once you get there, you'll realize some important things: nothing you've seen on a screen compares to the stunning beauty of the iconic coastline and nothing – absolutely nothing – beats a day traveling up and down the Pacific Coast Hwy, whether you're driving, biking or simply walking and taking in the beaches and the ocean beyond.

Those beach vibes infuse every inch of Orange County and you'll likely feel an instant serotonin boost from the massive dose of 'vitamin sea.' If you can tear yourself away from the water's edge, the area offers a lot more, like strollable historic downtown areas, art and culture museums, scenic hiking and biking routes and unmissable events. There's also a little matter of the Happiest Place on Earth – Disneyland is the state's biggest tourist draw, attracting 28 million visitors annually and could be a whole vacation unto itself. The 1955 attraction is worth a visit, even if you think you're not a theme park person. The Disney magic just might surprise you.

DISNEYLAND RESORT

THE MAIN AREAS

DISNEYLAND
A destination for kids and kids at heart.
p144

NEWPORT BEACH
A chic destination to see and be seen.
p156

LAGUNA BEACH
An artist colony turned beach oasis.
p164

For places to stay in Disneyland & Orange County, see p170

JON BILOUS/SHUTTERSTOCK

Left: Disneyland, (p144); Above: Laguna Beach (p164)

KNOTT'S BERRY FARM

Sierra Sidewinder, Knott's Berry Farm (p154)

Find Your Way

There's no wrong way to spend time in Orange County, but if you've only got a day or two, you'll likely want to stick to the coastal cities to maximize your ability to soak in the sun, sand and surf.

Newport Beach, p156

Don't be fooled by the megamansions and yachts: Newport Beach also has laid-back beaches and charming old-school boardwalk attractions.

Disneyland, p144

The Happiest Place on Earth has endless diversions for kids and adults. Nearby, Knott's Berry Farm is a theme park with a lot of delicious history.

Laguna Beach, p164

The artistic center of Orange County, Laguna Beach was founded as an artists colony and has become a destination for art, theater and singular events.

CAR

To make the most of your time, you'll need your own vehicle in order to explore more than one or two places in Orange County. Traffic can be intense, so use predictive software to gauge drive times as you're planning your itinerary.

METROLINK

Los Angeles's Metrolink trains go as far north as Ventura and Lancaster and as far south as San Diego County. There are no train stops at area airports, but there are bus connections. Use the Metrolink Mobile app to plan your route.

BUS

If you'd rather skip traffic and parking fees, try the robust bus system. Anaheim Regional Transportation (the ART bus) has easy access to Disneyland and local attractions. For other locations in OC, use the Orange County Transportation Authority (OCTA) app, called Transit Royale.

Plan Your Days

Orange County has a summer vibe all year long. Plan to bring layers, though: the mornings and evenings can be surprisingly chilly, especially near the water.

One Day in Orange County

- Spend the day exploring the Pacific Coast Hwy (PCH). Start in **Laguna Beach** (p164), spending the morning walking the scenic paths high above the beach, or down in the sand. The seaside shops are lovely to browse, but you'll get just as much enjoyment out of walking around downtown and seeing all the **public art** (p164).

- In the afternoon, head north to **Newport Beach** (p156). Stroll the Balboa Peninsula, especially the **Newport Beach Pier** (p159) and **Balboa Fun Zone** (p156), which is an old-time amusement park. Head to **Balboa Island** (p158) to sample one of the area's famous frozen bananas, or stroll the waterfront park in **Corona del Mar** (p159). Whatever you do, make sure you're somewhere for the sunset, whether that's the beach itself or a waterfront restaurant in **Mariner's Mile** (p156).

JON BILOUS/SHUTTERSTOCK

Balboa Pier (p156)

Seasonal Highlights

Orange County in the off-season is a delight, with smaller crowds, lower hotel prices and seasonal events.

MARCH

The superbloom is one of California's most elusive and unforgettable experiences, when massive swaths of wildflowers bloom at once. Try the **Laguna Coast Wilderness Parks** (p167) in Laguna Beach.

APRIL

You can watch surfers in Huntington Beach every day, but the **Jack's Surfboards Pro** (p160) is your chance to see some of the world's top surfers hit the waves as part of the World Surf League's qualifying series.

JULY

Laguna Beach's **Sawdust Art Festival** (p164), **Festival of Arts** (p164) and **Pageant of the Masters** (p167) happen every July and August. Browse works by hundreds of artists and see people immerse themselves in actual paintings.

A Weekend or More

- Before or after your PCH day, give yourself – and your inner child – an overnight at **Disneyland** (p144). While you can definitely get a lot out of a one-day visit, the best experience involves the nighttime shows like fireworks and parades, depending on the time of year. After a long park day, your body will thank you for booking a nearby hotel and not having to make a long drive.

- The Disneyland Resort has two parks, which can be accessed via single park tickets or a park hopper for same-day access to both. For classic attractions and pure nostalgia, head to **Disneyland Park** (p144. For thrill rides, excellent food and movie magic, choose **Disney California Adventure Park** (p147).

A Full SoCal Experience

- If you're planning to spend several days in Orange County, do yourself a favor and take it as slowly as possible – which means exploring by foot or bicycle. While a drive on the PCH is a supreme delight, it's easy to miss the small details that make places like **Seal Beach** (p162) and **Huntington Beach** (p160) truly memorable.

- Taking your time will give you opportunities to appreciate the surf monuments in Huntington, the public art in **Laguna** (p164), **Noguchi Garden** (p163) in Costa Mesa, the harbor boardwalks in **Dana Point** (p168) and a million other little details it's easy to overlook when you're trying to squeeze the most out of a short time. In **Newport** (p156), give yourself some time to get out on the water, whether it's on a whale watch or a sunset harbor tour.

AUGUST

Over a million people head to the **OC Fair** (p163) in Costa Mesa, which happens annually in July and August and includes concerts, a carnival, culinary demonstrations, agricultural contests and all the festival food you can handle.

SEPTEMBER

Halloween starts early at OC theme parks. Disneyland's **Oogie Boogie Bash** (p150) is a delightfully spooky and kid-friendly event, while the **Knott's Scary Farm** (p165) event is purely terrifying, in the best way.

OCTOBER

The **Newport Beach Film Festival** (p158) brings in nearly 60,000 attendees for red carpet events, film screenings, filmmaking Q&As and more. Expect to see early looks at movies that will end up at next year's Oscars.

DECEMBER

It doesn't get more OC than yachts decked out in holiday lights. The iconic Newport Beach **Christmas Boat Parade** (p158) usually happens the week before Christmas, but there are harbor tours of festive home and boat decor all month.

Disneyland

PURE NOSTALGIA | IMMERSIVE RIDES | MICKEY-SHAPED FOOD

TOP TIP

Bring a power bank for your smartphone. The Disneyland app is a must-have to keep track of wait times, book Lightning Lane passes, order food, make dining reservations and lots more.

GETTING AROUND

If you're not planning to rent a car – which, for a Disneyland-only trip, you likely won't need – the closest airports to Disneyland are Long Beach and John Wayne Airport in Santa Ana. Your flight will likely have a connection and cost more than the direct options into Los Angeles International Airport, about an hour away. Everything near Disneyland is walkable or easily accessible via rideshare or the ART Bus, and grocery delivery from nearby Target and Walmart is a cinch.

'Here you leave today,' the sign reads over the entrance into Disneyland Park, 'and enter the world of yesterday, tomorrow and fantasy.' It's easy to dismiss Disney as an only-for-kids attraction, but it's truly the kind of place where you can fully immerse yourself in the magic and take a break from the real world for a little while.

Walt Disney opened Disneyland in 1955, when it was just one park and admission cost $1. The idea was to create a place where kids and adults could have fun together, with everyone enjoying the same experience. It revolutionized family entertainment and set the standard for theme parks around the world. Today, the Disneyland Resort includes two separate parks – Disneyland Park and Disney California Adventure Park (DCA) – as well as three hotels and a shopping and dining district called Downtown Disney, which doesn't require a ticket to enjoy.

The Magic of Disneyland Park

Step into yesterday, tomorrow and fantasy

Walking into **Disneyland Park** *(disneyland.disney.go.com; from $104 per person for a single day ticket)* it's easy to see glimpses of Walt Disney's original park. The Disneyland Railroad puffs its way above the entrance and once you're walking down **Main Street USA**, there's joyful music, balloons flying overhead, the smell of popcorn and churros in the air, and cartoon mice waving at you as they walk by. Look to the left and you'll see a lamp in the window of the Disney family's personal apartment, lit in remembrance of Walt the day he died in 1966 and never turned off since. Look ahead and you'll see **Sleeping Beauty Castle**, a pink and blue dream that's the gateway to **Fantasyland**, where original opening-day rides like Peter Pan's Flight and the King Arthur Carrousel still spin today.

DISNEYLAND

Anaheim Majestic Garden Hotel (0.2mi)
Downtown Los Angeles (26mi)
Mickey & Friends Parking Structure
Star Wars: Galaxy's Edge
Mickey's Toontown
Disneyland Railroad
Fantasyland
Rivers of America
Frontierland
Disneyland Monorail
Bayou Country
DISNEYLAND PARK
Tomorrowland
New Orleans Square
Adventureland
Main Street, USA
Disneyland Park
DOWNTOWN DISNEY
Buena Vista St
Disney California Adventure Park (DCA)
Grizzly Peak
Hollywood Land
DISNEY CALIFORNIA ADVENTURE
Avengers Campus
Paradise Gardens Park
San Fransokyo Square
Paradise Bay
Cars Land
Pixar Pier
Disneyland Dr
Harbor Blvd
Disney Way
Katella Ave
JW Marriott Anaheim (0.3mi)
Anaheim Convention Center

HIGHLIGHTS
1 Disney California Adventure Park (DCA)
2 Disneyland Park
3 Star Wars: Galaxy's Edge

SIGHTS
4 Adventureland
5 Cars Land
6 Fantasyland
7 Frontierland
8 Grizzly Peak
9 Hollywood Land
10 Main Street USA
11 New Orleans Square
12 Pixar Pier
13 Sleeping Beauty Castle
14 Tomorrowland

SLEEPING
15 Alpine Inn
16 Anaheim Hotel
17 Candy Cane Inn
18 Disneyland Hotel
19 Disney's Grand Californian Hotel & Spa
20 Howard Johnson by Wyndham Anaheim Hotel
21 Pixar Place Hotel
22 Westin Anaheim

EATING
23 Blue Bayou
24 Carnation Cafe
25 Carthay Circle
26 Craftsman Grill
27 Goofy's Kitchen
28 Lamplight Lounge
29 Napa Rose
30 Paradise Garden Grill
31 Plaza Inn
32 Pym Test Kitchen
33 Ronto Roasters
34 Storytellers Cafe
35 Tiana's Palace

DRINKING & NIGHTLIFE
36 Broken Spell Lounge
37 Hearthstone Lounge
38 Trader Sam's Enchanted Tiki Bar

ENTERTAINMENT
39 Avengers Campus
40 Mickey's Toontown

TOP EXPERIENCE

Downtown Disney

A ticket to Disneyland has a hefty price tag, but there's an element of the Disneyland Resort that you can enjoy for free. Downtown Disney is the shopping and dining district that connects the two theme parks to the resort hotels. If a Disneyland day isn't in the cards for you on this trip, this outdoor pedestrian mall will give you a taste of the experience.

KIT LEONG/SHUTTERSTOCK

Disney Magic Without Disney Tickets

Downtown Disney has the same theming and feel as being inside the parks. There are character topiaries, fountains that do magic tricks and music wafting from the sky. During festival and holiday seasons, the area is also decorated the same way the parks are and sometimes has roving seasonal performers in addition to the nightly concerts at its performance stage. Downtown Disney is also the only place you can buy official Disney merchandise outside of the parks and hotel gift shops.

The Flavor of Downtown Disney

Downtown Disney has 26 dining options and has seriously upped its culinary game over the past few years. A trio of restaurants from Michelin-starred chef Carlos Gaytan (Paseo, Centrico, Tiendita) offer gourmet Mexican food at different price points and an outpost of the wildly popular dim sum restaurant **Din Tai Fung** serves 10,000 dumplings daily. Its newest restaurant, **Parkside Market**, is a food hall with an upstairs cocktail bar that has views of the Monorail and the Disneyland fireworks. Two more restaurants are coming: a fine dining steakhouse and a barbecue joint.

TOP TIPS

- $10 validated parking is available in the Simba Lot for four hours with validation from a store, or six hours with validation from a table-service restaurant.
- There's easy access into the Disneyland Hotel and Grand Californian Hotel to see and shop.
- Parking for the theme parks is not allowed.

PRACTICALITIES

Scan the QR code for more information on Downtown Disney.

The other lands of Disneyland aren't quite as storybook-like, but they are just as transportive. **Adventureland** is tropical-themed, with attractions like the delightfully punny Jungle Cruise and thrilling Indiana Jones Adventure: Temple of the Forbidden Eye. The Wild West–themed **Frontierland** has Big Thunder Mountain Railroad, a coaster where you escape an exploding mine. **New Orleans Square** has Pirates of the Caribbean (complete with a restaurant, Blue Bayou, inside the ride) and Haunted Mansion, the first truly immersive haunted house ever built. The retro-futuristic **Tomorrowland** offers a ride on Space Mountain and **Toontown** has the trackless dark ride Mickey and Minnie's Runaway Railway, the only ride dedicated to the mouse himself. The park's newest land, **Star Wars: Galaxy's Edge**, has the park's most technologically advanced ride: the 18-minute Star Wars: Rise of the Resistance. In this land, the park's nighttime fireworks have a special Star Wars projection show to match.

The Thrills of Disney California Adventure

A movie multiverse, with even bigger rides

If Disneyland is about making dreams real, then **Disney California Adventure Park** *(DCA; disneyland.disney.go.com; from $104 per person for a single day ticket)* is about making movies come to life. Instead of a Main Street USA modeled after Walt Disney's childhood, the land that greets you through the gates of DCA is the **Buena Vista Street** of 1920s Hollywood, when the Walt Disney Studios rose to prominence for making *Snow White and the Seven Dwarfs,* the first-ever full-length animated film.

Note: this is a separate park from Disneyland and requires separate admission or a park hopper ticket. It's not recommended that you visit both parks on the same day.

In **Hollywood Land**, which mimics Hollywood Blvd, there are meet-and-greets with Mickey and friends in Old Hollywood garb and the Animation Academy where you can learn to draw Disney characters. **Avengers Campus**, the Marvel-themed land, has rides like WEB SLINGERS: A Spider-Man Adventure and Guardians of the Galaxy – Mission: Breakout! That land, currently under expansion, is set to open a King Thanos multiverse ride and an Iron Man ride, likely in 2026.

On **Pixar Pier**, the Incredicoaster rockets you into the air with the Incredibles family and, in **Cars Land**, you can zoom through Ornament Valley on Radiator Springs Racers, a thrilling but kid-friendly car race ride. On **Grizzly Peak**, one of the

PLANNING AHEAD & SKIPPING LINES

Disneyland uses a reservation system to manage capacity, so while you can still buy a ticket in person, it's not a guarantee that you'll be able to go the same day. The much better way is to buy your tickets in advance online at *disneyland.disney.go.com*. Many Disney vacation planning sites offer discounted tickets.

On busy days, waits for the most in-demand rides can range from one to two hours, but the Lightning Lane Multi-Pass ($35 per day per person) allows priority access on many rides. For the most popular rides, including Star Wars: Rise of the Resistance and Radiator Springs Racers, there's an additional Individual Lightning Lane cost per ride – the good news is that you can purchase those without having to buy a Multi-Pass.

EATING AT DISNEYLAND: CHARACTER DINING

Goofy's Kitchen: In the Disneyland Hotel, this is a huge, kid-friendly buffet, with friends like Minnie and Pluto and a photo op with Chef Goofy. $$

Storytellers Cafe: An elevated buffet in the Grand Californian, serving wild Bloody Marys and an adventure theme. Mickey and friends come to every table. $$

Napa Rose: The Grand Californian's fine dining restaurant has an elegant Princess Breakfast, with high tea–like service and visits from Cinderella, Tiana and Elsa. $$$

Plaza Inn: Minnie and Friends Breakfast in the Park, inside Disneyland Park, is a morning buffet at Plaza Inn offering Minnie (not Mickey) waffles and comfort foods. $$

DISNEYLAND TURNS 70

Disneyland celebrates 70 years in May 2025 through summer 2026 with special entertainment, food and parades. Two additional nighttime spectaculars form part of the celebration: DCA debuted World of Color–Happiness, a fountain show with projections that include the Muppets and characters from Inside Out; and Disneyland brought back the fan favorite Wondrous Journeys fireworks show along with the Paint the Night parade. Disneyland 70 also marked the debut of a new show at the Main Street Opera House. In *Walt Disney: A Magical Life,* Disneyland debuted the first-ever Audio Animatronic figure representing Walt himself, using actual clips of Disney speaking as narration.

original lands from the park's 2001 opening, you can make a splash on the Grizzly River Run, or fly above the clouds on Soarin' Across the World, a 4D movie experience.

Disneyland Festivals

Lunar New Year Celebration (January & February)

Disney California Adventure marks the Lunar New Year with a celebration of East Asian food, culture and heritage. Food booths offer Disney takes on Chinese, Vietnamese and Korean street foods; and there are parades and musical performances. The year 2026 celebrates the Year of the Horse and 2027 marks the Year of the Goat.

California Adventure Food & Wine Festival (March & April)

The vast and varied landscape of California's regional cuisines are the spotlight for this highly anticipated annual festival at DCA. Not only are there food booths themed to different regions and iconic California foods – think an entire booth

EATING AT DISNEY CALIFORNIA ADVENTURE: OUR PICKS

Lamplight Lounge: Reserve this Pixar Pier place when World of Color is showing. The prime view is even sweeter with a bite and a cocktail. **$$**

Paradise Garden Grill: The Mexican food at this Paradise Gardens spot is always a winner, especially for its vegetarian fare and rotating menus. **$$**

Pym Test Kitchen: Avengers Campus spot inspired by Ant-Man's size: think tiny pasta with one giant, plant-based 'meatball' served in a huge spoon. **$$**

Craftsman Grill: This poolside restaurant is just through the Grand's dedicated park entrance. Its gourmet hot dogs (really!) and pizzas are the perfect break. **$$**

DISNEYLAND RESORT

Pixar Pier (p147), Disneyland

devoted to garlic, one of California's biggest crops – there are special dining events and chef demonstrations throughout the festival. As a special homage to its home state, the park brings back **Soarin' over California**, the original version of the ride, which showcases Golden State scenery like the Golden Gate Bridge and Big Sur.

Season of the Force (April & May)

If the phrase 'May the Force be with you' means anything to you, you might want to time your visit for Disneyland's **Season of the Force**, which celebrates Star Wars with specialty foods in Tomorrowland and a Star Wars overlay of Space Mountain, which becomes Hyperspace Mountain and puts riders in the battle between the Resistance and the First Order. During this time, Disneyland hosts **Star Wars Nite**, a specially ticketed after-hours event for fans who dress up as their favorite characters and wield their lightsabers with abandon. The dates vary, but there's always one on, you guessed it, May the Fourth.

HOW TO SKIP THE WAIT FOR NIGHTTIME SHOWS

On nights when Disneyland will have Wondrous Journeys fireworks, or DCA is showing World of Color, you'll likely see people staking out the best spots several hours in advance. If you only have a short time at the park, that's not the best way to utilize your time. There are two ways to guarantee prime viewing spots without the wait. Disneyland offers dessert parties, which are an additional cost, but come with seating for nighttime shows and parades. The parks also offer dining packages at certain restaurants: when you dine there with the package menu (just ask for it when you arrive), you'll receive a voucher for entry into a reserved viewing area for the nighttime Fantasmic! show or the Paint the Night parade.

DRINKING AT DISNEYLAND: BEST FOR COCKTAILS

Broken Spell Lounge: Sleeping Beauty–themed spot in the Disneyland Hotel; cozy couches, woodland-inspired cocktails and nightly live music.

Carthay Circle: Downstairs from the fine-dining restaurant, the lounge offers classic cocktails, including an unforgettable espresso martini.

Trader Sam's Enchanted Tiki Bar: Order the right drink at this Disneyland Hotel bar and it might do a magic trick. Bartenders are tiki aficionados.

Hearthstone Lounge: This Grand Californian spot has an excellent whiskey selection, a walk-up bar for drinks to enjoy by the lobby fireplace and a casual menu.

MUST-TRY SNACKS

Churros: A signature Disneyland treat, this cinnamon-sugar fried dough has endlessly delicious seasonal variations like s'mores and pumpkin spice. Snack carts open daily.

Dole Whip: No Disney day is complete without this frozen treat, in flavors like original pineapple and raspberry, best enjoyed sitting in Walt Disney's Enchanted Tiki Room.

Popcorn: Each cart has an adorable Roastie-Toastie animatronic inside that's themed to a specific land. The refillable popcorn buckets are seriously fun souvenirs.

Mickey-Shaped Foods: It's a proven fact that everything tastes better Mickey-shaped, including ice cream bars, hot pretzels, cookies and caramel apples.

DISNEYLAND RESORT

Tiana's Bayou Adventure, Disneyland

Halloween Time (September & October)

For those who love a spooky good time, there is no better season at Disneyland than **Halloween Time**. Both parks are fully decorated for the holiday, including an entire makeover of Cars Land with incredibly inventive Halloween decorations from auto parts: it includes a 'Haul-o-Ween' ride overlay for Mater's Junkyard Jamboree and Cars like Lightning McQueen and Mater dressed in Halloween costumes. Also in DCA, the Avengers Campus Guardians of the Galaxy – Mission: Breakout! becomes Monsters After Dark, an even more terrifying version of the drop ride. **Oogie Boogie Bash** is a highly anticipated, separately ticketed Halloween party with Disney villains and trick-or-treating. It sells out months in advance every year.

Halloween also brings the popular holiday overlay of Haunted Mansion, which becomes **The Nightmare Before Christmas**-themed and has a huge gingerbread house that changes every year. In past years, it has featured a guillotine that really dropped a blade and a moving gingerbread zombie.

EATING AT DISNEYLAND PARK: OUR PICKS

Blue Bayou: There's no more quintessentially Disneyland restaurant than Blue Bayou, inside Pirates of the Caribbean. Boats glide by as you enjoy your meal. $$$

Carnation Cafe: Southern-inspired comfort food is the order of the day at Carnation Cafe, famous for its fried pickles and Walt's Chili. $$

Ronto Roasters: Quick-service stand serving inexpensive, delicious sausage and veg 'Ronto Wraps' but the plant-based Rontoless Wrap is the star. $

Tiana's Palace: A counterpart to the new Tiana's Bayou Adventure ride, Tiana's Palace serves New Orleans–inspired food like jambalaya and muffaletta. $$

National Hispanic and Latin American Heritage Month & Dia de los Muertos (September–November)

National Hispanic and Latin American Heritage Month brings musical performances, special characters and incredible Mexican-inspired food to both parks. **Dia de Los Muertos** celebrates those who have passed with a huge, walk-through ofrenda in Disneyland's Frontierland. At The Tree of Life in the Paradise Gardens area of DCA, you can write a message to a departed loved one and hang it on the tree. By the end of the celebration, there are thousands of beautiful, moving messages.

The Holidays at Disneyland (November–January)

When it's snowing in Anaheim, it must be the **Holidays at Disneyland**. There's nothing like Disneyland Park at the Holidays, when Sleeping Beauty Castle's halls are decked with ornate decorations and, during the nightly fireworks, gingerbread-scented snow falls over Main Street. A **Christmas Fantasy Parade** brings Disney princesses through the streets, surrounded by dancing snowflakes and festive holiday music, followed by an appearance by Santa himself. The most in-demand treats at this time of year are the Mickey gingerbread cookies, which people buy by the dozen, and the hand-pulled candy canes, made fresh on a few select days: people arrive at the park hours early to make sure they'll be able to snag one.

During this time, It's a Small World becomes It's a Small World Holiday, a sweet celebration of holidays around the world and Haunted Mansion Holiday is still around after Halloween.

California Adventure Festival of Holidays (November–January)

Just like in Disneyland, DCA is absolutely laden with festive decor during the holiday months. While all the rides with holiday overlays are in Disneyland Park, DCA has a few special things going on during this season, like Santa appearing in the Redwood Creek Challenge Trail for holiday photos. The biggest event, though, is the **Festival of Holidays**, which celebrates Christmas, Hanukkah, Kwanzaa, Navidad, Diwali and Three Kings Day through food, musical performances and character appearances.

BEHIND THE SCENES

For fans who can't get enough of the mouse, Disneyland offers special ticketed tours that take guests into inaccessible areas like Walt Disney's personal apartment or the Lilly Belle, the Disneyland Railroad car reserved for visiting dignitaries. Those tours are add-ons to park admission and generally cost between $120 and $160 per person, depending on the experience. The multihour experience usually includes a snack, a collectible souvenir and Lightning Lane access to a ride. For the ultimate access, a VIP tour with a private guide allows you to skip all the lines and get priority access to shows. Book these experiences through the Disneyland website or at the Tour Booth inside the Town Square.

HELP ME PICK:

Hotels Near Disneyland

Unlike Walt Disney World® in Florida, which is the size of San Francisco and has multitudes of on-property hotels, Disneyland only has three of its own accommodations. The experience of staying at a Disneyland hotel definitely adds to the immersive experience, but it can be pricey. Within easy walking distance of the park, there are dozens of 'good neighbor' hotels, which tend to be more affordable and sometimes come with perks like free breakfast.

The main hotels

Disneyland Hotel

Disneyland Hotel is the resort's mid-tier property, but it absolutely has the most Disney magic, with touches like headboards that light up with Tinkerbell flying over the castle and playing *When You Wish Upon a Star* and luxury suites with pirate, jungle and Mickey themes. The hotel has four towers: the Fantasy Tower, the Adventure Tower and the Frontier Tower all match the theming of areas in Disneyland and those three have a huge central pool with hot tubs and Monorail-themed water slides. The newest tower, the Villas at the Disneyland Hotel, is an homage to animation with a smaller pool (still open to all hotel guests) with a Steamboat Willie-themed splash pad.

Disney's Grand Californian Hotel

With the ultimate convenience and the highest price tag, Disney's Grand Californian Hotel has an entrance directly into Disney California Adventure Park, which is especially convenient if you've got little kids who need to go back to the room to nap in the middle of the day. The Grand Californian has Craftsman-style architecture, woodsy Chip 'n Dale theming in the rooms and a rock waterfall in its pool area. Even if you aren't staying there, it's supremely pleasant to go sit in the soaring lobby with its overstuffed couches and rocking chairs by the fireplace and listen to music from the grand piano or enjoy a glass of wine.

Pixar Place Hotel

Formerly Paradise Pier Hotel, Pixar Place got a huge makeover in 2024 and is now themed to Disney's Pixar films like *Inside Out, Cars* and *Monsters, Inc.* The hotel is across the street from the main resort, but is still a very short walk and is the most affordable of the three. The Finding Nemo-themed waterslide and splash pad complex is fun and there's a patio area with lawn games for kids and adults to play together. The rooftop pool area offers some of the best fireworks viewing outside the parks. In the afternoons, Bing Bong from *Inside Out* makes appearances throughout the hotel and, in the evenings, Joe from *Soul* plays piano and tells stories in the lobby.

Disneyland Hotel

Disney's Grand Californian Hotel

Pixar Place Hotel

FROM LEFT: SIPA USA/ALAMY LIVE NEWS/ALAMY; JASON O. WATSON (USA: CALIFORNIA PHOTOGRAPHS)/ALAMY; SIPA USA/ALAMY LIVE NEWS/ALAMY

FELIPE SANCHEZ/SHUTTERSTOCK

Westin Anaheim

HOW TO

When to go The busiest, most expensive times are school vacations and the Halloween and holiday festivities. If price is a factor, choose an off-time.

Book ahead Disneyland hotel reservations can be made 180 days in advance, while local good neighbor hotels generally offer longer booking windows.

Before you go Necessities like refillable water bottles and bandages are pricey in the park; either pack them or order from a delivery service.

Budget If you're willing to book a few blocks further away, the good neighbor hotel prices drop dramatically and often have less expensive parking.

Affordable nearby options

The **Westin Anaheim** is newly renovated as of 2024 and the **JW Marriott Anaheim** opened in 2021. Both are excellent, higher-end options that have rooftop lounges where you can see the Disneyland fireworks. Slightly outside of walking distance, the **Hyatt Regency Orange County** offers similar quality for slightly more attractive prices, though without the rooftop.

For the ultimate in theming, choose the **Anaheim Hotel**, across the street from Disneyland's Harbor Boulevard entrance, which has mid-century vibes and mid-tier room rates. The **Anaheim Majestic Garden Hotel** has castle-inspired architecture and room decor; while it's not exactly walkable, the hotel offers a shuttle for a fee and has family suites for larger parties. The **Howard Johnson by Wyndham Anaheim Hotel** has a pirate-themed water park and a suite themed after one of Disney's long-gone attractions. The House of the Retro Future looks like the Monsanto House of the Future that was in Tomorrowland from 1957 to 1967.

Both **Alpine Inn** and **Candy Cane Inn** are directly adjacent to Disney California Adventure. Alpine has European theming that feels like it could be in the park right next to the Matterhorn and offers free parking. The Candy Cane Inn is even closer and offers free breakfast, free parking and a complimentary shuttle.

Find more places to stay on p170.

KNOTT'S BERRY FARM/SEAN TEEGARDEN PHOTOGRAPHY

Calico Mine Train

TOP EXPERIENCE

Knott's Berry Farm

What started as an actual berry farm in Buena Park in 1920 is now one of California's most beloved attractions. Today, Knott's Berry Farm is a hugely popular theme park with thrill rides, an Old West ghost town (which is more real than you might think) and unmissable seasonal events - but, at its core, the place is still all about the berries.

DON'T MISS

- Mrs Knott's Chicken Dinner Restaurant
- Calico Saloon
- Ghost Rider
- Calico Mine Ride
- Birdcage Theater

A Berry Amusing Park

Knott's Berry Farm has four main lands, all elements of the California experience. Calico Ghost Town is a fun version of the Old West. Fiesta Village, inspired by California's history as part of Mexico, celebrates the state's Mexican heritage and culture. The Boardwalk is a coastal-themed land with thrill rides like Hang Time, an intense plunge coaster inspired by surfing. Camp Snoopy, evocative of Northern California's redwood forests, is full of kid-friendly rides and Peanuts characters.

PRACTICALITIES

Scan the QR code for details of upcoming Knott's Berry Farm events and prices.

Calico Ghost Town

The centerpiece of Knott's Berry Farm is **Calico Ghost Town**, based on a real silver mining town in the Mojave Desert. Calico Ghost Town is the true heart of Knott's Berry Farm, not just because it feels so transportive, but because Walter Knott once lived in the real Calico and brought in historic buildings from the town (and other ghost towns across the West) to create the most immersive feeling.

The land includes **Calico Mine Train**, a dark ride through 'gold mines' complete with animatronic miners; the **Calico Railroad**, a real train that chugs around the park and has an unusually high rate of bandits aboard; a **Pony Express** coaster; and even real stagecoaches pulled by horses. Ghost Town is also home to **Ghost Rider**, the tallest, oldest, wooden roller coaster in the West.

Catch a 'burle-q revue' at the **Birdcage Theater**, visit the **Calico Saloon** or livery with live animals and go to 'school' and learn about the pioneer days of California. During the **Ghost Town Alive!** event, the town is full of characters like outlaws and sheriffs who give you interactive storylines to follow and solve.

IT ALL STARTED WITH A BERRY

When Walter and Cordelia Knott introduced the boysenberry – a mix of red raspberry, blackberry and loganberry – to their farm, the business took off. In 1934, they started serving fried chicken dinners and soon people were lining up for hours to dine. Walter started building small attractions to keep them busy. Soon, they had an Old West town and, by 1968, they had a bona fide theme park.

It's Always Boysenberry Season

Visit the park on any day and you can get a taste of the berry that made the farm famous. Knotts' boysenberry funnel cakes, topped with boysenberry preserves and boysenberry soft serve, are legendary, as are the freshly made boysenberry-filled churros, boysenberry pie, even boysenberry beer. But during March and April the park takes it to another level with its annual **Boysenberry Festival**, which incorporates the berry into foods in unexpected ways: think boysenberry beef chili over mac 'n cheese, boysenberry BBQ pulled pork over boysenberry corn bread, boysenberry lavender lemonade and boysenberry vanilla double hazy IPA.

TOP TIPS

- Knott's Berry Farm doesn't require advance park reservations and sells tickets at the gate, but they're cheaper if you buy online.
- Add a Fast Lane entry for an additional fee and you can skip the standby queues and use the speedier Fast Lanes on attractions.
- You can also pre-purchase meal packages online, which are a good value if you're planning on being at the park all day.

A Taste of Knott's Outside the Park Gates

Cordelia Knott's restaurant has come a long way from its start. Now, **Mrs Knott's Chicken Dinner Restaurant** feeds 1000 people daily. The restaurant is open to the public, so you can get a taste of the food that started one of California's most iconic destinations without paying admission. Even better: a chicken dinner includes chicken soup or cherry rhubarb, salad, vegetables, biscuits and preserves and a piece of boysenberry or apple pie for under $30.

A Halloween Scream

Knott's Spooky Farm is a kid-friendly Halloween experience, where rides like the Timber Mountain Log Ride and Calico Mine Train get festive seasonal makeovers. At night, the terror starts. **Knott's Scary Farm** is a separately ticketed event with intense haunted house mazes, delightfully creepy foods and fog-filled walkways where monsters emerge at any moment.

Newport Beach

PRISTINE BEACHES | LIVELY WATERFRONT | CHIC ATMOSPHERE

There's no city in California quite like Newport Beach. The upscale beach community has 10 distinct neighborhoods ranging from quiet and residential to bustling tourist draws. You'll likely spend most of your time at Balboa Island, the Balboa Peninsula, Lido Marina Village, Corona del Mar and Mariner's Mile, as they have the highest concentration of attractions for visitors.

So much of Newport Beach's allure involves the water. The city is home to the largest recreational harbor on the West Coast, with 10 miles of waterfront that offers boating and fishing, water sports and endless views. An enormous ecological wetland preserve is home to more than 200 endangered species. Beyond the shore, Newport Beach has some of California's most sought-after golf courses, beloved annual cultural events and shopping at Fashion Island that rivals Beverly Hills.

TOP TIP

Get a taste of the luxury life by doing a day rental of a sports car like a Ferrari or Aston Martin from one of Newport Beach's exotic car rental businesses.

GETTING AROUND

The closest Metrolink station is Tustin to the east. To access Newport Beach by bus from John Wayne Airport, take the bus to Huntington Beach and connect south from there. Since Newport Beach's main areas are somewhat spread out, you'll likely need to fill in some gaps with rideshare or bike/scooter rentals. If you're renting a car, expect to pay for parking most places; many restaurants offer valet parking for a fee.

Beach Vibes at Balboa Peninsula

A quintessentially beachy OC experience

Balboa Peninsula is where to head if you want a quintessential beach town experience. Stroll **Balboa Pier**, rent a bike and traverse the boardwalk, soaking in the sunshine and salt air. From here, you can hop the ferry to **Balboa Island** (also accessible by car or foot) or catch the **Catalina Flyer** *(catalinainfo.com)* to Catalina Island, a short sail away. In Balboa Village, there's **Balboa Fun Zone** *(balboafunzone.com)*, an old-time amusement park, with rides and midway games.

Make a Splash

If you don't get on the water, you didn't visit Newport

For an adventure by sea – or just to see the superyachts docked nearby – head to **Mariner's Mile**. This is where you'll disembark for water excursions like harbor tours, gondola rides

SIGHTS

1 Balboa Island
2 Balboa Pier
3 Corona del Mar State Beach
4 Crystal Cove State Park
5 Lido Marina Village
6 Little Corona del Mar Beach
7 Newport Beach Moke
8 Newport Beach Pier
9 The Wedge

ACTIVITIES

10 Duffy Electric Boat Rentals
11 Pelican Hill Golf Club

SLEEPING

12 Balboa Bay Resort
13 Crystal Cove Beach Cottages
14 Lido House
15 Resort at Pelican Hill

EATING

16 21 Oceanfront
17 Beachcomber Café
18 Crystal Cove Shake Shack
19 Dad's Donut & Bakery Shop
20 Nobu Newport Beach
21 RH Ocean Grill
22 Rusty Pelican
23 Sancho's Tacos
24 Sugar n' Spice
see 14 Topside

DRINKING & NIGHTLIFE

25 Billy's at the Beach
see 17 Bootlegger Bar
26 Louie's by the Bay
27 Under CdM

ENTERTAINMENT

28 Balboa Fun Zone
29 Christmas Boat Parade
see 5 Newport Beach Film Festival

TRANSPORTATION

30 Catalina Flyer

BEST FESTIVALS

Newport Beach Jazz Festival: *(festivals.hyattconcerts.com)* In June top jazz acts from around the world come to the Hyatt Regency Newport Beach.

Shakespeare By the Sea: *(shakespearebythesea.org)* In summer, the Bard's works feature in pop-up performances all around the city.

Newport Beach Film Festival: *(newportbeachfilmfest.com)* In October, Newport gets a taste of Hollywood.

Pacific Wine & Food Classic: *(pacificwineandfood.com)* Foodie festival in September.

Christmas Boat Parade: *(christmasboatparade.com)* The week before Christmas, but there are harbor tours all month.

and sailing lessons. Or rent your own **Duffy boat** *(duffyofnewportbeach.com)* and cruise around the harbor on your own. There are even sunset dinner **cruises** *(citycruises.com)* where you can enjoy dinner and drinks as you take in Orange County's singular sunset.

To enjoy the water from land, head to **Lido Marina Village** *(lidomarinavillage.com)*, a waterfront shopping and dining area with its own cinema, boutiques and an array of restaurants from casual to fine dining. Mariner's Mile and Lido Marina are also where you'll see boats decorated for the holidays.

Fun on Four Wheels

Moke cruising

A quintessentially SoCal experience is cruising around in a Moke. It looks a bit like a miniature Jeep, with an open top and a roll bar, but it's an electric vehicle that tops out at 25mph. It's perfect for cruising along the shore or any low-speed road, especially on a sunny day. Rent one from **Newport Beach Moke** *(newportbeachmoke.com)* or **Adventure OC** *(adventureoc.com)* in Huntington Beach (p160). Rentals are available by the hour, day or week.

Take a Swing

Some of California's best golfing

Newport is Orange County's most popular golf destination and has some of the state's most scenic and well-designed courses. **Pelican Hill Golf Club** *(pelicanhill.com/golf)* has two courses with panoramic ocean views all the way to Catalina Island. The membership-based club is open to the public for higher fees. For beginners, the **Newport Beach Golf Course** *(newportbeachgolfcoursellc.com)* is a nine-hole public course.

Visit the Banana Stand

Balboa Island has a surprising claim to fame

If you've ever heard the phrase 'there's money in the banana stand,' you already know something about **Balboa Island**. This area of Newport Beach is famous for its frozen

EATING IN NEWPORT BEACH: OUR PICKS

21 Oceanfront: In Doryman's Oceanfront Inn, this fine-dining seafood and steak restaurant serves up unparalleled beach views. *4pm-late* $$$

Nobu Newport Beach: Outpost of the legendary Japanese with two floors of water views. *noon-3pm Fri-Sun, Tanoshi 5-7pm Mon-Thu, dinner from 5pm* $$$

Rusty Pelican: An institution in Mariner's Mile since 1972, this harborside restaurant serves creative fish preparations with a robust wine list. *11am-10pm* $$$

Crystal Cove Shake Shack: Serving burgers and shakes on the beach since 1945; eat them on picnic tables and head straight back to the sand. *7am-9pm* $$

RH Ocean Grill: Elegant rooftop destination in Fashion Island housed in an all-season greenhouse lit with chandeliers. *10am-9pm* $$$

Sancho's Tacos: Once a backyard project but now with several OC locations, including Balboa Peninsula. Tacos on the patio, or take them to the beach. *9am-9pm* $$

Beachcomber Café: This lively, casual cafe at Crystal Cove is ideal for hungry diners walking in off the beach or wanting beach vibes. *7am-9.30pm* $$

Topside: On the roof at Lido House, Topside is a place to see and be seen with coastal-inspired small bites. *4-10pm Mon-Thu, to 11pm Fri, 2-11pm Sat, 11am-11pm Sun* $$

Corona del Mar State Beach

chocolate-dipped bananas, which inspired the family business on *Arrested Development*. Visit the 80-year-old original **Sugar n' Spice** *(sugarnspice.co)* or **Dad's Donut & Bakery Shop** for a taste. A note: in addition to getting there by ferry from Balboa Peninsula, the quaint island is easily accessible by foot, bike or car – but parking can be hard in the cozy community.

Nature, Preserved at Back Bay

This enormous ecological reserve is a natural dream

What's really the **Upper Newport Bay Ecological Preserve** *(ocparks.com)* is colloquially called Back Bay, with more than 1000 acres of protected coastal wetland and a 10.5-mile hiking and biking trail running through it. Admission to its Peter and Mary Muth **Interpretive Center** *(newportbay.org)*, dedicated to local wildlife programming and education, is free.

NEWPORT BEACH'S BEST BEACHES

Crystal Cove State Park: Appealing destination with three beaches, campsites, cabins and an underwater park for snorkeling and diving.

Corona del Mar State Beach: Known as Big Corona, this beach is family- and pet-friendly. If it looks familiar, you might recognize the beach from *Gilligan's Island*.

Newport Beach Pier: The stretch of sand on Balboa Peninsula around the Newport Beach Pier has fine sand and views and proximity to many shops and cafes.

Little Corona del Mar Beach: Calm beach known for snorkeling and tide pools, with no steps down to the sand.

The Wedge: This scenic beach's waves make it popular with surfers. In the summer, boards are prohibited between 10am and 5pm.

DRINKING IN NEWPORT BEACH: BEST COCKTAILS

Billy's at the Beach: Grab a seat at the harborside bar, watch boats pull up and get food and drinks to go. *11am-9pm Tue-Sat, to midnight Thu-Sat*

Bootlegger Bar: This casual bar at Crystal Cove State Park serves creative margaritas and a legendary Bloody Mary. *11am-9.30pm Mon-Fri, 10am-9.30pm Sat & Sun*

Under CdM: Under CdM is a speakeasy designed for tipplers who love an elevated smoked or infused cocktail. *by availability Thu-Sun*

Louie's by the Bay: Italian steakhouse offering refined cocktails like barrel-aged bourbon and gin drinks, plus a signature caviar martini. *happy hour 4-6pm, to late Wed*

Beyond Newport Beach

Places

GETTING AROUND

The closest Metrolink stations to Huntington Beach and Seal Beach are in Orange and Santa Ana, inland from the coast. Grab a rideshare or hop on an OCTA Bus to reach your final seaside destination. Costa Mesa is a short bus ride away. Find routes and timetables via the Metrolink Mobile app or the OCTA Transit Royale app. If you're driving, there are paid public lots on the Pacific Coast Hwy, but you can often get lucky and snag street parking, especially in the off season.

Head north on the Pacific Coast Hwy for incredible stretches of beach and the surfing capital of America.

Centrally located in Orange County's waterfront, Newport Beach is a great homebase to explore other areas up and down the PCH. North of Newport you'll find Huntington Beach, a haven for surfers and sun worshippers, where beach vibes are an entire lifestyle. Above that, Seal Beach is an idyllic postage stamp of a beach town with a very different vibe from the highly trafficked Huntington and Newport Beaches. It's perfect for people hoping to avoid crowds. Slightly inland, Costa Mesa offers a fun, artistic vibe, with must-see museums and performance spaces.

Huntington Beach

TIME FROM NEWPORT BEACH: **15MIN**

Welcome to Surf City, USA

There's no place in Orange County more closely associated with surfing than **Huntington Beach**, also known as Surf City, USA. It's where surfing first became popular in California and it's where the sport is celebrated every day by pros and first-timers alike, both on water and on land. There's an **International Surfing Museum** *(huntingtonbeachsurfing museum.org)* just blocks off the shore and a **Surfers' Hall of Fame** outside **Huntington Surf & Sport** *(hsssurf.com)*. Outside **Jack's Surfboards**, which has been an institution since the 1950s, is the **Surfing Walk of Fame** *(surfingwalkoffame.com)*. The Walk of Fame hosts an induction ceremony during the **US Open of Surfing** *(redbull.com/us-en/events/vans-us-open-of-surfing)*, the world's largest surfing competition, which happens in Huntington Beach in July. In April, Jack's hosts its own major surf competition, **Jack's Surfboards Pro** *(jackssurfboards.com)*, a qualifying event for the World Surfing League.

But you don't have to be a pro to surf in Huntington: many surf schools offer beginner's lessons. Head toward the water and you'll find one.

KK STOCK/SHUTTERSTOCK

Plaza, Huntington Beach Pier

Stroll the pier

At 1850ft long, **Huntington Beach Pier** is one of the largest piers on the West Coast. The pier has shops and dining and often artists selling their wares and street musicians performing. Before you arrive in Huntington Beach, you can scope out the scenery on the live-streamed webcam *(huntingtonbeachca.gov)*.

Beach all day, beach all night

Your beach vacation isn't complete without a beach bonfire. Three of Huntington's five beaches have fire pits available on a first-come, first-served basis: **Huntington City Beach**, **Huntington State Beach** and **Bolsa Chica State Beach**. Even though there are more than 500 available, they can be hard to come by in peak season, when people stake them out early in the day. However, there's a trick – rent a picnic spot through **California State Parks** *(parks.ca.gov)* and a fire pit comes with the rental. Be warned, though, the rentals can range from $200 to $300 a day, but are big enough to accommodate a larger group.

Appreciating the outdoors

Huntington's gorgeous scenery goes way beyond the beach. The 1300-acre **Bolsa Chica Ecological Reserve** *(bolsachica.org)* is the largest saltwater marsh in Southern California and has 5 miles of walking trails with scenic overlooks. Bird lovers flock here to see the more than 300 avian species that have been spotted in the last decade.

The 350-acre **Huntington Central Park** *(huntingtonbeachca.gov)* has horseback-riding trails, a playground, disc golf, a dog park and horseshoes, as well as a nature center showcasing local flora and fauna and three restaurants.

BEST BEACHES IN HUNTINGTON

Huntington State Beach: This 3-mile stretch of beach is popular with sunbathers, surfers, anglers and bird-watchers.

Huntington City Beach: Home to the Huntington Beach Pier; this beach is where the pro surfing happens.

Huntington Dog Beach: Unlike other OC beaches, you can have your pup here anytime. The Dog Beach has an annual SoCal Corgi Beach Day.

Bolsa Chica State Beach: Camping available across from Bolsa Chica Ecological Reserve and a visitors center with kid-friendly marine exhibits.

Sunset Beach: Ideal place to catch a perfect OC sunset. An attached park, the Green Belt, has a playground.

DEBBIE ECKERT/SHUTTERSTOCK

Huntington Central Park (p161)

Make a splash

Huntington Harbor is a must-see destination in the city. The harbor area is a collection of five human-made islands surrounded by more than 500 houses, many with truly remarkable (and remarkably quirky) architecture. During the holiday season, harbor homes are decked out for the **Huntington Harbor Cruise of Lights** *(cruiseoflights.org; adult/child $26/19)*, a narrated boat tour of the festive decorations that has been going on for more than 60 years.

The harbor area is an ideal place to get on the water if you're interested in water sports other than surfing. The calm waters are perfect for kayaking or stand-up paddleboarding and rental equipment is readily available at locations throughout. Private charters and electric boats are also available for hire.

Seal Beach

TIME FROM NEWPORT BEACH: **30MIN**

Sea the wildlife

Seal Beach gets its name from the seals that dot its shores. On any given day, you might spot them from the town's small pier or its quaint waterfront promenade. Many day-trippers bike to Seal Beach via the **San Gabriel River Bike Trail** *(trails.lacounty.gov/Trail/265/san-gabriel-river-trail)*, a 28-mile stretch of bike path next to the San Gabriel River that

EATING IN HUNTINGTON BEACH: OUR PICKS

Duke's: Founded by Duke Kahanamoku, surfer and Olympian, Duke's serves Hawaiian-inspired food on the beach. *11.30am-9pm Tue-Sat, 10am-8.30pm Sun* **$$$**

Jolie: Jolie has an elevated seafood menu and stunning water views. The Belle is a lively rooftop bar. *11am-10pm, to 11pm Fri-Sun* **$$$**

LSXO: This 28-seat restaurant is hidden within the Bluegold and serves refined Vietnamese cuisine and cocktails. *4-9.30pm Mon-Wed, 11am-10pm Thu-Sun* **$$$**

Pacific Hideaway: In the Kimpton Shorebreak Hotel, serves Asian- and Latin-influenced cuisine and has a dog menu. *7am-10pm* **$$$**

separates the city from Los Angeles County. Another attraction is the 965-acre **Seal Beach Wildlife Preserve** *(fws.gov/refuge/seal-beach),* on the grounds of the Naval Weapons Station Seal Beach military base. On the last Saturday morning of the month, you can take a free guided tour of the salt marsh. Aside from those tours, the refuge is not open to the public.

Shop and stroll

The charming town of Seal Beach is very small and walkable, which means you can take in most of it in an afternoon. After you've explored the beach, take some time to stroll and peruse independent seaside shops selling seashells, chocolates and beachy fashion. Because it's tucked away in the furthest northwest part of Orange County, Seal Beach tends to be less crowded than larger destinations.

Costa Mesa

TIME FROM NEWPORT BEACH: **15MIN**

A Renaissance city

Costa Mesa is a cultural hub in Orange County, with theater and fine art attractions worth detouring for. The **Orange County Museum of Art** *(ocma.org)* opened in its current home in 2022, with a collection focusing on California art, and is free to the public. The **Segerstrom Center for the Arts** *(sctfa.org)* has six venues. It's home to the Pacific Symphony and the Philharmonic Society of Orange County and hosts traveling Broadway productions. **South Coast Repertory** *(scr.org)* is a theater that has been debuting new works since 1966 and hosts an annual **Pacific Playwrights Festival**. The city is also known for its festivals: the **OC Fair** *(ocfair.com)* happens every July and August for food, festivities and concerts.

BEST FOR PUBLIC ART

Center Tower: This office building has several large-scale sculptures in the courtyard and lobby.

Noguchi Garden: At the Pacific Arts Plaza is this serene art garden.

19th Street & Wallace Avenue: Murals celebrate Dolly Parton and LA Lakers legend Kobe Bryant and his daughter Gianna.

Segerstrom Center for the Arts: The courtyard of this performance center has a striking 65ft steel sculpture.

South Coast Plaza: This huge shopping center has an enormous, vivid outdoor sculpture by Charles O Perry and a stained-glass dome skylight made of 7200 pieces of glass.

DINING IN COSTA MESA: OUR PICKS

Folks Pizzeria: Small but mighty pizzeria serving up inventive small plates and pies. *4-9pm Mon-Thu, 3-9.30pm Fri, noon-9.30pm Sat, noon-9pm Sun* **$$**

Descanso: Refined Mexican served a la carte, or meals cooked *à la plancha* at a grill directly at your table. *3-9pm Mon, 11.30am-10.30pm Tue-Sun* **$$**

AnQi by House of An: AnQi is a stylish restaurant that serves elevated California Asian cuisine. *noon-9pm* **$$$**

El Matador: A local favorite since 1966. Mexican classics are served alongside its 'wall of tequila' which has more than 400 selections. *11.30am-9pm* **$$**

Laguna Beach

LAID-BACK BEACHES | ARTISTIC VIBE | UNMISSABLE FESTIVALS

Laguna Beach has a singular energy all its own. Founded as an artist colony over a century ago, the city has evolved into a vibrant cultural center with events that draw visitors from near and far. But more than that, Laguna is just beautiful: there is public art nearly everywhere you look and where there isn't, there is some of the most scenic coastline imaginable. Its seven miles of beach is mostly connected and is easily accessible from the city's main waterfront thoroughfare. Watersports like surfing and kayaking are popular in Laguna, but the mountains and canyons offer outdoor recreation away from the shore. In short, there's a lot more to do than just hang out at the beach.

TOP TIP

Parking can be limited in the quaint downtown. In high season, consider taking the Laguna Beach Trolley, which services North Laguna, South Laguna and Dana Point. Download the Trolley Tracker app or access it online at *visitlagunabeach.com*.

GETTING AROUND

One of the supreme pleasures of an Orange County visit is biking along the Pacific Coast Hwy, a stretch of waterfront road about 40 miles long. It's also the single best way to beat the traffic and parking in crowded places like Laguna Beach and Newport. You can easily find bike rental shops up and down the PCH in beach towns like Laguna Beach, Huntington Beach and Newport Beach. Nearby Laguna Niguel is accessible via Metrolink; Laguna Beach is accessible by OCTA Bus.

A City of Art

Just walk around and you'll soak up creativity

Even if you're not into art, the city's artsy vibe is infectious. Stroll through downtown **Laguna Village** and you'll quickly notice that there's street art almost everywhere: phone booths, parking meters, alleyways, fences. Anywhere that can be made more beautiful has been made more beautiful by the city's artistic community.

The city is home to **Laguna Art Museum** *(lagunaart museum.org)*, which is a storied cultural institution that houses an all-Californian art collection. Throughout the city, there are over 80 art galleries and artists workspaces. Every first Thursday of the month, more than half of them open their doors on **First Thursdays Art Walks** *(firstthursdaysartwalk.org; free)*, an open gallery event with artist receptions and live performances, with free trolley transportation.

Every summer, two major art festivals light up Laguna Beach. The **Sawdust Art Festival** *(sawdustartfestival.org)* has been happening annually since 1967 and offers 500 art classes during its June, July and August event. The **Festival of Arts** *(foapom.org)* happens in July and August – the visual art portion of the festival showcases the works of more than 100 Orange County artists.

SIGHTS
1 Laguna Art Museum
2 Laguna Beach Cultural Arts Center
3 Main Beach
4 Thousand Steps Beach
5 Victoria Beach

ACTIVITIES
6 Aliso & Wood Canyons Wilderness Park
7 Divers Cove

SLEEPING
8 La Casa del Camino
9 Montage Laguna Beach
10 Ranch at Laguna Beach

EATING
11 La Sirena Grill
12 Larsen
13 Lost Pier Cafe
14 The Cliff
15 The Deck on Laguna

DRINKING & NIGHTLIFE
16 Laguna Beach Beer Company
17 Las Brisas
see 8 Rooftop Lounge

ENTERTAINMENT
18 Festival of Arts
see 1 First Thursdays Gallery Art Walk
19 Laguna Playhouse
see 18 Pageant of the Masters
20 Sawdust Art Festival

PREP FOR THE BEACH...OR DON'T

Don't stress about packing beach gear in Orange County. There are shops up and down Pacific Coast Highway that rent everything you need for the beach, including beach chairs, sand toys and boogie boards, in addition to selling items like sunblock and goggles. Some even sell bonfire kits for beach firepits once the sun goes down.

If you'd rather make it easier, there are companies all over Orange County that will deliver beach rentals to you and offer daily and weekly rentals, or longer. Try **Bliss Beach** *(blissbeach.co)*, which delivers gear packed in a wagon, or **Beach Bros** *(beachbrossharing.com)* or **SoCal Beach to You** *(socalbeach2you.com)*, which both hand-deliver supplies.

SUNFLOWERMOMMA/SHUTTERSTOCK

Thousand Steps Beach

The Beach & Beyond

Over 30 strips of sand to explore

Each of Laguna's 30-plus beaches has something unique. **Main Beach**, across from Laguna Village, is the one you might have seen on television before. It's famous for its scenery, beach volleyball and surfers and boardwalk. **Crescent Bay Beach** is popular with surfers; the adjacent **Crescent Bay Cove** is a green space with expansive views and tide pools. If that's the easiest to access, then **Thousand Steps Beach** is the hardest. Descend 218 steps to get to a secluded beach that has deep tide pools and a sea cave you can walk all the way through at low tide. **Diver's Cove** is ideal for snorkeling and has mild waves. **Victoria Beach** has a 'pirate tower' and a community-maintained swimming pool fed by ocean surf.

Most of the coves on Laguna's coast have tide pools that are protected environments, so they're thriving marine-life habitats which you can explore (look but don't touch). The best time to visit is at low tide, usually in the morning and evening.

EATING & DRINKING IN LAGUNA BEACH: WATERFRONT DINING

The Deck on Laguna: Dine at tables directly in the sand; also serves food and cocktails to the rentable beach bungalows next door. *11am-9pm* **$$$**

Larsen: Housed in the historic Laguna Hotel, this restaurant overlooks Main Beach and has outdoor tables and couches for lounging. *from 11am* **$$$**

Las Brisas: The water views are gorgeous at this Mexican-meets-Californian fine dining restaurant. *8am-10pm Sun-Thu, to 11pm Fri & Sat* **$$$**

Rooftop Lounge: On the roof of La Casa del Camino Hotel, the Rooftop serves creative cocktails and shared plates. Weekday happy hour. *11am-10pm* **$$**

A Haven of Performing Arts

The creative side of Laguna

Visual art isn't the only artistic medium prized in Laguna Beach. The **Laguna Beach Cultural Arts Center** *(lbculturalartscenter.org)* offers various events almost every day, from film screenings to gallery shows to opera and theater performances. The **Laguna Playhouse** *(lagunaplayhouse.com)* has been in continuous operation for over a century and regularly hosts world-premiere works and brings Hollywood celebrities to its stage.

The July and August Festival of Arts (p164) includes an art show, but also one of the most unique art events in the country: **Pageant of the Masters**. During this singular event, people create living dioramas of famous works of art. (If you've watched *Gilmore Girls*, you've seen this before – Stars Hollow hosts a Pageant of the Masters on the show.)

Take a Hike

Explore the coast and mountains

Much of Laguna Beach is high up above beach cliffs, making for stunning scenery and especially good visibility up and down the coast. The city has 20,000 acres of protected wilderness to explore in the **Laguna Green Belt** *(lagunagreenbelt.org)*, which is a series of linked parks: **Laguna Coast Wilderness Parks**, **Aliso & Wood Canyon Parks** and **Crystal Cove State Park**. Laguna Coast has more than 40 trails; in the spring, you might catch a wildflower superbloom. Crystal Cove has beaches, but also mountain biking trails that will bring you up to some of the best views in the city. Aliso and Wood Canyons have shadier trails through woodland.

TRAVELING WITH PETS

While many coastal communities in California are pet-friendly, Laguna Beach is especially accommodating for four-legged family members. Many places are open to well-behaved dogs and there are an abundance of shops that leave water bowls out on the sidewalk. On beaches, leashed dogs are allowed before 9am and after 6pm in the summer and all day the rest of the year.

Finding a pet-friendly hotel isn't challenging, either. **Visit Laguna Beach** *(visitlagunabeach.com)* offers an extensive and continuously updated list of accommodations that welcome dogs and sometimes other pets. Keep in mind that most hotels charge a pet fee, which can vary from $100 per stay to $50 or more per night.

EATING IN LAGUNA BEACH: PET-FRIENDLY RESTAURANTS

The Cliff: Terraced patio with water views and a dog-specific menu with choices like chicken breast or salmon with rice. *11am-9pm Mon-Thu, 8.30am-10pm Fri-Sun* $$$

Laguna Beach Beer Company: This brewery and kitchen serves seasonal beers along with pizza and tacos. Large dog-friendly patio. *noon-9pm, to 10pm Fri & Sat* $$

La Sirena Grill: This downtown Mexican kitchen prioritizes sustainability and welcomes dogs at its outdoor tables. *8am-8pm Mon-Sat* $$

Lost Pier Cafe: Beach cafe with casual vibe, upscale casual food and rentable fire pits to enjoy on the beach. *8am-6pm* $$

Santa Ana
Huntington Beach
Irvine
Newport Beach
Laguna Beach
San Juan Capistrano
Dana Point
San Clemente

Beyond Laguna Beach

Places

Head south on the Pacific Coast Hwy to find quieter shores, or escape to an island.

Driving (or biking) south from Laguna Beach on the PCH, the next beach town you'll reach is Dana Point. Known for its laid-back surf culture, it's also a destination for golfers and people looking for quiet, pristine beaches. But beyond the beach, Dana Point is full of attractions, from historic tall ships to an aquarium and public art. The city has a creativity all its own and hosts unusual and fascinating annual events like the Ocean Institute Maritime Festival and the Festival of Whales – in addition to Pearl Jam frontman Eddie Vedder's Ohana Festival, which brings in huge musical acts for beachfront concerts.

Dana Point

TIME FROM LAGUNA BEACH: **15MIN**

Set sail for adventure

If you've always wanted to learn to sail, **Dana Point** might be the place to do it. **Dana Point Charters** *(danapoint charters.com)* offers private sails for up to six people; you can even participate in the operating of the ship and learn from the captain and crew while aboard. The **Ocean Institute** *(oceaninstitute.org)* is home to *Spirit of Dana Point,* a replica of a 1770s privateer schooner that offers tall-ship sails where

GETTING AROUND

Driving or biking south along the coast, Dana Point is so close to Laguna Beach that you might not even notice that you've left one and entered the other. The Laguna Beach Trolley services North Laguna, South Laguna and Dana Point. Download the Trolley Tracker app or access it online via *visitlagunabeach.com*. If you're driving, expect to pay a nominal fee in public lots.

If you're headed to Catalina Island, there are only two places to hop on a ferry from Orange County. One is in Newport Beach and the other is in Dana Point. Once aboard the **Catalina Express** *(catalinaexpress.com)*, it's about 90 minutes from Dana Point to Avalon on Catalina.

guests can help with the rigging, sunset sails and adventure sails where they fire off a real cannon.

The Ocean Institute also offers sails on the Research Vessel *Sea Explorer*: take a whale watch in an area especially known for whale sightings, or go on a nighttime bioluminescence cruise in the summer months.

The organization hosts an annual **Maritime Festival** every September, which brings in other tall ships to Dana Point and features cannon battles, pirate school, sailor camp and a mermaid swim show.

Take a surfing lesson or learn to kayak

If watching all the surfers has you inspired to hit the waves, sign up for a lesson with **Girl in the Curl** *(girlinthecurl.com; from $150)*. This **Doheny Beach** surf shop offers private surf lessons for groups and individuals and provides all the equipment you need for the day.

Because of its calm water, Dana Point's **Baby Beach** is an easy place to try your hand at kayaking or stand-up paddleboarding. Many surf and sail shops by the beach offer day rentals of equipment with no reservations necessary – feel free to pop in and give it a shot.

Celebrate sea life

Dana Point has a front-row seat to the seasonal migration of gray whales from the colder waters of the West Coast to the warmer waters of Baja California. Every March, the city hosts a **Festival of Whales** *(festivalofwhales.com)* celebrating that unique gift, which includes whale-watching excursions, family entertainment and marine-themed activities.

Gather with your ohana

Founded by Eddie Vedder in 2016, the **Ohana Fest** *(ohanafest.com)* is a multiday music festival with a special mission: to educate people about conservation and environmental issues between performances from huge headliners like Stevie Nicks, Jack White, P!nk and Green Day.

The city also hosts the **Palm Tree Music Festival** *(palmtreemusicfestival.com)* in October, which features huge EDM acts like Martin Garrix and Calvin Harris.

Learn about the natural world

The **Headlands Conservation Area** *(danapoint.org)* has a network of easy and moderate hikes ranging from 1 to 2.5 miles, with scenic views from cliffs above the ocean and access to tide pools. The area is also home to the **Dana Point Nature Interpretive Center**, open every day but Monday, which has kid-friendly exhibits about the local environment and wildlife.

The **Ocean Institute** is also home to an aquarium that allows families to learn about the ocean, even if they don't want to sail. The aquarium has touch tanks, including one with sharks and rays and interactive exhibits.

THE BEST BEACHES IN DANA POINT

Doheny State Beach: A renowned surfing location that's also a popular camping spot; tide pools to explore at low tide.

Baby Beach: This family-friendly beach has a roped-off section of calm water perfect for kids to swim in.

Capistrano Beach: There's more to do than luxuriate in the sand: Capistrano Beach has beach volleyball courts and a boardwalk.

Dana Strand Beach: This beach, far below the parking lot, has a funicular that transports people down to the water.

Salt Creek Beach: Expect to see lots of surfers at Salt Creek Beach, where surf conditions are almost always ideal.

Places We Love to Stay

$** Budget **$$** Midrange **$$$ Top End

Disneyland & Anaheim

MAP P145

Alpine Inn $ An affordable motel very close to the park. Alpine Inn has the same aesthetic as Disneyland's signature Matterhorn. Free parking and free coffee in the morning.

Anaheim Hotel $$ This hotel matches Disneyland's retro vibe with mid-century chic decor and affordable room rates. It's located directly across from an entrance to Downtown Disney.

Anaheim Majestic Garden Hotel $$ This Fantasyland-inspired hotel has castle-like architecture both inside and outside. Not quite walking distance to the park, but offers a paid shuttle.

Howard Johnson by Wyndham Anaheim Hotel $$ Directly across from an entrance to Downtown Disney, this hotel has a pirate-themed water park attached and a singular Disneyland-inspired, art-filled suite.

Candy Cane Inn $$ Independently owned motel with free breakfast and free parking, which was recently refurbished. Very short walk to parks, or a free shuttle.

Disneyland Hotel (p152) $$$ Original Disneyland hotel, with four highly themed towers, two pools and Monorail-themed waterslides. Food options include a coffee shop and five restaurants.

Disney's Grand Californian Hotel (p152) $$$ The most convenient of the on-property hotels, the Grand Californian has a direct entrance into the park, plus a themed pool area, five restaurants and a soaring lobby with couches and a fireplace.

Pixar Place Hotel (p152) $$$ Newly renovated in 2024, Pixar Place has a themed pool, waterslide and lawn games area, plus excellent fireworks viewing and three restaurants.

Westin Anaheim $$$ A short walk from Disneyland, the newly renovated Westin has a luxury feel and a rooftop bar with fireworks views, plus attached restaurants including Fleming's.

JW Marriott Anaheim $$$ Opened in 2021, this hotel is attached to the Anaheim GardenWalk, an outdoor pedestrian mall with restaurants and entertainment. The hotel has a fine dining restaurant and a rooftop lounge with fireworks views.

Knott's Berry Farm

Knott's Hotel $$ The only hotel on Knott's Berry Farm property recently reopened with a top-to-bottom renovation, including a new restaurant showcasing the park's signature boysenberry.

Hilton Buena Park Anaheim $$ Close to Knott's, this Hilton has a heated rooftop pool, full-service breakfast and a 24-hour grab-and-go market.

Newport Beach

MAP P157

Crystal Cove Beach Cottages $$ These cottages in Crystal Cove State Park are unusually affordable for their beachside location between Newport Beach and Laguna Beach, but they sell out immediately when the six-month window opens.

Lido House Newport Beach $$$ This Autograph Collection hotel in the Lido Marina Village area has a fine dining restaurant, a rooftop lounge, a luxury spa and separate cottages apart from the main building.

Resort at Pelican Hill $$$ This sprawling oceanside resort has five restaurants and two golf courses and has been rated best resort in the country by Forbes Travel Guide. Accommodations go up to four-bedroom villas.

Balboa Bay Resort $$$ This AAA Four Diamond waterfront hotel has a lavish spa, on-site fine dining restaurant and a marina with boat rentals.

Huntington Beach

Surf City Inn $$ This quiet boutique hotel has harbor views and a short walk to Sunset Beach. Some rooms have Jacuzzi tubs.

Ocean Surf Inn & Suites $$ A quaint 30-room inn steps from the beach. Some rooms come with Jacuzzi tubs and water-view balconies.

Paséa Hotel & Spa $$$ Stylish beachfront hotel with a rooftop restaurant ideal for watching the sunset over the ocean.

Kimpton Shorebreak Hotel $$$ Get the daily surf report in this stylish hotel with lobby games and courtyard firepits, plus free breakfast.

Waterfront Beach Resort $$$ Relaxing Hilton resort with a spa and rooftop lounge, plus two waterslides in the lagoon-style pool.

Hyatt Regency Huntington Beach Resort & Spa $$$ Large beachfront hotel with two pools and amenities like bike rentals and beach bonfire packages.

Seal Beach

Pacific Inn $$ This beachside hotel offers free breakfast and provides a free local shuttle daily until 9pm.

Water Tower House $$$ Perched 85ft above the beach, this three-story rental is accessible via private elevator. It has four bedrooms and amenities including in-unit laundry.

Costa Mesa

The Westin South Coast Plaza $$ Extremely close to South Coast Plaza's shopping and dining, plus the Segerstrom Center for the Arts. This hotel has two restaurants and a market.

Avenue of the Arts $$ Tribute Portfolio Hotel overlooking Avenue of the Arts Lake and sculptures; a free airport shuttle and free pool cabanas.

Laguna Beach

MAP P165

La Casa del Camino $ The historic La Casa del Camino has water views, Mediterranean-themed rooms and a rooftop lounge.

Montage Laguna Beach $$$ An immersive resort with three pools, a spa, several restaurants and a museum-quality fine art collection.

Ranch at Laguna Beach $$$ California's only National Geographic Lodge of the World feels rustic yet refined in a secluded canyon and has beach access.

Dana Point

Waldorf Astoria Monarch Beach $$$ One of OC's most luxurious accommodations has its own beach club and golf course, plus six restaurants, including from acclaimed chef Michael Mina.

Laguna Cliffs Marriott Resort & Spa $$$ This resort is a short walk from Doheny Beach and offers beach gear for guests, as well as the ability to book gourmet lunches to-go. Three restaurants and a spa are on property.

STEVE CUKROV/SHUTTERSTOCK

Hyatt Regency Huntington Beach Resort & Spa

For places to stay in San Diego and Around, see p208

TOKAR/SHUTTERSTOCK

Above: Mission Beach (p190), San Diego; Right: Balboa Park (p184)

Researched by Julie Tremaine

San Diego & Around

CALIFORNIA'S MOST LAID-BACK CITY

The southernmost city in California is a low-stress paradise. San Diego's relaxed, beachy energy is more than a vibe – it's a lifestyle.

San Diego is a city unlike any other in California. The second-largest in the state by population, San Diego has everything you could ask for in a metropolis: vibrant arts and culture, diverse and varied neighborhoods, incredible food and one of the best zoos in America. But even with all that, the city manages to always feel relaxed. The chill coastal vibes and endless sunshine are ingrained in every corner of this Southern California paradise.

DANCESTROKES/SHUTTERSTOCK

Part of what makes San Diego so different is that it sits on the Mexican border and there's a real cultural influence from Tijuana, its neighbor to the south, in everything from food and festivals to art galleries showcasing Chicano and Latino works. Another thing that deeply influences the city's character: the beach. Nowhere in San Diego is more than a short drive from its 17 miles of coastline. There are beaches for families and for surfers, ocean caves to explore, tide pools to observe, boats to be chartered, seaside boardwalks to stroll and stunning sunsets to appreciate. Outside San Diego proper, smaller beach communities like La Jolla and Carlsbad have characters all their own and attractions worth driving to. And while Northern California is better known for its wine, the southernmost wine destination in California is worth a taste. Temecula is a wine lover's paradise, with idyllic scenery and hot-air balloons in the sky.

THE MAIN AREAS

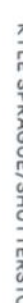

KYLE SPRAGUE/SHUTTERSTOCK

La Jolla (p192)

Find Your Way

San Diego International Airport (SAN) is in the city center and is easily accessible from almost anywhere. Amtrak's Pacific Surfliner train travels daily between Santa Barbara, Los Angeles and San Diego, with stops in between.

Temecula, p202

There are more than 50 wineries in Temecula Valley, an epicurean's destination with excellent dining and skies dotted with hot-air balloons.

San Diego, p178

The second-most-populous city in California, San Diego has plenty of sandy beaches and sunny neighborhoods worth exploring.

Carlsbad, p195

A beach town known for its Legoland theme park, expansive fields of flowers and pristine waterfront.

BICYCLE

The San Diego County Bicycle Coalition *(sdbikecoalition.org)* has extensive resources about the best, safest bicycle routes. If you're planning to get around on two wheels, you'll be well-covered.

TROLLEY & BUS

San Diego has a network of trolleys and buses. Not only do they get you where you need to go, but the trolleys also provide a fair bit of history and an overview of local points of interest as you ride.

CAR

If you plan to stay in and around San Diego, you can get away with not having a car. However, but if you plan to explore some of the surrounding areas or venture up into the mountains, you'll want to drive.

Plan Your Days

Exploring San Diego means going from the ocean all the way up into the mountains. Be prepared for a variety of climates, especially at higher elevations, where it can be chilly even in summer.

LARISA GRIB/SHUTTERSTOCK

Temecula

If You Only Do One Thing

- Give yourself one perfect day in **San Diego** (p178). Start with a morning on Imperial Beach, where you can take a serene walk on the **Silver Strand** (p188) watching the birds, take a swim in the surf or sit in the sand with a book.

- In the afternoon, head to **Balboa Park** (p184) and explore one or two of the many attractions there, from the **San Diego Zoo** (p184) and the art and science museums to the 34 different **International Cottages** (p185).

- Head to **Coronado** (p188) for dinner, where you can get a waterfront table at one of the restaurants at the **Hotel del Coronado** (p189) to watch the sunset. Then, follow up at a speakeasy with a secret entrance – San Diego has a lot of them – for a **nightcap** (p181).

Seasonal Highlights

When it feels like summer every day, you don't have to confine your travel to July and August. Any month of the year is a good time to visit San Diego.

MARCH

The superbloom at the **Flower Fields** (p195) at Carlsbad Ranch starts at the beginning of this month, when 55 acres of flowers burst into living color.

APRIL

The **Mission Fed ArtWalk** (p190) in San Diego's Little Italy is the largest art event on the West Coast, with proceeds going to nonprofit art education.

MAY

Arguably the most beautiful time to visit an already beautiful place is during the **Temecula Valley Balloon & Wine Festival** (p202), when hot-air balloons fill the sky.

Three Days to Travel Around

● Depending on whether you're flying into San Diego or driving down from the north, take a few days to go up or down the Pacific Coast Hwy. Either start in the city and make your way north to **La Jolla** (p192) and **Carlsbad** (p195), or start in a **smaller beach town** (p200) and finish in San Diego. Either way, you'll have a nice mix of laid-back time on the coast and an entertaining time in the city.

● Stay at least one night in a beachfront hotel and one night in the city center to truly give yourself a taste of everything San Diego has to offer.

If You Have More Time

● Venture out into the mountains around **Temecula** (p202). The idyllic city is only about 60 miles from San Diego, but the scenery is a world away. As the state's southernmost wine destination, Temecula Valley has over 50 **wineries and tasting rooms** (p206). Many of them are spread out in the hills and it's easy to hire a tour company to drive you around and spend a day tasting.

● Spend another day on two wheels taking in the scenery: with its 90 miles of bicycle trails, Temecula is especially suited to **cycling enthusiasts** (p205). Then there's the historic town center that has destination-worthy restaurants, antiques shopping and a **country music venue** (p205) known throughout the state for its line dancing and live bands.

JUNE

Make your way to Del Mar for the **San Diego County Fair** (p193), a month-long celebration with carnival games, concerts, festivals, performances and agricultural events.

SEPTEMBER

The **Festival of Sail** (p181) attracts tall ships from around the world to San Diego Bay, complete with food, games, pirates and a cannon battle.

NOVEMBER

Oceanside's **Dia de los Muertos** (p182) is a citywide celebration of Mexican culture, with live music, entertainment, food and altars remembering those who have passed.

DECEMBER

Celebrate the holidays SoCal style with the San Diego Bay **Parade of Lights** (p181), where sailing vessels are bedecked with thousands of Christmas lights.

San Diego

CULTURE | WALKABLE HISTORY | BEACHES

TOP TIP

San Diego's huge waterfront isn't just for the Navy; it's also a busy port for cruises. About 75 cruise ships dock in San Diego Bay every year and 10 cruise lines either stop as a port of call or start or end here. Many hotels offer cruise-related deals.

GETTING AROUND

San Diego's public transportation makes getting around the city without a car easy. The San Diego Metropolitan Transit System (MTS) has a network of buses and trolleys that service most of the city and has a route planner on its website *(sdmts.com; day pass $6)* that makes it simple to navigate. Even the airport is easy to reach on public transit: both bus route 992 and the Old Town Airport Shuttle offer frequent daily access; it's about a 15-minute ride.

San Diego is unlike any other city in California. It's huge – the second-most populous city in the state, just after Los Angeles – but the southerly city is a starkly different experience. Somehow, despite its size and how much it packs in, San Diego manages to exude a relaxed, sunny vibe no matter where you are or what you're doing.

And there's a lot to do: it has far more than you could possibly fit into a short visit. A stunning collection of museums in Balboa Park, the world-famous San Diego Zoo, the San Diego Padres baseball team and one of the largest naval bases in the country are just scratching the surface. Beyond the city center, there are a number of vibrant neighborhoods worth exploring, each with a character all its own. On top of that, the food and drink – especially the local craft beer – are divine. Is San Diego California's coolest city? You'll just have to visit to find out.

Savor the Gaslamp District

MAP P180

Dine, drink and shop downtown

The downtown **Gaslamp District** was named for the gas street lights installed here in the late 1800s. The glowing neon signs welcoming you to this historic neighborhood tell you exactly what you need to know: while the buildings are from the Victorian era, what's inside is totally modern. There are more than 100 places to eat, drink, shop and dance in the district's 16 square blocks – this is the place to come if you're just looking to walk around, explore and stumble on places that look enticing to stop for a bite or a drink. This is also where you'll head if you're looking for nightlife, or to have a cocktail on a rooftop lounge. Rumors of ghost sightings swirl throughout the neighborhood, especially at the **Gaslamp Museum at the Davis-Horton House** *(gaslampfoundation.org; admission $8)*, which offers walking ghost tours.

HIGHLIGHTS

1 Old Town San Diego State Historic Park

SIGHTS

see 1 Bazaar del Mundo
2 Cabrillo National Monument
see 1 Casa de Estudillo
3 Chicano Park
see 10 Heritage Park
4 Juniper Canyon
5 Junípero Serra Museum
6 Marston House
7 Mission Bay Park
8 North Park
9 South Park
10 Whaley House Museum

ACTIVITIES

11 Coronado Historical Association
12 Waterhorse Charters

SLEEPING

13 Hotel del Coronado
14 Humphrey's Half-Moon Inn
15 Kona Kai Resort & Spa
16 Mission Bay Resort
17 Wayfarer San Diego

EATING

18 Roberto's Taco Shop

DRINKING & NIGHTLIFE

19 Eppig Brewing Waterfront Biergarten
20 Hillcrest Brewing Company
21 North Park Flavordome
22 Part Time Lover

ENTERTAINMENT

23 Belmont Park
24 Lamb's Players Theatre
25 Parade of Lights

SHOPPING

26 Coronado Ferry Landing

TRANSPORTATION

27 San Diego International Airport

HIGHLIGHTS
1 New Children's Museum
2 USS Midway Museum

SIGHTS
3 Gaslamp Museum at the Davis-Horton House
4 Maritime Museum
5 Petco Park
6 San Diego Waterfront Park

ACTIVITIES
7 Flagship Cruises

SLEEPING
8 Guild Hotel
9 Ocean Park Inn
10 Omni San Diego
11 Pendry San Diego

EATING
12 Animae
13 Civico 1845
14 Fish Market
15 Headquarters at Seaport
16 Juniper & Ivy
17 Mona Lisa Italian Foods
18 Morning Glory
19 Werewolf

DRINKING & NIGHTLIFE
20 False Idol
21 Noble Experiment
22 Prohibition Lounge

ENTERTAINMENT
23 San Diego Comic-Con

SHOPPING
24 Seaport Village

Anchors Aweigh

MAP P180

Maritime history at the Embarcadero

Embarcadero, the waterfront area of downtown San Diego, has a lot to explore, especially when it comes to maritime history. Tour the **USS Midway Museum** *(midway.org; adult/child $39/26)*, a decommissioned aircraft carrier that served for 47 years. Independence Day is an especially good time to visit, when the museum hosts a July 4 Fireworks Viewing Party during the city's annual **Big Bay Boom** celebration.

The **Maritime Museum** *(sdmaritime.org; adult/child $24/from $12)* is a collection of historic ships that includes the 150-year-old *Star of India,* the oldest active sailing ship in the world. Families can even stay overnight on the ship and the museum offers an interactive pirate show. In September, the museum hosts the **Festival of Sail**, an enormous tall ships festival.

If you'd rather get out on the open water, it's easy to hop on a ship. **Flagship Cruises** *(flagshipsd.com)* offers seasonal whale watches, daily harbor tours, weekly dinner cruises, champagne brunch cruises and more.

Every December, more than 80 boats are aglow on San Diego Bay during the **Parade of Lights** *(sdparadeoflights.org),* when owners decorate their vessels with holiday lights and set sail.

If you'd prefer to enjoy the harbor from dry land, **San Diego Waterfront Park** *(sdparks.org)* is a public space with grassy areas for picnics, splash pads and water features to cool off in and seriously gorgeous water views. The **New Children's Museum** *(thinkplaycreate.org; adult/child $24/20)* has fun, interactive science exhibits where kids can play and learn. **Seaport Village** *(seaportvillage.com)* is a waterfront shopping and dining district that looks like a harbor village from a century ago, with live music every weekend.

More Than Baseball

MAP P180

Petco Park is a community gathering place

Petco Park *(petcoparkevents.com),* the home of the San Diego Padres, is located where the Gaslamp and East Village meet. Petco Park encompasses the stadium along with **Gallagher Square**, which is an outdoor concert venue that brings in huge national touring acts and is also a popular gathering spot on game days. Petco Park offers daily guided **stadium tours** *(mlb.com/padres; $43)* that take guests into the press box, the Hall of Fame, a luxury suite and down onto the field's warning track.

VISITING MEXICO

San Diego shares an international border with Tijuana and it's easy for US citizens with passports to head south and explore the Mexican border town. There's even a Cross Border Xpress skybridge connecting the Tijuana International Airport to San Diego. International visitors can also cross the border, but need a valid passport as well as a valid I-94 form or multiple entry visa or visa waiver, which can be managed through the US Customs & Border Patrol's CBP One app.

In TJ, as locals call it, you can shop duty-free, eat Mexican food and explore the city's sights, like **Tijuana Cultural Center**, which combines art galleries with a botanical garden, performance stages and an aquarium.

DRINKING IN SAN DIEGO: SPEAKEASIES

MAP P180

Prohibition Lounge: Open the door to 'Law Office, Eddie O'Hare, Esq' to find a Gatsby-esque lounge with elevated cocktails and live music. *8pm-1.30am*

Noble Experiment: Head to the back of Neighborhood, then push open the wall of kegs to reveal a cabinet of cocktail curiosities. *6pm-2am*

Part Time Lover: Walk into Purity & Accuracy Records and you'll find this vinyl listening bar and record store where guests can spin their favorites. *4pm-2am*

False Idol: San Diego's most-lauded tiki bar also happens to be a speakeasy, hidden behind a walk-in cooler at Craft & Commerce. *5pm-1am*

THE BIRTHPLACE OF CALIFORNIA

San Diego holds the distinction of being the first place in California that European explorers settled, on land belonging to the Native American Kumeyaay people. Portuguese explorer Juan Rodríguez Cabrillo first came ashore in 1542 in what's now Point Loma: you can visit the site of his landing at the **Cabrillo National Monument** *(nps.gov/cabr)*. The Mission San Diego de Alcalá was established in the 1769 in what's now the Old Town and was the first of 21 Spanish missions that stretched along the California coast, from San Diego to Sonoma. Today, you can still see buildings that date back to that earliest settlement in the Old Town, along with tributes to the Kumeyaay people.

Celebrate Chicano Culture

MAP P179

Explore Logan Heights and Barrio Logan

The city's oldest Mexican-American neighborhood is a living tribute to Chicano culture, especially in **Barrio Logan**, an art-filled neighborhood that represents the city's vibrant identity. The second Saturday of every month, the **Barrio Art Crawl** *(allforlogan.com)* is a self-guided tour through the cultural district's public art and galleries, with food and live music. Make sure to stop by **Chicano Park**, which has more than 100 Chicano murals and sculptures, plus gardens and green space.

Discover Old Town San Diego

MAP P179

Step back in time

Old Town San Diego State Historic Park *(oldtownmarketsandiego.com)* is a cluster of 19th-century buildings northwest of downtown, many of which date from San Diego's Mexican and early American eras. Arguably the most iconic of Old Town's historic buildings is the **Whaley House Museum** *(whaleyhousesandiego.com; adult/child $13.30/9.50)*, constructed in 1856 on the site where public hangings once took place. Today, it's rumored to be so haunted that it's been featured on many ghost-hunting television shows. At night, they offer ghost tours and after-hours paranormal investigations.

Casa de Estudillo is an original adobe building dating back to 1825 and is furnished with antiques from the 16th to the 20th century. **Heritage Park** nearby has a collection of preserved Victorian homes. The **Junípero Serra Museum** *(sandiegohistory.org; suggested donation $10)* commemorates Spanish Franciscan missionary Father Junípero Serra, who established the state's first mission; the event is widely considered to be the founding of California.

You can also make your own candles, buy penny candy and visit **Bazaar del Mundo**, which brings together merchants selling everything from jewelry to pottery.

Old Town is also the location of must-see events like May's **Fiesta Old Town Cinco de Mayo** *(oldtowncincodemayo.com)*, with *lucha libre* wrestling, music and entertainment. In November, Old Town celebrates one of the most important holidays in Mexican culture with a **Dia de los Muertos** *(dayofthedeadsd.com)* parade, music and entertainment in

(continued on p188)

DRINKING IN SAN DIEGO: CRAFT BREWERIES

MAP P179

Hillcrest Brewing Company: This beer haven and pizzeria claims to be 'the first gay brewery in the world.' *2-9pm Mon-Fri, 11am-10pm Sat, 10am-8pm Sun*

North Park Flavordome: Modern Times' tasting room is in the heart of the North Park beer neighborhood and has 20 brews on tap. *noon-9pm Sun-Thu, to 10pm Fri & Sat*

AleSmith: One of San Diego's biggest and most popular tasting rooms, Alesmith is kid- and dog-friendly. Food trucks too. *11am-10pm Mon-Thu, to 11pm Fri & Sat, to 9pm Sun*

Eppig Brewing Waterfront Biergarten: This Point Loma alfresco spot is BYOF, or you can hit up the on-site food trucks. *noon-9pm Mon-Fri, from 11am Sat & Sun*

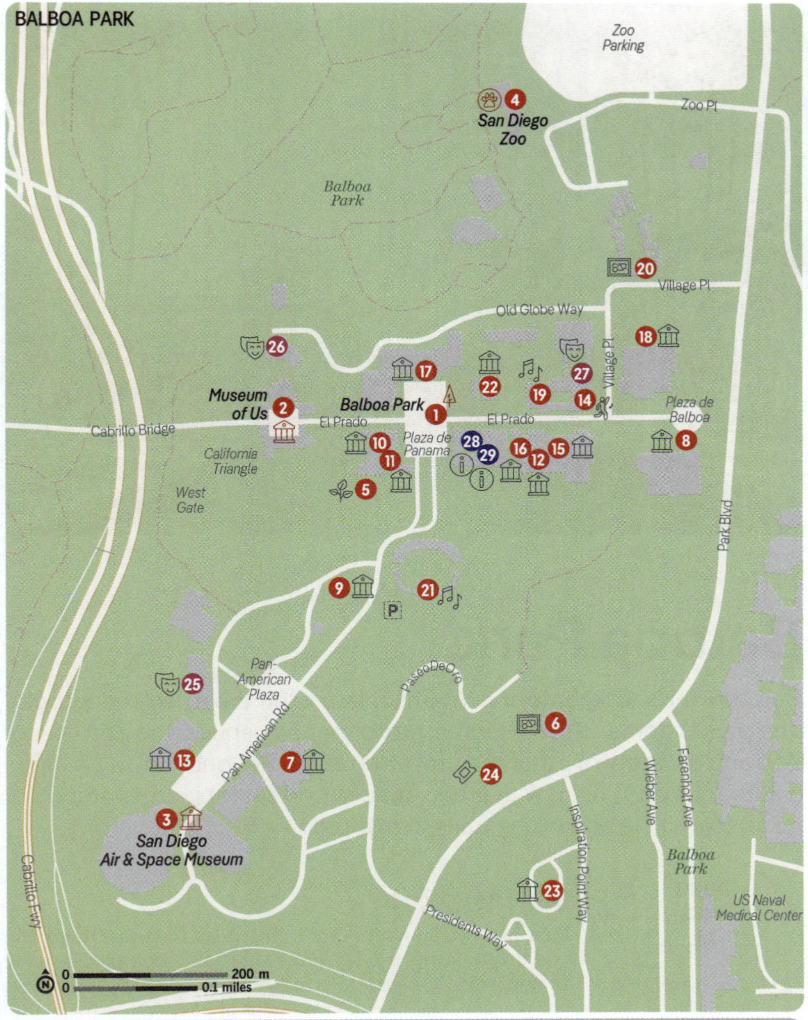

HIGHLIGHTS
1 Balboa Park
2 Museum of Us
3 San Diego Air & Space Museum
4 San Diego Zoo

SIGHTS
5 Balboa Park Gardens
6 Centro Cultural de la Raza
7 Comic-Con Museum
8 Fleet Science Center
9 House of Pacific Relations International Cottages
10 Institute of Contemporary Art, San Diego
11 Mingei International Museum
12 Museum of Photographic Arts
13 San Diego Automotive Museum
14 San Diego Civic Youth Ballet
15 San Diego History Center
16 San Diego Model Railroad Museum
17 San Diego Museum of Art
18 San Diego Natural History Museum
19 San Diego Youth Symphony
20 Spanish Village Arts Center
21 Spreckels Organ Pavilion
22 Timken Museum of Art
23 Veterans Museum of Balboa Park
24 WorldBeat Cultural Center

ENTERTAINMENT
25 Marie Hitchcock Puppet Theater
26 Old Globe
27 San Diego Junior Theatre

INFORMATION
28 Balboa Park Visitor Center
29 Park Ambassador Information Tent

VALERIA VENEZIA/SHUTTERSTOCK

TOP EXPERIENCE

Balboa Park

Balboa Park's nickname, the Smithsonian of the West, isn't hyperbole. The park is home to 17 museums, performance venues, the San Diego Zoo and a variety of other cultural attractions. Beyond that, it's simply a gorgeous park, filled with green spaces perfect for picnics and 65 miles of walking and biking trails to explore.

DON'T MISS

- San Diego Zoo
- San Diego Museum of Art
- Centro Cultural de la Raza
- Museum of Us
- The Old Globe
- Air & Space Museum
- Natural History Museum
- International Cottages

San Diego Zoo

Take everything you've ever heard about the **San Diego Zoo** *(sandiegozoo.org; adult/child $76/66)* and multiply it by two: that will give you some idea of how vast and wildly impressive the place is. The justifiably famous attraction has over 4000 animals representing more than 650 species in a beautifully landscaped setting. Typical enclosures replicate a species' natural habitat.

Specialized bioclimatic environments like the Elephant Odyssey, Panda Canyon and Monkey Trail are home to the zoo's many inhabitants: big cats (cheetahs, jaguars and leopards), elephants, giraffes, grizzly bears, red pandas, king cobras and much, much more.

PRACTICALITIES

Scan the QR code for details of upcoming Balboa Park events.

The San Diego Zoo has been instrumental in saving the endangered California condor, which you can also see while you're there.

Wear comfortable shoes: walking is the best way to get close to the animals. Alternatively, you can hop on a double-decker bus for a 35-minute narrative overview tour (free with your ticket): sitting downstairs puts you closer to the animals. Another option for those unable to walk far is the Kangaroo Bus, which lets you hop on and off at four stops. The **Skyfari** aerial tram flies from one side of the zoo to the other, with beautiful views of the rest of the park.

Arts Appreciation

For those who love the fine arts, there are several museums in Balboa Park worth checking out. The **Museum of Photographic Arts** *(mopa.org; by donation)* has a vast collection, ranging from Ansel Adams to avant-garde cell-phone photography. The **San Diego Museum of Art** *(sdma.org; adult/child $20/free)* has international exhibits that range from El Greco to Japanese woodblock prints, as well as an outdoor sculpture garden. The **Timken Museum of Art** *(timken museum.org; free)* has a collection of works by European old masters like Rembrandt.

The **Centro Cultural de la Raza** *(centrodelaraza.com; free)* is an arts center highlighting Mexican, Indigenous and Latino art and performance. The **Institute of Contemporary Art, San Diego** *(icasandiego.org; by donation)* exhibits the works of artists in Southern California from Los Angeles to Tijuana and has a second outpost in Encinitas. The round, steel building, originally a water tank, is impressively painted with 240ft of murals. The folk-art focused **Mingei International Museum** *(mingei.org; adult/child $15/free)* has exhibits showcasing handmade arts and craft from people and cultures around the world.

The **Spanish Village Arts Center** *(villageartscenter.org)* is a community of more than 200 local artists showing their works, with open studios and art demonstrations in a vibrant recreation of a Spanish village. It's also home to the **San Diego Mineral and Gem Societies' Museum** *(sdmg.org; free)*.

Science & Technology

To learn about the world, try the **Museum of Us** *(museum ofus.org; adult/child $19.95/16.95)*, dedicated to anthropology, human history and a deeper understanding of what makes us 'us.' Exhibits hopscotch from ancient Egypt to the Native American Kumeyaay people and from beer to the long-running cannibals exhibition. The **San Diego Air & Space Museum** *(san diegoairandspace.org; adult/child $35/22)* has the real *Apollo 9* Command Module and artifacts from Amelia Earhart and Charles Lindbergh. The **Fleet Science Center** *(fleetscience.org; adult/child $24.95/19.95)* has 100 interactive science exhibits that aren't just for kids; every month, the center hosts an adults-only 'after dark' event.

SAFARI PARK

In northern San Diego County is the San Diego Zoo's **Safari Park** *(sdzsafaripark.org; adult/child $76/66)*, where animals roam freely in savannas. There are a variety of experiences, ranging from the Sun Up Cheetah Safari – see cheetahs sprinting through the park before it opens for the day – to the Roar & Snore, where you camp in the park overnight.

INTERNATIONAL COTTAGES

If Disneyland's It's A Small World ride were a walk-through attraction, it would be the **House of Pacific Relations International Cottages** *(sdhpr.org)*. A gathering of 33 different 'houses,' each represents the traditions of its host country (from South Korea to Ukraine) through music, art, dance and food.

FINDING YOUR WAY

At more than 1200 acres, Balboa Park can be overwhelming to navigate – but there are two places that can help you get started. Pop into the **Visitor Center** at the House of Hospitality or the **Park Ambassador Information Tent** in the Plaza de Panama to get maps, recommendations and more information.

'The Nat,' as the **San Diego Natural History Museum** *(sdnhm.org; adult/child $24/14)* is called, offers a summer Fridays deal: admission is half-price after 5pm, the museum stays open until 10pm and there are special events throughout the night and dining on the rooftop. In addition to dinosaur fossils and a 'living lab,' the Nat offers lectures, events and hikes led by 'Canyoneers.'

For the Fun of It

Since 1970, the **San Diego Comic-Con** in late July has been a standard bearer for fandom events; its **Comic-Con Museum** *(comic-con.org/museum; adult/child $30/15)* celebrates all things superhero and fan culture. The **Marie Hitchcock Puppet Theater** *(balboaparkpuppets.com; $5)* stages whimsical performances every weekend. The park is also home to a 1910 carousel with hand-carved animals and a miniature, rideable antique railroad train.

History & Transportation

The **Marston House** *(sohosandiego.org; adult/child $20/7)* is a beautifully preserved example of California's signature arts-and-crafts architecture. The **San Diego History Center** *(sandiegohistory.org; by donation)* focuses on local history. The **Veterans Museum of Balboa Park** *(veteranmuseum.org; adult/child $5/free)* is housed in the former chapel of the naval hospital and is devoted to local military history.

For transportation nerds, there's the **San Diego Automotive Museum** *(sdautomuseum.org; adult/child $19.50/15)* that

ARTAZUM/SHUTTERSTOCK

Marston House

Public gardens

delves into car culture, and the **San Diego Model Railroad Museum** *(sdmrm.org; adult/child $20/free),* which has the world's largest operating model railroad running through a miniature California.

Public Gardens

Balboa Park started as a public garden and grew into what it is today thanks to the World's Fairs of 1915–16 and 1935–36. The natural landscape is still the heart of the park experience. The park has remarkable **public gardens**, including Palm Canyon, with 58 species of palm trees; Trees for Health, a medicinal plant garden; the Kate O Sessions Cactus Garden; the Inez Grant Parker Memorial Rose Garden, which has 130 varieties of rose and is in bloom almost all year; and the Zoro Garden, which was once a nudist colony and is now a butterfly garden.

All the Park's a Stage

Balboa Park hosts an incredible number of live performances, from the international dance-focused **WorldBeat Cultural Center** *(worldbeatcenter.org)* to the **San Diego Civic Youth Ballet** *(sdcyb.org),* **San Diego Junior Theatre** *(juniortheatre.com)* and **San Diego Youth Symphony** *(keynote-music.org).* The **Old Globe** *(theoldglobe.org),* based on the original theater in London, has three stages and hosts productions that often head to Broadway.

One of the most engaging things to do in San Diego is to attend a free Sunday afternoon organ concert at the **Spreckels Organ Pavilion** *(spreckelsorgan.org),* which has the largest outdoor organ in the world, with more than 5000 pipes.

FREE GUIDED TOURS

Every Tuesday and Friday morning, Balboa Park offers free guided tours *(foreverbalboapark.org)* of the Central Mesa. Guides talk about the history of the park, the attractions it holds and what events are currently on. Once a month, the park also offers a botanical tour, digging deep into the park's varied landscape.

TOP TIPS

- Save on admission fees by buying a Balboa Park Explorer Pass *(explorer.balboapark.org; adult/child from $60/39).* They're available for four museums in a single day or unlimited admission for a week.
- Give yourself plenty of time to explore. Balboa Park has miles of walking and biking trails and no matter what attraction you're going to see, you're almost guaranteed to see something else that catches your interest.
- Parking in the park is free, but the lots near attractions fill up quickly. Use the in-park shuttle system to catch a ride from a more distant lot.

SAN DIEGO'S BEST BIKE PATHS

San Diego has over 1800 miles of bikeways – use the *San Diego Regional Bike Map (sandag.org)* to find your route.

Bayshore Bikeway: A 24-mile loop from Coronado to Chula Vista, but you can stick to the beachside Silver Strand for a bike path-only route.

Mission Bay Bike Loop: Mission Bay, between SD and La Jolla, has a flat 12-mile bike path with gorgeous views.

Balboa Park Loop: Cruising around the park on two wheels offers a new perspective.

San Diego River Bike Path: This 20-mile car-free path follows the San Diego River from Mission Valley to Ocean Beach.

Los Penasquitos Canyon: This mountainous area has hiking and biking paths for all levels.

(continued from p182)

the streets and public *ofrendas* remembering those who have passed. December's **Old Town Las Posadas** is a Mexican celebration honoring biblical Christmas stories.

A Delicious Departure

MAP P179

Craft beers and vintage shopping in North and South Park

If you truly want to experience San Diego like a local, head to **North Park** and **South Park**, just beyond Balboa Park. North Park is often called the best beer neighborhood in the country because of the number of craft beer bars and breweries along University Ave and 30th St, like **North Park Brewing** and **Thorn Street Beer**. South Park has a distinctly indie vibe, with interesting, forward-thinking galleries and vintage shopping. Between the two, **Juniper Canyon** is an urban park with an easy 1-mile hike with gorgeous views.

Find the Silver Lining in Coronado

MAP P179

A sparkling beach destination

Dr Beach praised **Silver Strand State Beach** in **Coronado** as one of the best in the country – but if we're being honest, all of Coronado seems to shine. This coastal neighborhood, on a peninsula on the opposite side of San Diego Bay from the

EATING IN SAN DIEGO: GASLAMP & EMBARCADERO

MAP P180

Headquarters at Seaport: Village San Diego's old police HQ now offers food stalls, fine dining and shopping. *10am-9pm Mon-Sat, to 8pm Sun* $$

Fish Market: Freshly caught fish; straight from the sea to your plate at this Embarcadero restaurant. Del Mar outpost too. *11am-8.30pm Sun-Thu, to 9pm Fri & Sat* $$

Animae: Steakhouse infused with Japanese and Filipino influences from chef Tara Monsod. Seriously chic, art-filled dining room. *5-9pm Sun-Thu, to 9.30pm Fri & Sat* $$$

Werewolf: This lively brewpub in the Gaslamp is a high-energy destination serving brunch and elevated bar food. Nightly karaoke. *8am-2am* $$

MATTHEW JAMES FERGUSON/SHUTTERSTOCK

Coronado

mainland, is connected to downtown San Diego via bridges. It's an easy escape that's just a few minutes away. The area is full of beach cottages and boutiques. **Ferry Landing** is a strollable collection of shops, restaurants and galleries. **Lamb's Players Theatre** *(lambsplayers.com)* stages five productions a year and the **Coronado Historical Association** *(coronadohistory.org; adult/child $25/10)* offers daily walking tours of the island.

Coronado's best-known resident is the **Hotel del Coronado** *(hoteldel.com)*, one of the most famous hotels in California. The 1888 hotel was originally built for wealthy Victorians looking to take in the ocean air and has grown over the years to become a destination beloved for its location, historic architecture and, some say, its hauntings. Rooms can be very pricey, especially during high season. But the good news is that you don't have to be a guest to enjoy many of the hotel's attractions and restaurants, including year-round ghost tours and wintertime ice skating by the beach.

THE CALIFORNIA BURRITO

If you've ever had a California burrito outside of California, you've likely had one made with meat, beans, rice, cheese and guacamole. But that's actually a Mission burrito, invented in San Francisco. A real California burrito is a signature San Diego food and it's a must-try while you're in town. It features *carne asada* (grilled steak), *pico de gallo* salsa, guacamole, cheese and...french fries? Don't knock it until you've tried it.

Roberto's Taco Shop *(robertostacoshop.com)* is credited with inventing the California burrito in the 1980s – the local chain has locations across the city and beyond – but you'll find it's widely available at many taco shops and Mexican restaurants throughout the region.

Ocean Trash, Ocean Treasure

MAP P179

Go diving at Wreck Alley

A global destination for scuba enthusiasts, **Wreck Alley** is an artificial reef a few miles off the coast of Mission Beach.

EATING IN SAN DIEGO: LITTLE ITALY

MAP P180

Juniper & Ivy: One of the most decorated restaurants in San Diego, Juniper & Ivy has a seasonally driven fine-dining menu. *5-9pm Sun-Thu, to 10pm Fri & Sat* $$$

Mona Lisa Italian Foods: This grocery and restaurant is like the local version of Eataly. *deli 9am-10pm, restaurant 11am-9.30pm Mon-Sat, from noon Sun* $$

Civico 1845: In addition to freshly made pasta and Calabrian cuisine, this restaurant has a full slate of vegan offerings. *4-9pm Sun-Thu, to 10pm Fri, noon-10pm Sat & Sun* $$

Morning Glory: Whimsical brunch restaurant with a roving Bloody Mary cart and breakfast carbonara and chilaquiles. *8am-3pm Mon-Fri, to 4pm Sat & Sun* $$

OLD TOWN TROLLEY TOURS

One of the most entertaining and stress-free ways to see the city is on the **Old Town Trolley** *(trolleytours.com; $52/33)*, which is a hop-on, hop-off transportation that spans 25 miles over 11 stops. A two-hour loop on the Old Town Trolley will take you from Old Town to locations like the Gaslamp District, Barrio Logan, Seaport Village, the Embarcadero, Balboa Park and Coronado, and the tour guide provides local history and information about each area as you go. The best part: you do it on your own schedule. Trolleys run all day, so you can hop on and off the trolley to explore on your own, then catch a ride back when you're ready.

ROSAMAR/SHUTTERSTOCK

Mission Bay

A collection of intentionally scuttled boats, including an old Coast Guard ship and a Canadian naval destroyer, plus pieces of a former city bridge, have formed an artificial reef that's rich in marine biodiversity and perfect for diving. **Waterhorse Charters** *(waterhorsecharters.com; dives from $175)* takes divers out to the wrecks on public and private charters. Because there are both shallow and deep dive sites, the alley is suitable for divers of all levels.

On a Mission for Fun

MAP P179

Make a splash at Mission Bay and Mission Beach

Mission Bay Park, half waterfront and half water, is the place to go for water sports. This area offers everything from kayaking to water skiing, sailing and kitesurfing. If you want to charter a fishing or sailing excursion, this is the place to do it. **Mission Beach** has a classic beachside boardwalk with a vintage roller coaster, midway games, restaurants and beach bars at the 100-year-old **Belmont Park** *(belmontpark.com)*. Admission is free and each ride or game is paid individually.

Get a Taste of Italy in SoCal

MAP P180

Little Italy is a lifestyle

If you think the city's historic Italian neighborhood is just a place to go when you're craving pasta, think again. Just blocks from the harbor, **Little Italy** is full of art, outdoor markets and pedestrian spaces like Piazza della Famiglia, which really does feel like Europe. There's also, of course, a lot of pasta. Every April, Little Italy hosts the **Mission Fed ArtWalk** *(artwalksandiego.org)*, which brings together over 250 artists, performers and food vendors for a celebration of creativity.

Beyond San Diego

Coastal cities around San Diego have a charm all their own: explore an arts haven, a beach sanctuary and a superb aquarium.

You could spend an entire vacation within San Diego city limits and still not see everything the city has to offer – but you'd also be missing out on some truly special destinations that are a short distance away, whether you're driving, biking or taking the trolley.

La Jolla is similar to the Spanish phrase *la joya,* meaning 'the jewel.' Pronounced la-*hoy*-yah, the name may actually date from Native Americans who called the place *'mut la hoya, la hoya'* – the place of many caves.

Del Mar and Chula Vista are also easily reachable from San Diego without relocating your hotel accommodations or investing too much time in transit. Even if you only head to one of these destinations for an hour or two, it will be time well spent.

Places

Chula Vista

TIME FROM SAN DIEGO: **15MIN**

Sunny days, chasing the clouds away

Everyone's favorite monster-filled street comes to life at **Sesame Place San Diego** *(sesameplace.com; entry $95)*, a *Sesame Street* theme park for young kids in Chula Vista. There are parades and character meet-and-greets with Big Bird and friends, rides like Super Grover's Box Car Derby and experiences like Dine with Elmo. Water features like the Count's Splash Castle will help you stay cool. Pro tip: online tickets are substantially discounted from gate ticket prices.

How the other half trains

Future Olympians often find themselves at the **Chula Vista Elite Athlete Training Center** *(trainatchulavista.com)*, a massive campus that works with up-and-coming athletes at the highest level. The campus is open for tours; either take a self-guided tour and explore on your own or reserve spots on a guided tour on golf carts.

GETTING AROUND

The San Diego Metropolitan Transit System *(sdmts.com)* has trolley and bus services that connect the city to La Jolla, Chula Vista and Del Mar. Within the towns themselves, there are easy-to-navigate public transit systems. La Jolla has a hop-on, hop-off trolley *(trolleytours.com)* and Chula Vista has shuttle service on demand *(chulavistaca.gov)*.

TAKE A SWING AT TORREY PINES

This neighborhood in northern La Jolla has some of the city's most iconic destinations: **Torrey Pines Golf Course** *(torreypines.com)* and **Torrey Pines State Natural Reserve** *(torreypine.org; parking $10-25)*. The golf course, open to the public, is widely regarded as one of the best destinations in the country because of its sweeping cliffside location and the quality of its terrain. The natural reserve is a popular hiking spot prized for those same views. It's also home to a rare species of pine tree – *Pinus torreyana*, or Torrey pine – once prevalent in California and now preserved only in this reserve and on one island off Santa Barbara.

La Jolla

TIME FROM SAN DIEGO: **20MIN**

Stroll the Village

The Village is a picturesque collection of strollable shops and restaurants and includes many of **La Jolla**'s most notable attractions – including the sea lions the city is famous for. **Scripps Park** is especially picturesque. Most days you'll see street vendors set up in and around Scripps Park, selling everything from handmade jewelry to art painted in front of you.

Directly below Scripps Park in **La Jolla Village** is **La Jolla Cove**, one of the most famous beaches in Southern California, where you can swim and spot sea lions. Remember to keep your distance; some days, there are ropes in place to ensure the sea lions have enough space to themselves.

One of the most unusual places to check out is the **Cave Store** *(cavestore.com)*. This jewelry and gift shop is the entrance to a tunnel where you'll descend 144 steps carved out of pure rock, walking down and down until you arrive at **Sunny Jim's Sea Cave**, the only sea cave in California that's accessible by land. The tunnel has been open since 1902; legend has it that bootleggers smuggled alcohol through the cave during Prohibition.

One final note: don't confuse the Village with La Jolla Village, a more residential inland area.

The artful side of La Jolla

La Jolla has a robust art scene. On the **La Jolla Village Art Walk** *(lajollabythesea.com)*, you'll pass the Madison Gallery, Martin Lawrence Galleries and Peter Lik Gallery; the latter is one of the showrooms of the artist who allegedly sold the world's most expensive photograph, *Phantom,* in 2014 for $6.5 million.

La Jolla is also home to a standout local theater company, **La Jolla Playhouse** *(lajollaplayhouse.org)*, which is nationally renowned for the quality of its works and the star power it attracts. The playhouse hosts world premieres of innovative and forward-thinking works and brings in luminaries like Matthew Broderick to star in its productions.

Explore the ocean

La Jolla has two offshore marine reserves: the **San Diego-Scripps Coastal Marine Conservation Area** and the **Matlahuayl State Marine Reserve**. Both are ideal locations for snorkeling and scuba diving, but if you'd rather see marine

DINING IN LA JOLLA: OUR PICKS

George's at the Cove: This waterfront seafood restaurant has a dining room and a more casual rooftop terrace with gorgeous ocean views. *11am-10pm* **$$$**

Marine Room: A coastal seafood restaurant that's so close to the water that waves crash against the expansive windows at high tide. *5-9.30pm Wed-Sun* **$$$**

The Taco Stand: The first location of the Taco Stand serves killer tacos with handmade tortillas and slow-roasted and braised meats. *9am-9pm Sun-Thu, to 10pm Fri & Sat* **$**

Wayfarer Bread and Pastry: This bakery is beloved for its breakfast pastries and sandwiches perfect for the beach. *8am-2.30pm Tue-Sun, 4.30-8.30pm Tue-Sat* **$$**

CHRIS LABASCO/SHUTTERSTOCK

La Jolla Cove

life on land, then head to the **Birch Aquarium at Scripps** *(aquarium.ucsd.edu; adult/child $35/30)*. Part of University of California San Diego's **Scripps Institution of Oceanography**, the aquarium has more than 60 marine habitats on display, including an enormous two-story kelp forest. Among Birch's most famous residents: a pod of blue penguins, leopard sharks, seahorses and seadragons. The aquarium also has hands-on outdoor tide pool tanks and offers guided explorations of natural tide pools led by an aquarium naturalist, generally in the winter and early spring. Once per month, Birch hosts **Ocean at Night**, an after-hours event that celebrates bioluminescence in all its forms (including glowing cocktails).

Another part of Scripps that puts you close to the ocean is the **Ellen Browning Scripps Memorial Pier**, where oceanographic research takes place daily. You can only access the pier via student-led tours *(scripps.ucsd.edu/about/tours)*.

Del Mar

TIME FROM SAN DIEGO: **25MIN**

Visit the county fair

One of the most highly anticipated events of the year is the **San Diego County Fair** *(sdfair.com)*, which is so huge that it lasts a month. More than a million people visit the Del Mar Fairgrounds in June and July for the fair, which has

THE MURALS OF LA JOLLA

La Jolla sits atop bluffs with the ocean on three sides. But the city's natural beauty isn't the only thing worth admiring here. A massive public art program has been tasked with beautifying the city since 2010. Today, there are 16 large-scale **murals** on display and more than 50 pieces of public art. The Murals of La Jolla website *(muralsoflajolla.com)* details the art and the artists and offers a walking tour so you can see them for yourself.

BEST COCKTAIL BARS IN LA JOLLA

Le Coq After Hours: A bistro menu complements the next-level cocktails while DJs spin vinyl at this new-wave French restaurant. *5pm-midnight Tue-Sun*

Raised by Wolves: Make a reservation for this stylish cocktail bar with sophisticated libations. *11.30am-11pm Sun-Wed, to midnight Thu, to 1am Fri & Sat*

The Whaling Bar: Inside La Valencia Hotel, this swanky lounge revives a much-missed meeting spot, with original art and a daily martini hour. *3-11pm*

Birdseye: This rooftop restaurant and lounge serves bright, herbaceous cocktails. *11am-10pm Mon-Thu, 11am-11pm Fri, 10am-11pm Sat, 10am-10pm Sun*

HORSE RACING IN DEL MAR

Besides the San Diego County Fair, the Del Mar Fairgrounds are also home to the **Del Mar Racetrack** *(dmtc.com)*. Bing Crosby was an original owner and instrumental in getting the track built; on its opening day in 1937, the crooner was at the gate greeting the first guests. The first-ever nationally broadcast horserace was at Del Mar, where Seabiscuit won by a nose. Today, the thoroughbred racing season takes place from late summer to early fall.

KALJUNIOR/SHUTTERSTOCK

Del Mar

more than 2000 attractions and 1700 performers. There's a midway with carnival rides and games, concerts with major headliners, art and flower exhibitions, animal encounters, artisan craft demonstrations and wine, beer and spirits festivals. And that's just for starters.

Learn to surf

Because of its reliable surf conditions and less busy beaches, **Del Mar** is ideal if you've always wanted to take a surf lesson but never got around to it. Many surf shops and surf schools in Del Mar offer lessons that include board rentals, including **Rusty Del Mar Surfboards** *(rustydelmar.com; lesson $150, board and wetsuit rental $80)*, **Del Mar Surf Sessions** *(delmarsurfsessions.com; lesson $150)*, **Del Mar Surf School** *(delmarsurfschool.com; lesson $150)* and **Progressive Surf Academy** *(progressivesurfacademy.com; lesson $115)*.

DINING IN DEL MAR: OUR PICKS

Addison: The three Michelin-starred Addison offers tasting menus focused on local, seasonal ingredients and the flavors of Southern California. *6-9pm* $$$

Poseidon: This stylish seafood restaurant has incredible water views and a Mediterranean-inspired menu. *10am-9pm Sat & Sun, 4.30pm-9pm Mon, 11am-9pm Tue-Fri* $$$

Jake's Del Mar: Serves the same Hawaiian spirit of aloha as its sister restaurant Duke's, including its signature hula pie. *hours vary* $$

Viewpoint Brewing: This casual, fun brewery has swinging seats and water views, plus a huge selection of house-brewed beers. *noon-9pm Tue-Fri, from 10am Sat & Sun* $$

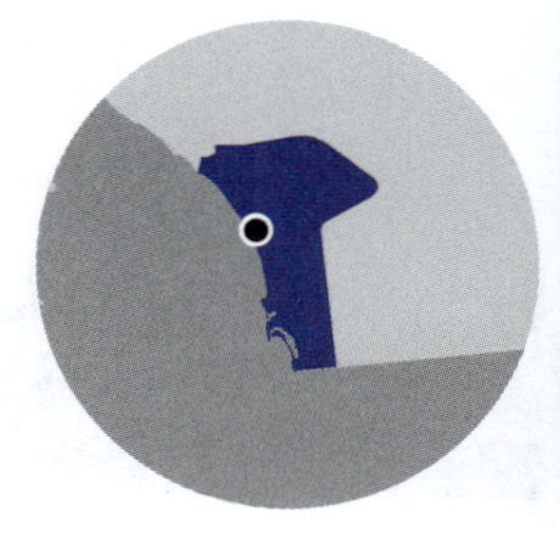

Carlsbad

MUSEUMS | NATURE | BEACHES

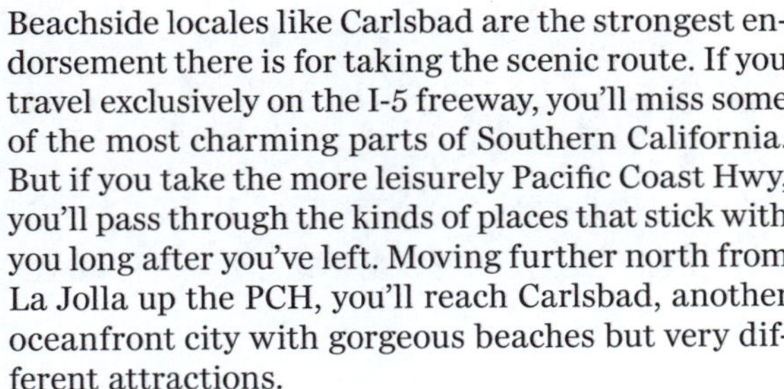

Beachside locales like Carlsbad are the strongest endorsement there is for taking the scenic route. If you travel exclusively on the I-5 freeway, you'll miss some of the most charming parts of Southern California. But if you take the more leisurely Pacific Coast Hwy, you'll pass through the kinds of places that stick with you long after you've left. Moving further north from La Jolla up the PCH, you'll reach Carlsbad, another oceanfront city with gorgeous beaches but very different attractions.

Carlsbad came into being in the 1880s when John Frazier, an early homesteader, sank a well and found water that had a high mineral content, supposedly identical to that of the spa water in Karlsbad, Bohemia (now in Czechia).

The city today is home to an aquarium, a gem institute, several intriguing museums and the first-ever Legoland theme park. Carlsbad also has some of the area's best golf courses.

Carlsbad in Flower

Where the superbloom hits different

There's no bad time to visit Carlsbad, but the best time is probably spring, when the **Carlsbad Ranch Flower Fields** *(theflowerfields.com; adult/child $27/17)* burst into vivid color. These 55 acres of carefully cultivated flowers bloom from March to May every year. Beyond the sea of color, there's also a floral hedge maze and kids' activities.

Where Learning Is Fun

One-of-a-kind museums

The city is home to a host of irresistible attractions, like the **Museum of Making Music** *(museumofmakingmusic.org; adult/child $15/10)*, which explores the history of music

(continued on p198)

TOP TIP

To help manage traffic and reduce emissions and help people find the best way of getting from Point A to Point B, the City of Carlsbad designed the Carlsbad Commuter app and website *(carlsbadcommuter.com)*

GETTING AROUND

Carlsbad is only about a 40-minute drive from San Diego International Airport, but if you'd rather take public transportation, it's very easy. The North County Transit San Diego Railroad *(gonctd.com; ticket $6.50)* connects Carlsbad and Oceanside to the north to downtown SD. If you're staying in Carlsbad and planning to explore on two wheels, the city is very bikeable, especially on the Coastal Rail Trail.

LEGOLAND CALIFORNIA

TOP EXPERIENCE

Legoland

This builder's paradise is more than just a theme park – it's an immersive land where Legos are life-sized, dragons are real and the only limit is your imagination. The first Legoland theme park in the country, Carlsbad's main attraction has two hotels, a separately ticketed aquarium and water park and a full schedule of fun seasonal events.

DON'T MISS

- Dino Valley Explorer River Quest
- Miniland USA
- Legoland Water Park
- Sea Life Aquarium
- Brick-or-Treat Monster Party
- Legoland Castle Hotel

Orientation

Just like Lego bricks themselves, the Legoland California park is small but mighty. The easily navigable campus includes the Legoland theme park, an attached Legoland water park and a separate Sea Life Aquarium – plus two themed hotels – all within a very short walk of one another. While there's fun for everyone, this is an ideal theme park to visit when your kids are younger (12 and under). The rides are fun but not too intense and many ride queues and waiting areas (even in the restaurants) have Lego play areas where kids can burn off extra energy during the boring parts when parents are

PRACTICALITIES

Scan the QR code for Legoland tickets and passes.

waiting in line. Everything from the food to the hotels (with free breakfasts) to the online ticket deals are a good value at this family resort.

Legoland Park

There are over 60 rides and attractions at **Legoland Park**, ranging from gentle rides for young kids to thrill coasters – but even the thrill coasters are still family-friendly. In Dino Valley, the park's newest land, you can search for dinosaurs on Explorer River Quest or escape the Coastersaurus. Search for treasure in the Lost Kingdom Adventure dark ride in the Land of Adventure, or tame the Dragon coaster on Castle Hill.

The central land at Legoland, **Miniland USA**, is a jaw-dropping attraction made of millions of Lego bricks. The enormous installation features scenery from Los Angeles, San Diego, San Francisco, New York, Washington, DC and Las Vegas. You can walk around and explore – there are even motorized functions like moving cars – or take the Coast Cruise, a boat ride across the park's central lake, to get a water's-edge view.

In addition to rides, Legoland has interactive shows and parades, like 'Once Upon a Brick – Tale of the Unicorn Knight' storytime and the Legoland Jam dance party. Meet characters from entertainment like *The Lego Movie* and *Lego Ninjago*.

Legoland's **Water Park** is within the gates of the theme park, but there's an additional charge for admission (note: there's no access without Legoland admission; it's an extra $35 if you buy discounted tickets online). Inside the water park, there are six waterslides, a pirate boat flume ride, a lazy river and Orange Rush, a raft slide half-pipe.

Sea Life Aquarium

Legoland's **Sea Life Aquarium** shares a central plaza with the theme park, but you can purchase a separate ticket for entry *($25, less if you have a park ticket)* without having to enter Legoland itself. Inside are over 350 species of marine creatures, most of them native to Southern California, and outdoor touch tanks.

Brick or Treat

In September and October, Legoland celebrates Halloween with **Brick or Treat**, featuring special entertainment like a dance party with Lego Dracula and in-park trick or treating. Costumes are encouraged and not even the zombie cheerleader Lego characters are too scary.

Accommodations

There are two Lego hotels here. The **Legoland Resort Hotel** has pirate- and adventure-themed rooms and the **Legoland Castle Hotel** is full of wizards and dragons. Both offer separate kids' sleeping areas in every room, a box of Legos to play with in the room, free breakfast and nightly family entertainment, like poolside movies.

GRANNY'S APPLE FRIES

If you know someone who's been to Legoland, they've likely said one thing to you: under no circumstances should you skip the apple fries. To confirm, they are 100% correct. The legendary apple fries are French fry-cut slices of apple, dredged in cinnamon sugar and lightly fried just long enough to crisp them up, served with whipped cream.

TOP TIPS

- Legoland is a Certified Autism Center. Its accommodations for neurodivergent guests, including sensory guides and quiet spaces, are top-notch.
- Single-park tickets can cost as much as $129 per person when purchased at the park, but online deals can be as much as 40% off.
- Both hotels share a small plaza with the front gate of Legoland and Sea Life Aquarium, so it's less than a minute's walk to get in and out of the attractions.
- From I-5, take the Legoland/Cannon Rd exit and follow the signs. Parking is $35.

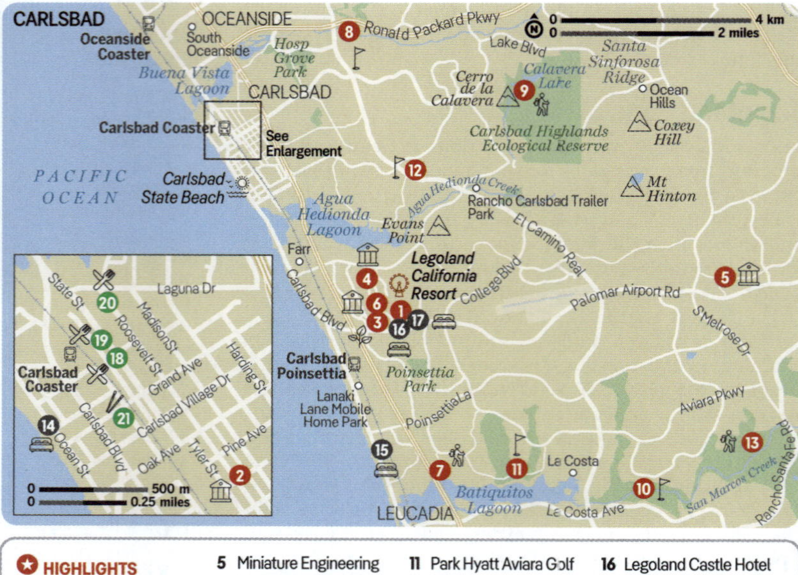

HIGHLIGHTS
1 Legoland California Resort

SIGHTS
2 Carlsbad Barrio & Museum
3 Carlsbad Ranch Flower Fields
4 Gemological Institute of America
5 Miniature Engineering Craftsmanship Museum
6 Museum of Making Music

ACTIVITIES
7 Aviara Trail System
8 Carlsbad Golf Center
9 Lake Calavera Preserve
10 Omni La Costa Golf Course
11 Park Hyatt Aviara Golf Club
12 Rancho Carlsbad Golf Course
13 Rancho La Costa Preserve

SLEEPING
14 Beach Terrace Inn
15 Cape Rey Carlsbad by Hilton
16 Legoland Castle Hotel
17 Legoland Resort Hotel

EATING
18 Campfire
19 Jeune et Jolie
20 Lilo
21 Same Same

(continued from p195)

and musical instruments. It hosts a concert series all year long. The **Carlsbad Barrio & Museum** *(carlsbadhistorical society.com; free)* celebrates the city's Mexican heritage and the families who established the area as a center of agriculture more than a century ago. The **Gemological Institute of America** *(gia.edu; free; reservations required)* houses a vast collection of stones, including the Tower of Brilliance, the world's largest crystal octahedron. The tiniest exhibits ever are at the **Miniature Engineering Craftsmanship Museum** *(craftsmanshipmuseum.com; free)*, which showcases teeny models.

Hike Carlsbad

Over 65 miles of trails

This oceanfront city has an abundance of scenic, relatively easy hiking trails. The **Lake Calavera Preserve**, adjacent to the Carlsbad Highlands Ecological Reserve, is a series of shorter trails, some going around the lake and others circling

NAYADADARA/SHUTTERSTOCK

Lake Calavera Preserve

its green space. The **Aviara Trail System**'s Lagoon Trail is a mostly flat 2.7-mile loop around its lagoon, with signage about the area's wildlife and flora. The more challenging **Rancho La Costa Preserve** is a 4-mile trail system that has some rugged spots, especially through Box Canyon.

Fore!

Carlsbad's top golf courses

Carlsbad is well known for its golfing and is even hosting the NCAA Division 1 Golf Championships through 2028. The **Carlsbad Golf Center** *(carlsbadgolfcenter.com)* has been consistently ranked as a top public range for more than 20 years and the **Rancho Carlsbad Golf Club** *(ranchocarlsbad golf.com)* is another excellent public course. Arnold Palmer designed the course at **Park Hyatt Aviara Golf Club** *(parkhyattaviara.com)* and legends like Jack Nicklaus and Tiger Woods have played at **Omni La Costa Golf Course** *(theclubatlacosta.com)*.

THE BIRTH OF MODERN SKATEBOARDING

In the 1970s, skateboarding was making a comeback from a lull in popularity and Southern California was the epicenter. In 1975, Del Mar hosted an enormous skateboarding competition, the Del Mar National Championships. The following year, Carlsbad opened one of the first skate parks in the world. Today, skateboarding is inextricable from Southern California's worldwide image, thanks to generations of skate kids who turned the pastime into a bona fide sport, like Carlsbad native Tony Hawk, who was just eight years old when the park opened. Widely hailed as one of the best skateboarders of all time, Hawk held the title of vertical skateboarding world champion for 12 straight years and inspired a skateboarding video game empire.

WHERE TO EAT IN CARLSBAD: OUR PICKS

Same Same: Modern Thai paired with Thai-tinged drinks, like nitro draft cocktails with tiki inspiration. *4pm-midnight Sun-Thu, to 1am Fri & Sat* $$

Campfire: New American restaurant serving a menu of wood-fired foods with an upscale rustic camping theme. *5-10pm Mon, Wed & Thu, 4:45-11pm Fri & Sat, 4-9pm Sun* $$$

Jeune et Jolie: A modern French restaurant serving four-course tasting menus, plus a more casual seafood-forward bar menu. *5-10pm Wed-Sun* $$$

Lilo: A truly curated dining experience, with a multicourse California coastal tasting menu served at an intimate chef's counter. *5-10pm Tue-Sat* $$$

Beyond Carlsbad

Oceanside and Encinitas are two charming beach towns that require you to slow down and enjoy the view.

Places

GETTING AROUND

The North County Transit San Diego Railroad *(gonctd.com; ticket $6.50)* connects Oceanside, Carlsbad and Encinitas to San Diego. Oceanside's gO'side shuttles are electric vehicles that you can request on-demand through the Ride Circuit app. A single passenger costs $3 and a group of riders is capped at $6 total.

When you're traveling, it's too easy to get caught up in wanting to see as much as possible and use every possible minute of your time. While that's tempting, especially in a place like California with its parade of unmissable attractions, it's antithetical to the spirit of the Pacific Coast Hwy. The coastal drive forces you to slow down and savor every moment – especially in smaller spots like Oceanside and Encinitas. Use your time in these beach havens as an antidote to the rush of city life. Take a walk, ride a bike, soak up the sun and let the laid-back Southern California energy take over.

Oceanside

TIME FROM CARLSBAD: **10MIN**

A California Cultural District

One of only 14 designated Cultural Districts in California, the **Oceanside Cultural District** is buzzing with local art, especially in Artist Alley. On the first Friday of every month, the district hosts **Art Walk Oceanside** *(oceansideartwalk.org)*, where galleries and artists' studios open their doors and offer demos, live music and refreshments. Every October, the district hosts the **O'Arts Festival**, which features visual art, performers, tattoo artists and culinary arts.

A short walk on a long pier

The **Oceanside Pier**, first constructed in 1888 and rebuilt through the centuries, is a must-stop in the city. Fishing is allowed without a license on the pier and there's a bait shop mid-pier that rents equipment. If you're just taking in the scenery, make sure to watch for sea mammals: dolphins and sea lions often swim up close, while it's not out of the question to spot a humpback whale in the distance. The amphitheater at the foot of the pier regularly hosts concerts and festivals.

A love affair with surfing

Every September, Oceanside hosts the **Super Girl Surf Pro** *(supergirlsurfpro.com),* a three-day event that's the largest all-female surf contest in the world. In addition to surf events, there are also concerts, a female art expo, beach sports and a festival village.

Oceanside is also home to the **California Surf Museum** *(surfmuseum.org; adult/child $7/free),* which is a tribute both to the sport and the distinctive SoCal surf culture that has grown from it. The museum regularly hosts film screenings and events like the Silver Skater Awards.

Encinitas

TIME FROM CARLSBAD: **15MIN**

Smell the flowers

Encinitas might be known for its beaches, but it's also got incredible scenery off the sand – specifically in the 37-acre **San Diego Botanic Garden** *(sdbg.org; adult/child $18/10).* It has 4 miles of walking trails and 29 different themed gardens, including the largest bamboo collection on the continent and the biggest children's garden on the West Coast, with interactive features and things to climb. Inside the enormous glass conservatory, plant islands hang from the ceiling.

The most fun on four wheels

On the third Thursday of the month during the summer, classic cars line up on Encinitas' Main St for **Classic Car Nights** *(encinitias101.com),* when hundreds of hot rods and vintage autos are on display; there's throwback live music, too. Every September for nearly five decades, the **Wavecraft Woodie Car Show** *(sandiegoassociationofcarclubs.org)* has been held on Moonlight Beach, where owners and enthusiasts of wood-paneled cars gather to talk shop.

TAKE MY BREATH AWAY

While it's not hard to find *Top Gun* filming locations in and around San Diego, arguably the most iconic – and inarguably the most delicious – is the **High Pie** *(highpie f10.com)* in Oceanside. The historic bungalow that was used as Charlie's (Kelly McGillis') house in the movie is now a bakery and pie shop, filled with *Top Gun* set photos and movie memorabilia, plus memorable art installations. The hand pies are small enough that you'll feel fine ordering one of every flavor, especially the ones that come warm with still-frozen ice cream inside. Outside, there's a Maverick-approved motorcycle to pose on and a waterfront porch where you can sit and enjoy the views.

DINING IN OCEANSIDE: OUR PICKS

Valle: This Michelin-starred Mexican restaurant has a seasonal tasting menu, plus a more casual bar experience. *5-9pm Tue-Sat* **$$$**

Little Fox Cups + Cones: To try Choco Tacos head to Little Fox for gourmet ice cream tacos alongside its sophisticated sweet and savory flavors. *11.30am-9pm* **$**

Wrench & Rodent Seabasstropub: This sushi gastropub offers inventive seafood- and plant-based rolls. *4-9pm Wed-Sun* **$$**

Dija Mara: Serves Balinese cuisine, like tofu *rendang* and *mie goreng,* with fun cocktails using ingredients like roasted pineapple and pandan. *5-9pm Tue-Sun* **$$**

Temecula

WINERIES | OLD TOWN | HOT-AIR BALLOONS

TOP TIP

The **De Portola Wine Trail** is a collection of 10 family-owned wineries along De Portola Rd in Temecula Valley and is a great place to start your tasting journey.

GETTING AROUND

About 60 miles from San Diego, Temecula isn't as easily accessed by public transit as other coastal locations. You might want to plan on driving to this sunny inland destination. Once you arrive, plan on leaving the car behind and use rideshares, bicycles or your feet instead.

Most people associate Napa Valley and Sonoma County with the best wines coming out of California – but the truth is that the entire state is littered with prime grape-growing areas, even down in the southernmost parts of SoCal. Temecula is only about an hour north of San Diego, but it feels like an entirely different world. Pull into Temecula Valley and you'll see row after row of grapevines dotted with picturesque tasting rooms, with the Temescal and Santa Ana Mountains rising up in the distance.

While you might be tempted to spend all of your time in Temecula tasting wine, you'd be missing much of what makes the valley great. Beyond the wineries (over 50), there are destination-worthy golf courses, 90 miles of bicycle trails, a children's museum and the Temecula Valley Symphony. Hot-air balloons are so popular in the area that there's an annual Temecula Valley Wine & Balloon Festival every May, with food, wine, concerts and 50 vividly colored balloons floating through the air.

A Taste of the Old West

Old Town Temecula is a place out of time

The heart of Temecula Valley was an important location in the Old West: after Mexico ceded California to the United States, Temecula served as a stagecoach stop and was also home to California's second-ever post office, after San Francisco. Following the Civil War, the town experienced an influx of settlers from the East. In 1882, the area saw the establishment of the Pechanga Reservation and the construction of a train station. The **Temecula Valley Museum** *(temeculavalley museum.org)* explores local history from the Native Luiseno

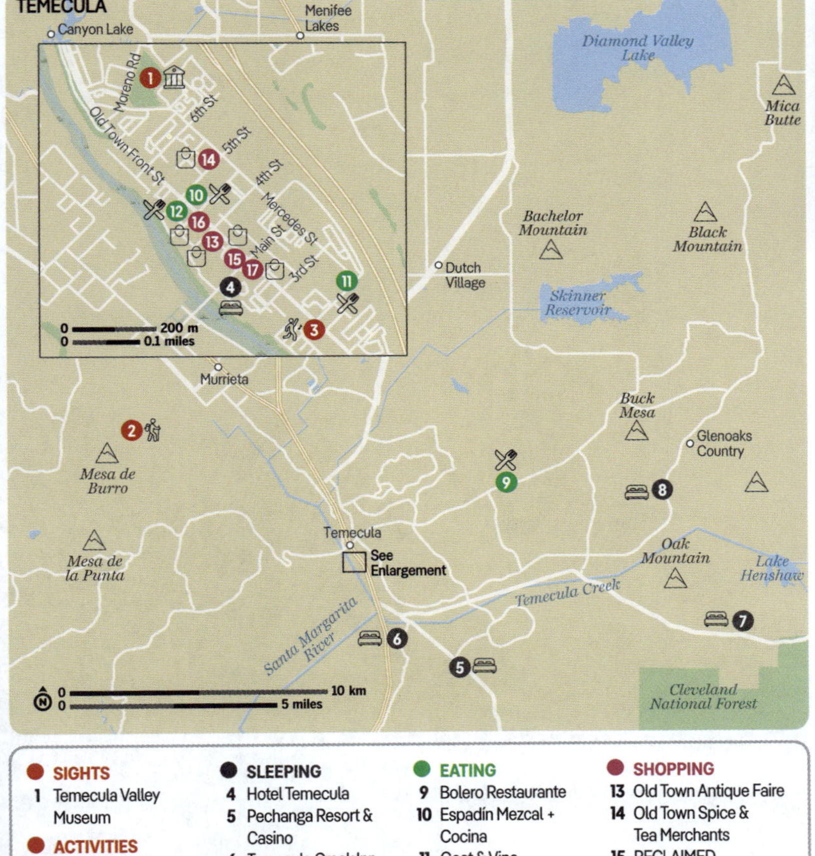

SIGHTS
1 Temecula Valley Museum

ACTIVITIES
2 Santa Rosa Plateau Ecological Reserve
3 Temecula Stampede

SLEEPING
4 Hotel Temecula
5 Pechanga Resort & Casino
6 Temecula Creek Inn
7 Vail Lake Resort
8 Vine House Bed & Breakfast

EATING
9 Bolero Restaurante
10 Espadín Mezcal + Cocina
11 Goat & Vine
12 Small Barn

SHOPPING
13 Old Town Antique Faire
14 Old Town Spice & Tea Merchants
15 RECLAIMED @ Main St. Market
16 Temecula Lavender Co
17 Temecula Olive Oil Company

tribe to Mission San Luis Rey (1798), with a miniature street scene for kids to play in.

Walking into Temecula's **Old Town** today recalls the late 1800s: there are still plenty of historic Old West buildings along Front St, but now they're home to antiques stores, boutiques, craft breweries and restaurants. **Temecula Olive Oil Company** *(temeculaoliveoil.com)* grows its own olives and presses them into robust olive oils; tastings are free in the shop. **Old Town Spice & Tea Merchants** *(spiceandteamerchants.com)* sells 350 spices and 100 loose-leaf teas. **Temecula Lavender Company** *(temeculalavernderco.com)* sells products made from flowers grown on its own local lavender

Temecula Valley

farm. One block on Fourth St holds several antiques shops, like **Old Town Antique Faire** and **RECLAIMED @ Main Street Market**, which refurbishes vintage furniture.

The largest country music venue on the West Coast, the **Stampede** *(thetemeculastampede.com),* has line dancing, bull riding and live music every weekend. It's located in the Old Town.

Explore the Outdoors

Cycle and hike the hills

Temecula Valley is a popular spot for cyclists, with more than 90 miles of biking trails and trail maps provided by the **Bike Temecula Valley** *(tvbikecoalition.com)* coalition.

In the **Santa Rosa Plateau Ecological Reserve** *(rivcoparks .org/srp),* you'll find a variety of terrains and ecosystems that are home to 200 species of native birds and 49 endangered or rare animal and plant species, including one that exists nowhere else on earth: the fairy shrimp.

WHY I LOVE TEMECULA

Denise and Stephen Otico are travel content creators. *@partyof4some times2*

We've called Temecula home for nearly 18 years and love how it's the perfect mix of peaceful living and vibrant experiences. From scenic wineries and outdoor adventures to the charm of Old Town dining and lively nightlife, there's always something to enjoy here. Whether we're exploring as a family or going out for a date – Temecula has a little bit of everything we love!

DINING IN TEMECULA: OUR PICKS

Bolero Restaurante: Serves Spanish tapas with a gourmet sensibility. Chef Hany Ali trained and cooked throughout Europe before arriving in California. *8am-9pm* $$

Small Barn: This farm-to-table restaurant and boutique winery evolved from the owners' backyard winemaking operation. *hours vary* $$

Espadín Mezcal + Cocina: Take a break from wine with inspired regional Mexican food and agave-based cocktails. *11am-9pm Sun-Thu, 11am-10pm Fri & Sat* $$

Goat & Vine: This stone-hearth kitchen might be casual, but its food is not: everything, from the pizza dough to the sauces, is made in-house daily. *11am-9pm* $$

Temecula Valley Wineries

Because the weather here is similar to a Mediterranean climate, Temecula is especially well-suited to growing Spanish, French and Italian grape varietals. Expect to sip Sangiovese, Montepulciano and Syrah – though vineyards cultivate more than two dozen different grapes.

Where to sip if you love...

Old World Wines

Doffo Winery At Doffo Winery, Marcelo channels his Argentine and Italian heritage to make outstanding Zinfandel and red blends. He also has a collection of vintage motorcycles at the winery.

Miramonte Winery Another standout, the Miramonte focuses on Spanish- and Portuguese-influenced styles like Tempranillo and medium-bodied red blends.

Robert Renzoni Vineyards A fourth-generation winemaker. Robert's great-grandfather worked in vineyards in northern Italy.

An Immersive Atmosphere

Briar Rose Winery If Disneyland owned a winery, it would be Briar Rose, which looks like it came straight out of *Snow White*. The compound was built by Beldon Fields, a former Walt Disney Imagineer, who designed it to look like his own fairy tale. Now owned by the Linkogle family, Briar Rose makes wines like Tempranillo, Syrah and Viognier.

Carter Estate Winery Known for its French-style sparkling wines, Carter Estate Winery is surrounded by blocks of vines and has an inn on site.

Palumbo Family Vineyards Known for its bigger reds like Cabernet Sauvignon and Cabernet Franc, Palumbo offers a 'Dirt to Bottle' tour of the winemaking process.

Europa Village This wine lover's compound has Spanish-influenced Bolero, French C'est La Vie and Italian Vienza wineries on site, as well as a Spanish restaurant and Italian market, an inn and casitas.

Wine & Food Pairings

Bottaia Winery Has wine and charcuterie pairings. If that's not enough, go to its wine blending lab and create your own custom bottle.

Herzog Wine Cellars At this winery's restaurant, Tierra Sur, every dish is prepared with a Herzog wine.

Leoness Cellars At the restaurant at Leoness, the menu changes with the seasons and takes into account what complements their new vintages and single vineyard reds.

Live Music & Entertainment

Ponte Winery There's a lot to keep you lingering at this Italian wine-focused estate, which has an inn, a restaurant and live music on Friday and Saturday evenings.

Rancho Guejito Vineyard Focuses on lighter-body reds and interesting whites and has live music on Sunday afternoons at its estate winery.

Callaway Vineyard & Winery Callaway brings in bands and a food truck for summer evening concerts. Sip wines like Sangiovese, Petite Sirah and Sauvignon Blanc.

THE IMAGE PARTY/SHUTTERSTOCK

Callaway Vineyard & Winery

HOW TO

When to go Every September, Temecula celebrates California Wine Month with events and live entertainment. Expect tasting tours, culinary events...even grape stomping!

Before you go Many wineries require reservations, so make sure to check in advance – or ask the tasting room staff for their recommendations on your next stop.

Remember to hydrate The Inland Empire is hot and dry, especially in the summer and fall. Make sure you've got a bottle of water and don't forget to drink it!

Budget Most wineries charge a tasting fee per person, but many also waive that fee with the purchase of a few bottles of wine.

Leave the keys at home

While driving is definitely the easiest way to get to Temecula Valley, once you're there, you might want to park your car and forget about it...especially if you're planning to go wine tasting. There are plenty of options for local wine tours and car services that will leave the responsibility of designated driving to a professional.

The **Temecula Wine Trolley** *(temeculawinetrolley.com; from $129)* has daily wine tours to three wineries; either buy a seat on a trolley or book a whole trolley for a private party. **Grapeline Wine Tours** *(gogrape.com; from $159)* runs wine tours and vineyard picnic tours. **Cable Car Wine Tours** *(temeculacablecar.com; from $110)* transports people in a restored 1914 San Francisco cable car.

Borrow Our Bikes *(borrowourbikes.com; from $53)* and **Temecula Wine Country E-Bikes** *(uyswines.com; from $60)* arrange e-bike rentals. Sidecar Tours *(sidecar toursinc.com; from $210)* has something totally unique: vintage motorcycles with sidecars modified to fit two people, which will transport you anywhere in the valley. There are even horse-drawn carriage wine tours courtesy of **Temecula Carriage Company** *(temeculacarriageco.com; from $215)*.

Places We Love to Stay

$ Budget $$ Midrange $$$ Top End

San Diego

Maps p179 & p180

Omni San Diego $$ High-rise hotel in the Gaslamp, connected to Petco Park and the San Diego Convention Center.

Wayfarer San Diego $$ On Pacific Beach, this newly renovated hotel has suites and rooms with gorgeous ocean views.

Mission Bay Resort $$ A newly renovated resort with a pool complex, beach access, spa treatments and three waterfront restaurants.

Ocean Park Inn $$ This mid-century modern hotel offers all-suite accommodations, many with kitchenettes and water views.

Kona Kai Resort & Spa $$ Shelter Island hotel with a private beach – a rarity in San Diego – and a tropical island feel.

Humphrey's Half-Moon Inn $$ This delightfully mid-century-inspired Shelter Island hotel radiates 'golden age of Hawaii travel.'

Guild Hotel $$$ Boutique hotel in a century-old building that was once a YMCA, with original architectural details.

Pendry San Diego $$$ Luxury hotel in the Gaslamp District with six restaurants and elegant decor.

Loews Coronado Bay Resort $$$ This luxury hotel has a private marina and offers shuttle service to Silver Strand Beach.

Hotel del Coronado $$$ One of the most historically significant and beautiful hotels in California, directly on the beach.

La Jolla

San Diego Marriott La Jolla $$ Closer to UCSD and Torrey Pines, this hotel has two restaurants and an outdoor pool.

Grande Colonial $$ Historic 1913 hotel with a Michelin-recommended restaurant and upscale accommodations and water views.

Estancia La Jolla Hotel & Spa $$$ AAA Four Diamond boutique hotel with luxury amenities and 10 acres of gardens and courtyards.

La Jolla Shores Hotel $$$ Request a water view at this oceanfront hotel that has easy access to the beach.

La Valencia Hotel $$$ Iconic pink hotel with Mediterranean inspiration and beach access, with pet-friendly rooms and dining.

Orli La Jolla $$$ Thirteen-room boutique hotel in a historic building, with thoughtful touches and a fun vibe.

Chula Vista

The Rambler Motel $$ This vibrant mid-century-inspired motel has bright colors and fun room decor, plus a pool.

Gaylord Pacific Resort $$$ On the Chula Vista Marina, this huge hotel has an expansive pool complex with waterslides.

Del Mar

L'Auberge Del Mar $$$ A luxury hotel with beach access, a spa, a fine-dining restaurant and pet-friendly accommodations.

Fairmont Grand Del Mar $$$ Next to Los Peñasquitos Canyon Preserve, this luxury accommodations has horseback riding, yoga and archery, plus a spa and golf.

Del Mar Beach Hotel $$$ The only beachfront hotel in Del Mar recently got a huge renovation; it's now a modern example of mid-century California architecture.

Carlsbad

Map p198

Beach Terrace Inn $$ This renovated beachfront hotel in Carlsbad has gorgeous views and easy access to the sand.

Cape Rey Carlsbad Beach $$ Carlsbad hotel with beach access and a large pool for when you've had enough of the ocean.

Legoland Resort Hotel (p197) **$$** Attached to Legoland theme park, this family hotel offers separate bunkbeds for kids, in-room Legos, free breakfast and pirate- and adventure-themed rooms.

Legoland Castle Hotel (p197) **$$** Also attached to Legoland, this property has the same amenities as the Legoland Hotel, but with a medieval fantasy theme.

Oceanside

The Seabird Ocean Resort & Spa $$ An elevated pool allows you to soak in the water while watching the waves roll in, which is especially perfect at sunset.

The Fin Hotel $$ A totally rehabbed 1920s hotel that's part of the Hilton Tapestry Collection – the Fin feels like a piece of California history.

Pacific Beach Resort $$$ Recently named *Travel + Leisure's* top US resort, this place is steps from the beach and has a fine-dining Mexican restaurant.

Encinitas

Surfhouse Boutique Hotel $$ Chic surf motel vibes combine with amenities like complimentary beach cruiser bikes and surfboards for guest use.

Alila Marea Beach Resort $$$ Luxurious rooms overlooking the ocean and Pacific Coast Hwy, with unparalleled sunset views.

Temecula

Map p203

Hotel Temecula $$ Old West vibes abound at this 1891 historic hotel in the heart of Old Town.

Vine House Bed & Breakfast $$ Luxury inn with vineyard views and complimentary breakfast, within walking distance to several wineries.

Pechanga Resort & Casino $$ One of the largest casinos in the country, Pechanga is a AAA Four Diamond property with fine dining and a huge pool complex.

Vail Lake Resort $$ This resort has campsites and cabins for rent, plus an enormous bass fishing lake, horseback riding, a mountain-bike park and 40 miles of hiking trails.

Temecula Creek Inn $$$ Idyllic resort with a 27-hole golf course, fine dining and complimentary shuttle service.

Hotel del Coronado

Researched by
Wendy Yanagihara

Palm Springs & the Deserts

DESERT CULTURE, ART AND EXPANSIVE WILDERNESS

California's vast desert landscapes await the adventurous soul with geologically diverse trails, environmental art, dark starry skies and the ever-sunny culture of Palm Springs.

The desert may evoke images of starkness and desolation, but a little immersion can quickly change that perspective. Much as the changing light can dramatically transform desert landscapes from moment to moment, living an off-grid desert minute reminds us how resilient the flora and fauna must be to survive in this boundary-pushing environment and how beautiful it is for its toughness.

Hollywood may have brought Palm Springs to the country's mainstream consciousness, but this land was home to the Cahuilla, Serrano, Chemehuevi, Kumeyaay, Cupeño, Diegueño and Mojave tribes long before. The lightly worn marks of their grinding mortars and rock art remain, while their trails became modern thoroughfares. The same mesquite, piñon and cactus that provided sustenance still flourish in the national parks and preserves today, supporting the wildlife that you may catch sight of, including desert tortoises and bighorn sheep.

Like the wildlife here, you'll have to adapt your rhythms to the desert environment. Self-sufficiency is key – always carry plentiful water, snacks and layers of clothing and stay aware of the changing weather. Keep an eye on the fuel gauge in your vehicle and the level in your water bottle. You'll often find yourself unplugged and offline whether you wish to be or not, so embrace the practice of attuning your senses to the desert's aliveness.

DANITA DELIMONT/SHUTTERSTOCK

THE MAIN AREAS

For places to stay in Palm Springs and the Deserts, see p260

CANADASTOCK/SHUTTERSTOCK

Left: Anza-Borrego Desert State Park (p246); Above: Zabriskie Point (p240), Death Valley National Park

Find Your Way

California's desert region stretches from the feet of the eastern Sierra to western Nevada and south to the Mexican border. These thousands of square miles represent a spectrum of desert ecosystems, including the buoyant urban version known as Palm Springs.

Death Valley National Park, p238

Death Valley's lowest low is 282ft below sea level, but its highs include a massive volcanic crater, multicolored mineral hillsides and singing sand dunes.

Mojave National Preserve, p253

Solitude is more easily found in the Mojave than in its more famous neighboring parks. Bighorn sheep, pristine sand dunes, Joshua trees and desert tranquility await.

Palm Springs, p216

As a mecca for mid-century modernism, gay culture and spa life, Palm Springs tempers indulgent living with outdoor recreation in the healing desert air.

Joshua Tree National Park, p227

With its weird beauty extending far beyond the eponymous trees, JTree spans the Mojave and Sonoran Deserts, dotted with boulders, cholla and ocotillo.

Anza-Borrego Desert State Park, p246

Wildflowers and bighorn sheep are the organic draws to California's largest state park, while Ricardo Breceda's metal sculptures complement these wide-open spaces.

CAR

A car or RV is the best way of getting around the region, allowing for maximum flexibility. The desert's state and national parks encompass thousands of square miles and are not served by public transportation.

BICYCLE

In Palm Springs, many motels offer free bikes or e-bikes for their guests to use. Cycling is a fun way to get around downtown when the weather isn't excessively hot.

WALKING

To hike the desert is the best way to know it, whether it's on a paved nature trail or through a slot canyon. Prepare well and allow for adjustment to plans, as the desert environment is extreme and conditions can change rapidly.

Plan Your Days

Balance holiday decadence in Palm Springs or shaking it at Coachella with outdoor adventures in desert wilderness, discovering outdoor art installations along the way.

NYKER/SHUTTERSTOCK

Palm Springs (p216)

If You Only Do One Thing

- Head straight to **Joshua Tree National Park** (p227) to get an up-close look at the park's iconic Joshua trees and chunky Flintstones-esque boulders. Take in the park's highlights on a **DIY driving tour** (p227), fitting in an easy hike along the **Barker Dam Loop Trail** (p230) or **Discovery Trail** (p229) if you have time.

- Alternatively, take a city break in **Palm Springs** (p216) for a day of sightseeing and self-care. Drive or hop on a bike for a **mid-century modern tour** (p221) to admire the city's signature architecture style. Then do some **vintage shopping** (p221) and **gallery hopping** (p222) downtown. Take time out for a spa treatment at **Spa at Séc-he** (p218) or log some pool time before dinner and cocktails at **Farm** (p223).

Seasonal Highlights

Summer can reach hellish temperatures above 120°F (49°C). The cooler high season runs mid-October through May. Spring brings wildflowers, but exact timing depends on rainfall.

FEBRUARY

Modernism Week (p216) celebrates all things mid-century modern in Palm Springs, its natural habitat. Lasting for 10 days, the festival includes tours, exhibitions and social events. A 'mini' version spans a long weekend in October.

MARCH

March is peak season for **wildflowers** (p250) in Anza-Borrego and the lower elevations of Joshua Tree and Death Valley, though depending on the season's climactic conditions, the season can begin in February and run through May.

APRIL

The region's most hyped happening, **Coachella Music Festival** (p237), draws the masses in mid- to late April. Spring break generally goes from late March through mid-April; it's best to book accommodations early.

Three Days to Play

- Start in **Death Valley National Park** (p238) to check off visits to **Badwater Basin** (p241), the lowest point in North America, and the spectacular colors of **Artists Palette** (p241) before spending the night in **Shoshone** (p244) for a warm-springs swim or hot-springs soak. Continue south through **Mojave National Preserve** (p253) for a beautiful, wild transect of this little-visited desert park, stopping to hike at **Kelso Dunes** (p255).

- Pick up lunch in the town of **Joshua Tree** (p233) or Twentynine Palms and head into **Joshua Tree National Park** (p227) for a day or two of hiking or climbing, ending with pool time and cocktails in **Palm Springs** (p216).

A Week or More

- Spend a few days exploring both **Death Valley National Park** (p238) and **Joshua Tree National Park** (p227), then rest and refresh for a day in **Palm Springs** (p216), perhaps fitting in a hike in the valley oasis of **Indian Canyons** (p223).

- Next, head south to the Salton Sea for a look at the shoreline art installations of **Bombay Beach** (p225). Keep following Hwy 111 south to **Salvation Mountain** (p226), the psychedelic religious monument on the edge of **Slab City** (p226).

- If you have time, end with a visit to **Anza-Borrego Desert State Park** (p246), with its variety of desert trails and badlands, plus whimsical metal sculptures dotting the roadsides.

MAY

The biannual **Joshua Tree Music Festival** (p237) showcases up-and-coming musicians and practices an ethos of radical inclusion. The spring edition happens mid-May in the town of Joshua Tree; the fall version comes around mid-October.

SEPTEMBER

Go **apple picking** (p251) in Julian through October, but try visiting midweek to miss the traffic, long lines and pedestrian traffic jams in this tiny hamlet.

NOVEMBER

Pride is a state of mind in Palm Springs, but **Pride celebrations** (p217) in America's gayest city happen in early November.

DECEMBER

Winter is a wonderful season to visit the desert, when temperatures dip but so do visitor numbers. Enjoy the parks with more space and peace, but remember to bundle up, as desert extremes can mean freezing temps.

Palm Springs

MID-CENTURY STYLE | ART AND ARCHITECTURE | R&R

TOP TIP

The greater Palm Springs area sprawls out from the city proper into eight other cities, including Desert Hot Springs, Rancho Mirage, Palm Desert and Coachella. Many of the area's attractions lie outside the city of Palm Springs.

GETTING AROUND

Getting around downtown Palm Springs is best on foot or by bike. Free parking is plentiful in the downtown lots; the Palm Springs Art Museum lot is a good choice. Many local lodgings offer free bike rentals to guests. When ranging beyond downtown and into the greater Palm Springs area, driving is the best way to get around.

One of the gayest cities in America in the best senses of the word, sunny Palm Springs has long been the desert retreat of celebrities and artists. When 1930s Hollywood studios instituted the 'two-hour rule,' requiring their film stars to stay geographically close enough to report to set on short notice, the city's reputation as a decadent playground took root. More recently, it established itself as the first city in the US to elect a 100% LGBTQ+ city council.

Palm Springs prides itself not only on its queer culture but also on its mid-century modern identity. The Mid Mod architecture and style that defined its heyday harmonized with the environment, establishing the distinctive desert aesthetic that endures to the present day.

Hike the trails of its Cahuilla lands, take design notes from the vernacular art and architecture, sip tiki cocktails in the desert sunshine and experience for yourself the ebullient appeal of Palm Springs.

Modernism Week Eternal

MAP P219

Revel in Desert Modern style

While mid-century modern design had a mainstream moment in the *Mad Men* era, it remains timelessly intrinsic to the Palm Springs aesthetic. But Mid Mod fever seizes the town during February's **Modernism Week** *(modernismweek.com; actually a 10-day affair)*. Design superfans, industry professionals and scholars alike flood into town each year to celebrate all things mid-century modern.

In addition to talks, book signings and art openings, the fun includes double-decker bus tours of notable architecture, rare tours of significant homes and countless soirées. The associated **Modernism Show & Sale** features exhibitors of vintage and contemporary design and art. Some events are free, as is the nightly illumination of prominent edifices along Palm Canyon Dr. A mini Modernism Week pops up in October over a long weekend, for those who need a fall fix.

HIGHLIGHTS
1 Sunnylands

SIGHTS
2 Backstreet Art District

ACTIVITIES
3 Andreas Canyon
4 Grounded Bodyworks
5 Indian Canyons
6 Mt San Jacinto State Park
7 Sunstone Spa

SLEEPING
8 The Cole

DRINKING & NIGHTLIFE
9 Paul Bar/Food

SHOPPING
10 Gypsyland
11 The Fine Art of Design

INFORMATION
12 Palm Springs Visitor Center

TRANSPORTATION
13 Palm Springs Aerial Tramway

But if your visit doesn't coincide with either main event, you can still take one of many year-round tours exploring Palm Springs modernism. Even tooling around the local neighborhoods on foot or bike, you'll come across showcase homes lovingly hewing to period architecture, design elements, color palettes and landscaping. Desert Modernism designs took the landscape into consideration, featuring walls of windows to frame the outdoors, breezeways to help cool the home and materials to insulate the interior from desert heat. Examples of Desert Modern homes designed by the likes of Richard Neutra and Albert Frey shaped Palm Springs' architectural aesthetic.

You can't help but visit some notable buildings over the course of your trip, simply because these architectural landmarks happen to house other points of interest. The cantilever-roofed **Palm Springs Visitor Center** on N Palm Blvd strikes a welcoming pose for those en route to the **Palm Springs Aerial Tramway** (p223), whose **Mountain Station** is the vision of mid-century architect E Stewart Williams. Another unmissable, grand work by Williams is the **Palm Springs Art Museum** (p220) anchoring downtown.

PRIDE SPRINGS ETERNAL

With almost 40% of its population identifying as LGBTQ+, queer culture is woven into the tapestry of Palm Springs. Pride and visibility are a perennial way of life, but they reach festive heights during the city's Pride celebrations in early November. **Palm Springs Pride** *(pspride.org)* festivities include a parade, live music, block parties and street fairs, as well as children's arts and crafts activities and youth zone.

YEAR-ROUND ARCHITECTURE TOURS

The Modern Tour: This long-running agency arranges intimate looks into the interiors of notable architectural gems, in their comfortable vehicles or your own.

Palm Springs Mod Squad: Admire from the outside and get a peek at the interiors of meticulously designed mid-century modern homes.

PS Architecture Tours: Insightful, insider tours guided by bike or car; it's best to book well ahead.

Palm Springs Historical Society: Themed tours featuring celebrity homes (Sinatra, Elvis, Elizabeth Taylor) and guided driving, biking and walking architectural tours.

Desert Tasty Tours: Get a taste of local history and architecture with a side of Palm Springs cuisine.

Agua Caliente Cahuilla Culture

MAP P219

Explore the Agua Caliente Cultural Museum

When you're strolling down Indian Canyon Dr, it's right there in the name: you stand on Indigenous land. A wonderful way to learn about the history and culture of the Agua Caliente Band of Cahuilla Indians is at the **Agua Caliente Cultural Museum** *(accmuseum.org; adult/senior $10/5)* on North Indian Canyon Dr. Opened in 2023 after years of anticipation, the museum features a short film illustrating the tribe's origin story. Historical photographs, interactive displays and audio components bring to life the Indigenous experience of colonialism and its effect on the culture, but also spotlight living traditions, cultural contributions and natural history of the area.

The lobby of the museum houses an art gallery featuring rotating exhibits, plus a gift shop. Outside, the curving wall of the larger Agua Caliente Cultural Plaza leads to the **Spa at Séc-he** *(thespaatseche.com)*. The 'Agua Caliente' in the tribe's name speaks to one of its ancestral land's sacred treasures: the mineral hot springs known as Séc-he. These waters' underground passages represent a link between the physical and spiritual worlds and were therefore historically used for ceremonial purposes as well as quotidian drinking and bathing. The spa welcomes guests to partake in these spiritually significant and mineral-rich thermal waters. Book ahead for luxury spa treatments or relax with a day pass that includes a 15-minute private soak.

Landscape & Art

MAP P217

Galleries, gardens and soft power

While Palm Springs might conjure technicolor visions of decadent pool parties and black-and-white Hollywood glamour, it's less well-known as an unofficial diplomatic retreat. Philanthropists and former diplomats Walter and Leonore Annenberg hosted foreign leaders and US presidents beginning in the 1960s at **Sunnylands** *(sunnylands.org; tours from $28)*, their Rancho Mirage estate, leaving it behind as a retreat for facilitating international peace and diplomacy.

Now free and open to the public, its serene gardens and walking trails are like an oasis impressionist painting come to life. Inside, there's an art gallery, cafe and home tours (when high-level retreats are not in session). The informative 20-minute film *A Place Called Sunnylands* screens at regular intervals in a small theater down the lobby's main hallway, introducing the estate's fascinating history.

A more organic and intimate desert refuge is the **Moorten Botanical Garden** *(moortenbotanicalgarden.com; adult/child $7/3)*, at the southern end of Palm Canyon Dr. A path leads through a beautifully landscaped array of cacti, succulents and desert flora from arid lands near and far. You may also see the resident desert tortoises

HIKING TRIBAL LANDS

Other places to enjoy tribal lands include hiking the shaded palm oasis of **Indian Canyons** (p223) or to the waterfall of **Tahquitz Canyon** (p222).

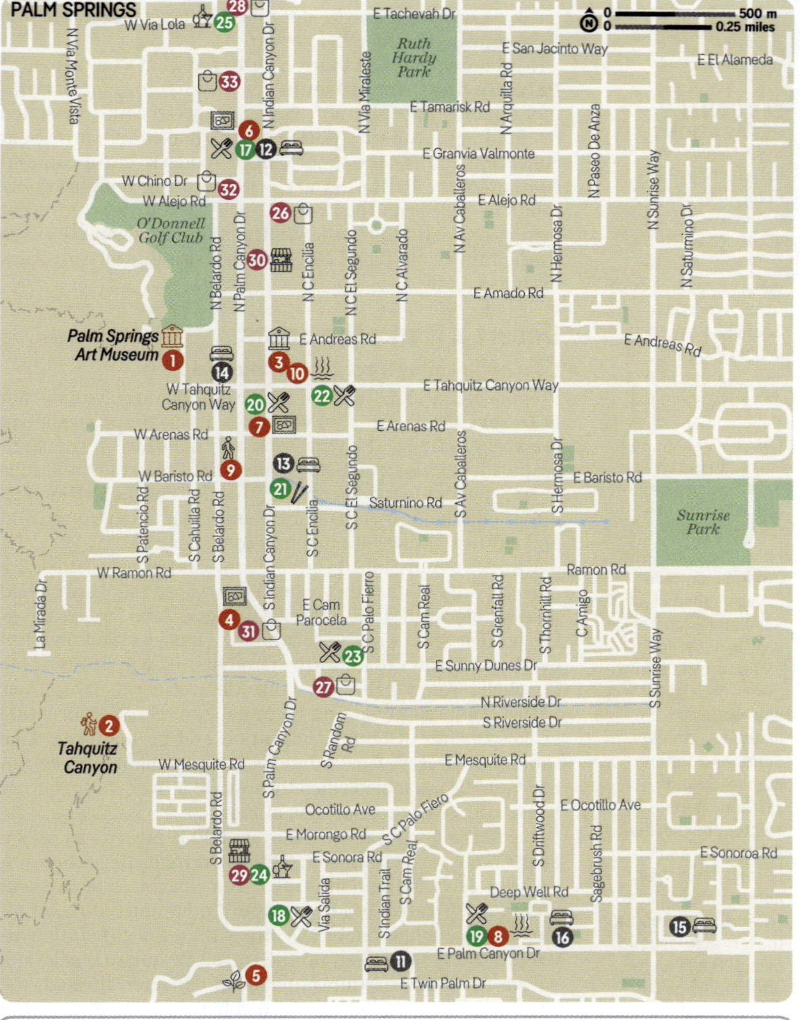

HIGHLIGHTS
1 Palm Springs Art Museum
2 Tahquitz Canyon

SIGHTS
3 Agua Caliente Cultural Museum
4 Moorten Botanical Garden
5 Rubine Red Gallery
6 Stewart Galleries
7 The Lofts Art District

ACTIVITIES
8 L'Horizon Resort and Spa
9 Palm Springs Historical Society Walking Tours
10 Spa at Séc-he

SLEEPING
11 Ace Hotel & Swim Club
12 Alcazar
13 Drift Palm Springs
14 Saguaro
15 Sparrows Lodge
16 The Rowan Palm Springs

EATING
see 15 Barn Kitchen
17 Cheeky's
18 El Mirasol
19 Elmer's
20 Farm
21 Rooster & the Pig
22 Sherman's Deli & Bakery
23 Townie Bagels

DRINKING & NIGHTLIFE
24 Bar Cecil
25 Bootlegger Tiki
see 16 High Bar

SHOPPING
26 Angel View Resale Store
27 Antique Galleries of Palm Springs
28 Iconic Atomic
29 Market Market
30 Mojave Flea Trading Post
31 Revivals
32 Seaplane
33 Trina Turk

SECTION 14 REPARATIONS

In December 2024, Palm Springs City Council unanimously approved a historic $5.9 million settlement for reparations to survivors of Section 14 evictions in the 1950s and '60s. Section 14 was owned by the Agua Caliente Band of Cahuilla Indians and leased to the city of Palm Springs in the late 1950s. At the time, the neighborhood was populated predominantly by lower-income Black and Latino families unable to settle elsewhere in the city due to discriminatory housing practices. In order to develop Section 14, the city of Palm Springs systematically evicted the families living there and burned down their homes. In addition to reparation payments, the city also issued over $20 million for affordable housing and entrepreneurship programs.

trucking around if they're not hibernating, a treat since tortoise sightings in the wild are rare.

Head north on Palm Canyon Dr to see what's on display at **Palm Springs Art Museum** *(psmuseum.org; adult/child $20/free),* a quintessentially Palm Springs structure designed by architect E Stewart Williams. The museum's permanent collection spans Mesoamerican to modern European and contemporary California art, with rotating temporary exhibitions reflecting the area's identity and history. A recent exhibition featured classic, digital and experimental works by the inimitable David Hockney in a suitably vibrant Palm Springs palette.

Desert X Marks the Spots

MAP P217

Coachella Valley's outdoor art biennale

Premiering in 2017, the site-specific outdoor art biennale that is **Desert X** *(desertx.org)* will make its next appearance in the spring of 2027. Playing with and building on the landscape, international artists create arresting art installations in unexpected locations around the **Coachella Valley**. The often monumental art is informed by social, environmental and cultural issues and inspired by the desert.

A work commissioned for 2025, for example, is called *The Act of Being Together* by Mexican artist Jose Dávila, who had massive blocks of stone quarried in Mexico and ferried across the border. Stacks of the rough-hewn blocks stand on a hill overlooking rows of uniform, aerodynamic windmills of the Coachella Valley below. Moving silent minerals from their native land and arranging them deliberately as if for ritual evokes themes of human migration and permanence. Like some of the Desert X installations, it may remain in place, but most are disassembled when the festival is over, disappearing like a mirage in the rearview mirror.

One of the temporary multilayered 2025 pieces was Alison Saar's *Soul Service Station*. This retro roadside station referenced early automobile travel, the weariness of the soul and the imperative of joy. Saar built a hammered-metal pit stop of hope inhabited by the larger-than-life gas station attendant Ruby who filled up the traveler's spiritual gas tank with a recording of an original song delivered through the conch-shell pump. Poignant and ephemeral like most of the biennale commissions, its short-lived existence makes it all the more memorable.

EATING IN PALM SPRINGS: BREAKFAST JOINTS

MAP P219

Townie Bagels: Get in line and perfect your order. Closing time is when they sell out; risk disappointment after 11.30am. *6.30am-noon Wed-Mon* $

Elmer's: A cozy classic serving crêpes and German pancakes along with typical hearty breakfast fare throughout opening hours. *6am-9pm* $

Cheeky's: Cute patio and seasonal menus featuring a bacon flight, avocado toast, cinnamon roll and Mexican options like chilaquiles. *8am-2pm Thu-Mon* $$

Sherman's Deli & Bakery: Enjoy NYC-deli comforts like pastrami on rye and lox with cream cheese in the bustling restaurant or order to go. *8am-9pm* $

STEVE CUKROV/SHUTTERSTOCK

Moorten Botanical Garden (p218)

A few artifacts from prior editions still remain, such as the 2019 *Visit Us in the Shape of Clouds* by Armando Lerma, a mural of stylized Southwest flora and fauna wrapping around a water tank just outside the town of **Coachella**. The removal of the temporary art follows Leave No Trace principles, ensuring that the installations create minimal environmental impact.

Channel Your Inner Desert Magpie

MAP P219

Treasure hunting, vintage and new

Palm Springs might be the best or worst place to hunt for mid-century modern vintage – you could unearth a mint Blenko vase amid estate castoffs, but you'll also pay a premium for it in the heart of the Mid Mod mecca. If you're just browsing for fun, this town has troves of vintage and retail shops to peruse.

Start on N Indian Canyon Dr at **Mojave Flea Trading Post**, a makers' market filled with artwork, clothing, homewares, jewelry, skincare and all manner of giftable baubles made in the Coachella Valley. This central spot has a mix of new and vintage, as well as a bougie bodega with snacks, wine and cold drinks. For a more upscale experience with a similar set-up of individual vendors in a 40,000-sq-ft open space, head

FESTIVE THURSDAYS IN PALM SPRINGS

It's like a holiday every Thursday evening when N Palm Canyon Dr is closed to vehicle traffic for **VillageFest**. Several blocks of the street are lined with food stalls emanating scents of tamales and falafel, alongside local artists selling their handblown glass, paintings, textiles and metal-work. There's live music and locals and visitors alike come out to enjoy the cool night air and festive atmosphere. If you're not into stand-up dining, the street's restaurants and bars remain open, so you can also grab an outdoor table and people-watch to your heart's content.

DRINKING IN PALM SPRINGS: COCKTAIL PAIRINGS

MAP P219

Paul Bar/Food: Open the door to what looks like a strip-mall dive and savor the speakeasy experience. *4-11pm Wed-Thu, to midnight Fri & Sat, to 10pm Sun*

Bootlegger Tiki: Scratch that itch for a rum cocktail at this campy tiki bar. Reservations recommended for timed slots. *3-11pm Sun-Thu, to 1am Fri & Sat*

High Bar: Best view for a sunset sip at the rooftop bar of the Rowan hotel downtown. Live music on weekends. *10am-11pm*

Bar Cecil: In-demand, stylish French-Californian spot. Didn't book months ahead? Turn up very early to try your luck as a walk-in. *5-10pm*

BEST ART SMORGASBORDS

Coachella Walls: A walkable series of murals around Coachella's tiny downtown, honoring the town's human history and current inhabitants.

Backstreet Art District: First Wednesday art walks from 5pm to 7pm, though you can wander the various galleries during their regular hours.

Lofts Art District (The): Peek into the studios of working artists every second Saturday; the artists also keep individual gallery hours.

Stewart Galleries: Features a mishmash of more traditional Western desert-ish art, ranging from modern sculpture to plein-air paintings.

Rubine Red Gallery: Rotating exhibits representing about 20 diverse artists working in contemporary, modern and mid-century styles.

TOM FORBES/SHUTTERSTOCK

Tahquitz Canyon

down to the Plaza del Sol shopping center on S Palm Canyon Dr – here you'll find **Market Market**, with flowy silk caftans among the high-quality vintage apparel, Desert Modern decor and furniture, Hawaiiana and vinyl, plus a bright, consciously stocked bottle shop.

Moving on to N Palm Canyon Dr, stroll along the north end in the Uptown Design District to find playful retro-patterned dresses at **Trina Turk** or men's shirts made with colorful but refined fabrics (think linen and silk-blend) at **Seaplane**.

Discerningly curated vintage spots include **Iconic Atomic** and **Gypsyland** for apparel, tchotchkes and furnishings. If thrifting is more your bag, pop into the **Angel View Resale Store**, part of a local chain benefiting its eponymous nonprofit organization that serves people with disabilities. Or pop into a **Revivals** to hunt for preloved clothing, homewares and furniture, supporting DAP Health in providing healthcare to everyone, regardless of ability to pay. For higher-end consignment apparel, venture out to **The Fine Art of Design** in Palm Desert.

South of downtown off S Palm Canyon Dr, **Antique Galleries of Palm Springs** occupies 12,000 sq ft of merchants selling vintage everything, spanning the eras. Find cocktail carts, Bakelite necklaces and possibly score the Eames of your dreams.

Hoofing It in Palm Springs

MAP P219

Hiking trails on city outskirts

Super-accessible trail adventures await just shy of downtown Palm Springs. Antsy feet can easily flee an afternoon of gallery hopping for an outdoor jaunt instead.

The Agua Caliente Band of Cahuilla Indians welcomes visitors to explore the inviting trails on their tribal land. Closest to downtown is **Tahquitz Canyon** *(tahquitzcanyon.com; adult/child $15/7),* named after a shaman who misused his great powers to harm the Cahuilla people and was subsequently banished to a remote cave in the canyon. The easy, mostly flat 2-mile loop leads to a seasonal waterfall and small riparian zone shaded by sycamores. Ranger-led hikes depart several times daily (at 8am only July through September) from the visitor center, taking a leisurely pace through the canyon to talk about the nature and culture.

For more options, head south to **Indian Canyons** *(indiancanyons.com; adult/child $12/6),* where over 60 miles of trail traverse the backcountry and cool oases with streams, ponds and waterfalls. In addition to the lovely fan palms, the scenic **Andreas Canyon** is notable for its mortars and *metates* (grinding stones) that silently evidence the canyon's long history of human habitation. Several loop trails begin along the oasis on the **Palm Canyon Trail**, where tall fan palms crowd over the creek bed. An attractive 3-mile loop connects with the scenic, cactus-dotted **Victor Trail**, opening to vistas of the valleys below.

For something completely different, hop the **Palm Springs Aerial Tramway** *(pstramway.com; adult/child $33/19, parking $15)* at the north end of downtown for the 10-minute ride to the 8516ft **Mountain Station**. Check the weather and layer up, as it can be 40°F (4.5°C) colder than in Palm Springs. After disembarking the slowly rotating tram at the Mountain Station, walk down the paved path to walk the easy 1.5-mile **Desert View Trail**. For longer hikes, stop by the San Jacinto State Park Ranger Station (p224) to check in and pick up a map. The 4.5-mile **Round Valley Trail** is a refreshingly forested alpine escape from the desert heat.

BEST DESERT SPAS

Spa at Séc-he: Soak at the source, whether with a spa treatment or day pass to enjoy the warm mineral pools.

Sunstone Spa: Make it a day of spa treatments, sauna and mineral pool at Agua Caliente Casino in Rancho Mirage.

L'Horizon Resort & Spa: Hollywood history lingers at this elegant, low-slung mid-century resort and spa with beautiful mountain views.

Spa at Two Bunch Palms: Relaxed oasis setting with palms and mineral waters in Desert Hot Springs.

Grounded Bodyworks: Lovely downtown Palm Springs day spa if you're simply seeking a massage or primping without the whole resort experience.

EATING IN PALM SPRINGS: OUR FAVORITES

MAP P219

Farm: Buzzy French-style simplicity. Breakfast and lunch are walk-in only; expect a wait. Reserve for the prix-fixe dinner. *8am-2pm daily & 5.30-9.30pm Fri-Tue* **$$**

Rooster & the Pig: No reservations; arrive before opening and come hungry for Vietnamese fusion. Asian-themed cocktails complement the cuisine. *5-9pm Wed-Sun* **$$**

El Mirasol: Family-run Mexican restaurant whose mole and *pipián* make a spicy change of pace from your favorite standbys. *9am-9pm* **$$**

Barn Kitchen: Locally sourced ingredients prepared beautifully for fresh American cuisine enjoyed in open-air elegance. *11am-9pm* **$$**

Beyond Palm Springs

Artsy communities thrive past the edges of Palm Springs, from alpine town to receding inland sea.

Places

GETTING AROUND

Both of these destinations require a car to visit, as neither is served by regular public transportation. Idyllwild is about an hour's drive from Palm Springs, heading south on Hwy 74 out of Palm Desert. Bombay Beach is less than 1½ hours to the south along Hwy 111, with Slab City another half-hour beyond. **Imperial Valley Transit buses** *(ivtransit.com; $1.25)* serve Salton Sea communities on Thursdays, once each way to and from Brawley.

From Palm Springs, heading up the hill to the forested mountains of Idyllwild is a cool change in perspective and temperature. Surrounded by the San Jacinto Mountains, this unpretentious little village (a dog has served as mayor for over a decade) is a great place to hike and relax.

In the other direction – geographically and culturally – the low-lying Slabs near the Salton Sea annually rotates in a new (human) fearless leader in 'the last free place.' Transient and permanent residents populate this veritable desert island of misfit toys.

While these communities couldn't be more different, the artistic soul in each place makes them fascinating counterpoints to easy-breezy Palm Springs.

Idyllwild

TIME FROM PALM SPRINGS: 1¼HR

Hiking and mountain biking

Miles of alpine hiking and mountain biking abound around the sweet hamlet of **Idyllwild**, nestled in the piney San Jacinto Mountains. About an hour's drive from Palm Springs, the temperatures cool perceptibly as you ascend into this wild and idyllic mountain village.

Local shop **Nomad Ventures** *(nomadventures.com)* is the place to stop for intel on trail systems, which are shared between **Mt San Jacinto State Park** *(parks.ca.gov; free)* and **San Bernardino National Forest** *(fs.usda.gov/r05/sanbernardino; free)*. It's a good idea to ask about conditions locally during your visit, as snow and fire damage may have recently affected trails, some of which are not clearly marked.

You'll need a free day-use permit, mostly so there's a record of your whereabouts and of visitor numbers. These are available 24/7 in front of both agencies' ranger stations and each honors the other's permits. Or you could opt to do the permit-free, family-friendly hike along the **Ernie Maxwell Scenic Trail**, a roughly 5-mile out-and-back through the pines and boulders with beautiful mountain views.

Browsing and carousing

If roaming around town is more your speed, grab a matcha latte at local favorite **Alpaca Coffee & Tea** before your walkabout in central Idy. Gift shops downtown carry souvenirs catering to a range of tastes, from garish psychedelia to organic body-care products; **Bubba's Books** remains a worthwhile stop for cheap road-trip reads and random vintage gems. The peaceful **Idyllwild Gardens** is worth a wander through its serene garden spaces; though it's largely a nursery and plant shop, you'll find some giftable garden-centric wares here.

If you're traveling with small kids, the **Idyllwild Nature Center** *(rivcoparks.org; adult/child $6/3)* can be a great place to check out live animals (and taxidermied critters), as well as displays on Native American culture. Afterward, you can explore over 5 miles of easy trails and end with a picnic under the pines.

Check the events page for **Idyllwild Arts Academy** *(idyllwildarts.org/events),* where you can catch student and faculty art shows, musical performances, lectures and other cultural events. Or see what's on at **The Rustic Theatre** *(rustictheatre.com),* where you could take in a concert, film or stage play from **Idyllwild Actors Theatre**.

MAYOR MAX III

Mayor Max III, the current mayor of Idyllwild, began his term in late 2022. The beloved golden retriever is the most recent civic leader in what is essentially a dynastic succession. Since 2012, the mayoral 'election' in the unincorporated town serves as a fundraiser for Idyllwild's animal rescue center and Mayor Max III takes his duties seriously. If you find yourself in town, ask around and he may grace you with a personal appearance to officially welcome you to his mountain community.

Salton Sea Communities

TIME FROM PALM SPRINGS: 1½HR

Bombay Beach

Turning off of Hwy 111 to **Bombay Beach** may feel like entering a postapocalyptic ghost town, but this former holiday destination on the eastern shore of the excessively saline, shrinking Salton Sea still retains over 200 residents. Outsider artists have replaced vacationing water-skiers, building kinetic sculptures from scrap and creating multimedia installations in unlikely places. There's even a **Bombay Beach Biennale** *(bombaybeachbiennale.org),* throwing art happenings from January through March. The beauty of this biennale is that you have to ask around to find out about the details and no one is solely an observer – this is a participatory, human-interaction function.

During the rest of the year, you can chat to the locals or catch live music at the **Ski Inn**, where you can fuel up with a hot dog and draft beer in the dollar-bill-papered bar or appealing garden patio. But the main event is cruising around town to see arted-up spaces along the eerily quiet streets. If

EATING & DRINKING IN IDYLLWILD

Cafe Aroma: Convivial, woodsy restaurant and gallery serving New American food, cocktails and live music. *4.30-8.30pm Tue-Thu & Sun, to 9pm Fri & Sat* $$

Idyllwild Brewpub: Taste a flight of house brews alongside good pub food on the patio in the pines. *11am-8pm Sun-Mon & Wed-Thu, to 9pm Fri & Sat* $$

Ferro: Cozy Italian bistro with cabin vibes and wood-fired pizza oven warming the outdoor patio. *3-9pm Mon-Thu, to 10pm Fri, 2-10pm Sat, 2-9pm Sun* $$

La Casita: Tucked amid the trees, this friendly spot serves tasty Mexican comfort food. *11am-8pm Thu-Tue* $$

THE SALTON SEA

The Salton Sea's existence sprang from a series of human interventions and heavy snowmelt in 1905 that caused the Colorado River to flood unnaturally for two years into Salton Sink. By the 1950s and '60s, the landlocked sea had become a holiday destination for boaters, water-skiers and migrating birds. The gradual concentration of agricultural runoff in the desert aridity caused fish and bird die-offs beginning in the 1970s. By the early 2000s, the Salton Sea had a higher salinity than the ocean. As the lake recedes and exposes the lakebed, blowing toxic dust becomes a growing health hazard, while the wetlands that once sustained life dry up. Environmental remediation remains a complex proposition as the inland sea continues to shrink.

LADYHOBO/SHUTTERSTOCK

Slab City

you're pressed for time, go straight to the **beach**. Along the sea's receding shoreline, landlocked boats, open-air bars and lounges, abstract sculptures and sensory art pieces form a slowly evolving open-air gallery populating the degrading ecosystem with a different kind of life.

The Slabs

About 20 miles southeast of Bombay Beach sits the area's most photographed monument, **Salvation Mountain** *(salvation mountain.org; donations welcome)*. This multicolored, psychedelic adobe piece of folk art was built by Leonard Knight, who passed away in 2014; it's now maintained by a devoted caretaker and supported by its eponymous nonprofit.

Salvation Mountain marks the entrance of **Slab City**, also known as the Slabs or 'the last free place' – an off-grid, alternative community of mostly peaceful anarchy. While some residents welcome visitors to their camps, art galleries and secret gardens, others have settled here precisely because they do not wish to be visited. Feel free to search out the community library, outdoor music venue and skate park, but respect the privacy of the residents.

Follow the signs through the Slabs to tiny **East Jesus**, founded by the late Charlie Russell. Intrigued with the freewheeling lifestyle of the community, he established this corner with a couple of art cars in 2007. Currently, its population of six maintains the solar-powered compound, inviting artists to contribute to its ever-changing desert installation.

Joshua Tree National Park

JOSHUA TREES | FUNKY ROCKS | MINING RUINS

Natural springs at the northern and southern edges of Joshua Tree National Park once sustained the local Indigenous Serrano, Chemehuevi and Cahuilla people. These water sources later enabled the cattlemen and gold prospectors who arrived in the 1870s to settle here.

The mining boom peaked in the 1920s and declined in the '30s, while activist Minerva Hoyt lobbied Congress to preserve her beloved desert environment from the human destruction she bore witness to. Her efforts culminated in President Roosevelt establishing 825,000 acres as Joshua Tree National Monument in 1936.

Acting as a backdrop for old Westerns, an escape and inspiration for artists and musicians and an irresistible playground for rock climbers, Joshua Tree attained national park status in 1994. JTree's desert mystique continues to attract and entrance visitors, who climb its rock faces, explore its trails and marvel at its funky geological formations and the wonky beauty of its namesake Joshua trees.

TOP TIP

Not only is Joshua Tree National Park irresistibly photogenic, it's only 2½ hours from LA, so on weekends it can seem as though all of SoCal is pouring in at once. If possible, time your trip during the week when it's less crowded.

GETTING AROUND

Driving is the best way to experience Joshua Tree National Park, as there is no public transportation and you'll be constantly tempted to pull over for unexpectedly stunning sights. Crossing north to south, expect the journey to take about 1¼ hours nonstop, but keep in mind that you'll probably stop along the way.

If you have a bike or e-bike with you, the park roads make for a gorgeous cycling tour. Always stay on established park roads.

JTree in a Day

One-day DIY highlights tour

Make a daylong loop through **Joshua Tree National Park** *(nps.gov/jotr; 7-day pass per car $30)*, using the town of **Joshua Tree** to access the park's West Entrance. You can easily reverse this loop to start from **Twentynine Palms**; the North Entrance is often much less busy. Alternatively, begin or end at the lower-elevation South Entrance – tailor to suit your travel plans.

Driving along Park Blvd from the West Entrance, you'll pass through swaths of Joshua trees in prickly, multiarmed welcome to their Mojave Desert zone. About 9 miles in, you'll come to **Intersection Rock** – look for climbers navigating its cracks.

Continue up this road to stretch your legs on the easy and

HIGHLIGHTS
1 Keys View
2 Wonderland of Rocks

SIGHTS
3 Cholla Cactus Garden
4 Desert Queen Well
5 Face Rock
6 Hall of Horrors
7 Heart Rock
8 Intersection Rock
9 Ryan Ranch
10 Skull Rock
11 Wall Street Mill
12 Wonderland Ranch

ACTIVITIES
13 Arch Rock Trail
14 Barker Dam Loop Trail
15 Cap Rock Nature Trail
16 Discovery Trail
17 Keys Ranch Tour
18 Lost Horse Mine Trail
19 Ryan Mountain Trail
20 Saddle Rocks
21 Split Rock Loop

SLEEPING
22 Belle Campground
23 Hidden Valley Campground
24 Jumbo Rocks Campground
25 Ryan Campground
26 White Tank Campground

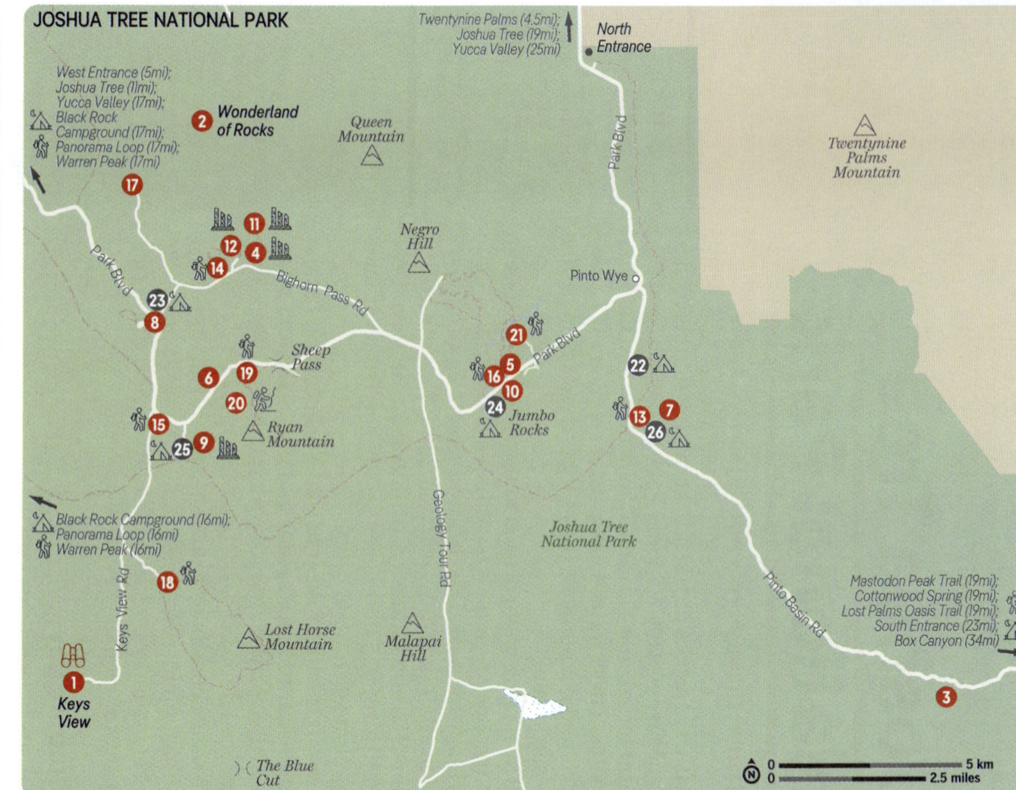

pretty **Barker Dam Loop Trail** (p230) for a deeper look at the ecosystem and natural history amid the fascinating boulder landscape of the **Wonderland of Rocks**. Afterward, detour south to check out **Keys View** for views over the San Andreas Fault, Salton Sea and out to the Mexican border. Enjoy a picnic lunch at **Cap Rock**.

Continue east along Park Blvd for another 3 miles. Stop to walk around the **Hall of Horrors** rock formation, or save the short walk for later as you continue another 6 miles to gawk at **Skull Rock**. Hang a right onto Pinto Basin Rd to head south 2.25 miles to park at Twin Tanks. Cross the road for the easy hike along the **Arch Rock Trail** and take the spur to pose lovingly with **Heart Rock**.

Keep driving south to the **Cholla Cactus Garden** to stroll the quarter-mile loop through teddy-bear cholla (avoid those snuggly barbed spines), then backtrack to exit through the North Entrance, or continue south to leave the park at the South Entrance. If taking the southern route and time allows, it's worth hiking at least part way along the **Mastodon Peak Trail**, which starts at Cottonwood oasis and passes by *metates* used by the Cahuilla people.

Hiking Joshua Tree's Varied Terrain

Explore classic JTree trails

Joshua Tree National Park's divergent landscapes, easing from the higher-elevation Mojave Desert to the lower Colorado Desert life zones, invite deeper exploration for those with more time.

If you're hiking with children, start at the trail designed by kids for kids – the **Discovery Trail** offers a bit of scrambling and interesting interpretive signs, making it a great park intro for grown-up kids, too. At less than a mile long, it's an easy hike and close to Skull Rock across the road. For classic bouldery Joshua Tree scenery, the 2.5-mile **Split Rock Loop** is another easy one, with a short spur leading to **Face Rock**.

Hikers wanting to gain elevation can head to the lesser-trafficked northwestern corner of the park, where the 6.5-mile **Panorama Loop** takes you through Joshua trees before rising into piñon-and-juniper forest atypical to most of the park. As the name suggests, you'll find panoramic views of the Coachella and Yucca Valleys along the 1200ft climb and another phenomenal view from **Warren Peak** (5103ft), off a spur trail on the western side of the loop. The trailhead begins at **Black Rock Campground**.

TREADING LIGHTLY

John Lauretig, president of Friends of Joshua Tree, muses on best practices in the desert. *@joshuatreefriends*

This is such a cool landscape if you've never been here: the diversity of Joshua trees, the exposed rocks and their cracks and the people climbing them. One can't-miss thing to do? When you see something that wows you, pull over and enjoy it!

One aspect that can elude visitors is how fragile the desert ecosystem is and how slow it is to recover. We all need to be good stewards of these special lands, whether it's staying on trail, picking up a little trash, respecting road closures so wildlife can access water sources – it all minimizes our impact on this unique environment.

EATING IN JTREE: PICNIC PROVISIONS

Campbell Hill Bakery: Pastries, soups, pizza and a line out the door in Twentynine Palms; check Instagram for current hours and arrive early. *6-9pm Thu-Sat* $

Dez (The): Grab-and-go sandwiches, salads, charcuterie and coffee in Joshua Tree for your national park picnic. *6.30am-4pm* $

Desierto Alto: Excellent bottle shop with a well-rounded selection of picnic goodies and gift-worthy edibles. *7am-7pm* $

Farmers market: Both Twentynine Palms and Joshua Tree hold year-round Saturday farmers markets. *8am-1pm* $

PLAN & PREPARE

All of the Leave No Trace principles *(lnt.org/why/7-principles)* apply when visiting Joshua Tree National Park, but it's particularly important to plan ahead and prepare. Once you enter the park, there are zero services aside from vault toilets at trailheads and campgrounds and running water is only found at the park entry points. Cell phone service is nonexistent inside the park. Bring everything you'll need: plenty of water (ie at least a gallon per person for the day), salty snacks to keep your electrolytes balanced and layers so you can adjust to sudden weather changes. Have all of the survival basics so you can fully enjoy the wondrous desert environment.

A more central high is the 3-mile **Ryan Mountain Trail**, rising over 1000ft in a mile-and-a-half – breathtaking in effort but also for the expansive vistas at the top. Be sure to pause along the way to notice the burly monzogranite tanks and piñon at the trailhead that transitions into cactus and yucca scrub as you climb.

Finally, at the southern end of the park, the 7.4-mile **Lost Palms Oasis Trail** begins at the small oasis at Cottonwood Springs, traversing boulder-piled hills and desert washes and ending at the gorgeous oasis named after its large grove of native California fan palms. The 3-mile Mastodon Peak Trail offers a shorter but just as sweet hit of varying terrain and human history with less of a time commitment.

Rock Art & Ruins

Remnants of JTree's human history

The mostly flat, rewardingly varied **Barker Dam Loop Trail** journeys into the park's natural history, with informative signage posted at regular intervals along the way. The 1.1-mile trail skirts the dam and cattle trough used in the early 1900s and a little spur leads to a shallow cave full of petroglyphs. At the trail's west end, an overlook in the boulders affords a view of Joshua tree plains below.

EATING & DRINKING: YUCCA VALLEY

Giant Rock Meeting Room: Rub shoulders with locals over pizza and wine north of Twentynine Palms Hwy; live shows too. *noon-11pm Wed-Sat, to 8pm Sun & Mon* $$

La Copine: Reserve months ahead or put your name on the list well before opening for sublime French brunch up Old Woman Springs Rd. *11am-4pm Thu-Sun* $$

Tiny Pony Tavern: Black velvet horse paintings, country music, good food and drag shows are a post-hike chef's kiss. *11am-1am Mon-Fri, from 9am Sat & Sun* $

Copper Room: Celebrate a special occasion at this historic resto next to the Yucca Valley airport, or just come for a cocktail. *4pm-midnight Wed-Sun* $$

FEEL4NATURE/SHUTTERSTOCK

Lost Palms Oasis Trail

An easy 2.2-mile out-and-back walk takes you to the well-preserved **Wall Street Mill**, passing ore-crushing ruins, the headstone of the unfortunate loser of a shootout and the **Desert Queen Well**, and continues to the crumbling pink ruins of **Wonderland Ranch**.

The **Ryan Ranch** ruins, an easy half-mile walk from the road, are worth a look as the Ryan brothers incorporated gold dust into the adobe bricks.

For a good hike, head further south down Keys View Rd to the **Lost Horse Mine Trail**, a roughly 4.5-mile out-and-back hike to an abandoned mine and equipment. As you climb, check out the views down on Pleasant Valley and the basalt-iced Malapai Hill popping up on the plain.

History buffs will want to book a tour of the national historic site **Keys Ranch**, accessible only by ranger-led walk from October to May. Exploring the small homestead brings to life the challenges of living in this environment.

At the park's southern end, it's only about a quarter-mile walk beyond the coolness of **Cottonwood Spring** to some trailside *metates* left by the Cahuilla. It's easy to imagine people gathering here and preparing food together near this life-sustaining water source.

CAMPING IN THE PARK

It's straight-up magical to experience sunset and sunrise in Joshua Tree National Park, to see the starry night sky above and hear coyote howls echoing off the boulders. Several of the park's campgrounds, including **Jumbo Rocks** (p260), are reservation-only up to six months in advance *(recreation.gov; $30 per night)*. **Hidden Valley**, **Belle** and **White Tank** *($25 per night)* campgrounds are first-come, first-served and best attempted midweek and outside of springtime for a chance of snagging a spot. All of the campgrounds in the park's interior have vault toilets, but no water or RV hookups.

Find **free dispersed camping** in the BLM land outside the park's southern border, or cross to the south side of I-10 to the more attractive **Box Canyon**.

EATING & DRINKING: TWENTYNINE PALMS

GRND SQRL: Welcoming gastropub and social hub with microbrews on tap, wine, good pub food and live music most nights. *noon-9pm Mon-Sat* $$

Jelly Donut: The doughnuts are great but you're here for the *pho* on the not-so-secret menu. Cash only. *5.30am-1pm* $

29 Palms Beer Company: The quality of the craft beers here makes it a rewarding stop after a hot day. Coffee too. *8am-9pm Sun-Thu, to 10pm Fri-Sat* $

Kitchen in the Desert: Indoor-outdoor dining experience with Caribbean-inflected shared plates and cocktails. *9am-3pm & 5-11pm daily, 3-5pm Fri-Sun* $$

JOSHUA TREE SURVIVAL

The Joshua tree, the elegantly Seussian namesake of the park, is showing some effects of climate change. While this plant species, known as *hunuvat chiy'a* or *humwichawa* in the Cahuilla language, continues to reproduce sexually in a symbiotic relationship with the yucca moth, research has shown it to reproduce asexually in parts of its cooler northern range. This cloning response embodies the species' resilience in the face of climactic change but also signals environmental stress. In the springtime, look out for its clusters of cream-colored blossoms signifying renewed hope for the future survival of this desert icon and tread carefully in its home.

JEANA LIM/SHUTTERSTOCK

Hidden Valley

Climbing Boulders, Cracks & Slabs

Guided climbing in the park

Standing at the base of the monzogranite, your hands begin to sweat through the chalk you've just dipped into for grippiness. Seeing some likely features to grab, you've never been so conscious of your fingers as you hold onto the cool rock before placing a foot on an obvious bump. Making your first move, you push yourself up with your foot to reach that higher depression that you saw from the start. Your other foot leaves the desert floor...and now you're on the rock, which suddenly seems a lot bigger than it did moments ago.

Fortunately, you are roped up and on belay with an experienced climbing partner. They've begun by introducing you to the basics while you're still on the ground, literally showing you the ropes.

The town of Joshua Tree has over 400 certified climbing guides and over 30 companies who offer climbing lessons. All certified guides have medical training and teaching experience, with permission to teach in the park. The best way to find the right guide is to call around and chat with someone personally to see if you vibe with them. If so, climb on.

Rates vary by outfit, but you can expect to pay roughly $300 to $400 for one or two people for a guided half-day or $425 to $525 for a full day. **Crash pads** *(small/large $18/25 per day)* can be rented 24/7 from lockers in the **Nomad Ventures** (p224) parking lot in JTree.

With over 10,000 climbs in the park, more experienced climbers can start with some bouldering and beta at **Hidden Valley** Campground (p260) and numerous centrally accessed climbs at Hall of Horrors or **Saddle Rocks**.

Beyond Joshua Tree National Park

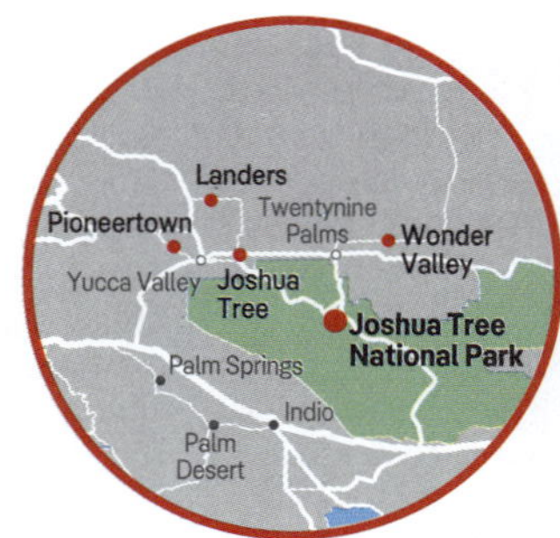

Find enduring outdoor art installations, new infusions of culture in gateway communities and a real town originally established as a film set.

Over the past few years, new energy has revitalized the park's gateway towns of Joshua Tree and Twentynine Palms along Twentynine Palms Hwy (Hwy 62), making it worthwhile to spend some time poking around the local shops and diverse eateries. Even more captivating are the outdoor sculpture gardens and art installations – both permanent and pop-up – dotting the desert. Moving through these human-made landscapes, often created with discarded objects, presents a compelling contrast to the natural artscapes of the park.

Branching off from Twentynine Palms Hwy, the road leads to another living art piece: Pioneertown, a film set constructed as a backdrop for old Westerns that was and still remains an actual tiny town.

Places

GETTING AROUND

You'll need a car to explore the sights outside the national park. The area's outdoor art installations are all over the map and spending half a day driving around finding them is part of the adventure.

Pioneertown Rd veers off of Twentynine Palms Hwy in Yucca Valley, winding 5 miles into the mountains.

Joshua Tree

TIME FROM JOSHUA TREE NATIONAL PARK: **10MIN**

Poking around downtown JTree

Joshua Tree: it's a tree, it's a national park and it's also a town. The most-trafficked West Entrance to the park is accessed from **Joshua Tree**, the town at this crossroads along Twentynine Palms Hwy and Park Blvd. It's where you'll find a busy national park **visitor center** and gift shop, a clutch of cafes and takeaway shops for your park picnic and the **Art Queen** complex containing the **World Famous Crochet Museum** *(sharielf.com/museum.html)*, a lime-green lozenge housing wall-to-wall crochet cakes, sea creatures, mushrooms and animals of all yarn species – all powdered with a bit of inevitable desert dust. The museum collection is made up of donated crochet work curated by Shari Elf, who also maintains her own gallery in this funky spot. Donations are accepted, but you can also purchase art and swag from any of the artists in the complex.

See what's going on at the **Alien Robot Museum** *(alienrobotmuseum.com)* – an outreach space for the yet-to-be-built **Joshua Tree Art Museum (JTAM)** – the vintage hairdressers'

BEST SHOPPING AT THE CROSSROADS

JT Trading Post: This spacious market carries new and vintage goods from local vendors and makers. Yoga too.

Nomad Ventures: Excellent outdoor shop for last-minute camping needs, climbing gear and local info.

The Station: Look for the giant cowboy looming in front of this repurposed gas station. Find eclectic, irreverent souvenirs, bumper stickers, T-shirts and more.

Sun of the Desert: Art, gifts, dude-centric clothes, accessories and body care (eg beard balm), plus locally themed lit. Sister store in Twentynine Palms.

Time Echo Vintage: Perfectly encapsulates the funky-fresh desert feel of JT in its clothing, cowboy boots, sun hats, jewelry and knickknacks.

chairs at **Beauty Bubble Salon and Museum** *(@beautybubblesalon)* and the other little galleries within Art Queen.

On the other side of the highway, **JT Trading Post** *(jttradingpost.com)* hosts an outdoor market on weekends, coinciding with Joshua Tree's Saturday **farmers market**. Pick up some fresh produce for hike snacks, or, on non-market days, roam the shops for a vintage fit. At some point you'll want to mosey over to the atmospheric **Joshua Tree Saloon & Grill** *(thejoshuatreesaloon.com)* to cool off with a margarita or replenish with a burger.

Open-air desert art

When you come to the high desert, you can't help but feel a sense of untethered freedom afforded by these wide-open spaces. And as you drive around the neighborhoods, you may notice a lot of eye-catching outdoor artwork in all that space. Some of it you have to look for, though.

For Noah Purifoy, who lived and made art in Joshua Tree throughout the last 15 years of his life, art was a means of creating social change. His first major work of assemblage art came from wreckage and found objects salvaged from the 1965 Watts Riots in Los Angeles, speaking to the social injustice of racial profiling.

The **Noah Purifoy Outdoor Desert Art Museum** *(noahpurifoy.com)* preserves these works he left behind, as pieces of it slowly succumb to the desert elements. The architectural and playful sculptures at his outdoor desert studio were constructed from discarded materials, including lunch trays, vacuum-cleaner parts, bicycle tires and even toilets. There's so much to look at and ponder with each turn through this space; allow yourself time to wander.

On the way in or out, stop to meander around the **Simi Dabah Sculpture Foundation** *(simidabahsculptures.com)*, where the large-scale steel sculptures of 98-year-old Simi Dabah will tune you into the works you'll recognize as you drive along Twentynine Palms Hwy. If you wish to take home a piece reflecting the area's spirit, you can purchase one of his sculptures or another of the artists who share the display space.

While in the neighborhood, make a detour to Daniel Popper's serene concrete-and-mosaic **Transmission** sculpture, located on private property. Note that a GPS will direct you to a gated driveway; drive past it to pull into the turnout directly after, where a trail leads you to the public viewpoint to this sculpture.

MORE OUTDOOR, OUTSIDER, OUTHOUSE ART

For a cheekier vibe, take Twentynine Palms Hwy east to Wonder Valley's **Glass Outhouse Art Gallery** (p237), whose actual glass outhouses hint at the founder's outlook.

Pioneertown

New fun in the Old West

TIME FROM JOSHUA TREE NP: **25MIN**

Purpose-built in the 1940s as a movie set for filming Westerns, **Pioneertown** has weathered its booms and busts. It was originally conceived as a permanent film set of an Old West town that could also house and support production staff, but its economy collapsed in the 1950s as the Western

ANNA KRASNOPEEVA/SHUTTERSTOCK

Pioneertown

genre faded in popularity. Since then, the town's population has ebbed and flowed over the decades. It is now enjoying a contemporary revival as a social-media backdrop.

A short 25-minute drive from the national park's West Entrance, Pioneertown still has human inhabitants and horses. And aside from its popularity for Instagram photo shoots, its block-long row of Old West facades on Mane St (get it?) house actual shops selling vintage clothes and cool locally made wares, including artisanal skincare, pottery and artwork. On Saturday afternoons you might witness **Wild West shootouts** in the street (donations appreciated).

Afternoons are best to find businesses open and weekends are typically way more crowded. But the best reason to head up to P-town is for a show at legendary music venue **Pappy & Harriet's Pioneertown Palace** *(pappyandharriets.com)*. It's a treat to see big-deal artists play in such a small setting – check the calendar ahead of your visit. You can't make dining reservations, so come early for the Santa Maria–style barbecue and expect a wait.

If it's two hours for a table – not unusual on weekends – head to the friendly **Red Dog Saloon** *(reddogpioneertown.com)* for some Mexican food and a beer. They've also got live local music on weekends and it's a great place to refuel

HI-DEZ ALLURE

Colleena Hake is an artist and gallerist at La Matadora Gallery in Joshua Tree. *@la.matadora.gallery*

Joshua Tree attracts artists for its surreal and natural beauty, but also because there's plenty of breathing room here to hide out and dive into art. When a distraction or inspiration is needed, so much is happening creatively and socially too. I still have much to discover and explore here, with its many layers of mystery and adventure. It's never boring in the hi-dez!

Every second Saturday of the month, Joshua Tree hosts an evening art walk. That's a fun time to meet the locals and check out art at **La Matadora** *(lamatadoragallery.org)*, **Art Queen** (p233) and other neighboring galleries.

EATING & DRINKING IN JOSHUA TREE: OUR PICKS

Joshua Tree Coffee Company: Nitro cold brew after a big night and before a big hike? Yes, please. Pick up beans while you're at it. *8am-5pm* $

JT Country Kitchen: Classic diner fare with fresh twists, breakfast served all day and happy customers since 1977. *7am-3pm* $

Crossroads Cafe: Perennial favorite, serving hearty breakfasts and sandwiches; also a great place for a post-hike beer and occasional live music. *7am-9pm* $

Joshua Tree Saloon & Grill: Serves saloon vibes, burgers, live music (weekends) and a happy hour menu (weekdays). *11am-11pm Sun-Thu, to midnight Fri & Sat* $

CHUCKWALLA NATIONAL MONUMENT

The 624,000-acre **Chuckwalla National Monument**, one of the country's newest, was designated by outgoing President Biden in January 2025. Of interconnected cultural significance to Native American tribes including the Cahuilla, Chemehuevi, Mojave, Quechua and Serrano, the monument connects 'islands' of desert ecosystems and protects 10,000-year-old petroglyphs and spiritual sites.

Stretching south from Joshua Tree National Park to the Arizona border, the monument protects the biodiversity that spans the Mojave, Colorado and Sonoran Desert zones, including the chuckwalla lizards for which the monument is named. These ecosystems support migrating birds who rely on its sustenance and water.

after a hike around the **Pioneertown Mountains Preserve** *(wild landsconservancy.org; donations appreciated)*. The preserve's several trails traverse the bouldery mountain landscape about 4 miles outside of P-town, offering a tranquil piñon-and-juniper-scented respite from the national park crowds. The 6.6-mile **Chaparrosa Peak Trail** (out-and-back) ends with views of San Jacinto Peak and San Gorgonio Mountain. Pick up a map at the ranger station; some trails were closed at the time of writing.

Book well in advance for the luxury of staying in stumbling distance of Pappy & Harriet's at the **Pioneertown Motel** *(pioneertown-motel.com)*.

Landers

TIME FROM JOSHUA TREE NATIONAL PARK: **45MIN**

Integratron sound bath

Former aerospace engineer George Van Tassel built the wood-domed **Integratron** *(integratron.com)* in the 1950s, incorporating structural elements based on writings of Nikola Tesla and, he claimed, direct communications from extraterrestrials visiting from Venus. He sited the dome in a precise location where he believed its structure would best amplify the intersection of geomagnetic forces. Channeling electromagnetic frequencies specified by the alien visitors, Integratron was designed as a machine for anti-gravity, rejuvenating cell tissues and even time travel.

Regardless of their provenance, the dome's acoustics provide a perfect setting for other frequencies, including **sound baths** using crystal singing bowls tuned to each of your chakras. Soak up the aural vibes in a one-hour public session *($55 per person)*. Walk-ins are not accommodated and you'll have to

GERALD PEPLOW/SHUTTERSTOCK

Chaparrosa Peak Trail

reserve a month or two in advance, as sessions sell out quickly. If you find that the calendar is booked out, check back frequently to snap up a last-minute cancellation. It's also possible to book the Integratron for private sessions with your own group of sound bathers.

Wonder Valley

TIME FROM JOSHUA TREE NATIONAL PARK: **10MIN**

View from the Glass Outhouse

The late artist Laurel Seidl fell in love with the quiet and open space of **Wonder Valley**. After raising rabbits on the property, she and her late partner eventually turned it into a cheeky sculpture garden filled with a delightful concatenation of kooky desert assemblage. He built for her the tiny chapel that you can enter, complete with pews and stained-glass window featuring a Joshua tree. Seidl's welcoming and irreverent nature still shines through the miniature Burma Shave–style road signs, the desert tableaux of skeletons working out and most especially in the functional glass outhouses clad in reflective glass that allows a user to gaze out at the surrounding desert in complete privacy.

Seidl's belief in inclusivity came from a disdain for the gatekeepers of the art establishment and her onsite **Glass Outhouse Art Gallery** was open to any artist who wished to exhibit there, as long as they paid a small fee and did their own catering for the art opening. Though Seidl passed away in 2024, her longtime friend and gallery caretaker Quisha Henderson continues to keep the exhibitions going and the spark of Seidl alive.

You'll know you've arrived when you spot the giant Pepsi can from the road.

FAMILY-FRIENDLY FESTIVALS

Grownups love the marquee superstars taking over multiple stages at **Coachella Music Festival** *(coachella.com)*, but the Joshua Tree area has its own family-friendly fests worth planning for. The biannual **Joshua Tree Music Festival** *(joshuatreemusicfestival.com)* comes around every May and October, bringing four days of genre-spanning music and DJs. In addition to music, attendees can enjoy workshops, yoga and dance classes, art and kids' entertainment outdoors at **Joshua Tree Lake Campground** *(joshuatreelake.com)*. Also taking place in October, **Pioneer Days** *(@cityof29palms)* in Twentynine Palms celebrates the community and its heritage with classic Americana.

Death Valley National Park

LOWEST LOW | VOLCANIC CRATER | PHENOMENAL GEOLOGY

TOP TIP

'Don't die.' This blunt message is on park signage everywhere, because the desert is not messing around. Have on hand at least one gallon of water per person per day, keep your gas tank topped up, know your limits and understand that your cell service will be mostly nonexistent. Plan wisely to play safely.

An ancestral and contemporary home to the Timbisha Shoshone people, the land now known as Death Valley National Park represents the largest US national park in the lower 48 states. The park is probably best known as the lowest point in North America at 282ft below sea level. Its highest point is Telescope Peak (11,049ft), making it a land of extremes, but not just in elevation.

Despite the ominous name, Death Valley's vast desertscapes are alive with geological wonders. Between the hexagonal quilt of salt flats at Badwater Basin, the startling greens and pinks of Artists Palette, the wind-sculpted sand dunes and the smooth marble-walled slot canyons, it may radically morph the image that the word 'desert' summons to your mind.

Borax mining put it on the proverbial map, but its fascinating austere wildness kept it there and garnered its protected status as a national park.

Rambling & Scrambling

Day hiking in Death Valley

True, it's the lowest place in North America (282ft below sea level), the hottest place in the world (it hit 128°F/53°C in the summer of 2022) and the driest of the US national parks – but **Death Valley** *(nps.gov/deva; 7-day pass per car $30)* is an amazing place to hike. Because of its brain-melting extremes,

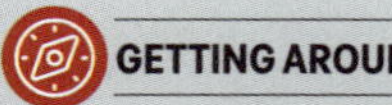

GETTING AROUND

As a car is necessary for traveling around the park and the distances are vast, make sure to check current road closures and conditions ahead of your trip at *nps.gov/deva*. There are three gas stations within the park at Panamint Springs, Stovepipe Wells and Furnace Creek (west to east). On roads that are accessible only with high-clearance 4WD vehicles, be sure to have a spare tire you can change yourself – or a satellite messenger – as cell phone service is nil throughout most of the park.

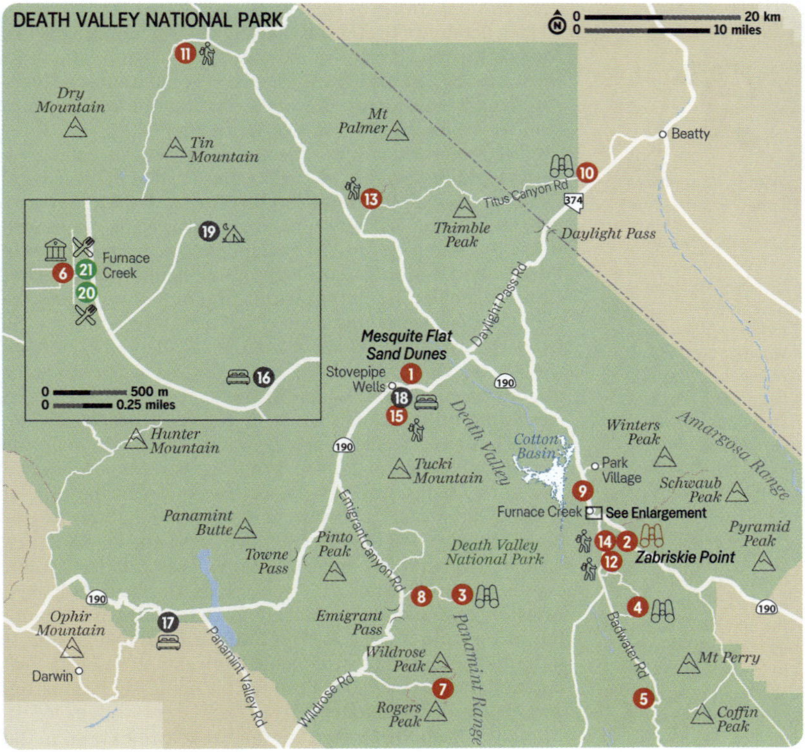

DEATH VALLEY NATIONAL PARK

HIGHLIGHTS

1 Mesquite Flat Sand Dunes
2 Zabriskie Point

SIGHTS

3 Aguereberry Point
4 Artists Palette
5 Badwater Basin
6 Borax Museum
7 Charcoal Kilns
8 Eureka Mine
9 Harmony Borax Works
10 Titus Canyon Rd
11 Ubehebe Crater

ACTIVITIES

12 Desolation Canyon
13 Fall Canyon
14 Golden Canyon
15 Mosaic Canyon

SLEEPING

16 Inn at Death Valley
17 Panamint Springs Resort
18 Stovepipe Wells Village Hotel
19 Texas Springs Campground

EATING

20 Last Kind Words Saloon
see 17 Panamint Springs Resort
21 Ranch 1849 Buffet
see 18 Toll Road Restaurant

EATING IN DEATH VALLEY: LAST CALL

Panamint Springs Resort: With an inclusive, sunny saloon ambience and good food, this family-run spot is a welcome stop at the park's west end. *7am-9pm* **$$**

Toll Road Restaurant: Buffet breakfasts and square meals at Stovepipe Wells, with a bar next door and nearby convenience store. *7-10am & 11.30am-9pm* **$$**

1849 Buffet: At The Ranch plaza in Furnace Creek, the buffet spread won't wow you, but the plentitude will satisfy. *6-10am, 11am-2pm & 5-9pm* **$$**

Last Kind Words Saloon: Burgers and pasta in Wild West-bedecked environs, complete with taxidermied critters and hammered-tin ceilings. *5-9pm* **$$**

WHY I LOVE DEATH VALLEY

Wendy Yanagihara, Lonely Planet writer

Every time I return to Death Valley, I discover something new about this extreme place – like when Badwater Basin fills with rainwater, it becomes Lake Manly (again) – until the water evaporates away. But even the things I already know about it reset my soul. Driving north along Badwater Rd, my heart still does a little leap seeing the hillsides pop in mineral swaths of red, pink, gold and green. Inexplicable-to-me geology on a canyon hike makes me feel small and awed at the forces that created them. And even sitting for a few minutes watching the light and shadow move across a nameless mountainside reminds me to simply experience the ever-changing beauty of this landscape and of life at large.

it's best to head out before 10am and after 4pm during the hottest seasons. Be prepared for dips in temperature after dark and stay aware of flash-flood warnings.

Flash floods are the reason that sinuously winding slots like **Mosaic Canyon** even exist and hikers have floods to thank for this canyon's beautifully exposed layers of juxtaposed Noonday dolomite and Mosaic Canyon breccia (mudflow carbonates studded with inclusions of rock fragments).

A different yet equally spectacular gallery of wondrous geology is **Golden Canyon**, off the northern end of Badwater Rd. Take the 4.3-mile **Golden Canyon–Gower Gulch loop** that starts in a narrow slot and climbs along a towering golden wall before dropping you into the badlands visible from **Zabriskie Point**. The 3.6-mile hike through the badlands of **Desolation Canyon** make this another stunner off of Badwater Rd. The trail follows a wash with splashes of pink, green and purple from iron oxides and chlorite and the payoff of an expansive, west-facing view at the end. This out-and-back involves some minor scrambling in a couple of spots.

Heading up the North Highway toward Ubehebe Crater, you've got two excellent choices to mull on the drive up the turnoff road to Titus Canyon. From the parking lot, you can hike into **Titus Canyon** – closed to vehicles at the time of writing, but usually a 27-mile, one-way drive that terminates here. At this end of the canyon, the breccia and colorful rock visible in the first few miles make it an easy and pretty hike, especially when you don't have to share the road with cars. Alternatively, take the little trail north from the parking lot that drops into a wash for the **Fall Canyon** hike, a 6-mile out-and-back. Though the color contrasts are not as eye-popping, the geology along the trail is endlessly fascinating and the trail ends at a dry fall.

Finally, **Ubehebe Crater**, the largest volcanic crater in the park, shows off a different side of Death Valley geology. The 1.5-mile hike around the rim is a fascinating look into the remains of a maar volcano, in which the meeting of magma and groundwater causes a steam explosion. In the springtime, desert flowers bloom in the pyroclastic pebbles.

Human History in Death Valley

Timbisha Shoshone and pioneer miners

As counterintuitive as it sounds, Death Valley may not have wound up as a national park were it not for mining.

For hundreds of years, the Timbisha Shoshone people lived seasonally in lands now known as Death Valley National Park, until the 1849 gold rush initiated the intermittent influx of prospectors and miners into the valley. Though miners often didn't succeed in the harsh conditions, Pete Aguereberry managed to work at his **Eureka Mine** for almost 40 years after discovering gold there in 1905. You can see the closed mine and camp, where his cabin compound still stands, and imagine the grit it took to survive here.

Continue down the road to check out the fantastic views from **Aguereberry Point**, 6433ft above the desert floor. The

DEATH VALLEY HIGHLIGHTS

If you're only driving through Death Valley between other destinations, you can still survey some of the park's must-sees.

START	END	LENGTH
Father Crowley Vista Point	Dante's View	125 miles; 3hr

From the west along Hwy 190, stop at 1 **Father Crowley Vista Point** for a view into Rainbow Canyon. After descending Hwy 190 and passing through Panamint Springs, turn right onto Emigrant Canyon Rd after 30 miles. Follow Emigrant Canyon 28 miles to the end of the road. Stretch your legs for a little wander into the 1870s-era 2 **beehive-shaped charcoal kilns** (p242) before heading back the way you came to Hwy 190. Continue east and stop to blaze your own trail through the entrancing, ever-shifting 3 **Mesquite Flat Sand Dunes**. Afterwards, stop at 4 **Furnace Creek** for a lunch break and gas before taking the turnoff down Badwater Rd.

Drive 17 miles to North America's lowest point, 5 **Badwater Basin**. Walk the half-mile out to the 6 **salt flats** for the full experience of strange awe, then backtrack up the road for the short detour onto Artists Dr to take in the colorfully otherworldly mineral hillsides of 7 **Artists Palette**.

Return to Hwy 190, now veering southeast, stopping at 8 **Zabriskie Point** for classic views of the badlands below in all their rugged gorgeousness. Try leaving enough time to drive the 14-mile road up to 9 **Dante's View** for a dramatic look down on Badwater Basin and the vastness of Death Valley before leaving the park.

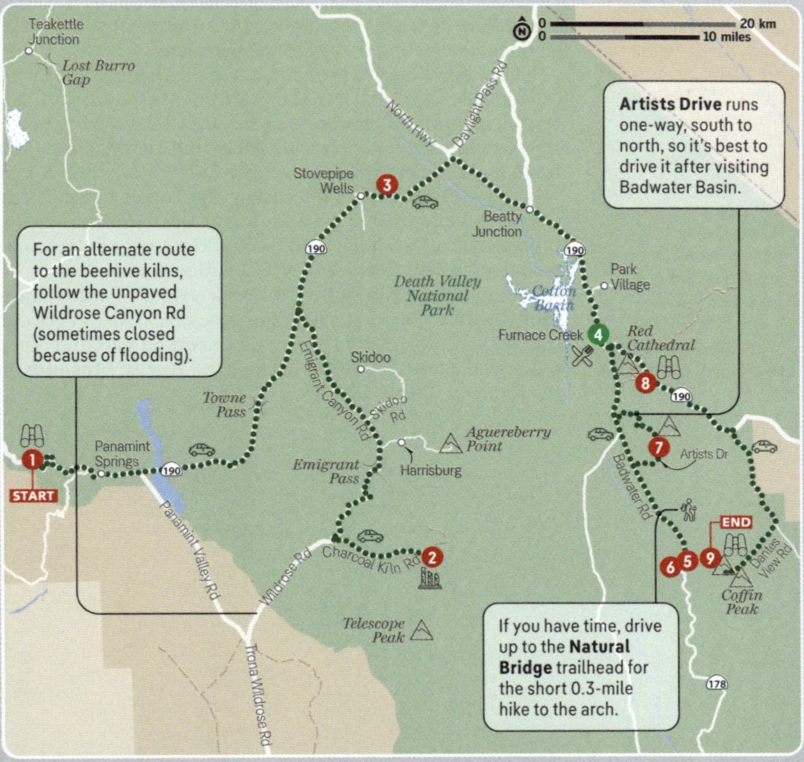

Artists Drive runs one-way, south to north, so it's best to drive it after visiting Badwater Basin.

For an alternate route to the beehive kilns, follow the unpaved Wildrose Canyon Rd (sometimes closed because of flooding).

If you have time, drive up to the **Natural Bridge** trailhead for the short 0.3-mile hike to the arch.

THE FIRST PEOPLE OF DEATH VALLEY

Timbisha Shoshone people lived in the Panamint Range for centuries, visiting the valley every winter to gather acorns, hunt waterfowl, catch pupfish in marshes and cultivate small areas of corn, squash and beans. After the federal government created Death Valley National Monument in 1933, the tribe was forced to move several times and was eventually restricted to a 40-acre village site. Years of protests and lobbying by tribal activists resulted in President Clinton signing the Timbisha Shoshone Homeland Act in 2000, transferring 7500 acres of land back to the tribe and creating the first Native American reservation inside a US national park. Today, a few dozen Timbisha live in the **Indian Village** near Furnace Creek.

NICHOLAS J KLEIN/SHUTTERSTOCK

Eureka Mine (p240)

6.5-mile road off Emigrant Canyon Rd is quite rough and best done in a high-clearance vehicle. Further south down Wildrose Canyon Rd, explore the **beehive-shaped charcoal kilns**. Built by the Modock Mines, the kilns were used to make charcoal for fueling ore-refining operations.

But it was the discovery of borax (used in detergents, among other purposes) that paved the way for tourism at Death Valley. Borax mining and processing began in Death Valley in the 1880s and was laboriously transported out via wagons pulled by 20-mule teams. When the lucrative mineral was discovered in a more easily accessed location, the Pacific Coast Borax Company built what is now the Inn at Death Valley, heavily promoting it as a holiday destination. The company later lobbied to establish Death Valley as a national park.

Nowadays, you can walk the interpretive trail at the **Harmony Borax Works** site near Furnace Creek. Also check out the rusty mining equipment, mule-drawn wagons and other sculptural skeletons in the back of the **Borax Museum** at the Ranch in Furnace Creek.

Beyond Death Valley National Park

These are lands of wide-open spaces, where the Sierra Nevada looms west of the park and tiny desert communities dot the east.

Hwy 395 runs north to south, near the west side of Death Valley. Along Hwy 395 lies the Eastern Sierra town of Lone Pine, a lovely gateway town on the park's west side. Stop here for a little mountain hiking, a big dinner and a fuel fill-up.

The park's eastern gateways are a different world altogether, where the desert stretches into Nevada, scattered with ghost towns, hot springs, oases and hidden rivers. Taking Hwy 127 south out of Death Valley Junction makes for a scenic road trip, meandering through small communities in greener desert zones to the Mojave National Preserve. Fascinating cave dwellings, reed-fringed hot springs and outdoor art are worth the stops on your drive.

Places

GETTING AROUND

As in Death Valley National Park, it's necessary to have a car to get around this area. Try to avoid driving in the area at night – the two-lane highways and rural roads are quite dark, especially if there's little to no moonlight.

Amargosa Valley

TIME FROM DEATH VALLEY NATIONAL PARK: **15–45MIN**

Ghost towns

The spectral white-and-turquoise adobe **Amargosa Opera House** *(amargosaoperahouse.org)* anchors Death Valley Junction with weather-beaten gravitas. Its story is compelling enough to have inspired a documentary about Marta Becket, the former ballerina who began performing one-woman shows here in 1968. Learn more on a twice-daily **tour** *(adult/child $15/5)*, or stay in the idiosyncratic adjacent hotel with basic rooms (some purportedly haunted) decorated with her hand-painted murals. Not much else exists here except for the road into the park, a 20-minute drive along Hwy 190, and the glorious dark sky above.

Further north on Hwy 95, **Beatty** (in Nevada) serves as the hub for the park's northeastern Daylight Pass entrance. Head west on Daylight Pass Rd (Hwy 374) for 6 miles through the hills and down to the ghost town of **Rhyolite**, once a prospering gold-rush town along the Las Vegas and Tonopah Railroad. Partial walls of the town's bank and shops lead up the road to the grand **Rhyolite Railroad Depot**, overlooking valley

DEVIL'S HOLE PUPFISH

East of Death Valley Junction, **Ash Meadows National Wildlife Refuge** *(fws.gov/refuge/ash-meadows)* protects habitat for 26 endemic species. Its most famous inhabitant is the endangered Devil's Hole pupfish, the rarest fish on the planet. Living in the 93°F (34°C) water of **Devil's Hole**, whose depth remains unknown, this little fish is a miracle that swam back from the brink of total extinction. Though near impossible to actually see the Devil's Hole pupfish deep within its gated enclave, other pupfish subspecies flourish in the warm springs of Ash Meadows and can be easily observed from the footpaths of Crystal Spring and Point of Rocks in all their captivating feistiness.

views. Interpretive signage helps to conjure up the bustling town in its prime.

Just outside Rhyolite, you may glimpse unexpected shapes in your peripheral vision. Whatever you look at first, you'll eventually stumble on the eerie figures of Albert Szukalski's *The Last Supper,* the flagship sculpture of the outdoor **Goldwell Open Air Museum** *(goldwellmuseum.org; donations welcome).* Walk around to view several artists' open-air work, day or night.

Shoshone

TIME FROM DEATH VALLEY NATIONAL PARK: **45MIN**

Ruins and restoration

Twenty-seven miles south of Death Valley Junction, **Shoshone** (population 17) may seem like a simple pit stop, but after gassing up the car, it's well worth walking the fascinating sights of this little oasis.

As ghost towns go, **Dublin Gulch** deviates from the norm with its cave dwellings carved out of the limestone by miners in the early 1900s. Insulating in the winters and cool in the blazing summers, these caves were ingeniously livable.

Learn more about the community's human and natural history, including the excavation of mammoth and mastodon bones nearby, in the tiny but mighty **Shoshone Museum** *(shoshonemuseum.org; donations welcome).*

More exceptional is Shoshone's extinction story gone right. The **Shoshone pupfish** was believed extinct by 1970, but in 1986 a small population was identified in a local ditch. Since then, habitat restoration efforts have resulted in the species bouncing back and it's now numbering at over 1000. From a little loop trail, you can see the current descendants energetically darting around the warm-springs pond habitats created expressly for them.

JAPANESE-AMERICAN GHOST TOWN

From Lone Pine, you can take a quick detour to the starkly beautiful **Manzanar National Historic Site**. This sensitively curated memorial of US government injustice is a must-visit in the Eastern Sierra.

SANDRA FOYT/SHUTTERSTOCK

Hot springs, Tecopa

Tecopa

TIME FROM DEATH VALLEY NATIONAL PARK: **1HR**

Hot springs and hiking

After exploring Death Valley, treat hike-weary muscles to thermal spring water at **Death Valley Hot Springs** *(deathvalleyhotsprings.com; day pass $35)*, formerly known as Delight's Hot Springs. There's an outdoor pool, clean showers and private pool cabanas where you can soak au naturel. Further south down Tecopa Hot Springs Rd, the small, spotless bath house at **Tecopa Hot Springs Resort** *(tecopahotsprings.org; day pass $25)* affords privacy, simplicity and peace, with showers and two private baths.

Both resorts have basic accommodations whose rates include hot-springs access; Tecopa also has a campground while Death Valley has a slightly higher-end range.

South of Tecopa, drive out to **China Ranch Date Farm** *(chinaranch.com)*, not for the date shakes – though you should definitely enjoy one – but to hike a refreshingly riparian section of the **Amargosa River Trail**. From the parking lot, take a shaded, verdant stroll around the ranch property, or opt for the longer 3-mile loop to a slot canyon with an additional spur to a waterfall and miles beyond in more arid Amargosa landscapes. Bring water and respect private property borders.

PRESERVING CULTURAL LANDSCAPES

Susan Sorrells is the fourth-generation owner of the town of Shoshone.

The Amargosa Basin is such a special place, not only for its beautiful wetlands and native flora and fauna, but for its spiritual value. Part of a physical spiritual path passes through here called the Salt Song Trail, which historically and spiritually connects multiple Native American tribes spanning California, Nevada, Arizona and Utah. The tribal knowledge that exists collectively among these tribes, like the Salt Songs that are still sung at memorial ceremonies, is vital to preserve. The traditional ways of caretaking these sacred lands are crucial to ensuring that the cultural landscapes, as well as the natural, are passed on to future generations.

EATING & DRINKING IN SHOSHONE & TECOPA

Crowbar Cafe & Saloon: Feeding weary travelers since 1920, the Crowbar offers breakfast, burgers and Mexican food, plus drinks at the saloon. *8am-9.30pm* $

Kit Fox Cafe: Coffee in the morning, wood-fired pizza in the afternoon. Hours can be erratic, but worth stopping to check. *8am-7pm Wed-Sun* $

Death Valley Brewing: Tecopa's first and best craft brewery uses water from the local mineral spring to brew interesting small-batch beers. *1-8pm Thu-Sun* $

Steaks & Beer: Vegas transplant Eric Scott prepares quality ingredients with simple yet sophisticated flair. Reservations recommended. *6-8pm Fri-Tue* $$

Anza-Borrego Desert State Park

WILDFLOWERS | BADLANDS | DARK SKIES

TOP TIP

In the mercurial way of the desert, Anza-Borrego's much-anticipated wildflower season is fleeting and unpredictable. Conditions have to come together with the right alchemy for desert wildflowers to blossom, but you can hear a weekly update on the **Wildflower Hotline** at 760-767-4684.

GETTING AROUND

If you plan on backcountry hiking or camping, it's ideal to have a high-clearance 4WD vehicle in Anza-Borrego. But even 4WD vehicles can wind up spinning their wheels in loose sand, so have gear on hand in case you need to dig out your rig. Bring a shovel and some carpet remnants or old floor mats for traction.

It's a superbloom superstar, an outdoor menagerie of metal-sculpture animals and an International Dark Sky Park. At over 1000 sq miles, Anza-Borrego is California's largest state park, with hundreds of miles of established roads and endless possibilities for backcountry camping under a shockingly starry night sky. The land was traditionally occupied by the Santa Rosa Band of the Cahuilla tribe and the Kumeyaay people and still bears the marks of their lives in the petroglyphs and *morteros* (mortars) visible today.

Anza-Borrego's high season runs from mid-February through March, when the wildflowers suddenly paint the desert in splashes of yellow, pink and magenta. The park's diminutive hub of Borrego Springs can quickly overflow with photo-hungry visitors when blooming peaks, but its all-season allure lies in its folded badlands, hidden oases, slot canyons and desert plains graced by joyous outdoor art.

Sky Art Safari

Borrego Springs' monumental sculpture garden

A **dragon** rears up from the desert floor, its serpentine back swelling and falling behind it, seemingly passing under the road. Nearby, saber-toothed tigers stalk a herd of horses on alert and a family of mammoths stretch out their trunks as they lope. They're all real, albeit in sculpture form, in the open plains of **Borrego Springs**. Artist Ricardo Breceda has created and installed over 130 sculptures – animals mythical, prehistoric and contemporary – that dot the landscape, all of which comprise the **Sky Art** of Galleta Meadows. The fantastical sculptures were commissioned by late landowner and philanthropist Dennis Avery, with the land they occupy intended for conservation, open to the public.

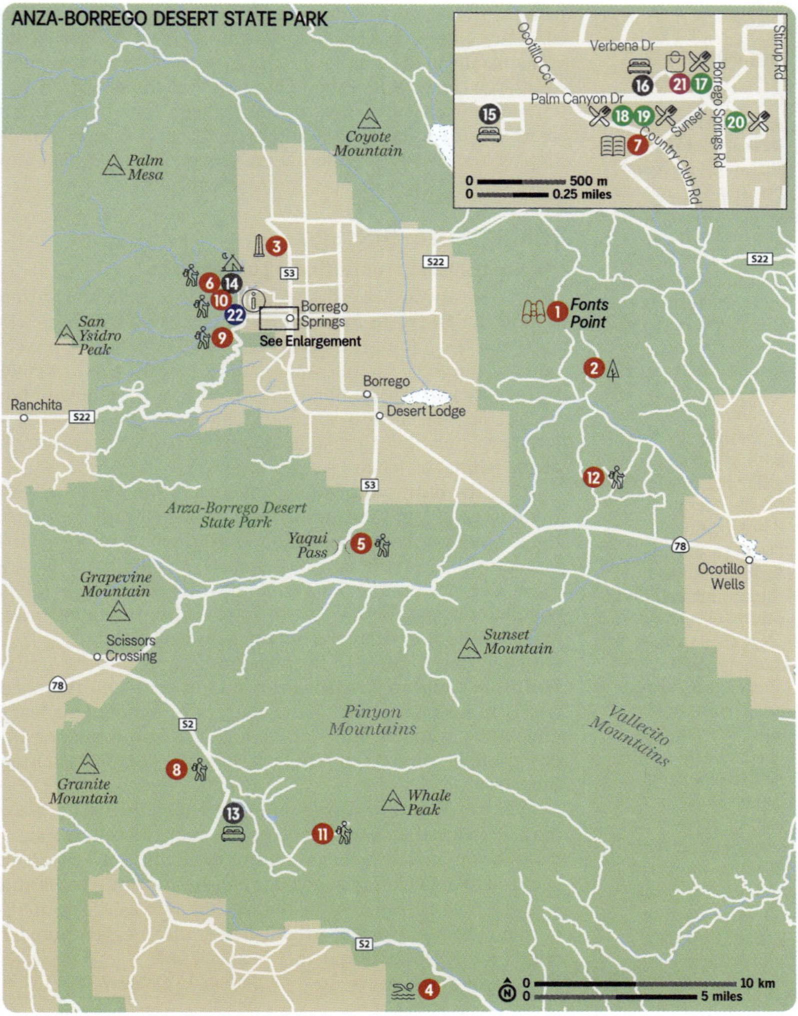

ANZA-BORREGO DESERT STATE PARK

Verbena Dr
Ocotillo Cct
Stirrup Rd
Palm Canyon Dr
Borrego Springs Rd
Sunset
Country Club Rd
0 500 m
0 0.25 miles

Coyote Mountain
Palm Mesa
San Ysidro Peak
Borrego Springs
See Enlargement
Fonts Point
Borrego
Desert Lodge
Ranchita
S22
S3
Anza-Borrego Desert State Park
Yaqui Pass
78
Ocotillo Wells
Grapevine Mountain
Scissors Crossing
Sunset Mountain
Pinyon Mountains
Vallecito Mountains
S2
Granite Mountain
Whale Peak
0 10 km
0 5 miles

HIGHLIGHTS

1 Fonts Point

SIGHTS

2 Sky Art Dragon Sculpture

ACTIVITIES

3 Agua Caliente Regional Park
4 Blair Valley
5 Borrego Palm Canyon Nature Trail
6 Borrego Springs Library
7 Hellhole Canyon Trail
8 Panorama Overlook Trail
9 Pictograph Trail

SLEEPING

10 Borrego Palm Canyon Campground
11 Borrego Valley Inn
12 Hacienda del Sol

EATING

13 Carlee's
14 Carmelita's Mexican Grill & Cantina
15 Kendall's
16 Red Ocotillo

SHOPPING

17 Anza-Borrego Desert Natural History Association

INFORMATION

18 Anza-Borrego Desert State Park Visitor Center

GET ORIENTED

Start at the **Anza-Borrego Desert State Park Visitor Center** *(day use $10)*, strategically designed to blend into the landscape. Paying the fee here also covers other stops where the fee is required. Find knowledgeable guides to help you plan your visit, as well as ranger programs and an interpretive path introducing visitors to the park.

In the heart of Borrego Springs, the **Anza-Borrego Desert Natural History Association** *(ABDNHA; abdnha.org)* carries gifts, clothing and books about desert hiking, natural history and more. Behind the building is the lovely **ABDNHA Borrego Desert Garden** with interpretive signage about the desert environment and tree IDs. Finally, the **Anza-Borrego Foundation** *(theabf.org)* organizes group hikes and educational events.

Part of the fun is stumbling upon them in the wild as you drive along the main artery that is Borrego Springs Rd. You'll glimpse them from a distance, noticing as you close in that even standing motionless, they appear on the verge of springing dynamically to life. But if you want to make a tour of the sculptures, you can download maps at *underthesunfoundation.org*.

The sculptures are a big draw to Borrego Springs and thousands of visitors come to see them each year. Try to keep your impact low by driving where there are preexisting tracks and not touching these beloved metal masterpieces.

Hiking Anza-Borrego

Nature trails and route-finding adventures

Many visitors to Anza-Borrego Desert State Park wind up hiking the **Borrego Palm Canyon Nature Trail** *(day use $10)* and it's popular for good reason. The trail is an easy one and fun for kids to explore and it ends at the **Borrego Palm Canyon Oasis**, named after its native California fan palms. The oasis itself is closed for restoration following a 2020 fire, but you can hike to an overlook to get a great look at the palms, which are recovering nicely.

To get the most out of your parking fee, you can follow up the Borrego Palm Canyon hike with some elevation gain on the 1-mile **Panorama Overlook Trail** that starts from a different trailhead at the same lot. Even as you climb, you'll enjoy expansive views of the desert floor below. Because this trail is completely exposed, it's best to start earlier in the morning and to avoid it entirely during the summer.

A longer alternative to Borrego Palm Canyon is the 5-mile **Hellhole Canyon Trail** nearby, taking you from the open desert to lush oases with little waterfalls, maidenhair ferns and palms untouched by fire. Though the trail is not strenuous, there is some scrambling over boulders before reaching the oases.

If your explorations take you further into the desert state park, it's a great idea to pick up a topo map and hiking guidebook so you have detailed directions in hand, as cell coverage is unreliable. Because flash floods can swiftly erase trails and signage, many hikes in Anza-Borrego follow washes, drainages and ridges in place of established trails. As ever, prepare wisely for desert hiking before heading out.

EATING & DRINKING IN BORREGO SPRINGS

Kendall's: Relaxed and nostalgic little diner with a patio on the strip mall, serving typical American breakfasts and Mexican options at lunch. *7am-2pm* $

Carmelita's Mexican Grill & Cantina: Down-home Mexican favorites tucked away in a corner of the mall, with shaded patio seating. *10am-8pm* $

Red Ocotillo: Crab-cake eggs Benedict for breakfast, lamb shanks for dinner. A lovely garden spot with a cute patio. *7.30am-8.30pm* $$

Carlee's: With hearty American food, wraparound bar (open later) and pool tables after food service has ended, this is the best evening hang in town. *11am-9pm* $$

HANS WISMEIJER/SHUTTERSTOCK

Borrego Palm Canyon Oasis

Anza-Borrego South to North

Petroglyphs, hot springs and diverse landscapes

Pack a lunch and start early for the drive south, through the park's **Pinyon Mountains** and beautiful higher-elevation piñon and juniper country. From the junction of Hwy 78 and County Rd S2, drive 6 miles to the Blair Valley turnoff, a dirt road at Mile 22.9. A map posted there shows the way to the **Pictograph Trail** (high-clearance vehicle recommended to the trailhead). The pretty hike to the **petroglyphs** is lined with small boulders, cholla and brittlebush, opening up to valley views at Smugglers Overlook.

If a hot-spring dip appeals to you, continue south about 15 miles to **Agua Caliente Regional Park** *(sdparks.org; parking $5)*, a San Diego County regional park within Anza-Borrego. Here, hot springs feed three indoor and outdoor developed pools, with $5 granting you access to showers and day use of the pools. Note: the indoor pool is adults only; weekends are often packed.

Return toward Borrego Springs the way you came, this time staying on Hwy 78 to the junction with the inconspicuous Buttes Pass Rd. It's 1.5 miles to the **Slot Canyon trailhead** *(day use $10)*. This is another easy hike through a cool slot canyon, ending at wind caves, so called because the wind eroded the sandstone into these smooth formations.

End your day with sunset at **Fonts Point**, with the dramatic panorama of **Borrego Valley** to the west, and the folded hills of the **Borrego Badlands** to the south in all their lit and shadowed glory.

GREAT HIKES NEAR BORREGO SPRINGS

Robin Halford, author of *Hiking in Anza-Borrego Desert, Vols 1-3,* suggests hikes located within 25 minutes of Borrego Springs.

Cannonball Run: In addition to the cannonball formations embedded in the mudstone here, you can also see the uplifting that occurred eons ago. It's almost like natural rock art.

Cool Canyon: A wonderful meandering canyon at a higher elevation, with different vegetation and cooler temperatures than on the desert floor.

Bill Kenyon Trail: This out-and-back isn't difficult, with wonderful cacti and other desert flora along the trail. You end up with a really nice view across Hwy 78 to a *bajada* (steep, curved descending trail), where several alluvial fans come together.

STARGAZING IN BORREGO SPRINGS

Approved in 2009 as the only certified Dark Sky Community in California, Borrego Springs is a stellar place for stargazing. The park's visitor center in Borrego Springs offers guided stargazing on dark new-moon nights and you may catch a star party behind the **Borrego Springs Library** *(sdcl.org/locations/6)*, where astronomers set up telescopes to tour the night sky. Check out the website of the **Borrego Dark Sky Coalition** *(abdnha.org/borregodarksky)* for upcoming events.

JNJPHOTOS/SHUTTERSTOCK

Wildflowers, Anza-Borrego Desert State Park

Wildflowers & Superblooms

Springtime blooms, sometimes in superlative

To some, Anza-Borrego is synonymous with superblooms. The park maintains its **Wildflower Hotline** *(760-767-4684)* to report on the season's conditions and bloom timing. When this desert floor lights up every spring, people can't resist the draw of flowers unfurling in swaths and spots of color, superbloom or not.

You don't even have to time your visit at peak bloom to spot flowers, as various flora show at different times – ocotillo flaming up in red tips in March and April and sometimes again in the fall. The many varieties of cacti start popping out with fat blossoms in white and pale yellow to shades of orange, pink, red and purple.

Anza-Borrego's most recognizable wildflowers are the bright yellow desert sunflowers, purple sand verbena and white dune evening primrose, which, when conditions are perfect, carpet the desert floor beginning as early as February and into March. Around that same time, look out for the pretty and hardy white flowers of the desert lily in sandy, inhospitable-looking places.

Desert scrub generally flowers in the springtime, with creosote blooming in sunny yellow blossoms and fuzzy white seed pods and the little red tubes of chuparosa attracting pollinators.

Unfortunately, especially in superbloom years, Anza-Borrego is inundated with people loving it to death. Instead of supporting life-sustaining bees and moths, human visitors wind up putting increasing pressure on the flora, stepping on plants and delicate root systems that sometimes can't bounce back the next season. We can all minimize our impact by parking in established areas, staying on paths and trails and visiting on off-peak days if possible.

Beyond Anza-Borrego Desert State Park

Discover the quaint mining town, forest lake and wolf conservation center west of Anza-Borrego.

Wild wolf encounters, lake fishing and mining-town ambience await in Julian, only an hour southwest of Borrego Springs but a world away at 4226ft. In contrast to Anza-Borrego's austere badlands and sun-baked valley floor, the mountains offer respite from the heat.

A popular midway point on the two-hour drive between San Diego and Anza-Borrego, Julian makes for a pleasant stop to stretch your legs and take in some cool mountain air. The old town's few blocks can get jammed with pedestrians and run out of street parking on the weekends. This is especially true during the fall, peaking for the Julian Apple Festival in October.

Places

Julian

TIME FROM ANZA-BORREGO DESERT STATE PARK: **25MIN**

Apple pies and mountain highs

Leaving Anza-Borrego from the west on Hwy 78, the road curves upward into oak and pine meadowlands, spilling into the little mountain town of **Julian**. Driving in, you'll see the Victorian-style shop fronts that date back to the early 1900s, when gold mining brought an influx of prospectors and settlers. Julian is most famous for its **apple pie**, abundant at bakeries along the main drag, though nowadays the apples hail largely from Washington state.

Stroll the few blocks of old-town Main St to shop for goat's-milk soap, sample a slice of pie and take the self-guided historical walking tour. From September through mid-October you can pick several varieties of your own apples at a local **u-pick orchard**. Year-round, book a beautiful guided trail ride on horseback with **Integrity Stables** *(integritystablesridingandtrainingcenter.com; 1hr ride $100 per person)*.

GETTING AROUND

You'll need your own wheels to get to Julian, which lies 30 miles southwest of Borrego Springs at the junction of Hwy 78 and Hwy 79. Note that in cooler seasons, snow and ice may present hazards on the twisty, two-lane mountain road; be sure to check weather conditions when planning your trip to or from Anza-Borrego. Once you've arrived, the little town is made for walking, as the downtown spans only a few square blocks.

JULIAN'S BLACK HISTORY

According to the US census of 1880, 33 of the 55 Black residents of San Diego County lived in Julian; several landmarks around town honor some of its notable Black citizens. **Coleman Creek** was named after AE 'Fred' Coleman, the local cattleman who first discovered gold in Julian, leading to the only gold rush in San Diego County and Julian's mining boom.

In town, former slave Albert Robinson and his wife Margaret Tull Robinson ran a successful restaurant, which they tore down to build the Robinson Hotel in 1897. Now the charming **Julian Gold Rush Hotel** *(julianhotel.com)*, it's the oldest continuously operating hotel in Southern California and is on the National Register of Historic Places.

CHRISTINAAIKO PHOTOGRAPHY/SHUTTERSTOCK

Julian Café & Bakery

One of the area's most worthwhile encounters is at the **California Wolf Center** *(californiawolfcenter.org; conservation tour $30 per person)* south of Julian, where you'll learn about wild wolf behavior, their populations and conservation efforts. Best of all, the guided walk around the grounds allows visitors to observe a few ambassador wolves that reside at the center. To be in the presence of such beautiful apex predators feels like an honor and, if you're lucky, they might give you chills with a collective howl while you're there. Advance reservations are required.

Find even more leisurely outdoor pursuits 9 miles south of Julian at the woodsy **Lake Cuyamaca**. The flat, 3-mile perimeter trail around the lake makes an easy, family-friendly walk with plenty of good lakeside picnic spots. You can also fish for rainbow trout, for which you'll need a **California fishing license** *(wildlife.ca.gov; 1-day license $21)*, conveniently procurable online. **The Tackle Shop** *(lakecuyamaca.net)* can rent you everything you need for a day of angling, from fish hooks to boat.

Exchange fish tales with a pint while enjoying views over the lake at **The Pub** *(thepubatlakecuyamaca.com)*. The Pub is an outpost of **Nickel Beer Company** *(nickelbeerco.com)*, whose little taproom on the east end of Julian occupies the former jailhouse. It's worth a look inside.

EATING & DRINKING IN JULIAN: BEYOND APPLE PIE

Purple Owl Cafe: Best place to caffeinate for the adventures of your day; good eats include savory and sweet crêpes. *6am-5pm Mon-Fri, from 8am Sat & Sun* $

Julian Café & Bakery: Show up early or be prepared to wait for rib-sticking goodness. *8am-7.30pm Mon-Thu, to 8.30pm Fri, 7am-9pm Sat, to 8.30pm Sun* $

Julian Beer Co: Pizza and barbecue feature prominently alongside the beer in this lively place; plenty of outdoor space, too. *11am-8pm Mon-Thu, from 9am Fri-Sun* $

Romano's Restaurant: Red-checkered-tablecloth family establishment serving Italian-American comfort food. No reservations. *11am-8.30pm Sun-Thu, to 9pm Fri-Sat* $$

Mojave National Preserve

SOLITUDE | DESERT WOODLAND | STUNNING DUNES

Occupying a swath of wilderness wedged between two interstate highways (I-15 and I-40), Mojave National Preserve is a less-visited desert park guaranteeing space for solitude. Spanning Mojave, Sonoran and Great Basin Desert zones, its landscape varies from sand dunes to piñon-and-juniper woodland. With a density of Joshua trees in some parts of the park that rivals the landscape of Joshua Tree National Park, the preserve offers all of the wild Mojave Desert beauty without the selfie-snapping human component.

Very few visitor amenities exist here, though the long-awaited reopening of the historic Kelso Depot visitor center is slated for 2026 and the Hole-in-the-Wall information center remains open 10am to 4pm Friday through Monday. But for the self-sufficient traveler, Mojave National Preserve is truly a refuge and a rich setting for sitting with the elemental delights of the desert.

TOP TIP

Before entering Mojave National Preserve, print a basic map showing passable roads, updated regularly by the National Park Service website *(nps.gov/moja/road-conditions.htm)*. GPS directions may be outdated and unreliable, sometimes leading travelers astray, so a quick NPS check-in and an old-fashioned map can save your day.

The Mojave's Greatest Hits

Lava tubes and great sand dunes

If you've only got a day to drive through **Mojave National Preserve** *(nps.gov/moja; free)*, choose your own adventure as suits your route.

GETTING AROUND

There is zero public transportation here, so you'll need your own vehicle to access Mojave National Preserve. The main paved roads connecting I-15 and I-40 are all open and most of the preserve remains accessible. Note that beyond the main arteries such as Kelbaker Rd, Cima Rd and Essex Rd, many of the connecting roads are unpaved and graded or washboard. Drive slowly on roads with scattered rocks, as some may be volcanic and sharp and flat tires on remote roads are not uncommon. Check road conditions ahead of your visit, as flash floods sometimes cause closures.

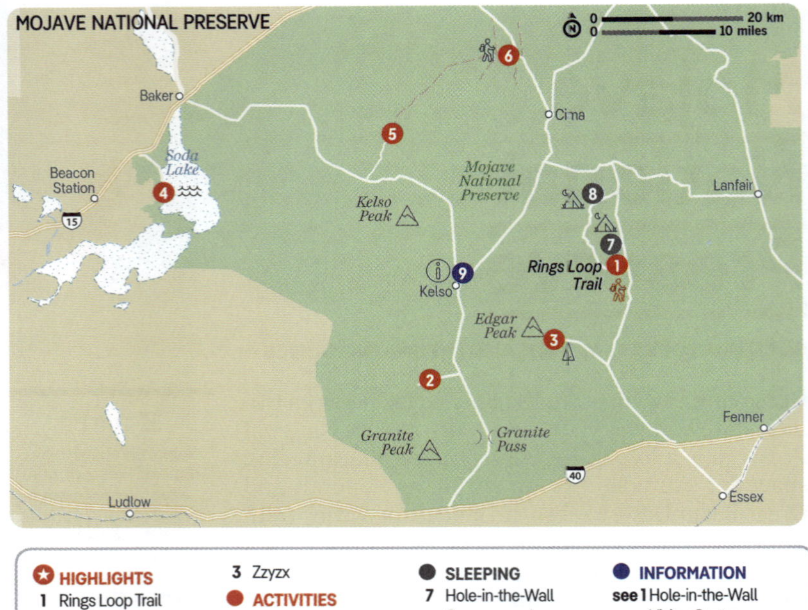

HIGHLIGHTS
1 Rings Loop Trail

SIGHTS
2 Kelso Dunes
3 Zzyzx

ACTIVITIES
4 Lava Tube
5 Mitchell Caverns
6 Teutonia Peak Trail

SLEEPING
7 Hole-in-the-Wall Campground
8 Mid Hills Campground

INFORMATION
see 1 Hole-in-the-Wall Visitor Center
9 Kelso Depot Visitor Center

From I-15 southbound from Vegas, take I-15 west, entering the preserve at **Cima Road**. Drive 12 miles through stands of Joshua trees, noticing the damage from the 2020 Dome Fire. Park in the small lot for the **Teutonia Peak Trail** (3 miles round-trip) and plan for about two hours hiking through Joshua trees and cactus scrub to the peak for marvelously wide-angle 360-degree views of the preserve. You can see clearly the delineation lines between healthy Joshua tree forest and the destruction of the burned zone. Back at the trailhead, consider picnicking under the huge juniper at the **White Cross WWI memorial** across the road before continuing to Kelso-Cima Rd and onto the graded turnoff for **Mojave Road**.

Mojave Rd cuts eastward across the park through robust Joshua tree habitat and into **Black Canyon**, where you'll travel south again through remote ranchlands between mountain ranges. About 10 miles south along Black Canyon Rd, stop at **Hole-in-the-Wall visitor center**. From here, walk the flat, 1-mile **Rings Loop Trail** clockwise (south from the parking lot). Shortly after the start of the trail, pause to look at the **petroglyphs** on the big boulder you'll round toward the backside of the Hole-in-the-Wall rock formation. Formed by a volcanic eruption whose gases left air bubbles in the cooling rock, the namesake holey walls on this fun hike include steep sections featuring bolted rings for handholds. Exit to I-40 along Essex Rd.

Alternatively, head 24 more miles westward along I-15 to Baker to take **Kelbaker Road** south into the park. At the **Aiken Mine Road** turnoff 19 miles in, drive another 5 miles through lava bed landscape to the cool, hilltop **lava tube** spotlit on one end by natural skylights. Look for the ladder descending into the cave.

Continue south on Kelbaker Rd, stopping at the **Kelso Depot Visitor Center** to learn a bit of preserve history. Seven miles further south, turn off toward the magnificent **Kelso Dunes**. Allow two to three hours for the round-trip hike to the top of the dunes. Empty out your shoes before driving on to I-40; stop for a photo at the picturesque Boulders viewpoint.

Avoid driving through the park around dusk when wildlife is active: scads of jackrabbits, chipmunks, owls, bats and other wildlife crisscross the remote park roads. If you must be on the road after sunset hour, take it slow.

Mitchell Caverns Detour

Geological salons of Mojave history

A little pocket of a California state park surrounded by the Mojave National Preserve, **Providence Mountains State Recreation Area** *(parks.ca.gov; $10)* is a high-altitude encapsulation of the Mojave's multifaceted geologic, natural and human history. Considered a sky island, the isolated mountains here support distinct species like rock squirrels that aren't found elsewhere in the preserve.

The main draw is **Mitchell Caverns** *(reservecalifornia.com; tour including day-use fee $20)*, a protected chain of strange and beautiful connected stalactite- and stalagmite-laden chambers created by the synthesis of time, water and minerals. You can only visit on a two-hour **ranger-led tour**, conducted twice daily on Fridays through Sundays, September to June by reservation. Tours explore the caverns with human context about their history (Chemehuevi, miner and entrepreneurial), as well as their past residents like the Shasta ground sloth and current denizens that include oddities like the blind pseudoscorpion.

Zzyzx

The last word?

Quack doctor and Methodist preacher Curtis Springer established **Zzyzx** as 'the last word' in health in 1944. The Bureau of Land Management evicted Springer 30 years later as he had no legitimate claim to the land; the structures were then left to the mercy of the unforgiving desert.

DESERT TORTOISES

The desert tortoise is a threatened species found in the Mojave Desert Preserve as well as California's larger desert regions. Though the species has been around for millions of years, its populations have declined over the past several decades. Stressors include rising temperatures from climate change, disease, human encroachment on desert habitats and even ravens, which prey on baby tortoises.

Consider it a blessing if you see a desert tortoise in the wild. In fact, always check under your parked car before driving away and watch out for tortoises trundling across roads.

BEEP BEEP!

You stand a fairly good chance of seeing a roadrunner cross your path in your desert travels, as these large, charismatic birds are diurnal and instantly recognizable. During the hottest seasons, roadrunners adjust their activity to dawn and dusk to avoid the scorching heat. Better at running than flying, they can hit speeds up to 20mph.

The greater roadrunner's scientific name of *Geococcyx californianus* means 'Californian earth cuckoo' (which could apply to many state residents) and its common name seems 100% accurate when you see them zipping across roadways. Roadrunners not only bravely mate for life but also prey on scary delicacies like scorpions and rattlesnakes.

ERIC M. WILLIAMS/SHUTTERSTOCK

Lake Tuendae (p255)

After following the shoreline of the **dry soda lake** to the parking area, walk the quarter mile to the spring-fed **Lake Tuendae** – time your arrival for the morning or evening and you have a good chance of spotting bighorn sheep quenching their thirst here. The reservoir is also a great locale for birding – spot hundreds of species, including the western tanager, various flycatchers, warblers and roadrunners. The quarter-mile loop trail around the lake is flat and an easy, accessible walk.

The north side of the road is open to the public from dawn to dusk. On the road's south side, the old resort buildings now house the **California State University's Desert Studies Center** *(fullerton.edu/dsc),* a working field station (private property). **UC Riverside Extension** *(extension.ucr.edu)* occasionally offers weekend courses open to the public, on such topics as photography, flintknapping and birding, offering the rare opportunity to overnight at the Desert Studies Center.

A little bit surreal and a lot tranquil, Zzyzx makes an excellent rest stop off the interstate, with picnic tables and vault toilets if you have time for a detour.

Beyond Mojave National Preserve

Embrace slow travel by taking yourself on a time-warp road trip along a stretch of the historic Mother Road.

Wide-open desert flies by as you travel the interstates to the north and south of Mojave National Preserve. But if you're not quite ready for highway travel and a straight shot back to urban hubs, take the long way to explore a smidge of old Route 66.

Flash flooding on Route 66 washed out several 1930s-era bridges and sections of roadway connecting Amboy with Goffs to the east, but the section between Amboy and Ludlow to the west has reopened. The romance of the Mother Road endures even in the short stretches, with unexpected roadside sights popping up through the shimmering heat waves.

Places

GETTING AROUND

You'll definitely need your own vehicle to get anywhere around the area. As is advisable around these parts, fill up your gas tank when you can. Roy's Motel & Cafe in Amboy is the only fuel stop along this lovely, lonely desert drive.

Amboy

TIME FROM MOJAVE NATIONAL PRESERVE: **20MIN**

Get your kicks in 2026

Crank up the '50s tunes for this mini road trip connecting Mojave National Preserve with Joshua Tree National Park (p227), in celebration of Route 66's 100th anniversary in 2026.

Leave Mojave via Kelbaker Rd, cross beneath I-40 and continue south about 11 miles until the road intersects with Route 66 (National Trails Hwy). The road eastward is blocked, so your only option is to turn right.

Route 66 stretches ahead of you for miles, passing the odd graffitied road sign. Look for the pair of **Chinese stone lions** guarding open desert on the south side of the highway, adding unexpected mystery to the archetypical-Americana mood. In about 6 miles you'll approach the town of **Amboy**, marked by its towering atomic-age sign for **Roy's Motel & Cafe** *(visitamboy.com)*. Though Roy's no longer offers lodging, you can fill up your gas tank here and grab a cold drink. Stretch your legs, checking out the active post office (serving the zero residents of Amboy) and the silent Amboy School.

WIRESTOCK CREATORS/SHUTTERSTOCK

Amboy Crater

Cut across the railroad tracks to check out **Amboy Crater**, a cinder cone in one of the youngest volcanic fields in the US (it last erupted around 10,000 years ago).

Return to Route 66, backtracking eastward about a mile to the turnoff on Amboy Rd, which travels south through the high desert to Twentynine Palms, gateway to Joshua Tree National Park. Or continue west to the ghost town of **Ludlow**, which spits you back onto I-40.

Circumambulate Amboy Crater

Eerily quiet but for your footsteps crunching along the lava-chunk-lined trail, **Amboy Crater's** remoteness, extreme heat and volcanic landscape feels like entering another world entirely. NASA thought so too, and test-drove the Mars Rover in these lava fields.

The trail from the parking lot leads into the breach in the crater where lava spilled out, providing entry into the crater itself. Trails traverse the interior of the crater, or you can follow the trail from the breach up to the rim (only 80ft up) and trek along its perimeter. Panoramic views from along the rim take in the dry **Bristol Lake** to the southeast and **Marble Mountains** to the northeast. Take care to stay on the main trail on the west side of the crater, as there's a steeper, narrow side trail descending along the exposed slope of loose volcanic pebbles.

Allow 1½ to two hours to complete the mostly flat, 3-mile hike to and around the crater. Bring at least a liter of water, try to finish your hike before 10am and avoid hiking during the summer in this particularly harsh environment.

An elevated, shaded observation terrace has views of the crater as well as picnic tables; it's accessible via a ramp from the parking lot.

PRONGHORN REDUX

Making surprising reappearances in the Mojave since the 2020s, the formerly extirpated **pronghorn** *(Antilocapra americana)* may be returning slowly to California deserts. Pronghorns, often mistakenly referred to as antelopes, are in a genus all their own. These swift ungulates can sprint up to 60mph, but fences and development have obstructed migration routes and livestock have displaced them from grazing land across the Mojave Desert.

Wildlife biologists posit that more northerly and easterly populations may have been growing for some time, expanding their range westward from Nevada in search of delicious California wildflowers. As the pronghorn brings a spark of hope for its comeback, keep a sharp eye out for an auspicious sighting.

ROAD-TRIP LINK

Make a grand desert road trip while getting from points A to B by stitching any or all of these drives together: **The Death Valley Highlights** (p241), **Mojave's Greatest Hits** (p254) and **JTree in a Day** (p227).

Places We Love to Stay

$ Budget $$ Midrange $$$ Top End

Palm Springs

Maps p217 & p219

Saguaro $ Colorful, playful pool-party atmosphere for the resort vacay experience, with poolside cabanas, spa and fabulous drag brunches on the weekends (reservations recommended).

The Cole $ Understated mid-century style at a slight remove north of downtown, with an enclosed patio area with pool.

Alcazar $$ Over-21s only at this stylish, relaxed boutique hotel walkable to downtown. Some rooms have a Jacuzzi, patio, fireplace or all three.

Ace Hotel & Swim Club $$ A solid, not over-the-top mid-century choice with DJs, dancing, pool parties and low-key spa – stay here to cement your status as a hipster not identifying as a hipster.

Rowan Palm Springs $$$ Memorable views from the upper-floor rooms and the rooftop pool deck with a restaurant and lively bar scene. Spacious rooms are sleek and contemporary.

Drift Palm Springs $$$ Spare, desert-inspired design in airy rooms and suites, downtown on Indian Canyon Dr with a chill atmosphere to escape to.

Sparrows Lodge $$$ An elegant, modern-farmhouse aesthetic creates an air of relaxation, aided by an E Palm Canyon location south of downtown.

Idyllwild

Fireside Inn $ Attractive cabins decked out mountain-home style, each with its own rustic decor. All include fireplaces and many have full kitchens or kitchenettes.

Idyllwild Inn $$ Cozy, wood-paneled mountain cabins and suites, featuring private terraces, full kitchens and fireplaces. Rooms also available at a separate lodge.

Joshua Tree National Park

p228

Jumbo Rocks Campground $ Classic bouldery JTree landscape in this popular campground with over 100 sites; reserve early to secure a spot.

Hidden Valley Campground $ Centrally located in the park amid the Wonderland of Rocks, where you can clamber around for innumerable sunset viewpoints. First-come, first-served at this favored spot.

Ryan Campground $ Lovely campground among big boulders with direct access to the 1-mile Ryan Ranch hiking trail. Reservations required.

Belle Campground $ Try your luck earlier in the week at this small, first-come, first-served campground near the crossroads of Pinto Basin Rd and Park Blvd.

Twentynine Palms

Harmony Motel $ U2 famously stayed at this cozy spot on Twentynine Palms Hwy, with homey, comfortable rooms and cabins around a pool and Jacuzzi. A fantastic deal.

29 Palms Inn $$ Tucked away at the Oasis of Mara, this family-owned gem has adobe rooms and bungalows scattered around a peaceful property, with central pool and excellent restaurant.

Hotel Wren $$$ A newly renovated boutique motel done in warm, minimalist design, with a peaceful pool area and slightly elevated location removed from the highway.

Joshua Tree Town

AutoCamp Joshua Tree $$ JTree is the picture-perfect setting for AutoCamp's vintage-Airstream aesthetic and glamping setup; cabins also available.

Joshua Tree Inn $$ Storied spot where Gram Parsons spent his last hours alive. Rooms decorated in Western-style painted brick and exposed beams make a lovely base for explorations.

Yucca Valley & Pioneertown

Field Station $ This AutoCamp spinoff revitalized an old Yucca Valley motor lodge with minimalist design and common spaces including espresso bar, pool, fire pit and gift shop.

Pioneertown Motel $$$ As befits Pioneertown, this old-timey miner's cabin opens into modern western comfort, the perfect spot to stay after a late night at Pappy & Harriet's.

Death Valley National Park

Map p239

Texas Springs Campground $ Central first-come, first-served campground near Furnace Creek with some greenery and no generators allowed. Open from mid-October to mid-April.

Panamint Springs Resort $ Spacious, family-run campground and rustic motel rooms at the park's western end, with sweeping views across the Panamint Valley, super-friendly restaurant, gas station and a stocked general store.

Stovepipe Wells Village Hotel $ Comfortable rooms and suites in a central location in the park, with pool, restaurant, bar and gas station across the road.

Inn at Death Valley $$$ The lush gardens and ponds of this hilltop resort are spring-fed and truly an oasis, creating a real sense of luxury in Death Valley.

Shoshone & Tecopa

Tecopa Hot Springs Resort $ The simple but comfortable accommodations here include access to the clean, two-room bath house as well as baths in the motel; pet-friendly cabins and camping also available.

Death Valley Hot Springs $$ Formerly Delight's Hot Springs, rooms range from basic to renovated; free-standing cabins, too. All include access to the hot spring-fed pool and private bath houses.

Shoshone Inn $$ High-standard, comfortable motel rooms in sweet Shoshone, with access to a warm, spring-fed pool a short walk away; RV and tent campground also available.

Anza-Borrego Desert State Park

Map p247

Borrego Palm Canyon Campground $ Popular spot for getting up early to look for bighorn sheep, with over 100 sites. Great location; reservations highly recommended.

Blair Valley $ With dispersed, primitive camping sites and vault toilets, Blair Valley is free, mostly flat and accessible to RVs as well as tent campers.

Borrego Springs

Map p247

Hacienda del Sol $$ Attractively restored motor lodge with modern, minimalist motel rooms and spacious casitas with kitchenettes and lounge areas. Pool, outdoor barbecue area and shuffleboard in the open courtyard.

Borrego Valley Inn $$$ Romantic, adults-only adobe compound with multiple pools, hot tubs and a serene ambience. The inn is sited between the town and park visitor center.

Julian

Julian Lodge $ This large and comfortably creaky historic lodge is off Main St, with snug little rooms. Note that there are stairs to both 1st- and 2nd-floor rooms.

Julian Gold Rush Hotel $$ Quaint, cozy bed-and-breakfast with a pioneer look and feel, appropriate for the oldest continuously operated hotel in SoCal. Two cottages offer additional privacy.

Mojave National Preserve

Map p254

Hole-in-the-Wall Campground $ A lovely, open setting against the backdrop of the Providence Mountains. By reservation, with walk-in sites if you want to take your chances.

Mid Hills Campground $ Further flung and 1000ft higher in elevation than Hole-in-the-Wall, this tranquil campground is set amid trees. Not recommended for larger RVs and trailers.

NOAH SAUVE/SHUTTERSTOCK

The Rowan Palm Springs

BADDIE
ALERT

TOOLKIT

The chapters in this section cover the most important topics you'll need to know about in Los Angeles and Southern California. They're full of nuts-and-bolts information and valuable insights to help you understand and navigate Los Angeles and Southern California and get the most out of your trip.

LA Pride parade (p274)

GERRY MATTHEWS/SHUTTERSTOCK

Arriving

Southern California has several airports with flights from out of state. Many have international services. You can also reach Southern California by train from neighboring states and beyond. Most domestic travelers, however, roll into the Southland in their own vehicles via interstate freeways, the backbone of road-tripping culture.

Easy Visas

Under the US Visa Waiver Program (VWP), visas are theoretically not required for citizens of about 40 countries for stays up to 90 days; however, entry is at the discretion of border agents. Check your home country's travel advice before departing.

Complex Visas

Regulations for non-VWP visas are in flux. Check the visa section on the **US Department of State** website *(travel.state.gov)* or contact a US embassy or consulate in your home country.

Cell Phones

Foreign phones usually work in California. Buy prepaid SIM cards locally or get an e-SIM. Coverage can be spotty in remote areas such as the deserts (where lack of signal can be a safety issue).

Wi-Fi

Wi-fi is nearly ubiquitous in the state that is home to Silicon Valley. Free networks abound in civic centers, restaurants, cafes, hotels and more.

Public Transport from Airport to City Center

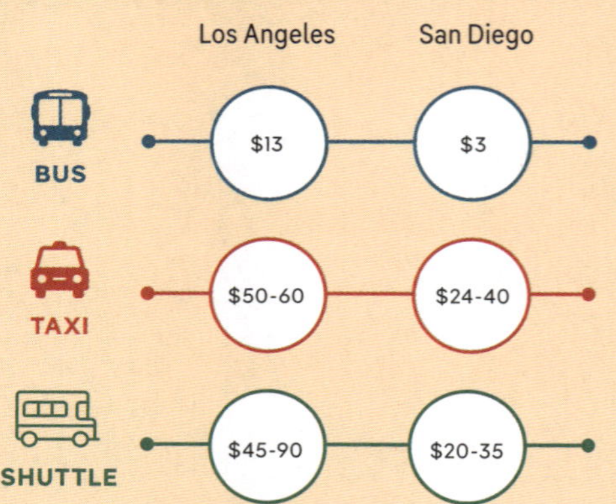

	Los Angeles	San Diego
BUS	$13	$3
TAXI	$50-60	$24-40
SHUTTLE	$45-90	$20-35

SCENIC WAYS TO SOUTHERN CALIFORNIA

There are four Amtrak routes to California from the rest of the USA. Each offers superb scenery.

From Seattle and Portland, the **Coast Starlight** serves the Bay Area and Santa Barbara, en route to Los Angeles. The ride along California's Central Coast is stunning.

From Chicago, the **Southwest Limited** reaches LA via the beautifully stark desert as does the **Sunset Limited** from New Orleans, Houston and Tucson.

Also from Chicago, the **California Zephyr** traces the route of the first Transcontinental Railroad as it reaches the Bay Area via the Sierras. You can connect to the **Coast Starlight** for Southern California.

FROM LEFT: FUSE/GETTY IMAGES, GEORGE MDIVANIAN/EYEEM/GETTY IMAGES

Getting Around

LA may be a freeway, but while the car is king in Southern California, there are many regional options to get around by train and bus.

TRAVEL COSTS

Car rental
$35-160/day

Gas
Approx $5/gallon

EV charging
$0.45/KWh

Train ticket from LA to San Diego
From $60

Hiring a Car

There's no inherent advantage between airport and city location rates for rental cars. Rates vary widely depending on season and demand. Don't rent a car if all you'll do is park it in the pricey city hotel garage; in LA, for example, ride the new Metro Rail line in from LAX, then get a rental when exploring further afield.

Road Conditions

After years of neglect due to fractured state finances, California's voters approved an extra gas tax, which is funding repair, rebuilding and construction of roads. You may get caught in work-related delays, but the result is that road conditions in the state are improving.

TIP

Download the Caltrans QuickMap app for road conditions statewide.

ROAD HABITS

Certain rules are enshrined in the state's road culture. On scenic and mountainous roads, pull over so that residents can whizz past. Motorcycles are allowed to ride between cars on freeways. Car-pool lanes are tightly regulated: if you have the right number of passengers, fly past coagulated traffic.

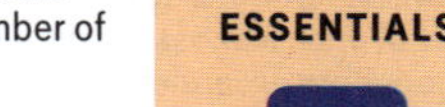

DRIVING ESSENTIALS

Drive on the right.

Speed limit is 65mph on freeways, 55mph on two-lane highways and 35mph in cities.

.08

Blood alcohol limit is 0.08%.

Bus & Train

Southern California has more public transit than many think. The LA region is well covered with a dense network; you can reach most of the major tourist areas without a car – and without traffic. Amtrak's regional trains, such as the lovely line between LA and San Diego, are reasonably frequent.

Public Transit Tickets

In LA, the TAP app works with over 20 systems, including Metro. It lets you ride the various forms of transit with a tap of your phone (or a physical card). Refill their stored value online, at a machine or just use your phone's payment options.

Plane

Californians use planes the way people in other places use trains. The environmental cost aside, service between the state's 12 major airports and numerous smaller ones is frequent and cheap.

Money

CURRENCY: DOLLAR ($)

Credit & Debit Cards

Visa and MasterCard are accepted everywhere, American Express and Discover are spottier. The US has finally fully adopted chip-and-pin systems for cards. Debit cards may require extra security checks at gas stations, rental-car counters, etc.

Digital Payments

Residents commonly pay with a tap of their phone and can go weeks without ever using cash. Save $1 bills (and other cash) for tip jars to ensure employees receive the full amount you tip.

Taxes & Refunds

California state sales tax (7.25%) is added to the retail price of most goods and services (groceries are exceptions). Local sales taxes may add on up to 3%. Tourist lodging taxes vary statewide, but average 10.5% to 14% in major cities. No tax refunds are available to international visitors.

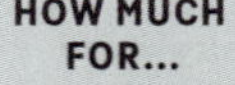

HOW MUCH FOR...

Beach parking
Free–$15

Bridge tolls
$9

Driving the Pacific Coast Highway
Free

ATM fees
$4

HOW TO... SAVE Dollars

An **America the Beautiful Pass** *(store.usgs.gov; $80)* grants unlimited entry to all US National Parks. It's valid for one year from the purchase date and can pay for itself through just three park visits. (The vehicle entrance fee at Joshua Tree is $30.)

Scan this QR code to buy an America the Beautiful Pass

WHAT TO TIP

Tipping is usually *not* optional; it's part of the workers' wages.

Bartenders 15% to 20% per round, minimum $2 per drink.

Concierges Nothing for simple information, but up to $20 for securing last-minute reservations etc.

Hotel bellhops $2 or $3 per bag, minimum $5 per cart.

Housekeeping staff $2 to $4 daily.

Parking valets From $2 to $5 when your car keys are handed back.

Restaurant servers 20% to 25%.

Counter service Optional. Generally 10%.

Taxi/rideshare drivers 10% to 15% of the fare, rounded up to the next dollar.

LOCAL TIP

Most passes for California's 280 state parks *(parks.ca.gov)* are best for year-round residents. Without a pass, for the parks that charge, do like many residents do: park outside and walk in.

Accommodations

A Bed for Every Taste

With its many beautiful destinations and innovative spirit, California has hundreds of cool, unique accommodations. Find solitude at a desert campsite or feed all your desires with decadent city luxury. Aside from the usual offerings, there are offbeat options like retro motels, vacation rentals right on the beach, campsites perched in dramatic locations and myriad forms of glamping.

Retro Motels

The humble motel has had a rebrand over the last few years, with many tired models receiving makeovers that have given them a second act. Designed with an eye to the mid-century aesthetic and consciously addressing contemporary needs, these roadside spots can be stylish but affordable options. Look for brilliantly restored neon signs along old Route 66.

Oceanfront & Beachfront

Seeing the surf and running out to the sand are quintessential Southern California fantasies. Plenty of hotels are ready to grant you your pleasure – for a price. But a few caveats are in order: always confirm that 'oceanview' means a real 'view' and not a mere glimpse. Conversely, the SoCal coast has some older motels in great spots that offer fine value.

Don't Camp, Glamp

California may not have invented glamping, but it has perfect backdrops and set pieces for the concept. Iconic national parks and private entities have placed canvas safari tents and yurts in gorgeous settings like the mountains and deserts. The coast maintains a temperate climate for most of the year, making glamping a realistic option, while inland is viable outside of summer.

Seeing the Forest from the Trees

Commune with nature in a tree house. Widely viewed on Instagram, human-size nests and birdhouse-clad pods are some of the more feral-feeling luxury aeries you can settle into for the night. Some meet the definition of shelter better than others, so check details, the weather report and your comfort zone before committing. Confirm basic details such as sanitation and water availability.

VACATION RENTAL LIMITS

Vacation rentals are a charged topic in California. In a state with a catastrophic shortage of affordable housing, any housing stock removed from availability for the general public provokes strong reactions. Once affordable rural areas have become weekend retreats for the urban affluent, forcing residents who work in the shops and cafes to scramble for housing they can afford. In wealthy areas, residents have grown weary of beach houses turned into party pads for tech bros. In response, cities and towns statewide have imposed limits on vacation rentals, especially ones listed on Airbnb.

CLOCKWISE FROM TOP LEFT: RED HERRING/SHUTTERSTOCK, NICK FOX/SHUTTERSTOCK, PIRTUSS/SHUTTERSTOCK

Family Travel

California is tailor-made for family travel. The kids will be begging to go to theme parks and teens to celebrity hot spots. Then take 'em into the great outdoors – from sunny beaches shaded by palm trees to misty redwood forests and four-seasons mountain playgrounds. Even getting around is fun, from stops at roadside diversions to the adventure of a train or ferry.

Traveling with Babies

Urban areas are great for strollers but if you plan on enjoying the great outdoors, child carriers are a better option. Some attractions offer rental strollers. Basics are available in supermarkets and drugstores 24/7, while organics and specialty items can be found at higher-end supermarkets and big-box stores. Family bathrooms and changing facilities are common.

Dining Out

Casual eateries typically have high chairs and children's menus. Roadside restaurants on tourist routes often have extra inducements for families to stop, such as playgrounds, amusing displays or a chance to pet a winsome barnyard animal.

Don't Get Caught Short

Some amusement park rides have minimum-height and/or age requirements. Let younger kids know about possible limitations in advance to avoid disappointment.

Car Travel

Children under eight must be buckled in a child or infant safety seat in the car's back seat; children under two must be in a rear-facing safety seat – reserve ahead when renting a car. Bring distractions for inevitable traffic delays.

KID-FRIENDLY PICKS

Disneyland Park (p144)
Kids of all ages adore the 'Magic Kingdom.'

Knott's Berry Farm (p154)
SoCal's original theme park.

Universal Studios Hollywood (p128)
Rides and thrills are pegged to popular characters.

Pacific Park (p121)
Famous amusement park delights on Santa Monica Pier.

San Diego Zoo (p184)
Deeply fascinating world-renowned institution.

La Brea Tar Pits & Museum (p108)
Kids love the smells and woolly mammoths.

KEEPING COSTS DOWN

Southern California is not cheap. Cost-conscious families need help to avoid sticker shock.

In hotels and motels, look for 'kids stay free' and/or 'free breakfast' promotions. Motels are cheaper on average, most have two queen- or king-size beds, and many have fridges and microwaves.

If you're visiting theme parks, carry a cooler in the car and have a picnic in the parking lot (ensure you have park re-entry permission before you do) to avoid expensive junk-food options inside.

From endless beaches, deserts and urban parks for frolicking, some of the most family-friendly activities in Southern California are free.

Health & Safe Travel

INSURANCE

Travel insurance to cover theft, loss and medical problems is essential. Domestic visitors should confirm they have proper coverage under their current plans. Some policies do not cover 'risky' activities, so read the fine print.

Earthquakes

If you're caught in a serious temblor:

- If possible, stay in an open outdoor space.
- If indoors, get under a desk or table or stand in a doorway.
- Protect your head and stay clear of windows, mirrors or anything that might fall.
- Don't head for elevators or go running into the street.

Wildfires

The wildfire season gets ever-longer (at least May through January.) Fires limit access to roads and parks, and can cause vacationers and residents to flee for their lives. Conflagrations can quickly overwhelm firefighters and outpace public warnings. If you see the sign of a wildfire, don't wait to be trapped – leave the area.

MARIJUANA

Cannabis is legal for medicinal and 21-plus recreational use. Shops sell myriad forms of marijuana. Driving under the influence is illegal.

BEACH LIFEGUARD FLAGS

Green
Water is safe.

Yellow/Blue
Potential dangers.

Orange
No lifeguard on duty.

Red
Beach is closed to the public.

Smoking

Smoking (tobacco, marijuana, vapes, anything) is prohibited inside all public buildings. Lighting up may be tolerated on outdoor restaurant patios or at sidewalk tables (ask first). At hotels, you must specifically request a smoking room. In some areas, you can't smoke outside near a business.

SHARKS

Despite the hype of TV channels seeking ratings, shark attacks are not a real concern in the ocean off the California coast. Since records began being kept in 1851, only 25 people have been killed by sharks in the state. Still, the image of a dead-eyed great white cruising along looking for a meal inspires fear at a base level.

LEFT: LJUPCO SMOKOVSKI/SHUTTERSTOCK; ABOVE: STOCKPHOTO-GRAF/SHUTTERSTOCK

Food, Drink & Nightlife

When to Eat

Breakfast Usually between 7:30am and 11am. Residents often grab this meal on the go, except on weekends.

Brunch Enjoyed from 11am until 3pm on weekends. Often boozy.

Lunch Generally served between 11:30am and 2:30pm. Lunch out tends to be for social or business purposes. Alcohol is mainly consumed at social lunches.

Dinner Between 5pm and 9pm.

MENU DECODER

Californian casual Few restaurants require more than a dressy shirt, slacks and shoes that aren't flip-flops. At most places, T-shirts, shorts and sandals are fine.

Corkage You can bring your own wine to most restaurants; a 'corkage' fee of $15 to $30 usually applies.

Entrée Always confusing to non-Americans – the word for the main course.

Heirloom Trendy term for types of produce meant to evoke varieties grown in the past.

Split-plate If you ask the kitchen to divide a plate between two (or more) people, there may be a small split-plate surcharge.

Vegetarian/vegan Travelers with food allergies or dietary restrictions are in luck – vegetarian and vegan fare is routine in Southern California and restaurants are used to catering to specific dietary needs.

Where to Eat

Cafes and diners Historically, diners were called 'coffee shops.' Hours vary, but expect breakfasts and comfort food.

Farmers markets Vendors selling superb local produce and prepared foods.

Food trucks Get fresh, imaginative food to go, often in a parking lot.

Destination dining Top restaurant in a high-end hotel or wine-country resort. Make reservations online at least a month ahead for top tables.

HOW TO... Dine Out in Southern California – Tips & Tricks

SoCal residents love to swipe right with restaurants, especially places deemed new and unmissable. It's essential to reserve a table as far in advance as possible at restaurants with buzz or perennial popularity. Hot tables in a trend-loving place like West Hollywood will be booked up weeks in advance.

Destination restaurants in Beverly Hills or Santa Monica have become tick boxes for some diners whose main interest is bagging another famous meal. An entire market exists for secondary sales of table reservations – people pay a huge premium for a booking. Trust us, there's always a fine alternative restaurant.

How to tip (p266) is a minefield for non-Americans not used to the practice. Some restaurants in LA have introduced mandatory tip fees, but they often leave the door open to additional tipping (!), meaning 'service fees' are the equivalent of the hated resort fee.

HOW MUCH FOR A...

Coffee
$3-7

Craft cocktail
$12 and up

Craft beer
$10

Burrito
$12

Non-designer doughnut
$2

Philippe French Dip sandwich
$14

California sushi roll
$12

Cup of artisanal ice cream
$6

HOW TO... Eat & Drink Like a Southern Californian

Start your morning with a pricey coffee. Some have it black, most adulterate their brew with something like oat milk and various flavorings. Breakfast might be a yogurt, something from an artisan bakery or one of LA's famous doughnuts. Diner fare is more common at weekend brunch.

Lunch can be from a food truck; 'taco trucks' are the most popular, but there are plenty of others, too. Lunch might also be a sandwich or salad consumed at one's desk.

After-work drinks outside on a patio at a brewery or bar are popular 12 months a year. Dinner at home might feature whatever is fresh at the local farmers market (many are open year-round). Favorite dining-out choices are Japanese, regional Chinese, Vietnamese, Italian, the catch-all Mediterranean (which is a lot like Californian!) and regional Mexican (of course).

Bars tend to close early, so even in cities like San Francisco or LA, the streets are quiet by midnight.

Food Trucks

California has about 1000 food trucks (p27) operating across the state. Some are found in clusters, others operate alone. Some are in the same spot every day, others move around. Sample widely!

COCKTAILS LIKE NOWHERE ELSE

The margarita (traditionally made with tequila, triple sec, and lemon or lime juice, either frozen and blended or served straight up 'on the rocks' with ice) is the drink of choice with Mexican cuisine. The finest are made using 100% agave tequilas. These higher-grade tequilas are also reputedly better for avoiding hangovers.

Quality underscores a growing number of SoCal cocktail bars, where bartenders are judged not by flashy tricks, but by their knowledge of the boutique liquors from California's burgeoning micro-distilleries. Knowledge of a drink's history is another source of kudos, as is the ability to competently reinterpret classics in clever ways.

The penchant for local, seasonal and organic ingredients on modern Californian menus also drives many of the region's best bars, where herbal and fruit infusions are often made in-house. Cocktail wizards pride themselves on creating their own infusions and combinations of flavors. They'll wow you with a gin like no other. The barkeeps at many LA bars will ditch the known drink list altogether and concoct libations with whatever fresh market produce is at their disposal.

And while neither LA nor San Diego can claim a world-famous namesake cocktail (New York, stop gloating...), SoCal is not without its own homegrown curiosities. Take LA-born Chareau, a delicate liqueur made by distilling Californian grapes into an eau-de-vie (clear brandy), infusing it with locally sourced cucumber, spearmint, muskmelon and lemon peel, before finally adding fresh-pressed aloe vera juice. Savor it in a Milano Swizzle, a refreshing combination of Chareau, citrus, Italian vermouth and strawberry-cucumber shrub.

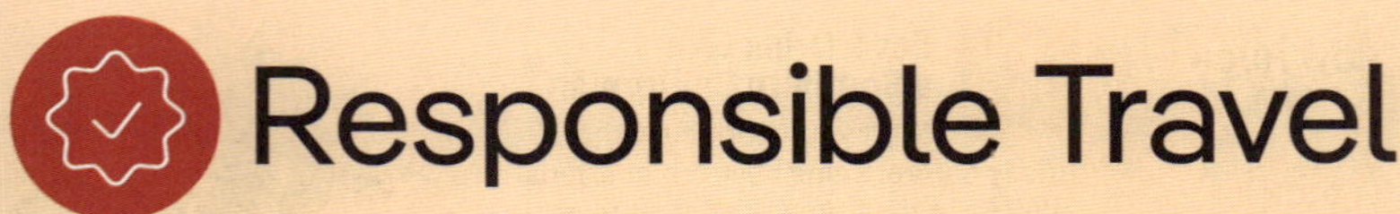

Responsible Travel

Climate Change & Travel

It's impossible to ignore the impact we have when travelling; Lonely Planet urges all travelers to engage with their travel carbon footprint, which will mainly come from air travel. While there often isn't an alternative, travelers can look to minimize the number of flights they take, opt for newer aircrafts and use cleaner ground transport, such as trains. One proposed solution – purchasing carbon offsets – unfortunately does not cancel out the impact of individual flights. While most destinations will depend on air travel for the foreseeable future, for now, pursuing ground-based travel where possible is the best course of action.

The **UN Carbon Offset Calculator** shows how flying impacts a household's emissions

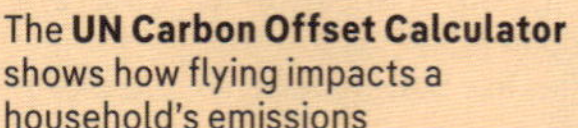

The **ICAO's carbon emissions calculator** allows visitors to analyze the CO2 generated by point-to-point journeys

Rent an Electric or Hybrid Car

California car rental companies have embraced hybrid and electric vehicles. The state has thousands of charging stations.

Scan this QR code to find charging stations

Where & How to Cycle

Bikes, e-bikes and e-scooters are easily rented at all of California's main tourist areas and beaches. Check out **CalBike** *(calbike.org/go_for_a_ride/map_routes)* for downloadable route maps. In LA, the 22-mile-long Marvin Braude Bike Trail (p119) runs right on the beachfront.

Southern California's near-permanent drought means everybody must reduce their water consumption. Visit saveourwater.com for things you can do.

A thicket of regulations governs California's fishing industry. Learn about sustainable seafood options at seafoodwatch.org.

Ride Local Trains

LA's Metrolink and Metro Rail system of subways and light rail are hugely useful. San Diego's Trolley has comprehensive service.

Don't Follow the Crowd

High-season crowds at popular spots like Joshua Tree exacerbate the environmental cost of over-tourism. Try off-the-radar spots instead.

Start Walking

SoCal defies clichés by being a walk-friendly place. LA, Santa Barbara and San Diego are wonderful places to explore on foot, as are the beaches.

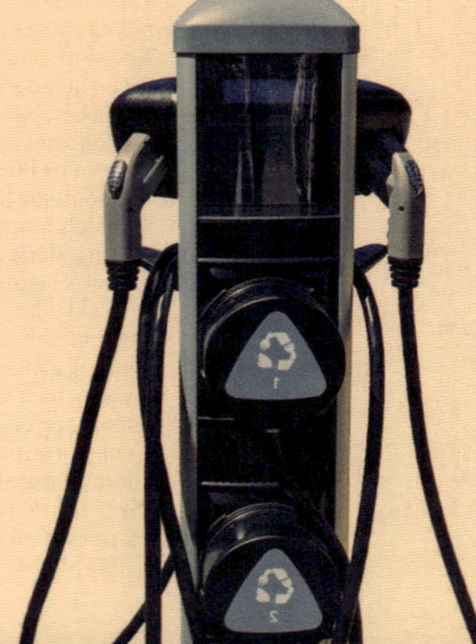

MARVEL AT AMTRAK'S VIEWS

Amtrak's regional service runs from San Luis Obispo to San Diego via Santa Barbara, Los Angeles and Anaheim plus a string of coastal towns. Oceanfront views are spectacular; trains are frequent and comfortable.

Get Cash for Containers

Look for 'CA CASH REFUND' or 'CA CRV' on beverage containers sold in California (although not wine bottles). Refunds range from 5¢ to 10¢. Find recycling points to collect the cash at calrecycle.ca.gov.

Scan this QR code to find bottle and can recycling points

Southern California has great drinking water and many water fountains have spigots for refilling water bottles easily, so pack a reusable water bottle.

Help clean up the beaches: adopt any trash you see as your own and toss it – works elsewhere too!

Save on Plastics

Rinse out resealable beverage containers and fill them with tap water. One plastic bottle will last the duration of your trip. If you're given a plastic straw (banned in many parts of Southern California), rinse and reuse it.

Environmentally Friendly Packaging

You'll find that California is good about mandating that goods, especially takeaway food and drinks, be sold in responsibly minded packaging. Sure, your straw may start to fail after a few minutes, but it also won't end up in the environment with a half-life of a few thousand years.

150kg

Driving from San Francisco to LA emits about 150kg of carbon dioxide per average-size car; per passenger, flying emits 160kg, bus travel 20kg and trains 40kg. Calculate your trips: native.eco/client-calculator/reverb/.

RESOURCES

greenbusinessca.org
Search for green businesses by category.

happycow.net
Vegetarian and vegan restaurants in California and beyond.

afdc.energy.gov/fuels/electricity_locations.html
California has thousands of EV charging stations.

CLOCKWISE FROM BOTTOM LEFT: IMAGENET SMOKOVSKI/SHUTTERSTOCK, LJUPCO SMOKOVSKI/SHUTTERSTOCK, ACRAMS/SHUTTERSTOCK

LGBTQ+ Travelers

Inclusivity tends to be the norm in California, and its embrace of all things LGBTQ+ brings visitors from around the world. Within Southern California, West Hollywood stands out as one of the LGBTQ+ centers, not just in the region but in the US. Attitudes narrow a bit in some parts of conservative Orange County.

Notable Times for LGBTQ+ Travel

There's no bad time for LGBTQ+ travel in California, but there are months made famous by their special events. Pride events from May through June bring parties and a whole lotta fun to LA, West Hollywood, Long Beach and even Disneyland.

In July, the action moves south to San Diego. Palm Springs lets its great weather shine for its November pride (p217). Other pride events can be found in towns across the Southland during the year.

GETTING MARRIED IN CALIFORNIA

Though it remains legal across the USA, many LGBTQ+ couples prefer to marry in a state known for its queer welcome. In California, you don't have to be a citizen or take a blood test: fill out a form at a county clerk's office, pay a fee and get a license.

Queer Havens

In Southern California, the following are notable both for their history on LGBTQ+ issues and culture today: West Hollywood (p113), with its extraordinary culture, and Palm Springs (p210), with its languid pool days. Though not as high-profile, other areas such as LA's Silver Lake neighborhood are well-regarded for their inclusivity.

DISCOVER LA'S LGBTQ+ HISTORY

For insight into LA's fascinating queer history, download the free **Pride Explorer app** thelavendereffect.org/pride-explorer, which offers self-guided walking tours. Drop by the Black Cat tavern in Silver Lake (p97), where the nation's first major gay rights demonstration took place in 1967.

LGBTQ+ Employment Rights

It is illegal for an employer to discriminate against anyone because of their sexual orientation, gender identity and/or gender expression.

LGBTIQ+ RESOURCES

Advocate *(advocate.com/travel)* News, LGBTQ+ travel features and destination guides.

Damron *(damron.com)* Advertiser-driven gay travel guides and app.

Out Traveler *(outtraveler.com)* Online magazine with travel tips, destination guides and resort reviews.

LGBT National Help Center *(lgbthotline.org)* Counseling, information and referrals.

Accessible Travel

California leads the way on accessibility in the USA. More populated areas of Southern California are reasonably well-equipped for travelers with disabilities, although older properties may have limitations.

Park Passes

US residents with a permanent disability can get a free lifetime pass, which waives entry fees to all national parks. California State Parks' disabled discount pass ($3.50) gives 50% off parking and camping fees.

Airport

California's airports comply with accessibility legislation, which includes provisions for assistance with boarding, access to disability supports and the right to be treated with dignity and respect. Assistance is available through your airline.

Accommodations

Hotels built since 1993 must meet the **Americans with Disabilities Act** accessibility requirements. These include regulations covering door widths, accessible bathrooms, and hearing and sight supports. That said, call ahead to confirm they have what you need.

RESOURCES

California State Parks *(parks.ca.gov/?page_id=21944)* Searchable online map and database of accessible features at state parks.

Discover Los Angeles *(discoverlosangeles.com/travel/the-guide-to-accessibility-in-los-angeles)* Extensive information detailing the many accessibility features found at museums and attractions.

San Diego Tourism Authority *(sandiego.org/plan-your-trip/visitors-centers-information/disability-accessible-travel-in-san-diego)* Lists extensive accessibility resources for travelers.

BEACH ACCESSIBILITY

California Coastal Commission *(coastal.ca.gov/access/beach-wheelchairs.html)* lists dozens of beaches with wheelchairs designed for use on the sand. Some can be reserved.

Buses

Public transit buses with ramps that deploy automatically when the bus is lowered to the curb are the norm. Drivers may have to assist with securing wheelchairs once inside.

Trains

Metrolink and Metro trains and stations in the LA region are all accessible, as is the Trolley system in San Diego. Amtrak requires advance notice for accessibility services.

DISABILITY RIGHTS

The US Department of Justice *(ada.gov)* enforces the **Americans with Disabilities Act** (ADA). It makes this statement on its website: 'Disability rights are civil rights.' The act covers many areas of public life, including travel and transport.

Rideshare services like Uber offer the option of accessible rides for people with mobility needs. In the Uber app, look for the 'Uber WAV' option when booking your ride.

Getting Studio Audience Tickets

You're in Hollywood, you don't want to keep watching TV shows on screens, you want to watch the TV shows being made. Around Hollywood, Los Angeles, Burbank, Culver City and beyond, there are game shows, talk shows, sitcoms and more being produced: most need audience members, but some need participants as well. Read on to see how this could be you.

Talk Shows

The big dog of the desk chat set is *Jimmy Kimmel Live!*, which is recorded at the El Capitan Theatre (p81) on Hollywood Blvd with A-list guests. It's necessary to secure (free) tickets well in advance, so head to **1iota** *(1iota.com)* three to six weeks ahead of your visit to check availability and request tickets.

Game Shows

There is a two-track system for game shows. If you want to be a contestant, there's a vetting process, even for a simple show like *Wheel of Fortune*. But all need audience members and even *The Price is Right* will have audience-only options for people who don't want to 'come on down.'

Sitcoms

Search for shows shot in LA, then find out when they're in production and go to their ticketing website.

Sourcing Tickets

It's always worth searching the name of the show that's your goal and 'studio audience' and 'tickets' (or if it applies, 'contestant') as there is no one source for tickets. However, there are a handful of ticket agents that handle most of the shows. And the good news is almost all audience tickets are free, which is good considering the hoops you have to jump through to get them. The main players are:

1iota *(1iota.com)* Major shows are *Jimmy Kimmel Live!* and *The Voice*.

On Camera Audiences *(on-camera-audiences.com)* Major shows include *Jeopardy!*, *Wheel of Fortune* and *The Price is Right*.

OS|LA Productions *(oslaproductions.com)* Major show is *Wheel of Fortune*. They also handle a vast number of minor shows, many of which may be unfamiliar.

HOW TO... Get On Air

If you want to be a contestant on a game show, there are several things to know: the most important – with the exception of *Jeopardy!* – is to be bubbly. In fact, be the most bubbly you've ever been in your life. Think 'we've just had triplets and won a million dollars' bubbly. The producers want positive energy that explodes off the screen. At the audition/vetting, hug everyone, be excited.

If it's a show where you bet your winnings, always bet EVERYTHING in the audition. Viewers respond to drama and risk. The shows want contestants who risk everything. And if you win? Jump up and down, shout and hug everyone!

ON THE DAY DETAILS

If you secure tickets to be in a studio audience, know the following:

- Having tickets doesn't mean you will get in. It's like the airlines: shows overbook to ensure a full studio. Get there early.
- Tapings last a long time. An hour-long show like *Jimmy Kimmel Live!* (which isn't broadcast live) may require you to be in the studio for three hours. Add to that queuing to get in, security checks and more, and it can add up to a five-or-more-hour commitment.
- Studios are cold. The talent under the hot lights demand that the air be cold to compensate, so dress warm in layers and stuff your pockets with snacks.

ABOVE: KENISHIROTIE/SHUTTERSTOCK

Nuts & Bolts

OPENING HOURS

Businesses, restaurants and shops may close earlier and on additional days during the winter off-season (November to March).

Banks 9:30am to 6pm weekdays

Bars 4pm to 1am (2am is the legal limit)

Restaurants 11am to 3pm and 5:30pm to 9pm daily, some open later Friday and Saturday

Shops 10am to 7pm Monday to Saturday, 11am to 6pm Sunday

Toilets

Free public restrooms are easy to find inside shopping malls, public buildings, libraries, fast-food restaurants and some transportation hubs, as well as at parks and beaches.

Water

Tap water in Southern California is good quality and is safe to drink.

Weights & Measures

Imperial system (except 1 US gallon equals 0.83 imperial gallons).

GOOD TO KNOW

Time zone
Pacific Time (GMT/UTC minus eight hours)

Country code
+1

Emergency number
911

Population
24 million

PUBLIC HOLIDAYS

New Year's Day January 1

Martin Luther King Jr Day Third Monday in January

Presidents' Day Third Monday in February

Cesar Chavez Day March 31

Memorial Day Last Monday in May

Independence Day July 4

Labor Day First Monday in September

Indigenous Peoples' Day Second Monday in October

Veterans Day November 11

Thanksgiving Fourth Thursday in November

Christmas Day December 25

Electricity 120V/60Hz

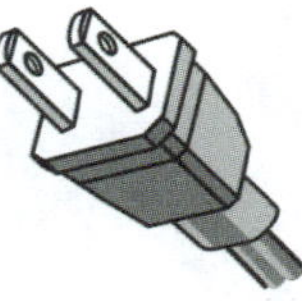

Type A
120V/60Hz

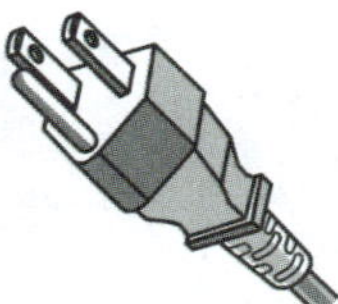

Type B
120V/60Hz

THE LOS ANGELES & SOUTHERN CALIFORNIA

STORYBOOK

Our writers delve deep into different aspects of Los Angeles and Southern California life

Annual Chumash (p280) Day Powwow and Intertribal Gathering in Malibu

HANNATOR/SHUTTERSTOCK

A HISTORY OF LOS ANGELES & SOUTHERN CALIFORNIA IN 15 PLACES

When European explorers first arrived in the 16th century, more than 100,000 Native Californians called this land home. Spanish conquistadors colonized the land before ceding to Mexico which in turn lost it to the fledgling United States in 1848. Waves of dreamers haven't stopped arriving in Southern California ever since. By Ryan Ver Berkmoes

THE FIRST PEOPLE started crossing from Asia into North America via the Bering Strait land bridge around 20,000 BCE. Human bones found in the Channel Islands suggest they reached Southern California 13,000 years ago.

Over the next millennia, the population remained sustainably modest. Perhaps 100,000 people were living in today's SoCal in 1542 when Portuguese navigator Juan Rodríguez Cabrillo sighted the west coast and anchored in today's San Diego Bay. More Europeans followed. In 1769, Spanish captain Gaspar de Portolá led the first European land expedition north, establishing the famous colonial missions with priest Junípero Serra.

Rapid colonization followed and continued under Mexican rule. Mexico controlled California from 1821 to 1848, and Spanish and Mexican culture remain strong in the region today. However, everything changed in two short years: the United States muscled in and took over, gold was discovered and in 1850, California became the USA's 31st state.

Over the next seven decades, orchards, oil and movies became huge industries in Southern California, fueled by water plundered from the Eastern Sierra and the Colorado River. WWII drove the aerospace industry, while in the post-war era, immigrants from across the US and the world flocked to the region. In return, SoCal gave the world Hollywood culture, rap and hip-hop, Richard Nixon and Ronald Reagan.

1. La Brea Tar Pits

TRAPPING CRITTERS, RELEASING WEALTH

So far, the oldest bones found of an animal trapped in the La Brea Tar Pits are 38,000 years old. Still bubbling away and stinky today, the sticky, oozing goo effectively ties several strands of Southern California history together. The Chumash were among the original inhabitants who used the tar found here to build things, including their redwood canoes. In the late 19th century, the tar represented the vast oil reserves found under large swaths of Southern California, which provided an early source of wealth. Drive to LAX on La Cienega Blvd today, and you can see the pumps still at work.

For more on La Brea Tar Pits, see page 108

2. The Chumash

THRIVING FOR THOUSANDS OF YEARS

The Chumash people and their ancestors lived in what is now known as Santa Barbara and Ventura counties for more than 10,000 years before Europeans arrived. They lived off both the land and sea, and adapted well to the bounty of Southern California. They were particularly skilled seafarers: with a *tomol* (plank canoe), the Chumash could fish the offshore waters out to the Channel Islands. You can see a recently constructed *tomol* at the Santa Barbara Maritime Museum (p46). Built in traditional fashion from redwood, members of the Chumash community paddle to the islands at least once a year.

For more on the Chumash tomol, see page 43

3. Indian Village

DEATH VALLEY'S ORIGINAL RESIDENTS

The seemingly forbidding Panamint Range in far eastern California was home to the Timbisha Shoshone people for countless centuries. They followed the same pattern year in and year out: in summer, they lived in the mountains and in winter, as temperatures moderated, they came down into Death Valley to gather acorns for food and plant small patches of maize, squash and beans.

However, in 1933, when Death Valley National Monument was created, the Timbisha were forcibly moved multiple times until they were stuck on a 40-acre plot. In 2000, 7500 acres were transferred back and you can visit the residents at Indian Village.

For more on Indian Village, see page 242

4. Mission Santa Barbara

TENTH OF CALIFORNIA'S 21 MISSIONS

Established in 1786, over 240 years after Europeans first arrived in Southern California, Santa Barbara's mission was well-named: Saint Barbara was a martyr whose father had beheaded her for converting to Catholicism. Conceived as a means to project the power of the Spanish empire, the mission was also meant to convert the local Chumash people into indentured servants.

Unsurprisingly, the Chumash proved unwilling and rebelled in 1824. After they were captured, there was a death march in which a number of elderly and infirm are reported to have died. Meanwhile, the church as you see it today has been regularly damaged by earthquakes and rebuilt even as branches of the church quarreled over its ownership.

For more on Santa Barbara, see page 42

Ávila Adobe (p92)

HELGA_FOTO/SHUTTERSTOCK

5. Ávila Adobe

GRACIOUS HOME TO DUBIOUS GUESTS

In the early 19th century, while Spanish priests were trying to keep the missions functioning, wealthy cattle barons of Mexican descent were living pretty good lives in the Southland. Francisco de Ávila was one such baron and he built what was for its time a gracious adobe home near the center of barely there Los Angeles in 1818.

He soon had some fateful guests: American fur trappers from back east who'd crossed the deserts and liked what they saw. They spread the word and it wasn't long before US troops showed up and the Mexican government was strong-armed into selling California in 1848. Meanwhile, the adobe went on to anchor the touristy El Pueblo de Los Ángeles.

For more on the Ávila Adobe, see page 92

6. Biddy Mason Memorial Park

HARD-WON FREEDOM

Born enslaved in Mississippi in 1818, Biddy Mason hoped for a new life in California. In 1856, she won a landmark court ruling in Los Angeles and prevailed in her fight to be a free individual. But the ruling was not a panacea. Despite what mythmakers say, California has been marred by racism since the arrival of Europeans. The first governor openly killed Native Americans, and when Nat King Cole moved to the white community of Hancock Park a century later, his dog was killed and the state's realtors invented restrictive covenants to keep neighborhoods white. Despite this, Biddy Mason turned her freedom into a fortune that she used to help others. Today, a Downtown park tells her story.

For more on the Biddy Mason Memorial Park, see page 92

7. Southern California's Orchards

MAKING LEMONADE FROM LEMONS

Carpinteria seems like another one of Southern California's idyllic little beach towns, only with a name harder to pronounce than most. Yet, look beyond the surf for the orderly rows of trees growing inland, especially those with deep green leaves or the ones bearing little balls of bright yellow. Avocados and lemons, respectively, are vestiges of the orchard industry that blanketed the region 100 years ago. Orange County didn't get its name from the color of its sunsets! Eventually, the value of the land outstripped the value of the harvest, but those remnants in Carpinteria represent what was once the landscape all the way to San Diego.

For more on Carpinteria, see page 51

8. Hollywood Sign

THERE'S NO BUSINESS LIKE SHOW BUSINESS

The 1906 earthquake hobbled San Francisco, opening the door for Los Angeles. SoCal boosters like Los Angeles Times publisher and real-estate developer, Harry Chandler, were busy building an empire out of what had been Spanish and Mexican land-grant ranches and desert.

In 1923, Chandler had a 'Hollywoodland' sign erected in the hills to advertise a luxury home development (the first of many!). Conceived as temporary, the sign arrived with the meteoric rise of the film studios. Soon, 'land' decayed away and, as they say, a star was born as the sign became the literal symbol for the entertainment industry, known generically as Hollywood.

For more on the Hollywood Sign, see page 80

9. Warner Bros Studio

PLAY IT SAM

Although no one ever held Culver City in high esteem, it was home to the studio held in highest esteem – MGM. Once the most prestigious of the major movie studios, what's remains today has even lost its name.

But head north to another underrated town, Burbank, for the real survivor of the studio system. Still going strong on its lot of 100 years, Warner Bros has been feisty since the early days when Jack Warner grabbed credit from his three brothers: it was the first to make anti-Nazi movies in the 1930s and it has churned out hit movies and series for decades. On tours, little has changed from when they were shooting *Casablanca*.

For more on Warner Bros Studio Tours, see page 129

10. Santa Monica Pier

GAUDY END TO A JOURNEY

With its flashing neon and spinning Ferris wheel, the Santa Monica Pier makes the perfect end point for the 2400 miles of Route 66 that angled southwest across the USA to Los Angeles from Chicago.

The storied road's heyday spanned the 1930s to the 1950s, when it was superseded by wide and straight Interstate highways. But in its day (it turns 100 in 2026), the Mother Road, as it was dubbed after a line in John Steinbeck's *The Grapes of Wrath*, held out the promise of a new life in a new state for countless millions.

For more on Santa Monica Pier, see page 119

11. USS Midway Museum

SYMBOL OF A VICTORIOUS NATION

Now a museum ship in the longtime naval port of San Diego, the USS *Midway* was completed too late for service in WWII, but embodied every lesson the US Navy learned from that war, where its carriers revolutionized the war at sea.

A perfect natural port, San Diego was the Navy's main base on the west coast and remains so today. To see what aircraft carriers the *Midway* replaced, visit the WWII battleship USS *Iowa* up the coast in Long Beach, which was obsolete the day it was launched.

For more on the USS Midway, see page 181

12. Disneyland

NOTHING MICKEY MOUSE ABOUT IT

It was the dawn of the California dream in 1955, when California's middle class exploded along with the population. Increased wages allowed the whole family to take a holiday and drive the Chevy on a new freeway to Disneyland, Walt's new idealized fantasyland.

Families flocked here from their new tract houses spreading like crabgrass in suburbs across the LA Basin, the San

M. VINUESA/SHUTTERSTOCK

Entrance, Universal Studios Hollywood (p128)

Fernando Valley, across San Jose up north and all around the San Francisco Bay and beyond. Today, Disneyland is yet another California first and, at its core, is remarkably unchanged from Walt's original vision for Main Street USA, Sleeping Beauty Castle, Frontierland, Adventureland and Tomorrowland.

For more on Disneyland, see page 144

13. Al & Bea's Mexican Food

WHAT'S A BURRITO?

This family-run Mexican restaurant embodies a lot of LA stories that belie its tiny size. First, there's the neighborhood: Boyle Heights. If LA is a melting pot for America, this neighborhood is the melting pot for LA. Now mostly Hispanic, over the last 100 years, Boyle Heights has been home to Eastern European Jews, Japanese, Italians, Irish, African Americans from the South and Mexicans.

Al & Bea's little shop speaks to the time when immigrant families added a retail outlet to their house. It's been open so long (60 years!) that back then, everybody asked what that burrito thing was on the menu.

For more on Al & Bea's Mexican Food and Boyle Heights, see page 90

14. Space Shuttle Endeavour

ON A MISSION TO NOWHERE

The space shuttle *Endeavour*, one of five space shuttles built that went into space (three survive, two blew up), is getting a soaring new home at the California Science Center in LA. It flew 25 missions between 1992 and 2011. The huge white machine was built in LA County, out in the desert town of Palmdale, during the decades when Southern California's aerospace industry was like no other in the world.

Companies like Lockheed and McDonnell Douglas built thousands of military and passenger planes in LA. The command modules that took Apollo astronauts to the Moon were also built there. Today, there is little manufacturing left.

For more on the Endeavour and the California Science Center, see page 102

15. Universal Studios Hollywood

THE STUDIOS ARE IN THE NAME

Always playing catch-up, always wearing a chip on its shoulder, Universal Studios started producing films at its studios just over the hill from Hollywood in 1915. By the 1930s, it was giving the world Frankenstein and Dracula. By the 1970s, it had become the center of TV series production, a virtual factory of hundreds of episodes a year. This continued into this century when streaming upended everything and series production scattered to tax havens around the globe. Today, there are days when nothing can be heard on the Universal lot except the sounds of the ever-expanding theme park, where the 'backlot tour' is just another thrill ride.

For more on Universal Studios Hollywood, see page 128

MEET THE SOUTHERN CALIFORNIANS

Culturally diverse and aware of how lucky they are to live in such a geographically stunning place, Southern Californians are laid-back nature lovers. Amelia Mularz introduces her people.

CLOCKWISE FROM TOP LEFT: RAWPIXEL.COM/SHUTTERSTOCK, HALBERGMAN/GETTY IMAGES, ONEINCHPUNCH/SHUTTERSTOCK, VLAD TEODOR/SHUTTERSTOCK

MY DAD, A lifelong Midwesterner, once told me that if you want to be productive, you have to live in cold weather. I'm not sure that he was making a direct comparison between life in Chicago (his hometown) and Southern California, but regardless, he touched on a stereotype we hear all too often.

Here in Southern California we're perpetually at the beach. Work hours are only suggestions and when the swell is right, we cut out of the office early to ride the waves. We skateboard to the office (when we actually go in) and live on green juice and good vibes. Or at least that's what the stereotypes say.

In reality – and I hate to break this to my dad, who has suffered through seven decades of frigid winters – Southern California has both beautiful weather and productive people. And no, that doesn't mean just actors and influencers.

Southern Californians work in aerospace, healthcare, finance and technology – four of the largest industries in the region. Entertainment, it's true, is also a top moneymaker. However, changes over the last decade in TV and film have brought significant challenges for workers in those fields. Multiple factors – including higher labor costs, more difficult permitting and the rise of streaming services with smaller budgets – have sent filming outside the state, significantly affecting job opportunities. Today, only about 20% of American TV shows and movies are filmed in LA.

As diverse as Southern Californians are in their work, they're also a vibrant mix culturally. In the state as a whole, over 27% of the population is made up of immigrants. But that number is even higher in SoCal's largest metropolitan area, Greater Los Angeles, where over 33% of its residents are foreign-born. And while the state is 39% Latino, it's 49% in LA, with the majority hailing from Mexico. LA is also home to the largest number of Armenian, Filipino, Iranian and Korean populations outside their respective home countries.

It's true that we love our warm weather, though it's worth noting that not everybody lives near San Diego or Laguna Beach's breezy swaths of sand. Southern Californians also live in the desert, where they regularly battle triple-digit temps, as well as in snow-covered mountains where they're more likely to ride a black diamond than a wave. Speaking of which, there's a popular notion that in SoCal you can ski and surf on the same day – it's called the California double. Technically you can, but nobody actually does that. And it's not because we're not productive, it's because we know better than to rush through each experience. We're laid-back in the best way possible, taking our time to soak up all that SoCal has to offer.

Who & How Many?

SoCal's population is roughly 24 million, which means 60% of all Californians call the region home.

Pictured clockwise from top left: People on a Ferris wheel, Santa Monica Pier (p119); Wine tasting, Californian vineyard; Surfers, Malibu (p119); Traveling in Coachella Valley (p220)

SOCAL OR SOMEWHERE?

Before I moved to LA, where I've lived for a decade, I spent 11 years in NYC. New Yorkers are extremely loyal to their city, donning "New York or Nowhere" hats and tees. But now that I'm on the other side, I'm going to let you in on a secret... New Yorkers are very curious about life in SoCal.

Before my West Coast leap, I constantly wondered, what if? Could I trade the subway for freeways, crisp fall weather for perpetual sunshine, late nights for early mornings? It turns out I could and I did.

However, the things I thought I'd love most about SoCal, namely the beach, aren't what I gravitate toward now. These days you're more likely to catch me on the hiking trails of Griffith Park or cruising inland to explore deserts around Palm Springs. But one thing has remained constant: every so many months I get a message from a friend in NYC saying, "psst... what's it like?"

Skate park (p125), Venice Beach

JON CHICA/SHUTTERSTOCK

SKATE OR DIE THE SOCAL WAY

Tony Hawk, Vans and vert skating – they all hail from Southern California. Here's a look at how the region has shaped everyone's favorite new Olympic sport. By Amelia Mularz

LONG BEFORE THE world learned of the legends of wthrough a popular documentary (more on this later), and decades before I'd make Los Angeles my home, I already had a sense that Southern California and the sport of skateboarding were inextricably linked.

When I was a kid in the late 1980s, my family took a vacation from our suburban Chicago town to San Diego, where my brothers and I were mesmerized by the skaters speeding along the Mission Beach boardwalk. My oldest brother, Greg, was especially enamored by the sport and returned home intent on learning. To pick up tricks, he began renting VHS tapes from a local bike shop (these were the pre-internet days, after all), and I noted that they all featured sun-kissed kids, palm trees and beachside stretches of concrete. I don't remember Greg mastering any of the moves on his California-designed Powell-Peralta board, but he did get a skater haircut that was particularly edgy (for our town anyway) and he did graffiti our basement walls (in chalk, no less) with the name of his own personal Dogtown: Craphead City. Skate culture had taken a hold of him, and Southern California had found its way into our home via the VCR.

It's impossible to track down the birthplace of the very first skateboard, since the sport began in a makeshift way. Adrenaline seekers, usually surfers, fashioned their own boards from plywood and attached roller-skate wheels. But in 1959, Albert Boyden filed the very first patent for a skateboard-like creation: a board, described as a 'child's coaster,' that could be steered by leaning side to side. Boyden then teamed up with John Humphrey, a distinguished US naval pilot, to release one of the first commercially manufactured skateboards. The Humco Surfer skateboard, made in San Diego, hit the market in 1963.

That same year, the first organized skateboarding competition took place at Hermosa Beach's Pier Avenue Junior High. Larry Stevenson, a Venice Beach lifeguard who had founded his own skateboard company, Makaha, staged the event. An innovator in addition to an organizer, Stevenson would go on to invent the kicktail. In 1969, he filed a patent for a deck with 'an inclined foot depressible lever,' dramatically improving the skateboard.

Style & Substance

Things really changed for the sport in the 1970s when a ragtag group of kids from the proverbial wrong side of the tracks on LA's West Side formed a skate team based out of a Santa Monica surf shop. The Zephyr skateboard team, aka the

Z-Boys, dubbed their home stretch of Santa Monica and Venice Beach 'Dogtown.' The team made waves at the Bahne/Cadillac National Championships at the Del Mar Fairgrounds, their first appearance, when they introduced a lower-to-the-ground, more surf-inspired style of skating.

The Z-Boys would again make their mark on the sport when they helped usher in vert skating, as they were among the first to skate empty swimming pools and pioneer aerial tricks. The 2001 documentary *Dogtown and Z-Boys*, co-written and directed by Stacy Peralta, a Z-Boy himself, spread the stories of these skateboarding revolutionaries.

Even before the documentary, Peralta had a hand in sharing the sport with the wider public. After launching his company, Powell-Peralta Skateboards, in 1978, he devised a way to attract potential new customers: creating skateboarding videos on VHS. And thus, a new genre of action sports film was born. These Peralta-produced videos were the ones my brother got his hands on in the late '80s in the suburban Midwest.

Speaking of the '80s, you can't talk about California skate culture – or skateboarding in general – without mentioning Tony Hawk. Another SoCal creation, Hawk was born in Carlsbad and turned pro in 1982 at the tender age of 14. He'd go on to be the first to land a 900, as well as win 12 consecutive vert skateboarding world championships and nab six gold medals at the X Games. In 2014, the city of San Diego declared May 29 'Tony Hawk Day.'

The 1990s and early 2000s were a time when Southern California skatewear brands truly flourished. These included Vans, Vision Street Wear, Etnies, DC Shoes and Volcom – all founded in SoCal between the 1960s and mid-90s. Also in the '90s, legislation in the Golden State helped make it possible for municipalities to build skate parks around the country. In 1999, Jim Fitzpatrick, founder of the International Association of Skateboard Companies, helped push through California Senate Bill 994, which limited liabilities for injuries at public skate parks.

STACY PERALTA DEVISED A WAY TO ATTRACT POTENTIAL NEW CUSTOMERS: CREATING SKATEBOARDING VIDEOS ON VHS. AND THUS, A NEW GENRE OF ACTION SPORTS FILM WAS BORN.

Stacy Peralta

ED SOQUI/CORBIS VIA GETTY IMAGES

Olympic Dreams

In recent years, arguably the biggest news in skateboarding has been its inclusion in the Olympics. In 2021, the sport made its Olympic debut in Tokyo with two events: street and park. Not only was the first US skateboard team made up largely of Southern Californians, the region also served as Team USA's official training grounds, with preparation taking place at the California Training Facility (CATF) in Vista. In fact, the company behind CATF, California Skateparks, designed and built the street and park skateboarding facilities used at the Tokyo Olympics.

Three years later, my dad and I stood outside Place de la Concorde during the 2024 Olympics in Paris. Skateboarding was by far one of the most popular events and tickets were totally untouchable. We settled for secondhand spectating, enjoying the near deafening roar of the crowd inside as athletes from 23 nations ollied and kickflipped in the same square that was central to the French Revolution.

My dad confirmed that our basement walls are still emblazoned with my brother's 'Craphead City' tag and I laughed, thinking about Dogtown and that motley crew from Santa Monica. Skateboarding – and particularly SoCal's flavor of the sport – had truly gone worldwide.

THE CLIMATE CRISIS

California is on the leading edge of the global climate crisis, facing both the repercussions and the need to pioneer initiatives to fight back.

ALTHOUGH THE WHOLE world is facing up to the reality of the climate crisis, California is especially vulnerable to its effects. The challenges - wildfires, swings between drought and floods, plus rising seawater levels - are a continuous threat to life, property and landscapes.

The State of Things

According to the California Environmental Protection Agency's Office of Environmental Health Hazard Assessment (OEHHA; *oehha.ca.gov*), annual air and ocean temperatures have been rising since records began in 1895. This has been scientifically proven to be due to human activity. Average temperatures have risen by 2.5°F and the rise is accelerating rapidly: it's projected to increase by another 4.4°F to 5.8°F degrees by 2050. It's most noticeable in Southern California and more than half of the 20 warmest years in California have occurred after 2000.

Warmer seas mean rising sea levels and this is a huge problem for coastal populations in a state where more than

Death Valley National Park (p238)

STEVEN GROUP/SHUTTERSTOCK

26 million people live near the sea. Authorities are fast-tracking the expensive work of 'coastal armoring,' and California has already spent billions of dollars improving seawalls and fortifying wetlands. Not only has the sea risen by six inches since 1950, but the rise has accelerated to a pace of one inch per decade.

Extreme Weather Events

Rising tides and rising temperatures are also causing an increase in extreme weather events. The Indicators of Climate Change in California report (2022) warned that weather extremes are getting more intense and less predictable – which plays dangerously into California's seasonal wildfires.

The 2020 wildfire season broke records when more than 6565 sq miles burned; 2024 saw the state's fourth-largest fire, the Park Fire; and 2025 started as a brutal year with the Palisades Fire. The world watched as Los Angeles burned: decimating Pacific Palisades, Malibu and Altadena. Though Californians are fighting back and CAL FIRE has put in place an expanding network of high-tech cameras in fire-prone areas (speeding up firefighting responses) and scientists are harnessing AI to model wildfire behavior, the human capacity to curb Mother Nature is limited.

You also can't ignore the extreme smoke pollution hanging thick in the air during large fires. On September 9, 2020, the infamous 'orange sky day,' San Francisco Bay Area residents woke to a sun that never appeared, so thick was the smoke brought in by high winds.

Speaking of winds (which also exacerbate fires)...El Niño and La Niña wind changes and weather events like atmospheric rivers, which bring intense rainfall, mean more Californians than ever are at risk of experiencing floods and landslides. The impact of the climate crisis on Californians intersects with racial and economic inequalities. A study by UC Irvine showed that Black and low-income households in the Los Angeles Basin are at the greatest risk of impact by flooding – up to 79% higher risk than white residents.

AUTHORITIES ARE FAST-TRACKING THE EXPENSIVE WORK OF 'COASTAL ARMORING,' AND CALIFORNIA HAS ALREADY SPENT BILLIONS OF DOLLARS IMPROVING SEAWALLS AND FORTIFYING WETLANDS.

Cyclone, Capitola

ROSANGELA PERRY/SHUTTERSTOCK

Lessons from California's First Nations

Climate change isn't the only accelerant of California's worsening wildfires; forest management also holds a key. In 2022, the Wildfire and Forest Resilience Task Force (*wildfiretaskforce.org*) announced a plan to expand the use of 'beneficial fire,' a concept passed down through generations of Native American people.

A UC Berkeley study showed that the Klamath Mountains forests have doubled in size since the native Karuk and Yurok tribes were able to steward the land. These original custodians carried out controlled burns to prevent overgrowth and keep the forest floors in healthy balance. Europeans, in contrast, carried out extensive logging, followed by replanting trees close together. Much modern forest management has focused on preventing burns, the end result is an overgrown carpet of forest and undergrowth that can carry fires over a devastatingly wide area. CAL FIRE and other organizations now manage prescribed burns.

San Francisco skies glow orange from wildfires in 2020

LARRY ZHOU/SHUTTERSTOCK

The Impact of Tourism

When visitors encounter California's natural splendor and learn about the state's complex environmental challenges, an uncomfortable truth arises. The fragile beauty that draws around 270 million visitors to California in a single year is at the mercy of their behavior. At popular destinations like Big Sur and Lake Tahoe, where overtourism has caused soil erosion and other problems, many blame social media for having popularized the areas' photogenic locations.

Sustainable Futures

Fortunately, California has an extensive set of programs to encourage sustainable travel (*travelmattersca.com*). The National Park Service is increasingly shifting to renewable or alternative energy sources, with some parks heading toward carbon-neutral status. One example is the Golden Gate National Recreation Area (the USA's most visited park in 2024) which buys 100% renewable electricity for park operations. Winter sports giant Vail Resorts has committed to achieving carbon-neutral status by 2030, while the SIP (Sustainability in Practice) certified program highlights increasing numbers of wineries using sustainable practices.

CALIFORNIA MAY BE AT THE SHARP EDGE OF CLIMATE CHANGE, BUT IT'S ALSO MOUNTING SOME OF THE MOST ROBUST MEASURES TO MEET THESE CHALLENGES.

California may be at the sharp edge of climate change, but it's also mounting some of the most robust measures to meet these challenges. The state has been reducing its greenhouse gas emissions since 2007 (except for a hiccup during the COVID-19 pandemic). The state enacted regulations banning the sale of new fossil-fuel-powered cars from 2035, but this was blocked by the Trump administration in May 2025. Legal battles will ensue.

There are also efforts to harness California's abundant sunshine for solar power. Rooftop solar alone won't meet the population's energy needs, but devoting land to this use is hotly debated. Wildlife conservationists want solar sites in the cities, far from protected land, meanwhile urban dwellers want the sites far from view.

Many more hurdles lie ahead, but the urgency of California's climate crisis, mixed with its cutting-edge technology and research, are equipping the state for a fight.

Learn more about how to be a responsible visitor on p272.

Desert Sunlight Solar Farm, Mojave Desert (p253)

THE DESERT PHOTO/SHUTTERSTOCK

CRUISING CALIFORNIA

Turning on some tunes, finding a glorious stretch of open road and going for a drive just might be the state's most quintessential activity. By Amelia Mularz

NATIVE CALIFORNIAN Joan Didion famously described the experience of driving on LA's freeways as 'the only secular communion Los Angeles has.' The 2004 film *Sideways* turned the rural routes of Santa Barbara's wine country into big-screen stars, while the hit HBO series *Big Little Lies* elevated maneuvering the throughways of Big Sur to an art form.

The Birthplace of Car Culture

Practically speaking, driving in the Golden State is all too often a headache. Traffic-riddled freeways around every major metropolis devour our time. Rural roads navigate coastal, mountainous and sometimes windswept desert stretches, requiring the utmost concentration and speeds much slower than some would prefer. And then there's the pain that come with parking (limited spaces, impossible-to-comprehend signs, expensive tickets, the list goes on...). But culturally speaking, driving in California is a phenomenon. Dubbed the world's first 'auto-civilization,' California is obsessed with driving. And that obsession has shaped not only how the state's residents live, but how people across the country live.

Many point to the Arroyo Seco Parkway (aka the 110), which connects Los Angeles with Pasadena, as the birthplace of California's car culture. Dedicated on December

Pictured clockwise from top left: Intercity freeway, San Diego (p173); Tesla factory, Fremont; Highway intersection, Los Angeles (p73); In-N-Out Burger, Ventura (p63)

30, 1940, this was the first freeway in the US and considered an engineering marvel at the time. City plans preceding the Arroyo's unveiling, back in the early 1900s, had included Parisian-style grand boulevards. But because California and especially LA, came of age at the same time as the car, the boulevards were scrapped and plans featuring massive, limited-access highways to alleviate car congestion were chosen instead. This freeway system would soon become a model for urban roadways around the world.

Freeways enabled Californians to live even farther from work and while the state can't claim to be the birthplace of the modern-day suburb (most give that honor to New York), residential sprawl has certainly flourished here. California was also an early adopter of suburban America's favorite amenity: the drive-thru. In-N-Out Burger opened one of the very first drive-thrus, complete with two-way speakers, at their Baldwin Park location in 1948.

Because they were spending so much time in their cars, Californians naturally began to use the automobile as a means of entertainment and self-expression. Drag racing got its start on the dry lake beds of California's Mojave Desert. Lowriders, with their bold custom paint jobs and ground-grazing bodies, have their roots in the Mexican-American communities of Southern California.

From Smog to Sustainability

Never ones to rest on their low-riding laurels, Californians have continued to innovate car culture, zeroing in on zero-emission rides in recent decades. In the early 1990s, the state issued a Zero-Emission Vehicle (ZEV) mandate as part of a move to improve air quality. The mandate required all automakers to sell a small percentage of ZEVs in the state. And while car technology wasn't quite up to the task, the mandate did inspire some feats of engineering. In 1997, a San Dimas car company called AC Propulsion unveiled the first electric sports car, called the tZero.

It's probably no wonder then that the Golden State was also the base for a small Silicon Valley startup called Tesla Motors. In 2006, the company announced it was starting production of a luxury electric sports car that could get 200 miles on a single charge. Another California car company, Rivian, based in Irvine, became a pioneer in the industry 15 years later when they released the first electric pickup truck in 2021.

Today, California leads the country in both electric vehicle ownership and charging locations. According to the US Department of Energy, 35 percent of the country's electric vehicles are registered in California. So should you rent an electric ride on your visit, you'll be in good company and well accommodated.

Beyond electric cars, the state has also been a leader in rethinking how car culture affects wildlife. At the time of publication, the Wallis Annenberg Wildlife Crossing outside of Los Angeles was on track to open in early 2026. When it does, it will be the largest wildlife corridor in the world. Covered in vegetation and reaching across Hwy 101, the bridge will provide safe passage for many wildlife species – including bobcats, mountain lions, mule deer and gray foxes – between the Santa Monica Mountains and the Sierra Madre Range.

This is welcome news for nature lovers who, like so many of us, feel the paradox of wanting to see and celebrate as much of the environment as we can, while also striving to protect it.

Scenic Byways

Speaking of seeing some awe-inspiring environments, California has a number of iconic roadways that'll run you past countless natural wonders. The legendary Route 66 enters the state in the Mojave Desert near Needles and drops off drivers right by the beach in Santa Monica. Yosemite's seasonal Tioga Road, only open in the summer, is the highest elevation highway in the state: a scenic 47-mile journey past meadows, forests and granite domes. Then there's the Pacific Coast Highway (aka Route 1), which is road trip royalty. Hugging the Pacific along some breathtaking stretches, the state's longest route runs 656 miles from Dana Point in Orange County to Leggett in Mendocino County.

And if you're the one behind the wheel and terrified of tackling California's notoriously wide freeways (Orange County has an interchange with a whopping 26 lanes), take some advice from Didion herself and think only about where you are, instead of where you're going. Then all that's left to do is enjoy the ride.

CLOCKWISE FROM TOP LEFT: IDOGORA SUN/SHUTTERSTOCK, FELIX MIZIOZNIKOV/SHUTTERSTOCK, TIERNEYMJ/SHUTTERSTOCK, ROBERT V SCHWEMMER/SHUTTERSTOCK

INDEX

Map Pages **000**

Map Pages **000**

Map Pages **000**

"Following human footprints into Kelso Dunes (p255), I delighted in the crazy criss-crossing tracks of beetles, lizards and kangaroo rats."

WENDY YANAGIHARA

"Stumbling across Sunny Jim's Cave & Store (p192) was such a magical discovery. It has the most stunning and unusual view in La Jolla."

JULIE TREMAINE

FROM LEFT: ROBERT HARDING VIDEO/SHUTTERSTOCK, DIAMOND W/SHUTTERSTOCK

Mapping data sources:
© Lonely Planet
© OpenStreetMap http://openstreetmap.org/copyright

THIS BOOK

Destination Editor
Melissa Yeager

Production Editor
Sarah Farrell

Image Editor
Katherine Marsh

Cartographer
Anthony Phelan

Coordinating Editor
Lauren O'Connell

Cover Researcher
Katelyn Perry

Thanks
Alexis Averbuck, Liana Cafolla, Lucy Jones, Alison Killilea, Kate Mathews, Jennifer McCann, Jeremy Toynbee, Saralinda Turner

Paper in this book is certified against the Forest Stewardship Council™ standards. FSC™ promotes environmentally responsible, socially beneficial and economically viable management of the world's forests.

Published by Lonely Planet Global Limited
CRN 554153
6th edition – Jan 2026
ISBN 978 178701 708 5

10 9 8 7 6 5 4 3 2 1
Printed in Malaysia